U. S. Money

vs.

Corporation Currency

"ALDRICH PLAN"

**30
ILLUSTRATIONS**

BY

ALFRED OWEN CROZIER

PRICE 25 CENTS

COMING MONEY TRUST

U.S. TREASURY · U.S. CAPITOL · WHITE HOUSE

RESERVE

NATIONAL — ASSOCIATION

(PRIVATE) — SYNDICATE)

N.Y. STOCK EXCHANGE

WALL STREET

BANK · FARM · FACTORY

THE OCTOPUS — "ALDRICH PLAN" (SEE LAST CHAPTER)

U. S. MONEY

VS.

CORPORATION CURRENCY

"ALDRICH PLAN"

WALL STREET
CONFESSIONS!

GREAT BANK COMBINE

By
ALFRED OWEN CROZIER
Author of the financial novel, *"The Magnet"*
Cincinnati, Ohio

THE MAGNET COMPANY
PUBLISHER
PROVIDENT BANK BUILDING
Cincinnati, Ohio

Printed and Bound
By
M. A. DONOHUE & CO.
Chicago

To

Reverend Owen R. L. Crozier

¶ Now ninety-two years of age with clear mind, whose whole life has been an unselfish public service, this volume is affectionately inscribed by his son, the author.

¶ Before the Civil War he and his good wife, Maria P. A. Crozier, who went to her final rest this year, were zealous for abolition of human bondage. During the '70s they joined the movement to resist the growing aggression of Wall Street and the big banks and preserve the life and integrity of government money.

¶ Author, born in midst of civil conflict, 1863, now gladly takes up the struggle they pioneered. Surely there can be no more inspiring mission than to fight for the things absolutely necessary to conserve popular government and preserve the Republic's life.

ILLUSTRATIONS

ILLUSTRATIONS—Continued

CONTENTS

CONTENTS—Continued

CONTENTS—Continued

LIST OF LETTERS

LIST OF LETTERS—Continued

(See affidavit on next page.)

AFFIDAVIT
SWORN PROOF AS TO LETTERS

State of Wisconsin)
)
) ss
)
County of Milwaukee)

    August Frey, of the Fairbanks-Frey Engraving Company,
Milwaukee, Wisconsin, having been duly sworn says

    That he carefully examined the originals of the
photographically reproduced letters printed in Alfred
Owen Crozier's new book, "U. S. Money vs Corporation
Currency" and that his firm made the photographic
reproductions and cuts of said letters as shown in
said volume and that same are accurate and genuine.

                August Frey

    Subscribed and sworn to before me this 29th day
of May, 1912

                Aug E Brown
                Judge of Civil Court
                Milwaukee County Wis

CHAPTER I.

CENTRAL MONEY TRUST.

A Warning. Wall Street and Big Banks Promoting the "Aldrich Plan." Patriotic Bankers Are Fighting the Measure. Will This New Issue Create a New Political Party—the National Progressive Party? "Shall the People Rule"—Their Money Supply?

The New York Chamber of Commerce is conceded to be the confederated brains of all the great interests of Wall Street. It was founded April 5, 1768. It is dominated by the masters of high finance and is the official voice of Wall Street on governmental action and financial policies. Frank A. Vanderlip, president of Standard Oil's National City Bank, and others comprised the "Special Currency Committee" of the Chamber. Its exhaustive report, adopted by the Chamber October 4, 1906, is given in this volume. It advocated a great Central Bank or Association with the identical powers and functions proposed for the National Reserve Association under the pending "Aldrich Plan."

Wall Street's Own Views!

Describing the precise power such a central financial institution issuing and controlling the volume of the public currency and fixing the discount or interest rates would have, such report significantly says:

"By the control of its rate of interest and of its issues of notes it would be able to exert great influence upon the money market and upon public opinion. Such power is not possessed by any institution in the United States."

This was a heart-to-heart talk by the committee with the other great financial leaders to induce them to join in pro-

7

moting the scheme. It was showing them truthfully the power such an institution would put into the hands of those controlling same. The report bluntly said that such central institution not only could control the "money market," but also the "public opinion" of the United States, by arbitrarily increasing and decreasing interest rates and inflating and contracting its circulating notes, or currency. This power to increase and decrease the supply or quantity of money and credit, and the interest or price charged for same, is the power of absolute life and death over the 24,392 banks and the business of every individual and corporation in the United States. If carried to extremes it would cause general panic, disaster, bankruptcy and ruin. By this means it could at will raise and lower the prices of all securities, property and human labor. The committee truthfully said: "Such a power is not now possessed by any institution in the United States." Even the Federal Government itself has no such enormous and dangerous power. It is power to do all these things that Wall Street seeks. With it, the few who will control this private corporation easily can soon own the entire republic and its 94,000,000 inhabitants in fee simple.

The pending Aldrich measure by far is the most daring and dangerous scheme ever introduced into Congress. Any unprejudiced person will so conclude from the plain evidence writer has accumulated by years of effort and thousands of dollars of expense, and now gives to the public in this volume. The facts are official and incontrovertible. They are documentary, from the public records, and letters of the biggest banks and financiers in the country; also conflicting letters from various members of the Monetary Commission. The originals all are now in writer's possession. It is earnestly hoped that publicity of the true inwardness of this evil measure will render some public service by warning the people of their approaching danger.

It is certain that the bill will become law and fasten upon the country for fifty years this great incorporated money trust unless the rank and file of the people take matters into their own hands. The Wall Street and bank combine are now dickering for support with the management of both parties. It is said to be offering to finance the campaign of both sides if friendly candidates are nominated, and a real investigation of the "money trust" is prevented. It is willing to spend millions, because the play is for future billions and the political control of the republic for the next half century.

The people can defeat the measure only by making it the leading public issue in the 1912 campaign. It will be the secret issue anyway, engineered by Wall Street and the banks. The plan is to keep down all discussion in Congress or the campaign prior to election and then force the bill through Congress under whip and spur before the expiration of the present session and presidential term March 4, 1913, or later, if the "interests" control the nomination and election in 1912. The people should publicly pledge every delegate, candidate and convention. Take no man high or low for granted. Count as secretly pledged to the bill every man refusing to declare against it publicly. There will be no neutrals. Talk with your friends and neighbors and beg them to immediately join in this fight. The entire money supply is at stake. Your business and the welfare of your family is involved. The issue will be: "Government Money vs. Corporate Currency." Do the people want their Government to continue to issue and control the public currency? Or, shall Congress grant to a mere private corporation owned by the banks controlled by Wall Street an absolute monopoly of the printing and issuing of all public currency? Remember, those who have power to make money scarce or plenty have power over the business of every man, the happiness of every home, to make or break, to confer or destroy general prosperity. It gives them a hunger-hold on every man, woman and child. Shall this autocratic power be granted without reservation, effective regulation or restraint for fifty years to just one

private corporation? Even the suggestion is criminal! Yet, there is serious probability of its being done. Wall Street and the banks feel sure of it, and generally they know.

The people can kill the scheme. But will they do it? Public sentiment, lashed to indignation and fury by knowledge of this dangerous and daring legislative "hold-up," can smash the entire conspiracy. But will the people wake up; will they realize their peril and act in time? *It must be war!*

If the Aldrich measure is passed it cannot be repealed. It will be a contract, a "vested right" for fifty years; 94,000,000 Americans and all their interests will by act of Congress be put in financial and political bondage for a half century to a cold, calculating, merciless, greedy and soulless incorporated money power—a central money trust. We are at the "parting of the ways." Shall the country hereafter be ruled by the people, or by a single private corporation?

To a greater extent than during any national crisis since 1776, the life of the republic is now in danger!

Banks Promoting Aldrich Scheme.

The American Bankers' Association at New Orleans in November, 1911, by resolution officially committed itself and the banking fraternity to the Aldrich private central bank plan. This makes it proper and necessary to examine and publish the history and record of the national banking system and the conduct of bankers generally. Only in this way can the country determine whether it is safe by law to turn over to a private corporation owned by the banks a monopoly for fifty years of the entire public currency and the other enormous powers granted by the Aldrich bill. By seeking thus vastly to increase their profits and power by act of Congress the banks have made themselves and their practices a public political issue. Therefore startling facts about banks and bankers will be revealed herein plainly and without bias or apology.

Wealth honestly and fairly gained by individual effort, whatever the size, may put upon the owner a public responsibility, but no stigma. It should receive the full protection of the law. But law-made wealth, that obtained improperly by private interests through acts of Congress or State Legislatures, if it tends to increase the burden upon the people for the profit of the few, should be either confiscated or strictly regulated for the public benefit. This line of distinction between law-made and individually earned wealth should ever be kept in mind.

No honest person will be prejudiced against any man simply because he is a banker, or rich. On the other hand, because a man is a banker, rich and powerful, is no reason why he should be shielded or feared if he has been guilty of graft, fraud and criminal conduct. Writer's brother and many of his personal friends are bankers, so he has no class prejudice whatever. But a deep sense of duty impels the publication of the official evidence conclusively proving the existence of a great and dangerous conspiracy between Wall Street and the big banks for the creation of a giant central money trust that in time through the 24,392 banks and their grip on all business will rule the republic and destroy genuine popular government.

The gold standard no longer is an issue. It is firmly and permanently established. The silver question is gone forever. And no one wants fiat paper currency or irredeemable greenbacks. But the action of Wall Street and the big banks has precipitated on the country a new financial and political issue more important to the people than all former financial issues combined. There are two branches to this one new issue:

1. The trust question. Shall Congress take from Government and the people all power to issue and regulate the quantity of the public currency and grant it unreservedly for fifty years to a private corporation controlled by the big banks owned by Wall Street? Shall it by law create and turn loose for half a century a huge incorporated central

money trust in private hands to monopolize and control without any effective regulation or restraint the country's entire supply of money and bank credit?

2. The money question. Shall the future currency of the country be full legal tender ("lawful money"), the direct obligation of the Government, redeemable on demand in gold, secured by a reserve of at least one-third the volume in actual gold, issued through the banks on fair but business-like terms under strict legal regulations by a great and independent public institution so created as absolutely to exclude all Wall Street and political control? Or, shall it be as proposed by the Monetary Commission, a partial legal tender (not "lawful money") corporate paper currency, the mere obligation of a private corporation and not guaranteed by the Government, issued for private profit without legal limit as to quantity by a corporation controlled by the big banks owned by Wall Street? Shall it be Government money, or corporate currency?

Around this new financial and trust issue soon will be waged the greatest political contest since the Civil War. It touches the pocket-interest of every citizen. The people will be on one side and the "special interests" on the other. It will be a finish fight. The victors will rule the republic for all future time, the vanquished being subservient.

It is history that no question so interests and stirs the American people as does the money issue. They are intelligently and wisely jealous of their money supply. Instinctively they realize that whoever controls money and credit, the life-blood of all business, soon can control everything else, including government itself. Therefore the people will fight to the last ditch to retain in their government control of the issuance and volume of the public currency.

Party lines are likely to be shattered and perhaps destroyed. If the present efforts of the promoters of the Aldrich scheme to control the nominations and policies of both parties are successful, the progressive and patriotic men and women of both parties may come together on this great issue, form the National Progressive Party, and in a whirlwind campaign sweep the country. Broadly, it is the same old issue, "Shall the people rule?"

The contents of this volume is not an attack upon individual bankers or banks as such or upon Wall Street and its financiers. It is only intended to lay bare the defects and evils of the present financial and banking systems in the hope that by informing the people it will aid them to defeat the unpatriotic and dangerous Aldrich scheme that would financially and politically enslave for fifty years the banks, all American business and the 94,000,000 people of the United States.

It is possible that slight errors in the large amount of data and figures herein produced have escaped author's notice in the short time allowed for its preparation, but in all essentials it will be found substantially accurate and reliable, the sources of the astonishing official evidence being given, date and page.

This volume is not intended to be a scientific and technical financial treatise. It is chiefly issued to expose the dangerous designs of high finance and increase popular knowledge, thought and discussion.

"U. S. Money vs. Corporation Currency" is a book of pregnant facts. Author's financial novel, "The Magnet," was preliminary. That volume, written in 1906 and the early part of 1907, although in form of fiction, is almost an exact history in every detail of subsequent and current financial and political events. Its plot is woven around the identical private central bank scheme reported to Congress by the Monetary Commission on January 8, 1912. The chapter, "The Artificial Panic," is a history of the panic of 1907, and yet it was all in type long before the panic occurred. These facts are here mentioned only to show the accuracy of the information obtained by author from Wall Street sources in 1906 that high finance and the big banks were about to promote a great central bank trust that would be a huge money monopoly, taking away from the Federal Government and putting into private hands all control over the issuance and volume of the public currency.

Writer then believed, and does now, that if Congress creates such an institution it will be the beginning of the end of real popular government. Therefore he deliberately began the campaign that already has occupied five years to alarm the people and make them suspicious of Wall Street and the high finance banks that he knew then were secretly promoting the dangerous scheme and soon would bring it into the open and try to drive it through Congress. For that reason he wrote "The Magnet." For that purpose he attended the currency conference of the National Civic Federation in New York on December 16, 1907, and there openly denounced the program of high finance and obtained from the prominent Wall Street bankers present the important public admission that they sought to obtain private control of the public currency. Other similar steps have been taken from time to time, and now that the measure actually has been introduced into Congress and the lines are being formed for a final mighty struggle between the people and the "interests" over the control of the nation's entire supply of money and credit, this new volume and its serious contents is given to the public in the hope that it may aid the people in their unequal fight for financial, industrial and political independence against the most powerful nation-wide combine ever formed to accomplish the selfish conquest of a republic.

Patriotic Bankers Oppose Measure.

Fortunately there are many honest and patriotic bankers who refuse to barter away the interests of their customers, neighbors and friends and the welfare of their communities and the nation for a little more profit that they do not need. The number of bankers opposed to the Aldrich bill will increase as they come to realize the dangerous character of the measure. They will see that the alternative plan herein proposed confers all the benefits claimed for the Aldrich plan, but avoids the very apparent grave evils.

Andrew Jay Frame, president of Waukesha National Bank, ex-president of the Wisconsin Bankers' Association, and now a member of the Executive Council of the American Bankers' Association, is recognized generally as a financial authority, speaker and writer, of the highest national standing. He is not a radical, but a strict conserative. He is utterly opposed to the pending Aldrich central bank bill and considers it not only unpatriotic and evil, but highly dangerous to the banks; and in unmeasured terms he denounces the means being used to promote the measure through Congress and the gag rule methods employed at New Orleans to force approval of the Aldrich scheme by the American Bankers' Association.

In an address, "Diagnosis of the National Monetary Commission Bill," made on March 5, 1912, before the Bankers and Business Men's Club of Memphis, Tenn., Mr. Frame denounced the pending Aldrich bill as opposed to independent banking, a move to create a great banking or money monopoly, a scheme for wild and dangerous currency and credit inflation certain to react on the banks and the country in the shape of frequent panics following periods of excessive expansion and speculation, and that the proposed remedy is worse than the claimed disease. He said he was invited to present the revised Aldrich plan to the American Bankers' Association at New Orleans for its approval, but refused to stultify himself by doing so. He favors a more elastic currency system, chiefly for emergencies instead of rediscounting for the convenience of banks in normal times, and urges centralization of bank reserves in one institution, but only for protective purposes. He says any solvent bank can now easily rediscount or sell at another bank any good paper. He warns the banks and the country in effect that destruction of the independent banking system and substitution of the Wall Street branch banking plan that means ultimately a universal banking trust to control the cash and credit of the entire country is the real aim and object of the pending Aldrich measure.

He further said:

"Senator Aldrich submitted an amended tentative plan, just before the American Bankers' Association met in New Orleans in November. Without waiting for the bankers to calmly and deliberately digest the subject, as has been the custom for ten years past under ring control the steam roller worked overtime and an 'ex-parte' miscarriage of Justice occurred.

"A bombardment of attorneys for the prosecution with no one invited to defend took place. Another 'unqualified' indorsement of the new plan passed with only one 'No,' even if others for divers reasons failed to vote at all. I simply cite these facts not to air them in public, but to show the Congress the undignified and unfair methods pursued by the powers that be in the great American Bankers' Association.

"I again assert that if the American Bankers' Association is to preserve its usefulness, it will overturn ring control and make an open forum for fair discussion by both sides to any controversy and let the majority rule. * * *

"Further, I appeal to the intelligent bankers of the country, even if the bill is complex, to ponder carefully this analysis before swallowing the bait, hook and all, as it takes ten years after the bill is passed to amend it in any manner. Remember 'an ounce of prevention is worth a pound of cure.' Do not sleep in the confident peace that your interests will be fully safeguarded by the Currency Committee of the American Bankers' Association. It is a well known fact that the guiding spirit of this committee, if in his power, would crush the independent banking system and substitute therefor branch banking and asset currency. The balance of the committee heretofore seems to have acquiesced.

" * * * tends toward a monopoly that sooner or

later a second Andrew Jackson will throttle. * * *

"The world is now agitated over high prices partly caused by the wonderful production of gold in the last twenty-five years, which has exceeded in quantity the world's gold production since the discovery of America. In view of this it is our bounden duty to limit running the printing presses to supply a fictitious substitute, except in emergencies to prevent the paralyzing effects of cash suspension by banks. Heed the warning or compound the trouble.

"Therefore, give us a reserve bank that will be our servant and not our dictator. * * * Give us a bank that under no circumstances will undermine our independent banking system, or serve to inflate either currency or credit. To quote an eminent authority, 'we certainly cannot cure defects by opening numerous doors to additional dangers.' "

This terrific indictment of the Aldrich private central bank scheme, and the high finance "ring" or clique running the American Bankers' Association that is said to have joined with Wall Street in a great conspiracy to force the sinister measure through Congress, is significant. It is made by a gentleman who for fifty years has been an eminent banker and actually is now a member of the Executive Council of the American Bankers' Association. But he is of that independent and patriotic class of bankers who put the welfare of the community and the nation first. He is not one of those modern fly-by-night high finance bankers who have seized control of big institutions containing vast accumulations of the deposit savings of the people which they freely use legally and illegally to bolster up their high finance flotations and gambling ventures that rob the people, endanger the solvency of the banks and menace the whole country with frequent panics that their practices cause or intensify.

If the Wall Street element for ten years has maintained "ring control" and flattened all opposition with the "steam roller" in the American Bankers' Association representing every bank in the country, when each bank has had an equal voice, as Mr. Frame declares, will not the same element establish "ring" rule in the National Reserve Association where each bank does not have equal power, but only in proportion to the size of its capital stock, a Wall Street $25,000,000 bank owning one thousand times as much association stock as the $25,000 country bank. The central bank is rigged to rule absolutely each of the 24,392 National and State banks and trust companies, the big banks will control the central bank and Wall Street owns the big banks. Thus will high finance obtain mastery over every bank and through the banks of all American business and establish a central money trust to legally corner and control for private profit every dollar of public currency and the bank credit of the whole United States for the next fifty years. It is to be a trust of the trusts, with imperial powers that will make it absolute dictator for half a century of all American finance, industry and politics.

Then we shall have only corporate currency, and a government of the corporations, by the corporations and for the corporations—a "soulless" corporate republic.

CHAPTER II.

⌐THE ALDRICH PLAN.

The Bill in Full Reported to Congress by Monetary Commission Analyzed. Amazing and Dangerous "Jokers." 24,392 Banks Legally Tied Together in Great Money Trust for 50 Years.

The bill attached to the National Monetary Commission's report to Congress made January 8, 1912, now pending, is herein printed in full. After each section the comments of writer analyzing the measure will be found. Only a few brief points are so made, because the entire contents of this volume in one way or another bears on some feature of the bill, or on subsequent conditions likely to prevail if the measure becomes law. Comparison of its provisions with those of the two plans for a central bank originated by the New York Chamber of Commerce, one in October, 1906, and the other in January, 1911, reproduced elsewhere in this book, will conclusively show that the proposed functions of the National Reserve Association and of such central bank are practically identical. The chief material change since 1906 is in the management or control. In 1906 Wall Street only proposed a *Government Central Bank* with the Federal Government in absolute and supreme control. In 1912, emboldened by the panic of 1907 and its results, and belief that the Administration and Congress can be induced to entirely surrender to Wall Street and the banks, it is now actually demanded that Congress create a *Private Central Bank* named "National Reserve Association," with the banks in absolute and supreme control, the Government selecting 4 and the banks 42 of the 46 directors. The governmental function of issuing and regulating from day to day the volume of the entire public currency, that in 1906 was to be granted because it was to be a public institution under absolute Government control, is now to be delegated to and exercised by this mere private corporation.

The Aldrich plan bill is as follows:

A BILL

To Incorporate the National Reserve Association of the United States, and for Other Purposes.

Be it enacted by the Senate and House of Representatives of the United States of America in Congress assembled, That the National Reserve Association of the United States be, and it is hereby, created and established for a term of 50 years from the date of filing with the Comptroller of the Currency a certificate of paid-in capital stock as hereinafter provided. It shall have an authorized capital equal in amount to 20 per centum of the paid-in and unimpaired capital of all banks eligible for membership in said National

*Reserve Association. Before said association shall be au-
thorized to commence business $200,000,000 of the capital
stock shall be subscribed and $100,000,000 of its capital shall
be paid in cash. The capital stock of said association shall
be divided into shares of $100 each. The outstanding capital
stock may be increased from time to time as subscribing
banks increase their capital or as additional banks become
subscribers or may be decreased as subscribing banks reduce
their capital or leave the association by liquidation. The
head office of the National Reserve Association shall be located in Washington, in the District of Columbia.*

June 7, 1911, the 24,392 reporting national and state
banks and trust companies had a combined capital stock
of $1,952.411,085.

If all joined, the reserve association stock would be about
$400,000,000. That size capital is "authorized" whether
they all join or not. The figure is 20 per cent of combined
capital of "all banks eligible for membership." If only
the 7,331 national banks join, their combined capital on
October 31, 1911, being $1,032,632,131, the total reserve
association stock will be about $200,000,000, the amount
that must be "subscribed" (one half being paid in) before
the association can "commence business." Evidently when
the $200,000,000 minimum was fixed, it was anticipated
that probably only national banks would join; and possibly
such state banks and trust companies as are directly controlled by national banks. Although there is no important
advantage to be gained by state banks and trust companies
by joining, and very serious disadvantages, it was necessary
to make a show of impartiality to keep state institutions from
fighting the scheme in Congress. Apparently state institutions can join or not, as they like. Subsequently, however,
they will be forced to surrender and become a minor part
of this universal banking trust or see their deposits and
business gradually diverted to national banks by the cry that
only such banks as join the association have been made
"panic-proof" by the Government. Once the law is passed,
every bank can be forced into the combination; and once
in they are powerless and never can get out, except by
insolvency or liquidation. If necessary, another little panic
easily can be sprung as an "object lesson" to accelerate the
decision of all banks to join this salvation corporation.
Elsewhere we shall see that every bank joining must in
everything submit to the orders of the central bank. A

universal bank trust—a great money combine—is certain
the moment Congress passes and the President approves
this bill. The President has indicated that he will approve
it, so Congress is the only protector of the country and
the people against the imperial money monster this bill
would bring into being. And the "interests" believe they
can control a majority of the present Congress. If they can,
then only the people can block the measure. The total
capital of this financial colossus, and its power, is to automatically increase as new banks are organized or old banks
increase their stock, Congress having no voice in the matter
during the next 50 years. While the official head-office is
to be in Washington, of course the real headquarters will
be at the New York Branch in Wall Street. The moment
this bill becomes law it will be an enforceable contract, a
"vested right," that neither Congress or any other authority
can cancel or change to the financial disadvantage of the
corporation. A member of the Monetary Commission so
stated to writer recently.

SEC. 2. *Upon duly making and filing with the Comptroller of the Currency the certificate hereinafter required
the National Reserve Association of the United States
shall become a body corporate and as such and by that
name shall have power—*

First. To adopt and use a corporate seal.

*Second. To have succession for a period of 50 years from
the date of said certificate.*

*Third. To make all contracts necessary and proper to
carry out the purposes of this act.*

*Fourth. To sue and be sued, complain and defend, in
any court of law or equity, as fully as natural persons.*

*Fifth. To elect or appoint directors and officers in the
manner hereinafter provided and define their duties.*

*Sixth. To adopt by its board of directors by-laws not
inconsistent with this act, regulating the manner in which its
property shall be transferred, its general business conducted,
and the privileges granted to it by law exercised and enjoyed.*

*Seventh. To purchase, acquire, hold, and convey real
estate as hereinafter provided.*

*Eighth. To exercise by its board of directors or duly
authorized committees, officers, or agent, subject to law,
all the powers and privileges conferred upon the National
Reserve Association by this act.*

This lax-wild-cat form of incorporation is enough to make corporations under the laws of New Jersey, Delaware or Arizona turn green with envy. It was not considered by the fathers safe to allow even the Federal Government to exercise any functions or powers except such as were delegated to it by the States and specifically enumerated in the Constitution, even with the people constantly in control for the benefit of the people. This private corporation owned by the banks for the benefit of the banks is granted life for 50 years, a half century, almost half as long as the republic has existed, and it is practically given legal power to do anything and everything without limitation, restraint, regulation or serious government supervision, except as to a few minor and relatively unimportant things specifically mentioned. No public regulation or supervision of its investments or conduct is provided. Paragraphs "third," "sixth" and "eighth" grant the corporation practically unlimited power and turn it loose to work its will and pleasure for 50 years. Granting its board of directors this wide-open power to "adopt by-laws" is giving the corporation legal authority for 50 years to legislate for itself on all subjects not expressly illegal, except that such by-laws must be "not inconsistent with this act." The unconditional grant of power "to make all contracts necessary and proper to carry out the purposes of this act" enables it to do practically everything; for almost anything can be made "necessary and proper" by the by-laws. The two former central banks, abolished by Congress refusing to renew their charters because of their political activity and because they had too much power, did not have a tenth of the power this bill would confer upon this corporation, and the length of their charters was but 20 years.

In the whole measure there is not provided even one criminal penalty upon any officer, director or agent of the association, or any of its branches, or upon the corporation itself, for the violation of one or all of the provisions of the bill.

Paragraph "second" almost confers immortality on this "soulless corporation," and "fourth" seems to grant it "human rights" as well as corporate powers by making it equal to "natural persons." Individuals do not have corporate powers and ordinary corporations do not have "natural human rights," but this bill seems to endow this money octopus with both corporate powers and human rights.

It was unnecessary expressly to say that it shall be equal to Omnipotence in authority, because that is practically assured by the other sections of the bill.

Sec. 3. *All national banks, and all banks or trust companies chartered by the laws of any State of the United States or of the District of Columbia, complying with the requirements for membership in the said National Reserve Association, hereinafter set forth, may subscribe to its capital to an amount equal to 20 per centum of the paid-in and unimpaired capital of the subscribing bank, and not more nor less; and each of such subscribing banks shall become a member of a local association as hereinafter provided. Fifty per centum of the subscriptions to the capital stock of the National Reserve Association shall be fully paid in; the remainder of the subscriptions or any part thereof shall become a liability of the subscribers, subject to call and payment thereof whenever necessary to meet the obligations of the National Reserve Association under such terms and in accordance with such regulations as the board of directors of the National Reserve Association may prescribe.*

The subscriptions of a bank or trust company incorporated under the laws of any State or of the District of Columbia to the capital stock of the National Reserve Association shall be made subject to the following conditions:

First. That (a) if a bank, it shall have a paid-in and unimpaired capital of not less than that required for a national bank in the same locality; and that (b) if a trust company, it shall have an unimpaired surplus of not less than 20 per centum of its capital, and if located in a place having a population of 6,000 inhabitants or less shall have a paid-in and unimpaired capital or not less than $50,000; if located in a city having a population of more than 6,000 inhabitants and not more than 50,000 inhabitants, shall have a paid-in and unimpaired capital of not less than $100,000; if located in a city having a population of more than 50,000 inhabitants and not more than 200,000 inhabitants shall have a paid-in and unimpaired capital of not less than $200,000; if located in a city having a population of more than 200,000 inhabitants and not more than 300,000 inhabitants shall have a paid-in and unimpaired capital of not less than $300,000; if located in a city having a population of more than 300,000 inhabitants and not more than 400,000 inhabitants shall have a paid-in and unimpaired capital of not less than $400,000,

*and if located in a city having a population of more than
400,000 inhabitants shall have a paid-in and unimpaired
capital of not less than $500,000.*

*Second. That it shall have and agree to maintain against
its demand deposits a reserve of like character and proportion to that required by law of a national bank in the same
locality: Provided, however, That deposits which it may
have with any subscribing national bank, State bank or trust
company in a city designated in the national banking laws as
a reserve city or central reserve city shall count as reserve in
like manner and to the same extent as similar deposits
of a national bank with national banks in such cities.*

*Third. That it shall have and agree to maintain against
other classes of deposits the percentages of reserve required
by this act.*

*Fourth. That it shall agree to submit to such examina-
tions and to make such reports as are required by law and
to comply with the requirements and conditions imposed
by this act and regulations made in conformity therewith.*

*The words "subscribing banks" when used hereafter in
this act shall be understood to refer to such national banks,
and banks or trust companies chartered by the laws of any
State of the United States or of the District of Columbia, as
shall comply with the requirements for membership herein
defined.*

Paragraph "second" of Section 3 indicates that bank reserves are to be as now kept in other banks in reserve cities
instead of in the "Central Reservoir" of the National Reserve Association as had been represented. In fact, this bill
seems to force all joining State banks and trust companies to
send their reserves to Wall Street or to put the same in the
national banks that now are constantly sending hundreds of
millions of dollars of the deposit savings of the people to
Wall Street and thus are depriving the communities where
such deposits are owned of their use. Paragraph "fourth"
legally binds all joining State banks and trust companies
to forever "comply with the requirements and conditions
imposed by this act and regulations made in conformity
therewith."

The association is empowered to adopt by-laws containing
such "regulations" as it may from time to time care to
impose. The courts will compel all banks and trust companies to obey the regulations or orders of the Central
Association, for each in advance by adopted resolution and

in writing legally binds itself to do so. Every act of each bank thus can be regulated or dictated by the association, such as interest rates, paid to depositors or charged on loans, investments, loans made, securities bought, expansion and contraction of the volume of its loans, etc. Under this power a mere circular order or "round robin" to the banks by the association can suddenly contract the volume of bank loans to business men to the extent of billions of dollars. The power of the association over every bank and trust company is about as great as it would be if it owned all of the stock of each bank and trust company. Instead of the association being a subsidiary of the banks, the 24,392 banks all are to be mere helpless subsidiaries of the National Reserve Association. Thus the new born child is stronger than its parents. Through this clever means the big banks controlled by Wall Street that will dominate the association will be able to rule every individual bank and trust company in the United States. Country bankers thereafter will be mere clerks for Wall Street. There never was such a big, powerful, nation-wide complete combine in all trust annals. It will be a trust of the trusts, and it is all to be done by act of Congress. And yet in his message indorsing this measure, President Taft said, "And I trust also that the new legislation will carefully and completely protect and assure the individuality and independence of each bank to the end that any tendency there may ever be toward a consolidation of the money or banking power of the nation shall be defeated." If he meant what he says, he will have to veto this bill. If he did not mean it, why did he say it? Did he in a public message to Congress indorse a measure of great importance without knowing its provisions, and this only a few days before the bill was introduced into Congress? Or, did Aldrich conceal from the President the already prepared bill while inducing him to publicly indorse the same?

SEC. 4. *The Secretary of the Treasury, the Secretary of Agriculture, the Secretary of Commerce and Labor, and the Comptroller of the Currency are hereby designated a committee to effect the organization of the National Reserve Association, and the necessary expenses of said committee shall be payable out of the Treasury upon vouchers approved by the members of said committee, and the Treasury shall be reimbursed by the National Reserve Association to the full amount paid out therefor.*

*Within sixty days after the passage of this act said com-
mittee shall provide for the opening of books for subscriptions to the capital stock of said National Reserve Association in such places as the said committee may designate.
Before the subscription of any bank to the capital stock of
the National Reserve Association shall be accepted, said
bank shall file with the organization committee or after
organization with the National Reserve Association a certified copy of a resolution adopted by the board of directors of
said bank accepting all the provisions and liabilities imposed
by this act and authorizing the president or cashier of said
bank to subscribe for said stock.*

This and other provisions tend to give the impression
that the association is a public institution, being promoted
by the Government, when it is only a mere private corporation. Morally it binds the Government, which is to
have responsibility without power. The Government should
not go into partnership with, or loan its credit or influence
to, any private individual or corporation. It is deceiving
the people into believing that the association and its paper
currency has behind it the credit of the Government, which
it is claimed is not a fact. Under this bill the Government
has no stock or financial interest in or the slightest effective
control over the private corporation to which Congress is
asked to grant power to issue and regulate the volume of
the public currency. Making four appointed public officers
ex-officio directors in a board of 46, and allowing the President to appoint the Governor, but only from a list of three
nominated by such board, gives not the slightest power of
public control. It is intended to mislead the people. And
if it is made to appear a Government action, the banks more
generally may promptly respond by joining. There is no
legitimate reason why members of the President's Cabinet
should solicit subscriptions to the stock of this private corporation and have the expenses paid from the public
treasury. It is, of course, a mere bluff.

SEC. 5. *When the subscriptions to the capital stock of
the National Reserve Association shall amount to the sum
of $200,000,000 the organization committee hereinbefore
provided shall forthwith proceed to select 15 cities in the
United States for the location of the branches of said National Reserve Association: Provided, That one branch shall
be located in the New England States, including the States
of Maine, New Hampshire, Vermont, Massachusetts, Rhode*

Island and Connecticut; two branches in the Eastern States, including the States of New York, New Jersey, Pennsylvania and Delaware; four branches in the Southern States, including the States of Maryland, Virginia, West Virginia, North Carolina, South Carolina, Georgia, Florida, Alabama, Mississippi, Louisiana, Texas, Arkansas, Kentucky, Tennessee and also the District of Columbia; four branches in the Middle Western States, including the States of Ohio, Indiana, Illinois, Michigan, Wisconsin, Minnesota, Iowa and Missouri; four branches in the Western and Pacific States, including the States of North Dakota, South Dakota, Nebraska, Kansas, Montana, Wyoming, Colorado, New Mexico, Oklahoma, Washington, Oregon, California, Idaho, Utah, Nevada and Arizona.

When the cities in which the branches are to be located have been selected the organization committee shall forthwith divide the entire country into 15 districts, with one branch of the National Reserve Association in each district: Provided, That the districts shall be apportioned with due regard to the convenient and customary course of business and not necessarily along State lines.

The districts may be readjusted, and new districts and new branches may from time to time be created by the directors of the National Reserve Association whenever, in their opinion, the business of the country requires.

It is made to appear that the Government is to control the dividing of the country up into districts. It is loudly claimed that Wall Street control is forever barred by this particular arrangement of districts. But the directors of the association expressly are given power to change the districts at will. In other words, they can immediately "readjust" so Wall Street will have complete control. And these district associations choose the directors of the National Reserve Association.

SEC. 6. *All subscribing banks within a district shall be grouped by the organization committee or after organization, by the National Reserve Association, into local associations of not less than 10 banks, with an aggregate capital and surplus of at least $5,000,000, for the purposes hereinafter prescribed: Provided, That the territory included in each association shall be contiguous and that in apportioning the territory due regard shall be had for the customary course of business and for the convenience of the banks forming the association: Provided further, That in* *apportioning the territory to local associations comprising a district every bank and all of the territory within said district shall be located within the boundaries of some local association: And provided further, That every subscribing bank shall become a member only of the local association of the territory in which it is situated.*

The banks uniting to form a local association shall, by their presidents or vice presidents, under authority from the board of directors, execute a certificate in triplicate setting forth the name of the association, the names of the banks composing it, its principal place of business, its territorial limits, and the purposes for which it is organized. One copy of this certificate shall be filed with the Comptroller of the Currency, one copy shall be filed with the National Reserve Association, and one copy shall be filed with the branch of the National Reserve Association of the district in which the local association is included. Upon the filing of such certificates the local association therein named shall become a body corporate and by the name so designated may sue and be sued and exercise the powers of a body corporate for the purposes mentioned in this act, and not otherwise.

The local associations in each district may be readjusted from time to time and new associations may be authorized by the directors of the National Reserve Association.

Local associations with their boasted republican form of government can be changed, "readjusted," at will by the imperial board of directors of the central association. The whole management is despotism disguised as a democracy.

SEC. 7. *Each local association shall have a board of directors, the number to be determined by the by-laws of the local association. Three-fifths of that number shall be elected by ballot cast by the representatives of the banks that are members of the local association, each bank having one representative and each representative one vote for each of the positions to be filled without reference to the number of shares which the bank holds in the National Reserve Association. Two-fifths of the whole number of directors of the local association shall be elected by the same representatives of the several banks that are members of the association, but in voting for these additional directors each representative shall be entitled to as many votes as the bank which he represents holds shares in the National Reserve Association: Provided, That in case 40 per centum of the capital stock in any subscribing bank is owned directly or*

*indirectly by any other subscribing bank, or in case 40 per
centum of the capital stock in each of two or more subscribing banks, being members of the same local association, is
owned directly or indirectly by the same person, persons,
copartnership, voluntary association, trustee, or corporation,
then and in either of such cases, neither of such banks shall
be entitled to vote separately, as a unit, or upon its stock,
except that such banks acting together, as one unit, shall
be entitled to one vote, for the election of the board of directors of such local association. In no case shall voting by
proxy be allowed. The authorized representative of a bank,
as herein provided, shall be its president, vice president, or
cashier.*

*Each director shall take an oath that he will, so far as
the duty devolves upon him, diligently and honestly administer the affairs of such association and will not knowingly
violate or willingly permit to be violated any of the provisions of this act.*

*The directors originally elected shall hold office until the
second Tuesday in February immediately following their
election, and thereafter the directors shall be elected annually on that date and shall hold office for the term of one
year.*

*The board of directors of the local association shall have
authority to make by-laws, not inconsistent with law, which
shall be subject to the approval of the National Reserve
Association.*

If Congress exists to serve the people instead of the
banks, it will consider immaterial the method of electing
directors so long as the banks select all and the people none
for the local associations. The whole scheme is for the
benefit of the banks and not the people. All local by-laws
must be approved by the supreme association. Sec. 7 seems
to authorize ownership of one bank by another, branch banking, now illegal; 40, 51 or 75 per cent of a bank's stock
could be put in one or more coöperating holding companies
and thus easily evade the restriction.

Each director of a local, a branch, or of the national association must take an oath that he will faithfully perform his
duties. This is a joke, in view of the U. S..Comptroller's
charges that about 40,000 bank officers and directors almost
every day knowingly violate their oaths which all take as
bank officials. This oath is to serve the bank or the association, not the Government. No penalty or method of im-

peachment is provided in the bank act or this bill against directors who break their oaths. The provision is a mere bluff. There should be a penalty of fine and imprisonment against bank officers and directors who knowingly violate their sworn duty. This would at least modify the evils and somewhat improve administration. The central association can approve or veto the by-laws of local associations. It is the autocrat.

SEC. 8. *Each of the branches of the National Reserve Association shall have a board of directors, the number, not less than twelve in addition to the ex-officio member, to be fixed by the by-laws of the branch. These directors shall be elected in the following manner:*

The board of directors of each local association shall elect by ballot a voting representative. One-half of the elected directors of the branch shall be elected by the vote of such representatives, each representative having one vote for each of the positions to be filled, without reference to the number of shares which the banks composing the association which he represents holds in the National Reserve Association. One-third of the elected directors shall be elected by the same voting representatives, but each voting representative in this case shall have a number of votes equal to the number of shares in the National Reserve Association held by all the banks composing the local association which he represents. The remaining one-sixth of the directors shall be chosen by the directors already elected and shall fairly represent the agricultural, commercial, industrial, and other interests of the district and shall not be officers nor while serving, directors of banks, trust companies, insurance companies, or other financial institutions. The manager of the branch shall be ex-officio a member of the board of directors of the branch and shall be chairman of the board.

Each director shall take an oath that he will, so far as the duty devolves upon him, diligently and honestly administer the affairs of such association and will not knowingly violate or willingly permit to be violated any. of the provisions of this act.

All the members of the board of directors of the branch except the ex-officio member shall at the first meeting of the board be divided into three classes. One-third of the directors shall hold office until the first Tuesday in March immediately following the election; one-third of the directors shall hold office for an additional period of one year after the first Tuesday in March immediately following the election; the remaining one-third of the directors shall hold office for an additional period of two years after the first Tuesday in March immediately following the election. All elections shall be held on the first Tuesday in March of each year, and after the first election all directors shall be elected for a term of three years: Provided, That the by-laws of the National Reserve Association shall provide for the manner of filling any vacancies which may occur in the board of directors of the branches.

The board of directors of the branch shall have authority to make by-laws, not inconsistent with law, which shall be subject to the approval of the National Reserve Association.

One-sixth of the directors of branch boards "shall fairly represent the agricultural, commercial, industrial," etc. This is advisory only, not mandatory, because there is no way provided to determine, and no penalty if it is not done. It is largely buncombe, for the banks will select only such men for "one-sixth" as the banking "five-sixths" consider friendly. The entire 24 directors of the great bank of England are all from these classes. No bankers can be on that board. This is because that bank issues the public currency and regulates the discount rate for the whole nation. It was feared that bankers, if directors, would manipulate the currency supply and discount rates for selfish objects, as surely they will do with this association. The central association may approve or veto the by-laws of branch associations.

SEC. 9. *The National Reserve Association shall have a board of directors, to be chosen in the following manner:*

First. Fifteen directors shall be elected, one by the board of directors of each branch of the National Reserve Association. In case the number of districts shall be increased hereafter, each additional district shall be entitled to elect an additional director of this class.

Second. Fifteen additional directors shall be elected, one by the board of directors of each branch of the National Reserve Association, who shall fairly represent the agricultural, commercial, industrial, and other interests of the district, and who shall not be officers nor, while serving, directors of banks, trust companies, insurance companies, or other financial institutions. In case the number of districts shall be increased hereafter, each additional district shall be entitled to elect an additional director of this class.

Third. Nine additional directors shall be elected by voting representatives chosen by the boards of directors of the various branches, each of whom shall cast a number of votes equal to the number of shares in the National Reserve Association held by the banks in the branch which he represents. Not more than one of the directors of this class shall be chosen from one district. Directors of each of the three classes named above shall be residents of the district from which they are elected.

Fourth. There shall be seven ex-officio members of the board of directors, namely: The governor of the National Reserve Association, who shall be chairman of the board, two deputy governors of the National Reserve Association, the Secretary of the Treasury, the Secretary of Agriculture, the Secretary of Commerce and Labor, and the Comptroller of the Currency.

No member of any national or State legislative body shall be a director of the National Reserve Association, nor of any of its branches, nor of any local association.

All the members of the board, except the ex-officio members, shall at the first meeting of the board be divided into three classes. One-third of the directors shall hold office until the first Tuesday in April immediately following the election; one-third of the directors shall hold office for an additional period of one year after the first Tuesday in April immediately following the election; the remaining one-third of the directors shall hold office for an additional period of two years after the first Tuesday in April immediately following the election. All elections shall be held on the first Tuesday in April of each year, and after the first election all directors shall be elected for a term of three years: Provided, That all directors provided for in sections seven, eight, and nine of this Act shall serve until their successors have qualified: And provided further, That the by-laws of the National Reserve Association shall provide for the manner of filling any vacancies which may occur in the board of directors of the National Reserve Association.

Each director shall take an oath that he will, so far as the duty devolves upon him, diligently and honestly administer the affairs of such association and will not knowingly violate or willingly permit to be violated any of the provisions of this act.

The board of directors of the National Reserve Association shall have authority to make by-laws, not inconsistent with law, which shall prescribe the manner in which the business of said association shall be conducted and the privileges granted to it by law exercised and enjoyed.

The public is not interested in the complicated and confusing method of voting or choosing directors. It is an affair of the banks only. The people have no hand or voice in the selection of the governing board of this private association or syndicate that is to control their entire money supply and fix the interest rates that the whole country must pay. Of the 46 directors, 42 are chosen by the banking fraternity. The other four are appointed public officials, ex-officio directors. Congressmen and legislators, officials for whom the people have voted are blacklisted. They cannot be upon local, branch or national boards; yet the people's elected Congressmen are expected to grant all these privileges and powers to the banks. But there is nothing to prevent Wall Street high financiers being directors. Directors of the National Association serve until their successors are chosen, and they determine how vacancies shall be filled. Could not vacancies be "induced," to change control, the board filling the vacancies? As they can revise and perhaps abolish the local and branch associations, there is nothing to prevent the first board constituting itself an autocratic self-perpetuating body in absolute control of a fifty year charter, a legally enforcible "vested right" giving imperial power over all banks, controlling the public currency, and enjoying privileges obtained free that former Secretary of the Treasury Shaw is reported as saying are worth to the private interests in control more than the entire national debt, about one billion dollars. The power to make by-laws is a grant practically unlimited. The effect if not the design of the complicated system of electing directors is to confuse and divert public attention away from other provisions of the bill that really are important and dangerous.

Sec. 10. *The executive officers of the National Reserve Association shall consist of a governor, two deputy governors, a secretary, and such subordinate officers as may be provided by the by-laws. The governor of the National Reserve Association shall be selected by the President of*

the United States from a list of not less than three sub-
mitted to him by the board of directors of said association.
The person so selected shall thereupon be appointed by the
said board as governor of the National Reserve Association
for a term of ten years, subject to removal for cause by
a two-thirds vote of the board. There shall be two deputy
governors, to be elected by the board, for a term of seven
years, subject to removal for cause by a majority vote of
the board. The two deputy governors first elected shall
serve for terms of four years and seven years, respectively.
In case of any vacancy in the office of deputy governor his
successor shall be elected to fill the unexpired term. In the
absence of the governor or his inability to act the deputy
who is senior in point of service shall act as governor. The
board of directors shall have authority to appoint such other
officers as may be provided for by the by-laws.

Three men will be selected by the banking interests.
The President can say which of the three shall be "governor." No doubt the other two will be the "two deputy
governors." This puts a serious responsibility upon the
President and Government without power of free discretion. He should not mix in the matter unless he can select
whom he thinks best suited in the public interest. If he ap-
points the governor he should both deputies, and have
power of removal. Otherwise the association should have
the entire responsibility, the Government and all public officials keeping out so not to even morally bind the Government to policies and acts that it is powerless to block, regulate or execute. The Government should have full and
supreme control, or no part whatever in the management.
There can be no safe compromise on this point. Even a
bare majority would not be safe. It must be a genuine
public institution or an absolute private corporation. A
mixed deal will be dangerous, if not utterly unlawful. The
plan of having the President appoint the "governor" from a
list of three furnished him by the banking fraternity would
be matched if the law was so changed that the President
must appoint the Comptroller who supervises and regulates
the banks from a list of three persons given to him by the
banks to be regulated. In France the Chief of State selects
as governor of the Bank of France a man of his own choice,
and it is conceded that no disadvantage to the bank or the
country therefrom ever has been experienced. The promoters intend that the association shall be the "Govern-

ment," exclusive, supreme and imperial, in the world of banking, business and finance.

SEC. 11. *When the National Reserve Association is duly organized its board of directors shall call upon the subscribing banks for a payment of 50 per centum on the amount of their subscription to the capital stock of said association. When $100,000,000 of capital have been paid in the board of directors shall at once proceed to execute and file with the Secretary of State a certificate showing the payment of $100,000,000 on capital stock, and they shall further file with the Comptroller of the Currency a certificate showing the title and location of each bank which has subscribed to the capital stock of the National Reserve Association, the number of shares subscribed by each, and the amount paid thereon.*

$100,000,000 probably is all the banks ever will pay in. The balance of the money needed will be manufactured on the association's printing press, circulating notes of the association, corporate currency, which it is to be authorized to issue without limit. This $100,000,000 no doubt will be paid in U. S. bonds (Under Sec. 49), the association getting with the bonds the $100,000,000 bank-note currency based thereon. The association can hand this currency bank to the banks for their free use permanently, except 1½ per cent tax. And lo, and behold! The banks have bought and own $200,000,000 reserve association stock on which they have paid $100,000,000, the association has obtained $100,-000,000 of assets in shape of U. S. bonds, has deposited the bonds with the U. S. Treasury and obtained $100,000,000 of bank-note currency which it has permanently loaned to the banks for the mere government tax, and the whole thing is completed without the banks supplying a single dollar of their money! Then the banks through their association will get the 2 per cent interest on the deposited $100,000,000 U. S. bonds, will receive 4 per cent or 5 per cent on the $100,000,000 of association stock and say 6 per cent for use of $100,000,000 bank-note currency when loaned to customers, less 1½ per cent tax. This confederated banking fraternity invests $100,000,000, but gets interest on $300,000,000. That's financiering! The "joker" is the fact that the Government issues the $100,000,000 of currency, hands it over to the banks, allows the banks to have the interest on the bonds and what they can get loaning out the money and then charges banks only a nominal tax. Under the present system banks get two profits, but under the Aldrich plan they get three. In fact, under Sec. 23 the Government must deposit all its public moneys with this corporation immediately and then keep on doing so, without interest. This fixes it so that as soon as the association is formed the Government must hand over about $150,000,-000 of cash belonging to the people, 50 per cent more than the $100,000,000 paid in by the banks, same to be loaned out at 6 per cent to the people through the banks for the profit of the banks' association. And based on this $150,-000,000 of public money, if it is put into bank cash reserves, the banks actually can loan an additional $1,500,000,000 "credit" to the people at 6 per cent. Or, better yet, the association can hold this $150,000,000 of Government money, using it as its own cash reserve instead of gold, issue based on this reserve $450,000,000 of its own corporate currency, and hand this $450,000,000 of corporate paper currency over to its banks to be held by them as their "legal cash reserve" on which the banks then lawfully can loan $4,500,000,000 of additional credit loans to the people at 6 per cent. This huge increase of bank loans is based wholly upon the original $150,000,000 of Government money belonging to the people of the United States, and the banks are enabled to increase the quantity of their bank loans over four billion dollars and to collect 6 per cent thereon from the people each year just because the people's Congress authorizes by law this astonishing power. And for all of this enormous increase of the profits of banks through use of public revenues the Aldrich bill does not propose to insure one cent of compensation to the Government or the people.

There is no objection to the Government using the banks as a means of putting currency into circulation among the people, but the Government should receive the full value to the banks of the currency it so supplies. If this had been done continuously in the past it would have yielded to the Government without unfair burden on the banks enough to have paid off the entire national debt, now nearly $1,000,-000,000.

Much loud talk by Aldrich has conveyed the impression that banks would make only 4 per cent. We now see they will get at least double that profit direct, and vastly more indirectly.

SEC. 12. *Shares of the capital stock of the National Re-*

serve Association shall not be transferable, and under no circumstances shall they be hypothecated nor shall they be owned otherwise than by subscribing banks, nor shall they be owned by any such bank other than in the proportion herein provided. In case a subscribing bank increases its capital it shall thereupon subscribe for an additional amount of the capital of the National Reserve Association equal to 20 per centum of the bank's increase of capital, paying therefor its then book value as shown by the last published statement of said association. A bank applying for membership in the National Reserve Association at any time after its formation must subscribe for an amount of the capital of said association equal to 20 per centum of the capital of said subscribing bank, paying therefor its then book value as shown by the last published statement of said association. When the capital of the National Reserve Association has been increased either on account of the increase of capital of the banks in said association or on account of the increase in the membership of said association, the board of directors shall make and execute a certificate showing said increase in capital, the amount paid in and by whom paid. This certificate shall be filed in the office of the Comptroller of the Currency. In case a subscribing bank reduces its capital it shall surrender a proportionate amount of its holdings in the capital of said association, and if a bank goes into voluntary liquidation it shall surrender all of its holdings of the capital of said association. In either case the shares surrendered shall be canceled and the bank shall receive in payment therefor a sum equal to their then book value as shown by the last published statement of said association.

If any member of the National Reserve Association shall become insolvent and a receiver be appointed, the stock held by it in said association shall be canceled and the balance, after paying all debts due by such insolvent bank to said association (such debts being hereby declared to be a first lien upon the paid-in capital stock), shall be paid to the receiver of the insolvent bank.

Whenever the capital stock of the National Reserve Association is reduced, either on account of the reduction in capital of members of said association or the liquidation or insolvency of any member, the board of directors shall make and execute a certificate showing such reduction of capital stock and the amount repaid to each bank. This certificate shall be filed in the office of the Comptroller of the Currency.

The association and the banks, instead of the Government, get the excess profits going to surplus in addition to the 4 or 5 per cent cumulative dividends, by figuring the basis as "book value" instead of par. Membership, which is a privilege and not an enforcible legal right, is forfeited just as soon as a bank gets into trouble and a receiver is appointed. The association has a first lien (ahead of depositors) on the funds of a bank invested in association stock, for any debt of the bank to the association. It is by law to be made a preferred creditor.

SEC. 13. *The National Reserve Association and its branches and the local associations shall be exempt from local and State taxation except in respect to taxes upon real estate.*

This creature corporation of the banks may become a ready means, under this section, for dodging local taxes on hundreds of millions and perhaps billions of dollars of otherwise taxable assets. Many big banks and bankers are said to now evade taxes by tricks of bookkeeping, thus increasing the taxes of other people.

SEC. 14. *The directors of the National Reserve Association shall annually elect from their number an executive committee and such other committees as the by-laws of the National Reserve Association may provide. The executive committee shall consist of nine members, of which the governor of the National Reserve Association shall be ex-officio chairman and the two deputy governors and the Comptroller of the Currency ex-officio members, but not more than one of the elected members shall be chosen from any one district.*

The executive committee shall have all the authority which is vested in the board of directors, except the power of nomination, appointment, and removal of the governor and deputy governors and except such as may be specifically delegated by the board to other committees or to the executive officers, or such as may be specifically reserved or retained by the board.

The States reserved all power not expressly delegated to the Federal Government. Congress by law is to grant all power to this executive committee of 9 that is not specifically reserved by action of the board of 46 directors of the Reserve Association. The executive committee of 9 is given all the power over the business and operations possessed by the 46 directors, and 5 is a working majority. Twenty-four of the 46 directors can select this committee and 5 members of the committee, the governor, two deputy governors and two others; just five persons will absolutely rule the National Reserve Association and wield its limitless and dangerous powers. This will be the secret "holy of holies," and these five men will be selected by and ever do the will of Wall Street. These five men will decide from day to day the amount of money 94,000,000 people shall have for their use and the interest rate they must pay. They will have power to rediscount or aid any and every bank, and to refuse to do so. They will each day determine the quantity of bank credit the business of the country can borrow, who shall have it, and what must be paid therefor. These five men without prior public notice will be able suddenly to contract and cancel say $500,000,000 of corporate currency and thus force the federated banks to contract their loans of credit and make their customers pay up immediately $5,000,000,000 of their debts to the banks. This is the power to wreck prices, slaughter securities and property, shut down industries, forcing labor into idleness, causing general bankruptcy, panic, ruin. These five will be the executioners, the "headsmen," of all American business.

Congress is asked to grant power to do all these things to *five irresponsible men,* who are certain to be the dummies of the high financiers, and who with all power and no public responsibility, *in secret* will sit in unchallenged final judgment *with life and death power* over the welfare and very existence of every bank and through the banks *over the business of every individual and corporation in the United States.* And as is usual in such cases, one man, probably the governor, perhaps dominated from the outside by special interests, will rule the five and be sole master of the association and all its vast powers.

Do business men want Congress to grant for 50 years to five persons whom they do not know and never will see, absolute power to crush their business by subtle means any time without a moment's notice?

SEC. 15. *There shall be a board of examination elected annually by the board of directors from among their number, excluding the members of the executive committee, of which the Secretary of the Treasury shall be ex-officio chairman. It shall be the duty of this board to carefully examine the condition and the business of the National Re*

NATIONAL RESERVE ASSOCIATION EXECUTIVE COMMITTEE
ALDRICH PLAN

A QUORUM (5) OF EXECUTIVE COMMITTEE OF NATIONAL RESERVE ASSOCIATION IN SECRET SESSION PASSING DEATH SENTENCE ON "GENERAL PROSPERITY." CHAIRMAN:— "THE MOTION: TO CONTRACT AND CANCEL 1,500,000,000 OF THE ASSOCIATIONS CURRENCY IS CARRIED. THIS WILL FORCE THE BANKS TO CALL IN FIVE BILLION DOLLARS OF BUSINESS LOANS, CAUSE PANIC AND SMASH PRICES. "MUMS THE WORD BOYS UNTIL OUR BROKERS SELL SHORT FOR OUR SEVERAL ACCOUNTS, THEN LET HER RIP!

*serve Association and of its branches and to make a public
statement of the result of such examination at least once a
year.*

The association thus is empowered to regulate itself.
No public regulation or control is provided. The corporation is to be independent of government, supreme.

SEC. 16. *Each branch shall have a manager and a deputy
manager appointed from the district by the governor of the
National Reserve Association with the approval of the
executive committee of said association and the board of
directors of the branch, and subject to removal at any time
by the governor with the approval of the executive committee of the National Reserve Association. The powers
and duties of the manager and deputy manager and of the
various committees of the branches shall be prescribed by
the by-laws of the National Reserve Association.*

SEC. 17. *The directors of each local association shall
annually elect from their number a president, a vice-president, and an executive committee, whose powers and duties
shall be determined by the by-laws of the local association,
subject, however, to the approval of the National Reserve
Association.*

SEC. 18. *The National Reserve Association shall cause
to be kept at all times, at the head office of the association, a full and correct list of the names of the banks owning stock in the association and the number of shares held by
each. Such list shall be subject to the inspection of all the
shareholders of the association, and a copy thereof on the
first Monday of July of each year shall be transmitted to the
Comptroller of the Currency.*

The association rules absolutely its branches and the
local associations. The Government and the people have
no effective voice in this private corporation that is to get
the free use of all public moneys and for 50 years issue and
control for its own profit all public currency.

SEC. 19. *The earnings of the National Reserve Association shall be disposed of in the following manner:*

*After the payment of all expenses and the franchise and
other taxes not provided for in this section the shareholders
shall be entitled to receive an annual dividend of 4 per
centum on the paid-in capital, which dividend shall be cumulative. Further annual net earnings shall be disposed of as
follows: First, a contingent fund shall be created, which
shall be maintained at an amount equal to 1 per centum*

on the paid-in capital, and shall not exceed in any event
$2,000,000 and shall be used to meet any possible losses.
Such fund shall, upon the final dissolution of the National
Reserve Association, be paid to the United States and shall
not under any circumstances be included in the book value
of the stock or be paid to the shareholders. Second, one-
half of additional net earnings shall be paid into the surplus
fund of the National Reserve Association until said fund
shall amount to 20 per centum of the paid-in capital, one-
fourth shall be paid to the United States as a franchise tax,
and one-fourth shall be paid to the shareholders, until the
shareholders' dividend shall amount to 5 per centum per
annum on the paid-in capital: Provided, That no such divi-
dends, exclusive of the cumulative dividends above provided
for, shall at any time be paid in excess of 5 per centum
in any one year. Whenever and so long as the contingent
fund has been provided for and the 5 per centum dividend
has been paid to shareholders one-half of the additional
earnings shall be added to the surplus fund, and one-half
shall be paid to the United States as a franchise tax. When-
ever and so long as the surplus fund of the National Re-
serve Association amounts to 20 per centum of the paid-in
capital and the shareholders shall have received dividends
not exceeding 5 per centum, all excess earnings shall be
paid to the United States as a franchise tax.

Right here the game of Euchre begins, the Government
getting plenty of experience, but the banks taking all the
tricks. This reads like the Government might get a lot of
money as its share of the partnership profits. But under
the above provision probably it will never get one cent. The
$2,000,000 "contingent fund" it can not get until the end
of the charter, 50 years. If the association never earns net
over 4 per cent and sufficient to keep its $2,000,000 "con-
tingent fund" to pay losses intact, clearly nothing would go
to the Government. It no doubt will keep its profits down
to that basis by cutting its discount rates charged banks for
rediscounting (under Sections 26, 27, 28, 29), because then
banks will get all the excess profits, in form of lower discount charges. Whereas, if the discount rate was kept up
the association would have excess profits that the banks
must divide with the Government, although on a grossly
unfair basis. As the banks own all of the association's stock
and pay to the association all the revenue it receives, what
is the use of letting the Government get away with any of

the profits when the banks can keep all by simply manipulating the interest or discount charges? And Carnegie says we cannot trust the "human nature" of big financiers when their interests are at stake. We must expect them to grab every dollar they can get and keep out of jail—and then some. But if this bill passes, this method by which the banks will euchre the Government out of all of the joint profits will be made lawful. If the association keeps its reserve intact (Sec. 41) and issues no more than $900,000,-000 of its corporate currency (Sec. 51), there is no other provision under which the Government can receive a dollar of profit or benefit. Section 56 gives it 1½ per cent annual tax on the bank-note currency or bonds taken over by the association from the banks, but 1 per cent of this is given back by exchanging 3 per cent 50-year Government bonds for the present 2 per cent bonds. This leaves only ½ per cent, the same amount the Government now is receiving as a tax on bank-note currency, which only about covers the expense. The history of the banking system given in another chapter proves that the banks always take advantage of the Government when they have the power so to do.

The greatest high finance minds in the world have spent months, years, helping to devise the provisions of this bill. It is a great success—for the banks. Its ingenious, sly and crafty wording and provisions makes the measure a genuine wonder. Every little sentence has a meaning of its own. Every addition to "surplus" increases the "book value" of the association stock, the benefit all going to the banks besides their liberal dividends.

SEC. 20. *Any member of a local association may apply to such association for a guaranty of the commercial paper which it desires to rediscount at the branch of the National Reserve Association in its district. Any such bank receiving a guaranty from a local association shall pay a commission to the local association, to be fixed in each case by its board of directors. Expenses and losses in excess of commissions shall be met by an assessment of the members of the local association in proportion to the ratio which their capital and surplus bears to the aggregate capital and surplus of the members of the local association, which assessment shall be made by its board of directors, and the commission received for such guaranty, after the payment of expenses and possible losses, shall be distributed among the several banks of the local association in the same proportion.*

*A local association shall have authority to require security
from any bank offering paper for guaranty, or it may decline to grant the application. The total amount of guaran-
ties by a local association to the National Reserve Association shall not at any time exceed the aggregate capital and
surplus of the banks forming the guaranteeing association.*

A local association may legally refuse to aid a particular bank. This puts any bank or trust company at the
mercy of any local dominant clique among banks. The
bank has paid its quota, is obligated, yet aid in time of need
can be refused and this notwithstanding Section 22, which
extends to each bank the privileges of the national association; for the local has power, under Section 20, to block
such help. Discrimination and favoritism as between banks
would be legal and probable. One bank can be charged a
mere nominal commission and another a prohibitory figure.
A bank is made legally liable without limit for losses by a
local association under its guarantee on paper certified for
rediscount, and this without the consent or knowledge of
such bank. It is made liable without limit for acts of others
whom it cannot control or restrain.

SEC. 21. *Any local association may by a vote of three-
fourths of its members and with the approval of the National Reserve Association, assume and exercise such of the
powers and functions of a clearing house as are not inconsistent with the purposes of this act. The National Reserve
Association may require any local association to perform
such services in facilitating the domestic exchanges of the
National Reserve Association as the public interests may
require.*

For many years banks have sought means to legalize
and incorporate clearing houses, and now here it is in
smoothest and broadest form. Sections 6 and 21 do the trick.
Every local association is made a distinct corporation.
Every bank clearing house is a local trust for regulating
competition between banks so as to keep low the rate of interest paid to depositors and high the rates charged borrowers. This destruction of competition between banks and
the fact that no new competing banks will be permitted to be
established in any city or town to compete with the banks
joining this association, are among the chief arguments
being made directly to banks by the promoters of this
scheme to induce the co-operation of all banks. But what
are the business men and the people who must depend upon

bank loans and pay the interest rates going to say about this plan of establishing in every town a monopoly of money and bank credit and destruction of competition?

SEC. 22. *All of the privileges and advantages of the National Reserve Association shall be equitably extended to every bank of any of the classes herein defined which shall subscribe to its proportion of the capital stock of the National Reserve Association and shall otherwise conform to the requirements of this act: Provided, That the National Reserve Association may suspend a bank from the privileges of membership for refusal to comply with such requirements or for failure for thirty days to maintain its reserves, or to make the reports required by this act, or for misrepresentation in any report or examination as to its condition or as to the character or extent of its assets or liabilities.*

The National Association can suspend any bank refusing to comply with the requirements imposed on it, deprive it of all aid and benefit. The "child" can discipline its parents. If a bank does not "conform to the requirements of this act," for example, does not instantly obey an order to contract its loans to its regular customers, say half, it can be "suspended," denied aid, even in a panic.

SEC. 23. *The National Reserve Association shall be the principal fiscal agent of the United States. The Government of the United States shall upon the organization of the National Reserve Association deposit its general funds with said association and its branches, and thereafter all receipts of the Government, exclusive of trust funds, shall be deposited with said association and its branches, and all disbursements by the Government shall be made through said association and its branches.*

SEC. 24. *The Government of the United States and banks owning stock in the National Reserve Association shall be the only depositors in said association. All domestic transactions of the National Reserve Association shall be confined to the Government and the subscribing banks, with the exception of the purchase or sale of Government or State securities or securities of foreign governments or of gold coin or bullion.*

SEC. 25. *The National Reserve Association shall pay no interest on deposits.*

The total general-fund receipts of the government for the fiscal year to June 30, 1911, were $759.707,100.03. The association thus will receive Government deposits amounting during each year in the aggregate to more than three-fourths of a billion dollars, or $40,000,000,000 during the next 50 years, for nothing. June 30, 1911, the balance on hand was $140,176,926.13. December, 1907, it was over $240,000,000.

These vast sums of public money raised by the taxation of the people are all to be turned over free to this private corporation for deposit and by it to be loaned to the people through its banks for the exclusive profit of the corporation. And Sec. 25 (aimed at the Government exclusively) prevents Government getting one cent for the use of these vast sums. Yet the members of the Monetary Commission who prepared this bill, were paid and sworn "servants" of the people. Section 23 requires that every dollar paid out by the Government must be paid through this corporation, thus virtually making it the guardian of the Republic.

The Central Bank is prohibited from doing any "domestic" business except with banks, but it can do business abroad without restriction or limit. It can legally take the Government's deposited revenues raised by taxation that it gets the use of free, and loan the same to carry on business in Europe or Asia, but not in the United States.

SEC. 26. *The National Reserve Association may through a branch rediscount for and with the indorsement of any bank having a deposit with it, notes and bills of exchange arising out of commercial transactions; that is, notes and bills of exchange issued or drawn for agricultural, industrial, or commercial purposes, and not including notes or bills issued or drawn for the purpose of carrying stocks, bonds, or other investment securities.*

Such notes and bills must have a maturity of not more than twenty-eight days, and must have been made at least thirty days prior to the date of rediscount. The amount so rediscounted shall at no time exceed the capital of the bank for which the rediscounts are made. The aggregate of such notes and bills bearing the signature or indorsement of any one person, company, firm, or corporation, rediscounted for any one bank, shall at no time exceed ten per centum of the unimpaired capital and surplus of said bank.

SEC. 27. *The National Reserve Association may through a branch also rediscount, for and with the indorsement of any bank having a deposit with it, notes and bills of exchange arising out of commercial transactions as hereinbefore defined, having more than twenty-eight days, but not exceeding four months, to run, but in such cases the paper must be guaranteed by the local association of which the bank asking for the rediscount is a member.*

SEC. 28. *Whenever, in the opinion of the governor of the National Reserve Association, the public interests so require, such opinion to be concurred in by the executive committee of the National Reserve Association and to have the definite approval of the Secretary of the Treasury, the National Reserve Association may through a branch discount the direct obligation of a depositing bank, indorsed by its local association, provided that the indorsement of the local association shall be fully secured by the pledge and deposit with it of satisfactory securities, which shall be held by the local association for account of the National Reserve Association; but in no such case shall the amount loaned by the National Reserve Association exceed three-fourths of the actual value of the securities so pledged.*

SEC. 29. *The power of rediscount and discount granted to the National Reserve Association by sections twenty-six, twenty-seven and twenty-eight of this act shall in each case be exercised through the branch in the district in which the bank making the application is located.*

Can any one read these provisions and deny that the association is a Central Bank? If so, what is a Central Bank? The "lid is off." The association can discount and rediscount for the banks practically without limit. The foundation is laid for the wildest wild-cat banking inflation ever dreamed of. It is an "endless chain." It is "wide open." When the bubble bursts no doubt it will exceed any financial catastrophe in all history. Any and all kinds of "securities" and "paper" in one way or another can be juggled and used as "security," and basis for inflating and issuing hundreds of millions of corporate currency claimed not to be guaranteed by the Government.

In a great stock market campaign, when call loan rates are bid up high, banks can rediscount at the Central Bank their ordinary 6 per cent commercial paper, and get printing press corporate currency in unlimited amounts to loan at 10, 30, 50 or 100 per cent to the stock gamblers for use in fleecing the public in the speculative struggle. The whole scheme is rigged for the convenience of Wall Street.

SEC. 30. *The National Reserve Association shall have authority to fix its rates of discount from time to time,*

THE EXECUTIONER
"ALDRICH PLAN"

INCREASE INTEREST RATES

BANK LOANS CONTRACTED

ELASTICITY

NAT. RESERVE ASSOCIATION

ALL BUSINESS

BANK

Crozier

THE ALDRICH BILL GRANTS TO THE NATIONAL RESERVE ASSOCIATION UNLIMITED POWER TO RAISE AND LOWER THE DISCOUNT OR INTEREST RATES AND TO INFLATE AND CONTRACT THE VOLUME OF CREDIT LOANS MADE BY THE 24,392 BANKS TO BUSINESS MEN. THIS IS THE POWER OF ABSOLUTE LIFE AND DEATH OVER ALL AMERICAN BUSINESS.

which when so fixed shall be published, and shall be uniform throughout the United States.

Power to raise and lower the general discount rate is the power to increase and decrease interest rates and the prices of all securities, property and labor. It is the power to veto prosperity, curtail credit and the volume of business, and if carried to extreme to cause panic. Inflation and contraction of the currency and bank credit is an equally dangerous power. And this power is to be exercised each day in secret by five irresponsible men for the whole United States.

SEC. 31. *National banks are hereby authorized to accept drafts or bills of exchange drawn upon them, having not more than four months to run, properly secured, and arising out of commercial transactions as hereinbefore defined. The amount of such acceptances outstanding shall not exceed one-half the capital and surplus of the accepting bank, and shall be subject to the restrictions of section fifty-two hundred of the Revised Statutes.*

SEC. 32. *The National Reserve Association may, whenever its own condition and the general financial conditions warrant such investment, purchase from a subscribing bank acceptances of banks or acceptors of unquestioned financial responsibility arising out of commercial transactions as hereinbefore defined. Such acceptances must have not exceeding ninety days to run, and must be of a character generally known in the market as prime bills. Such acceptances shall bear the indorsement of the subscribing bank selling the same, which indorsement must be other than that of the acceptor.*

SEC. 33. *The National Reserve Association may invest in United States bands; also in obligations, having not more than one year to run, of the United States or its dependencies, or of any State, or of foreign governments.*

SEC. 34. *The National Reserve Association shall have power, both at home and abroad, to deal in gold coin or bullion, to make loans thereon, and to contract for loans of gold coin or bullion, giving therefor, when necessary, acceptable security, including the hypothecation of any of its holdings of United States bonds.*

SEC. 35. *The National Reserve Association shall have power to purchase from its subscribing banks and to sell, with or without its indorsement, checks or bills of exchange, arising out of commercial transactions as hereinbefore de-*

fined, payable in such foreign countries as the board of directors of the National Reserve Association may determine. These bills of exchange must have not exceeding ninety days to run, and must bear the signatures of two or more responsible parties, of which the last one shall be that of a subscribing bank.

SEC. 36. *The National Reserve Association shall have power to open and maintain banking accounts in foreign countries and to establish agencies in foreign countries for the purpose of purchasing, selling, and collecting foreign bills of exchange, and it shall have authority to buy and sell, with or without its indorsement, through such correspondents or agencies, checks or prime foreign bills of exchange arising out of commercial transactions, which have not exceeding ninety days to run, and which bear the signatures of two or more responsible parties.*

The association thus is legally authorized to sit in and play the international game of financial poker with all of the world's gold in the jack-pot. Section 36 equips it to take its position as the American branch of the coming great international money combine that will soon eliminate or suppress all serious competition for important loans and double the burden on the human race by increasing universally the rates of interest for money and credit.

SEC. 37. *It shall be the duty of the National Reserve Association or any of its branches, upon request, to transfer any part of the deposit balance of any bank having an account with it to the credit of any other bank having an account with the National Reserve Association. If a deposit balance is transferred from the books of one branch to the books of another branch, it may be done, under regulations to be prescribed by the National Reserve Association, by mail, telegraph, or otherwise, at rates to be fixed at the time by the manager of the branch at which the transaction originates.*

SEC. 38. *The National Reserve Association may purchase, acquire, hold, and convey real estate for the following purposes and for no other:*

First. Such as shall be necessary for the immediate accommodation in the transaction of the business either of the head office or of the branches.

Second. Such as shall be mortgaged to it in good faith by way of security for debts previously contracted.

Third. Such as shall be conveyed to it in satisfaction of

debts previously contracted in the course of its dealings.

Fourth. Such as it shall purchase at sales under judgments, decrees, or mortgages held by said association, or shall purchase to secure debts due to it.

But the National Reserve Association shall not hold the possession of any real estate under mortgage or the title and possession of any real estate purchased to secure any debts due to it for a longer period than five years.

There will be a big saving for the banks in reduction of the cost of transferring funds. This cost can be paid by the association, if necessary to reduce profits so as to avoid paying anything to the Government.

SEC. 39. *All subscribing banks must conform to the following requirements as to reserves to be held against deposits of various classes, but the deposit balance of any subscribing bank in the National Reserve Association and any notes of the National Reserve Association which it holds may be counted as the whole or any part of its required reserve:*

First. On demand deposits: National banks in different localities shall maintain the same percentages of reserve against demand deposits as is now required by law, and the same percentages of reserve against demand deposits shall be required of all other subscribing banks in the same localities.

Second. On time deposits: All time deposits and moneys held in trust payable or maturing within thirty days shall be subject to the same reserve requirements as demand deposits in the same locality. All time deposits and moneys held in trust payable or maturing more than thirty days from date shall be subject to the same reserve requirements as demand deposits for the thirty days preceding their maturity, but no reserves shall be required therefor except for this period. Such time deposits and moneys held in trust, payable only at a stated time not less than thirty days from date of deposit, must be represented by certificates or instruments in writing and must not be allowed to be withdrawn before the time specified without thirty days' notice.

Note that the present reserve law is not repealed. The changes herein made do not require the banks to take any of their reserves out of Wall Street or to put same in the association's "central reservoir."

Bank-note currency is not "lawful money." It never could be counted as part of bank cash reserves. It would be too much like a man writing and signing his own promissory note for a million and then claiming that this made him a millionaire. But what the law prohibits banks doing singly they now propose to do collectively through their association by counting its corporate currency as part of bank reserves. It is a dangerous, reckless plan. The bill, like all legislation in recent years, reduces the duties and increases the privileges of the banks.

Sec. 39 authorizes mere commercial paper dumped onto the Association by a bank and re-discounted to obtain a "deposit balance" at the National Reserve Association to be counted as "legal cash reserve," on which such bank then lawfully can inflate its credit loans ten times the increase of its "reserve" so obtained. This opens the way for an "endless chain" inflation. No reserves at all are to be held against "time deposits" by the banks. This may reduce by half the $1,500,000,000 cash the banks now must hold as a reserve to protect depositors. Stating it differently, if half of present bank liabilities are converted from "demand deposits" into such "time deposits," the banks will be able to inflate and double their loans of "credit," getting say 6 per cent interest on at least $15,000,000,000 of extra "loans," without furnishing one more dollar of capital, or money. It will further raise prices and start an era of wild and dangerous speculation. On the average it would reduce by half the cash reserves the law now requires banks to hold. This would enable banks to loan about $20,000 instead of $10,000 of "credit" for each $1,000 of cash they possess. It would enable the 24,392 banks ultimately to practically double their annual net profits without one dollar of extra investment or expense. This is part of the bribe offered by Wall Street to the banks through the Aldrich measure to induce them to join the conspiracy and help force the bill through Congress.

Sec. 40. *National banks may loan not more than thirty per centum of their time deposits, as herein defined, upon improved and unencumbered real estate, such loans not to exceed fifty per centum of the actual value of the property, which property shall be situated in the vicinity or in the territory directly tributary to the bank: Provided, That this privilege shall not be extended to banks acting as reserve agents for banks or trust companies.*

National banks are by law prohibited from loaning on real estate. They were created to serve trade and commerce, banks of discount instead of mere loan agencies. Their assets were to be kept in quick, liquid form, not tied up in stationary loans. This bill authorizes national banks to loan on real estate up to "thirty per centum of their time deposits" and permits a bank, if it desires, to convert all its liabilities into "time deposits." This gives national banks a club to force all state banks and trust companies into this bank combine, or to take away from state institutions a large portion of their business and profits. It also tends to take the business of making real estate loans away from attorneys and other individuals and give banking corporations a complete monopoly of making loans of every character. Every lawyer and all business men not owned or ruled by the big national banks will fight this bill, if they wish to protect their own interests and welfare. The great menace to the legal profession is the increasing monopoly by a few corporations of business formerly conducted by lawyers exclusively. This bill makes it worse.

SEC. 41. *All demand liabilities, including deposits and circulating notes, of the National Reserve Association shall be covered to the extent of fifty per centum by a reserve of gold (including foreign gold coin and gold bullion) or other money of the United States which the national banks are now authorized to hold as a part of their legal reserve: Provided, That whenever and so long as such reserve shall fall and remain below 50 per centum the National Reserve Association shall pay a special tax upon the deficiency of reserve at a rate increasing in proportion to such deficiency as follows: For each 2½ per centum or fraction thereof that the reserve falls below 50 per centum a tax shall be levied at the rate of 1½ per centum per annum: Provided further, That no additional circulating notes shall be issued whenever and so long as the amount of such reserve falls below 33⅓ per centum of its outstanding notes.*

SEC. 42. *In computing the demand liabilities of the National Reserve Association a sum equal to one-half of the amount of the United States bonds held by the association which have been purchased from national banks, and which had previously been deposited by such banks to secure their circulating notes, shall be deducted from the amount of such liabilities.*

This is designed to make it appear that a 50 per cent reserve of actual gold will be behind the corporate currency. But in fact the bill does not make necessary one dollar of actual gold. Wall Street and the big banks forced Congress to adopt the gold standard, and now this bill leaves the entire burden of maintaining the gold standard and insuring gold payments upon the Government instead of upon this corporation that is to issue the public currency without limit and get the profits therefrom.

No tax is imposed if a 50 per cent reserve is maintained. If the reserve should fall, say to 33⅓, a tax equal to about 9 per cent per annum is required, but only on the deficiency below the 50 per cent reserve while so deficient. But this is not a serious burden because the Association would be getting from the banks say 3 per cent interest on corporate currency amounting to three times such reserve deficiency, which lets the Association out even. But it enables the banks to inflate their credit loans ten times such amount of currency and thirty times such reserve deficiency. And all that it costs the banks is 3 per cent per annum for the use of such corporate currency put into their cash reserves.

Sec. 41 says, "A reserve of gold * * * or other money," etc. Now, "other money" includes the $346,000,-000 of greenbacks, about $900,000,000 of gold certificates and a large amount of silver dollars and certificates, or between 1,200 and 1,500 million dollars, most of which is in the reserves of the banks now. This government paper money, under this bill, can be used instead of gold by the association as a "reserve" to secure its corporate currency, and there is enough of such Government currency, if acquired by the association, to enable it to issue nearly $3,000,-000,000 of its corporate currency, an amount nearly equal to all the money, gold, silver, greenbacks, gold and silver certificates and bank-note currency now in circulation, held by banks and possessed by the Government. Thus the way is opened for an unlimited inflation of corporate paper currency issued by a mere private corporation with relatively small net assets and no Government guarantee, every dollar supposed to be redeemable in gold, but with not a single dollar of gold necessarily held in the reserves of such corporation to accomplish such redemption. It is proposed to force the Government to provide all the gold by having the law keep all Government currency redeemable in gold. When the corporation wants gold it will take Government currency, present it for redemption and demand the gold. If the Government does not have the gold, the gold standard law of March 14, 1900, requires it to sell its bonds and buy the gold needed. So the entire burden is on the Government and the profits go to the banks.

This is wildcatting. It will lead to inflation and a depreciated paper currency, for the people will not take it at par without Government guarantee. Under Sec. 42 no reserve of any kind behind half the bonds taken over and the bank-note currency with such bonds is required.

Under Sec. 41 no tax is paid if the reserve of gold or "other money" is kept up, and only a nominal tax in any case. A 33⅓ per cent reserve is legalized, and if the reserve to secure the corporate currency goes below that, or is wiped out entirely, there is no remedy in the hands of the Government or in the people who may then hold a billion or more dollars of this wildcat corporate currency, except that the printing press shall be stopped and no more currency notes issued. But suppose the association don't stop? Suppose it prints and emits five, ten or fifty billion dollars of this wildcat corporate paper currency, not guaranteed by the Government, and without a dollar of gold or anything else to secure it? The bill fixes no limit in quantity and provides no penalty for violations, and all "thou shalt nots" in the law unenforced by penalties usually are ignored by bankers. This is the wildest, most unsafe and unsound currency plan ever suggested to Congress. Even free silver coinage was vastly more safe and sound, for the Government was behind every silver dollar and pledged to maintain it at par, and the silver in each dollar is worth 53 cents as bullion; but the paper and ink as such in this corporate currency will be worthless.

Sec. 43. *The National Reserve Association shall make a report, showing the principal items of its balance sheet, to the Comptroller of the Currency once a week. These reports shall be made public. In addition, full reports shall be made to the Comptroller of the Currency by said association coincident with the five reports called for each year from the national banks.*

Sec. 44. *All subscribing banks shall, under regulations to be prescribed by the National Reserve Association, make a report monthly, or oftener if required, to said association showing the principal items of their balance sheets.*

Sec. 45. *All reports of national-bank examiners in regard to the condition of banks shall hereafter be made in duplicate, and one copy shall be filed with the National*

*Reserve Association for the confidential use of its executive
officers and branch managers.*

SEC. 46. *The National Reserve Association may accept
copies of the reports of the national-bank examiners for
subscribing national banks and also copies of the reports
of State-bank examiners for subscribing State banks and
trust companies, in States where the furnishing of such information is not contrary to law: Provided, however, That
the standard of such examinations, both National and State,
meets the requirements prescribed by the National Reserve
Association. The National Reserve Association shall have
the right at any time to examine or cause to be examined
by its own representatives any subscribing bank. The
National Reserve Association may make such payments to
national and State examiners for such services required of
them as the directors may consider just and equitable.*

This private corporation through examiners and reports
is to have its nose in the private business of every individual and corporation that deals with banks. And no
effective way is provided to prevent this information being
communicated to, and used by, the special interests of Wall
Street. Espionage into everybody's affairs and improper
use of the confidential information will be possible. Not
only will the central bank get copies of the reports of all
banks and bank examiners, but each bank must make a
monthly report and special reports when required, and permit agents of the central bank any time to investigate every
detail of the bank's business and operations. Every bank
must disclose everything to the central bank and then obey
its orders or be "suspended," blacklisted.

SEC. 47. *All provisions of law requiring national banks
to hold or to transfer and deliver to the Treasurer of the
United States bonds of the United States other than those
required to secure outstanding circulating notes and Government deposits are hereby repealed.*

(A little provision for the benefit of the banks.)

SEC. 48. *There shall be no further issue of circulating
notes by any national bank beyond the amount now outstanding. National banks may maintain their present note
issue, but whenever a bank retires the whole or any part of
its existing issue its right to reissue the notes so retired shall
thereupon cease.*

This is to open the way for the association's corporate
currency, from which the federated banks will in one way or

another make much more profit than from present bank-note currency.

SEC. 49. *The National Reserve Association shall, for a period of one year from the date of its organization, offer to purchase at a price not less than par and accrued interest the 2 per centum bonds held by subscribing national banks and deposited to secure their circulating notes. The National Reserve Association shall take over the bonds so purchased and assume responsibility for the redemption upon presentation of outstanding notes secured thereby. The National Reserve Association shall issue, on the terms herein provided, its own notes as the outstanding notes secured by such bonds so held shall be presented for redemption and may issue further notes from time to time to meet business requirements, it being the policy of the United States to retire as rapidly as possible, consistent with the public interests, bond-secured circulation and to substitute therefor notes of the National Reserve Association of a character and secured and redeemed in the manner provided for in this act.*

October 31, 1911, there was $744,071,715 of bank-note currency outstanding on an equal quantity of United States bonds deposited as security, the banks getting 2 per cent interest on the bonds and say 6 per cent for use of the currency loaned to the people, less a Government tax of ½ per cent.

The association, owned by and for the benefit of the banks exclusively, will quickly "purchase" from the banks all these bonds, getting therewith the currency privilege. This can be done without a dollar of money. The banks by an assignment written on the receipts given when the bonds were deposited with the treasury can transfer the $744,071,715 of bonds to the association and for their pay can keep, loan out and permanently use the $744,071,715 of bank-note currency now held by the banks against such bonds. Or, the association's corporate currency may be issued in place of such bank-note currency. The association, which is but the banks themselves in federated form, agrees to "redeem" such bank-notes if any of them happen to be presented for redemption, in which case they will be paid, not in gold or "lawful money" but in corporate currency of the association, the product of its printing press. The association then, under Sec. 55, can require the Government to take back these 2 per cent bonds and give in exchange 3 per cent bonds running fifty years, an increase of 50 per cent in the annual interest expenses of the Government. The 3 per cent fifty-year U. S. bonds, even without any currency issuing privilege, should now, or soon will, sell on a 2 per cent or 2½ per cent interest basis. If at 2½ per cent, the $744,071,715 of 3 per cent fifty-year bonds so obtained by the association would at once increase about one-sixth in value and be worth a premium above par amounting to $124,012,000. This net profit for the association would be equal to 124 per cent on the entire $100,000,000 paid in by all the banks for its capital stock. No wonder former Secretary of the Treasury Shaw said, as reported, that private interests could afford to pay a billion dollars for such a charter from Congress. Note particularly that Congress, by Sec. 49, would solemnly bind the Government and the faith of the United States to the permanent "policy" of a private corporate paper currency, to "notes of the National Reserve Association of a character and secured and redeemed in the manner provided for in this act." This would be the beginning of *the downfall of all Government currency of every kind* and the ultimate substitution of *mere corporation paper currency* issued by and for the exclusive profit of *a private banking syndicate.* That is the big issue presented by this bill: "GOVERNMENT MONEY VS. CORPORATE CURRENCY." The fight will center around this one proposition. There is little else in the bill. There should be no compromise. The country must have all Government or all corporate currency. The chief aim of the promoters of this measure was to impose upon the United States corporate currency exclusively and get control of its volume into their own private hands.

SEC. 50. *All note issues of the National Reserve Association shall at all times be covered by legal reserves to the extent required by section forty-one of this act and by notes or bills of exchange arising out of commercial transactions as hereinbefore defined or obligations of the United States.*

The word "and" may make "notes or bills of exchange" usable in the "reserve" in place of "gold and other money."

SEC. 51. *Any notes of the National Reserve Association in circulation at any time in excess of $900,000,000 which are not covered by an equal amount of lawful money, gold bullion, or foreign gold coin held by said association, shall pay a special tax at the rate of 1½ per centum per annum, and any notes in excess of $1,200,000,000 not so covered* *shall pay a special tax at the rate of 5 per centum per annum: Provided, That in computing said amounts of $900,000,000 and $1,200,000,000 the aggregate amount of any national-bank notes then outstanding shall be included.*

No tax is paid on the first $900,000,000 of corporate currency, and none on currency in excess of that huge figure if the excess is "covered" as provided. If the bill becomes law the next Congress no doubt will be asked to amend the act and turn over to the association, subject to the outstanding certificates, the nearly one billion dollars of gold held in trust by the Government, and the $150,000,000 gold reserve in the Treasury. The $346,000,000 of greenbacks then would be burned up and corporate currency issued in their place. This we believe is part of the agreed program, but is being kept out of sight for prudential reasons, to stifle opposition that might kill the whole scheme. It is the same old fight that has been on constantly between the banks and the people for fifty years. This time, however, it takes a vastly more daring and dangerous form than ever before.

SEC. 52. *The circulating notes of the National Reserve Association shall constitute a first lien upon all its assets and shall be redeemable in lawful money on presentation at the head office of said association or any of its branches. It shall be the duty of the National Reserve Association to maintain at all times a parity of value of its circulating notes with the standard established by the first section of the act of March 14, 1900, entitled "An act to define and fix the standard of value, to maintain the parity of all forms of money issued or coined by the United States, to refund the public debt, and for other purposes."*

Corporate currency can be redeemed in greenbacks instead of gold, for both are "lawful money." So are silver dollars, the present bullion value of which is about 53 cents on the dollar. Is it not amusing to see the very interests that in 1896 opposed *free coinage of silver by the Government* when the bullion value of silver was 53 cents on the dollar, now they devoutly "pray" for *free coinage of paper and ink by their private corporation* to the extent of more than a billion dollars, the paper and ink as such being worthless? It is made the "duty" of the association to maintain its notes on a parity with gold. But suppose it don't, won't or can't? There is no penalty imposed or remedy provided. The "duty" is meaningless and impotent.

SEC. 53. *The circulating notes of the National Reserve Association shall be received at par in payment of all taxes, excises, and other dues to the United States, and for all salaries and other debts and demands owing by the United States to individuals, firms, corporations, or associations, except obligations of the Government which are by their terms specifically payable in gold, and for all debts due from or by one bank or trust company to another, and for all obligations due to any bank or trust company.*

Corporate currency is to be only a "limited legal-tender," not a full legal-tender for all debts, public and private, between individuals, or between ordinary corporations and individuals. The $50,000,000 of greenbacks issued under acts of July 17 and August 5, 1861, were made "full legal-tender" by act of March 17, 1862, and never depreciated but always were equal with gold in value. The $450,000,-000 of greenbacks issued under acts of February 25, 1862, July 11, 1862, and March 3, 1863, were made only a "limitel legal-tender" at the demand of the Wall Street financiers engaged in cornering the gold and forcing the Government to pay ruinous prices for it to carry on the war to preserve the Union. These "limited legal-tenders," although an obligation of the Government, depreciated to less than 50 cents on the dollar. Will not corporate currency that likewise is only a "limited legal-tender," and does not even have the obligation of the Government behind it, also depreciate? No person will be obliged to accept corporate currency when tendered in payment of a private debt, because it is not a "full legal-tender." This will make it less valuable and cause ultimate depreciation, after it has been floated at par out into the hands of the people, like the oceans of watered Wall Street stocks, and the people will be the losers. It is a step toward returning to the old wildcat corporate currency that generally prevailed prior to 1860, when 10,000 different kinds of corporate currency notes were issued by the banks of the country without any Government credit behind them, and most of this corporate currency became utterly worthless, entailing frightful losses on the people and demoralizing all business.

SEC. 54. *The National Reserve Association and its branches shall at once, upon application and without charge for transportation, forward its circulating notes to any depositing bank against its credit balance.*

This is for the benefit of the banks.

SEC. 55. *Upon application of the National Reserve Association the Secretary of the Treasury shall exchange the 2 per centum bonds of the United States bearing the circulation privilege purchased from subscribing banks for 3 per centum bonds of the United States without the circulation privilege, payable after fifty years from the date of issue. The National Reserve Association shall hold the 3 per centum bonds so issued during the period of its corporate existence: Provided, That after five years from the date of its organization the Secretary of the Treasury may at his option permit the National Reserve Association to sell not more than $50,000,000 of such bonds annually: And provided further, That the United States reserves the right at any time to pay any of such bonds before maturity, or to purchase any of them at par for the trustees of the postal savings, or otherwise.*

SEC. 56. *The National Reserve Association shall pay to the Government a special franchise tax of $1\frac{1}{2}$ per centum annually during the period of its charter upon an amount equal to the par value of such United States bonds transferred to it by the subscribing banks.*

Sec. 55 is discussed following Sec. 49 above. The tax, Sec. 56, is to offset the difference between 2 per cent and 3 per cent bond interest and ½ per cent in place of the present circulation tax on bank-note currency. If the banks decide not to turn their U. S. bonds over to the association, but retain and continue to enjoy their present currency privilege, as they are authorized by Sec. 48 to do, then the Government will get nothing under Sec. 56. If the Government pays the $744,000,000 of bonds, the proceeds held as "reserve" would form the basis of $1,488,000,000 to $2,732,000,000 corporate currency. If the bonds run the fifty years, the Government must pay as interest thereon $1,116,000,000.

SEC. 57. *That banking corporations for carrying on the business of banking in foreign countries and in aid of the commerce of the United States with foreign countries and to act when required as fiscal agents of the United States in such countries may be formed by any number of persons, not less in any case than five, who shall enter into articles of association which shall specify in general terms the object for which the banking corporation is formed and may contain any other provisions not inconsistent with the provisions* of this section which the banking corporation may see fit to adopt for the regulation and conduct of its business and affairs, which said regulations shall be signed, in duplicate, by the persons uniting to form the banking corporation and one copy thereof shall be forwarded to the Comptroller of the Currency and the other to the Secretary of State, to be filed and preserved in their offices.

That the persons uniting to form such banking corporation shall under their hands make an organization certificate which shall specify, first, the name assumed by such banking corporation, which name shall be subject to approval by the Comptroller; second, the foreign country or countries or the dependencies or colonies of foreign countries or the dependencies of the United States where its banking operations are to be carried on; third, the place in the United States where its home office shall be located; fourth, the amount of its capital stock and the number of shares into which the same shall be divided; fifth, the names and places of residence of the shareholders and the number of shares held by each of them, and, sixth, a declaration that said certificate is made to enable such persons to avail themselves of the advantages of this section.

That no banking corporation shall be organized under the provisions of this section with a less capital than $2,000,000, which shall be fully paid in before the banking corporation shall be authorized to commence business, and the fact of said payment shall be certified by the Comptroller of the Currency and a copy of his certificate to this effect shall be filed with the Secretary of State: Provided, That the capital stock of any such bank may be increased at any time by a vote of two-thirds of its shareholders with the approval of the Comptroller of the Currency and that the capital stock of any such bank which exceeds $2,000,000 may be reduced at any time to the sum of $2,000,000 by the vote of shareholders owning two-thirds of the capital.

That every banking corporation formed pursuant to the provisions of this section shall for a period of twenty years from the date of the execution of its organization certificate be a body corporate, but shall not be authorized to receive deposits in the United States nor transact any domestic business not necessarily related to the business being done in foreign countries or in the dependencies of the United States. Such banking corporations shall have authority to make acceptances, buy and sell bills of exchange, or other *commercial paper relating to foreign business, and to purchase and sell securities, including securities of the United States or of any State in the Union. Each banking corporation organized under the provisions of this section shall have power to establish and maintain for the transaction of its business a branch or branches in foreign countries, their dependencies, or the dependencies of the United States, at such places and under such regulations as its board of directors may deem expedient.*

A majority of the shares of the capital stock of such banking corporation shall be held and owned by citizens of the United States or corporations chartered under the laws of the United States or of any State of the Union, and a majority of the members of the board of directors of such banking corporations shall be citizens of the United States. Each director shall own in his own right at least one hundred shares of the capital stock of the banking corporation of which he is a director.

Whenever the Comptroller shall become satisfied of the insolvency of any such banking corporation he may appoint a receiver who shall proceed to close up such corporation in the same manner in which he would close a national bank, the disposition of the assets of the branches to be subject to any special provisions of the laws of the country under whose jurisdiction such assets are located.

The annual meeting of every such banking corporation shall be held at its home office in the United States, and every such banking corporation shall keep at its home office books containing the names of all stockholders of such banking corporation and members of its board of directors, together with copies of the reports furnished by it to the Comptroller of the Currency exhibiting in detail and under appropriate heads the resources and liabilities of the banking corporation. Every such banking corporation shall make reports to the Comptroller of the Currency at such times as he may require, and shall be subject to examinations when deemed necessary by the Comptroller of the Currency through examiners appointed by him; the compensation of such examiners to be fixed by the Comptroller of the Currency.

And such banking corporation may go into liquidation and be closed by the vote of its shareholders owning two-thirds of its stock.

Any bank doing business in the United States and being

the owner of stock in the National Reserve Association may subscribe to the stock of any banking corporation organized under the provisions of this section, but the aggregate of such stock held by any one bank shall not exceed 10 per centum of the capital stock of the subscribing bank.

This is practically a separate federal incorporation law. It is enormously broad and dangerously lax. It should not be a part of this bill at all. Evidently it was tacked on at the instance of powerful Wall Street interests that desire to incorporate their foreign financial operations under the protection of federal law so that they can invoke the aid of the diplomatic and consular representatives of the Government, "dollar diplomacy," to further their. games of international high finance. It has no necessary connection with this bill. By slipping it in here instead of in a separate bill it can not be repealed for fifty years. This would make Wall Street banks incorporated thereunder almost legally immortal.

Sec. 58. *Congress reserves the right to alter or amend the provisions of this act to take effect at the end of any decennial period from and after the organization of the National Reserve Association.*

"Decennial" means "tenth anniversary." If this bill becomes law there will be no power on earth that can amend this act against the will of the association for ten years, and during successive periods of ten years. This amending clause is unusual, impertinent, insolent and dangerous. Congress is asked to tie its own hands and make this private corporation above and independent of Government and the people, under any and all circumstances that may arise during that time. Before ten years, during this long period of immunity, no doubt the corporation and the federated banks will by means of the enormous advantages granted by this bill obtain such political mastery over the Government and the people that all changes thereafter made will be for the benefit of the association and its allied banks, and not for the people. This provision startlingly reveals the character or lack of character and fairness of the powerful and crafty special interests, Wall Street and the big banks, allied in a great conspiracy for promoting this private central bank bill through Congress.

It was a surprising argument of the President in his message to Congress on December 21, 1911, in effect suggesting that Congress need not hesitate or be over-par-

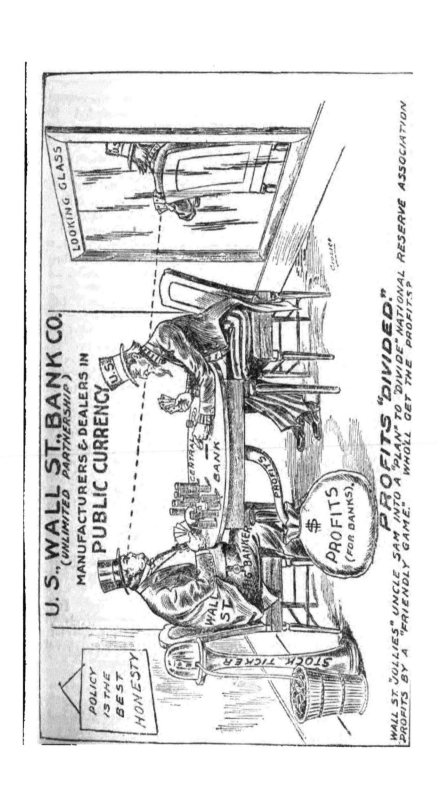

ticular, because if after the law is passed it is discovered
that a mistake has been made, the law can be amended. In
other words, pass the bill first and look into it afterwards
and correct by amendment any mistakes made. This is
strange doctrine for a learned judge, the trusted executive of
the republic. If he saw this amending clause, Sec. 58, before
writing his message, it is astounding. If he did not, the
man who, if anybody, induced him to insert in his official
message to Congress that suggestion, which was calculated
to put the people to sleep and unduly hasten careless action
on the measure by Congress, grossly deceived the President
by concealing from him the language of this amending
clause that makes the President's suggestion ridiculous.
This bill introduced into Congress by the Monetary Commission on January 8, 1912, no doubt was completed long
before the President wrote his message of December 21,
1911. It is to be hoped that the President will inform
Congress whether he had seen Sec. 58 before writing his
advice to Congress, and if not, then he should state whether
Chairman Aldrich, of the Monetary Commission, while concealing this amending clause, induced the President to include in his message the suggestion mentioned. Congress
is entitled to this information. It is also entitled to definitely
know whether other suggestions on this subject in the
President's message were proposed to him by any member
of the Monetary Commission. The usual reservation by
Congress of the right to repeal this act is nowhere in this
bill. There will be no power in Government or the people
to get rid of this corporation for fifty years, for it will be a
"vested right."

SEC. 59. *All acts or parts of acts inconsistent with the
provisions of this act are hereby repealed.*

This is very broad and sweeping. It should be examined carefully to find just what laws or parts of laws will
be wiped out.

"Selfishness defeats itself," is an old wise saying. It is
likely to prove true in this case. In trying, figuratively, to
corner the whole earth with the provisions of this one bill,
the greedy interests are likely to fail to secure enough for
a cemetery lot in which to bury their blasted hopes.

CHAPTER III.

FOOLING THE PEOPLE.

Bank Reserves to Be Left in Wall Street, Not Put in Central Reservoir?

Mr. Frank A. Vanderlip, president of the National City Bank of New York, on February 25, 1911, delivered an address on "The Aldrich Plan for Banking Legislation," before the Commercial Club of Chicago, praising the plan without qualification. He has been a consistent advocate of a central bank for ten years, ever since he retired as Assistant Secretary of the Treasury, and became vice-president of the great "Standard Oil" Bank. He was one of the five members of the "Special Committee of the New York Chamber of Commerce" that originated and devised the first plan for a central bank, adopted by that body on October 4, 1906, hereinafter fully described. And that first plan and the present Aldrich plan are practically identical as to their functions and powers.

The plan of 1906 called it a "Central Bank," the plan of 1912 a "National Reserve Association;" but a pickle by any other name is just as sour. The said report of 1906, signed by Mr. Vanderlip, says on page 9:

"In our opinion the best method of providing an elastic credit currency, the volume of which could never be excessive, would be the creation of a central bank of issue under the control of the Government. This central bank should have branches in the leading cities, and should have dealings only with banks, although its capital stock might be privately owned or distributed among the banking institutions of the country, it should be under the direct control of a board of governors appointed, at least in part, by the President of the United States, for it should perform some of the functions now imposed upon the United States Treasury, and should at the same time be managed not exclusively for private gain, but for the public good as well." On page 24 the report says: *"In its management representatives of the government shall be supreme."*

That report was a reasonable, logical, statesmanlike utterance. We take it as the guide in the plan hereinafter suggested, accepting in detail practically all of its provisions. Will the gentlemen who originated that plan join us now on that basis? Or will they insist on blocking all legislation unless they can put through the Aldrich plan for a *Private Central Bank* or association controlled by the banks instead of the Government?

Were those gentlemen insincere, not frank, in 1906, or have they backslid since? We prefer to believe that they have changed their minds, perhaps due to the fact that since 1906 the riches and power of Wall Street have grown so enormously that they now seem to consider Wall Street and its banks of more consequence than the United States Government and its 94,000,000 people.

Mr. Vanderlip in his Chicago address strongly urges the present Aldrich plan. He reverses his 1906 position. In that speech, which is being sent out by the banks as a campaign document, on page 8 he says: "We are now more than amply supplied with reserves. The difficulty is not in amount, but in mobility. * * *

Today the secondary reserves of the banks of the whole nation flow to one center and must of necessity be employed in one way. Such part of our banking funds as experience has taught may be needed on instant notice can be loaned in just one place in the United States where the lender can get them back with substantial certainty on demand. That place is Wall Street."

This foremost of Wall Street's bankers thus confesses that under the reserve law the country's cash goes to New York and is loaned in Wall Street. And he says the greatest danger is this lack of mobility of bank reserves. And yet he is urging the Aldrich bill that leaves the reserve law as it is and the country's money in Wall Street. It seems strange that the 24,000 banks are unwilling for the safety of the public and depositors, who furnish them most of the money, to hold $1,500,000,000 in their vaults or in a central "reservoir" and out of Wall Street when by law they have been given a monopoly of the rich privilege under which on a total capital stock of two billions they have loaned to the people at 6 per cent or other going rate a total of twenty-three billions, most of it being mere credit, inflated financial wind, that costs the banks nothing. The fact is the banks hope that by getting control of the public currency they can print money enough to protect the banks in emergencies without taking the reserves away from Wall Street. Instead of using their own capital and consolidating their reserves for mutual protection, they are going to keep their own money busy making profits in Wall Street and let the private central reservoir be filled with a billion dollars of public currency furnished free by act of Congress. Mr. Vanderlip adds: "I would, then, say that the four things we must seek to accomplish by a properly designed financial measure are, first, mobility of reserves; second, elasticity of note issue; third, certainty that solvent banks can rediscount; and, fourth, the creation of a discount market."

The first, enforced mobility of ordinary cash reserves, has been abandoned. The third, rediscount, and fourth, a discount market, can easily be furnished under the present law by the banks themselves without any action by Congress. They can without new legislation incorporate a big central bank to rediscount for other banks. And no one in the United States would object. The second, issuing of currency, is the only thing left. It is the one important thing in the pending bill that can not now be done by the banks without new legislation. Therefore, it is the sole object of the Aldrich plan and of the entire campaign being waged by Wall Street and the banks. It is the one thing that should not be done. The main thing that should be accomplished is to reform the reserve system; but that is left out entirely. And this is called "reform"!

Writer foresaw that this would be the program when, at the National Civic Federation meeting in New York on December 17, 1907, he forced from the Wall Street bankers present, through Mr. Seligman, chairman of the committee on resolutions, a public admission that they sought private control of the public currency, when they opposed writer's amendment which read:

"PROVIDED, THAT POWER TO ISSUE AND REGULATE THE VOLUME OF THE PUBLIC CURRENCY SHALL NOT BE TAKEN AWAY FROM THE FEDERAL GOVERNMENT AND BE PUT INTO PRIVATE HANDS."

With all the dense dust kicked up by Aldrich, the banks and Wall Street to hide the real issue now blown away, and the actual bill brought out of hiding and into the spot-light of public congressional scrutiny, investigation and criticism, the Aldrich plan, stripped of "tentativeness" and mystery, is found to seek just one new thing, namely, PRIVATE CONTROL OF THE PUBLIC CURRENCY.

In "The Magnet," written in 1906 and 1907 to combat this measure, we warned the country that private control of the public currency was to be attempted. Writer gave the same warning on December 17, 1907, at the National Civic Federation meeting when a majority present were Wall Street bankers and their friends, and in his petition read to the Senate and printed in the Congressional Record February 10, 1908, in his address on "Wall Street and Its Currency Measures" before the Boston City Club March 5, 1908, in his argument against the Aldrich emergency currency bill, a measure paving the way for the central bank scheme, delivered on invitation before the House Banking and Currency Committee in Washington, on April 16, 1908, in his speech on "Panics, Their Causes and Cure," before the National Reform Association at Wilmington, Del., on June 4, 1908, in many articles and interviews on the subject sent over news association wires and printed throughout the country in the public press, and in personal interviews with and letters to President Roosevelt and President Taft, judges of the Supreme Court, senators, congressmen, governors and many other public men.

That author's fears were justified and his early information accurate, the pending Aldrich bill is convincing and conclusive evidence. *It is just a private grab at the public currency.* The warnings that at the time to many seemed over-radical, now are found to have been rational and conservative.

Whatever sentiment there may be favorable to the Aldrich plan among the masses of the people has been almost wholly created by the plausible and convincing argument that all bank reserves should be taken out of Wall Street and merged into one central reservoir, to be drawn upon for adequate relief in an emergency by any bank located any place in the United States.

For years this has been heralded broadcast through the public press by the Monetary Commission (specifically stated in their report to Congress) by high government officials, in the speeches of President Aldrich and many leading bankers and by letters and literature now being circulated throughout the country by the big banks and the American Bankers' Association. The very name "National

Reserve Association" was selected for the same purpose, to convey that impression to the people. That the whole argument is a cheat and fraud upon the people and Congress is proved by the fact that the bill prepared by the Monetary Commission, hereinbefore given in full, does not contain a single provision requiring the banks to withdraw a cent from Wall Street or to deposit and maintain with the National Reserve Association, in the "Central reservoir," even one dollar of their $1,500,000,000 of "legal cash reserve." This revelation no doubt will shock the confidence of the whole country in the genuineness of the proposed "reform" in President Aldrich, and in the big banks and powerful Wall Street interests promoting the scheme for their own benefit. The chief curse and evil of the present banking system is the law that years ago was instigated by Wall Street, under which a large portion of the entire cash of the country held by the banks, nearly one-third of it, by means of the reserve system is concentrated in a few big Wall Street banks, where much of it is used by the stock gamblers to fleece the people in flotation schemes and dishonest manipulation of the prices of listed securities. And this Aldrich bill practically makes no change in this reserve system. The banks of the entire country can go on depositing their "cash reserve" in Wall Street, and will do so, because Wall Street banks pay interest on such deposits and the National Reserve Association is prohibited from doing so.

We now find that instead of merging their cash reserves in the central bank or association for mutual protection, there to be held ever ready for use at any point of danger, as loudly proclaimed, the banks are allowed to continue sending the same proportion (three-fifths) of all their reserves to Wall Street hunting interest. And that instead of using or depending upon their own capital reserves, in case of trouble they propose to make the government supply' the capital or money to protect the 24,000 banks in emergencies, and to maintain the gold standard and rediscount for the exclusive benefit of the banks. This is to be done under act of Congress, the law of the land, with a public corporate currency issued and controlled by a private corporation owned by the banks themselves. Thus the great powers of government are delegated to a private banking syndicate and made to continuously enrich the banks at the expense of the people and to serve the evil ends of Wall Street.

The present law permits a bank to deposit three-fifths of its 15 per cent "legal cash reserve" in a Central Reserve city bank. This bill *does not require* but *merely gives the option* to a bank to deposit the other two-fifths of its reserve (that now must be held in cash in its vault) with the Reserve Association. The association uses this money to rediscount with, for the profit of all the banks. This plan puts every dollar of the bank at work earning profits, three-fifths in Wall Street and two-fifths through the association. It gives the banks extra profits from use of the $600,000,000 now idle as reserve in bank vaults.

Note that the association itself is not *required* to retain in its own vaults, in the "Central Reservoir," as a reserve to protect the banks or their depositors, any of this $600,000,000 representing two-fifths of the cash reserve money of all the banks. It can pay out every dollar of it for commercial paper, and such *rediscounted paper thus becomes "reserve" instead of actual gold*. Only corporate currency, made on the association's printing press, will be used for the protective reserve. *The law thus supplies money ad libitum to a private corporation solely for private profit and advantage.* Why should it not be as proper for the Government by act of Congress thus to furnish gratis capital and credit without limit for other private corporations and individuals, as well as for the banks and their private association? *The whole scheme is a vicious graft of doubtful legality.*

In an address before the Economic Club of New York (widely circulated by the Monetary Commission), made by President Aldrich early in his campaign for his *predetermined "plan"* (on November 29, 1909), in praising the Central Bank Systems of Europe, he said: "These Central Banks hold practically the entire specie reserves of all the banks and other financial institutions of their respective countries. * * * The great difference between foreign banking systems and our own is found in the *concentration and mobilization of reserves,* which is the distinctive method of the European systems. * * * It is the policy of the joint-stock banks in times of stress to strengthen their reserves by increasing their balances at the central bank. * * * It matters not whether the use suggested is in London, Birmingham, or in Australia; this reserve can be drawn upon, as water is drawn from a *great reservoir* in order to put out a fire before it becomes a conflagration, and before the time when the application of water would be as useless as if it were poured into the ocean.

The European banks take these matters at their inception, and, by means of a *concentration of reserves*, they are ready at any minute to furnish the necessary means and the necessary credits to prevent disasters such as those we have suffered, and from which we shall continue to suffer unless we do something to reorganize and strengthen our financial system."

He praises the Central Bank system and then, to fool the Democrats, says the National Reserve Association will not be a Central Bank. Here we have President Aldrich threatening or predicting a return of heartrending panic, the terrors of which over and over he has publicly described and enlarged upon, unless Congress adopts his then concealed "plan." At the same time he leads the country to believe that his "plan" *will require the withdrawal from Wall Street and concentration of the cash legal reserves of all banks in one central "reservoir."* When on January 8, 1912, the bill containing his *real* plan is reported to Congress by his monetary commission, *no such thing is required of the banks.*

Former Congressman Robert W. Bonynge, a member of the Monetary Commission, now is traveling about the country and by speeches and interviews helping to promote the Aldrich plan. The Chicago Daily News on February 23, 1912, reported him as saying that the greatest evil of the present system is concentration of bank reserves in Wall Street, and that *the Aldrich plan takes these reserves away from Wall Street and puts them in the Central Association as custodian.* He spoke to the same effect in the speech made at St. Paul, February 3, 1912, now being circulated by the "National Citizens' League," the stated title of said speech being, *"Reform Banking Legislation. A plan to Break Wall Street Control of American Finances."*

The evidence is conclusive, and the country now can see that. Is Aldrich, with the aid of his supine "non-partisan" commission, the big banks, the Bankers' Association and Wall Street, trying to work on the people and Congress a clever, cold, heartless, gigantic and dangerous political confidence game? And it seems to be intended instantly to more than double the possible earning power of all the banks by act of Congress.

The play began way back in 1901 when in his report Secretary of the Treasury Gage began the argument for a central bank and concentration of bank reserves in one central reservoir. Mr. Gage went out of office and became president of a great Wall Street trust company. His assistant, Frank A. Vanderlip, went out of office and became vice-president, and now is president, of that great Standard Oil institution, the National City Bank, that had just purchased from the Government the old Custom House in Wall Street, which it now occupies for its bank purposes. That bank, or interests affiliated therewith, is the real originator and promoter of the Aldrich plan. As the deal has progressed, a general concentration of banking capital and control has been effected until the various financial groups practically are all one and united in support of Aldrich, and they have made a deal through the terms of the "plan" changed to suit the big bankers by which the American Bankers' Association and the big national banks of the country have joined the alleged conspiracy or are co-operating to drive the Aldrich scheme through Congress at all hazards and at the earliest possible moment, before Congress and the people come to realize the true character and ultimate effect of this evil measure. Because of the tremendous power of these great financial allies, reaching through the banks, railroads and trusts into every congressional district in the United States, there is danger, yes probability, that this bill, the greatest graft, the most sinister, far-reaching and dangerous measure ever presented to the Congress of the republic, will become the law of the land.

Then beware! The American people can be enslaved to the masters of high finance by Congress and the President, but they cannot permanently be kept in bondage. Must it be like France, *"After that, the deluge"?*

CHAPTER IV.

A DISCOVERY.

**Is the Government to be Liable on a Billion Private Corporation
Currency? Conflicting Statements by Bankers and Members
of Monetary Commission. Great Inflation Bubble.**

President Aldrich, the monetary commission and the
banks all have led the public to believe that the Government in no way will guarantee or pledge its credit to sustain
the corporate currency of the National Reserve Association.

The letters of the National City Bank and the National
Bank of Commerce of New York and Continental and
Commercial National Bank of Chicago, printed in the next
chapter, expressly state that in no way will the Government
be liable.

Congress surely would not knowingly grant to a private
corporation power to run the Government into debt more
than a billion dollars for the exclusive benefit and profit of
such corporation. It would not make the Government a
mere accommodation indorser and liable on a billion dollars
or more of the circulating notes of the National Reserve
Association, any more than it would grant to it power to
issue without the consent of the Government a billion dollars of binding Government bonds and to sell the same, and
forever keep the entire proceeds and use same for the
exclusive profit of such corporation.

To settle this important matter authoritatively, writer
mailed the following letter:

"MILWAUKEE, WIS., NOV. 21, 1911.

Hon. Nelson W. Aldrich,
        President National Monetary Commission,
            Washington, D. C.

Dear Sir: Kindly have your office favor me with a copy
of your revised monetary plan.

Many doubt whether currency issued by the proposed
National Reserve Association will be accepted at par unless

the faith and credit of the Federal Government is pledged to maintain it at par. Please state whether or not it is intended that the Government shall be obligated.

Under your plan will a bank receive the minimum dividend of 4 per cent on the face of its subscription to National Reserve Association stock, or on only the cash actually called in on such subscription?

Thanking you, I remain,
Very truly yours,
ALFRED O. CROZIER."

This was a civil letter to President Aldrich officially on a relevant subject. It called for an answer under every rule and practice of the public service. It was ignored. Why?

At the time, writer believed the apparent desire of President Aldrich to evade committing himself meant that before the bill finally passed, an amendment pledging the Government credit to the corporate currency would be inserted. Or, that in later years this would be done, after a billion or more currency had been put into circulation and depreciated. Failing to get any reply from Chairman Aldrich, writer tried to get the information from the other members. A similar inquiry addressed to Senator Burton, a member of the monetary commission, brought only a reply from the commission's librarian saying:

"I am directed by Senator Burton to reply to your letter of inquiry of January 27, 1912. The information you desire is set forth in the report of the National Monetary Commission of January 8, 1912, pp. 16-20, and in Sec. 52 of the bill reported by the commission."

The reference does not give the information asked, nor is it anywhere in the commission's report or bill.

The following reply to the above letter of the Commission's Librarian was not answered. It was ignored:

"The Romaine, Middleton Avenue,
"Cincinnati, O., Feb. 3, 1912.
"National Monetary Commission, Washington, D. C.

"Gentlemen: Your reply to my letter to Senator Burton and the copy of the commission's report and bill are received. I do not see that the sections you cite, or in fact any other section of the bill specifically states either that the Government will be or will not be in any way obligated or liable on the currency of the National Reserve Association, if the pending bill becomes law.

"Kindly advise me as to what is the fact on that point. Thanking you, I remain,

"Very respectfully yours,

"ALFRED O. CROZIER."

Former United States Senator Julius Caesar Burrows, who is a member of the National Monetary Commission, writing to a gentleman on February 26, 1912, said:

"Your valued favor of the 7th inst., you mailed to Kalamazoo, and did not reach me until a few days since, hence the delay in reply. In your communication you inquire as to whether, 'in case of the passage of the National Monetary Commission bill, the Government would be responsible for the currency issued by the National Reserve Association,' and in reply I would say that the Government would be in no way liable for the notes of the National Reserve Association. Provision is made, however, that the Government shall receive these notes at par in payment of all taxes, excises and other dues, and the redemption of the notes is insured by requirements as to reserve, and by provision that they shall have a first lien upon all of the assets of the Reserve Association, including the uncalled liabilities of the stockholders."

On January 31, 1912, writer met Robert W. Bonynge, a member of the Monetary Commission, who had addressed the Merchants and Manufacturers' Association of Milwaukee on the Aldrich plan the previous evening. In response to a question, Mr. Bonynge then stated that the Government in no way would be obligated or made liable for the currency issued by the National Reserve Association.

A similar inquiry written to the Secretary of the Treasury brought this reply:

Office
of
Assistant Secretary.

"TREASURY DEPARTMENT,
WASHINGTON, January 29, 1912.

Mr. Alfred O. Crozier,
    The Romaine, Middleton Ave.,
        Cincinnati, Ohio.

Sir: In reply to your inquiry as to whether the faith and credit of the United States would be pledged to maintain at par the currency issued by the National Reserve Association, if the pending bill framed by the National Monetary Commission should become law, I would say that this is a hypothetical question which the department cannot undertake to answer.

Respectfully,

A. PIATT ANDREW,
Assistant Secretary."

TREASURY DEPARTMENT

WASHINGTON

January 29, 1912.

Mr. Alfred O. Crozier,
The Remains, Middleton Avenue,
Cincinnati, Ohio.

Sir:

In reply to your inquiry as to whether the faith and credit of the United States would be pledged to maintain at par the currency issued by the National Reserve Association, if the pending bill framed by the National Monetary Commission should become law, I would say that this is a hypothetical question which the Department cannot undertake to answer.

Respectfully,

Assistant Secretary.

Now, A. Piatt Andrew is not only Assistant Secretary of the Treasury, but he is also "assistant to the National Monetary Commission" and as such signed the commission's report to Congress. Also, he has been making public addresses explaining and booming the Aldrich plan. He has been actively searching the records and helping to prepare the elaborate data issued by the commission. If anyone knows whether the Government would be legally liable for the corporate currency of the National Reserve Association, he does. If he did not desire to answer that

House of Representatives U.S
Washington, D.C.

February 12, 1912,

Morris N. Webb, Esq.,
#1204 Pleasant Street,
Wilmington, Del.

My dear Sir:-

I beg to acknowledge the receipt of yours of
February eighth, relating to the currency which it is proposed shall be issued by the National Reserve Association.

The credit of the Government is not behind this circulation, but it is provided that it shall be redeemable in
gold on presentation at the Reserve Association or any of
its branches, at any and all times. Furthermore, in issuing this circulation one-half of its value must be in
gold, in the hands of the Association, and the other half
fully covered by Government bonds or commercial paper,
which must be of the standard fixed by the terms of the bill.
On the whole, I think it is agreed that it is amply covered,
and that there can be no possible failure of its redemption
in gold, in case anyone desires it. No action is likely to
be taken on the proposed bill at this session of Congress.

Yours very truly,

"hypothetical question" as Assistant to the Treasury, why did he not do it as assistant to the commission? Would not such palpable evasion and the action of Chairman Aldrich in ignoring that question tend to make one suspicious? Then there was Senator Burton's action. Instead of answering "yes" or "no," he turns it over to the Librarian, who evades and gives an irrelevant answer. What is the game, if it is a game? The following from Congressman John W. Weeks, of Massachusetts, who was a member of the National Monetary Commission, explains itself:

Here are more letters on the letterhead of the Monetary Commission:

"WASHINGTON, D. C., January 30, 1912.
Mr. Alfred O. Crozier,
   The Romaine, Middleton Avenue,
     Cincinnati, Ohio.

Dear Sir: Replying to your letter of the 27th instant, I write to say that the United States is not responsible for the parity of the currency issued by the National Reserve Association. That, as in the case of gold, silver and greenbacks, is cared for by a statute which provides that the Secretary of the Treasury shall see that all forms of the circulating medium are kept at par. The subject is covered in Sections 52 and 53 (pages 67 and 68) of the pamphlet, which has been sent to you by this mail, containing the report of the National Monetary Commission and the draft of a bill to cover the suggestions made therein. From a reading of the foregoing and those provisions, you will see that there is not the slightest danger.
          Very truly yours,
            H. D. MONEY. (a)"

Former U. S. Senator Money, a member of the commission, thus contradicts himself, as do other members. He first asserts that the Government will not be obligated for the corporate currency, and then says that under the (gold standard) statute the Secretary of the Treasury must keep such currency at par the same as gold, silver and greenbacks. If the Secretary must under the Act of 1900 sell Government bonds to get gold to keep this corporate currency at par, why will not the Government be legally obligated?

WASHINGTON, D.C.

January 30 - 1912

Mr. Alfred O. Crozier

The Romaine,

Cincinnait, Ohio.

Dear Sir :-

I have your letter asking me whether
the faith and credit of the government would be pledged
to maintain at par the currency issued by the National
Reserve Association under the proposed bill of the
Monetary Commission.

As I understand it, the note issue of the Reserve
Association would have the same relation to the government
that notes issued by national banks have under the existing
law. My understanding of the Financial Act of 1900 is
that the Secretary of the Treasury is required to maintain
at par with gold all currency issued by the government or
under its authority.

The marked difference, however, would be that under
the legislation proposed by the Monetary Commission is
obliged to maintain its own notes at par with gold.

Very truly yours,

His reference to the bill gives no information on the subject. His assurance, therefore, that there is not the "slightest danger" must be taken with a "grain of salt."

Congressman Edward B. Vreeland, vice-president of the National Monetary Commission, writes:

"WASHINGTON, D. C., January 30, 1912.

Mr. Alfred O. Crozier,
 The Romaine,
  Cincinnati, Ohio.

Dear Sir: I have your letter asking me whether the faith and credit of the Government would be pledged to maintain at par the currency issued by the National Reserve Association under the proposed bill of the Monetary Commission.

As I understand it, the note issue of the Reserve Association would have the same relation to the Government that notes issued by national banks have under the existing law. My understanding of the Financial Act of 1900 is that the Secretary of the Treasury is required to maintain at par with gold all currency issued by the Government or under its authority.

The marked difference, however, would be that under the legislation proposed by the Monetary Commission the Reserve Association is obliged to maintain its own notes at par with gold.

    Very truly yours,
      EDWARD B. VREELAND."

Mr. Vreeland's first letter, we see, was on the letterhead of the National Monetary Commission. His second on the letterhead of the "Committee on Banking and Currency of the House of Representatives of the Sixty-second Congress," which shows the membership of such committee to be as follows:

Arsene P. Pujo, La., Chairman.

Carter Glass, Va.	Robt. L. Doughton, N. C.
J. F. C. Talbott, Md.	Hubert D. Stevens, Miss.
Geo. W. Taylor, Ala.	James A. Daugherty, Mo.
John H. Moore, Tex.	John J. Kindred, N. Y.
James P. Latta, Nebr.	James F. Byrnes, S. C.
Chas. A. Korbly, Ind.	Edward B. Vreeland, N. Y.
Wm. G. Brown, W. Va.	Henry McMorran, Mich.
Robert J. Buckley, Ohio.	Geo. D. McCreary, Pa.

Everis A. Hayes, Calif.   Frank E. Guernsey, Me.
James McKinney, Ill.   Philip P. Campbell, Kans.

The members of the National Monetary Commission are:
Nelson W. Aldrich, R. I., Chairman.
Edward B. Vreeland, N. Y., Vice Chairman.

Julius C. Burrows, Mich.   Arsene P. Pujo, La.
Eugene Hale, Me.   H. D. Money, Miss.
H. M. Teller, Colo.   Geo. W. Prince, Ill.
Theodore E. Burton, O.   James P. Taliaferro, Fla.
Boies Penrose, Pa.   L. P. Padgett,
John W. Weeks, Mass.   Geo. F. Burgess,
Robt. W. Bonynge, Colo.   James McLachlan, Mich.

It will be seen that Chairman Pujo of the Committee and Vice Chairman Vreeland of the Commission are members of both bodies. Why, during the past three years, did not the Monetary Commission investigate the "money trust" as now it is proposed to have this committee do under the lead of a member of the Monetary Commission? It had the time, money and power to do so. No practicable monetary and banking system can be devised without taking into account the conditions that would be revealed by an investigation of that kind if it was honest, thorough and patriotic. The character and contents of the Commission's bill shows that such conditions were ignored. Failure to require all bank reserves to be taken out of Wall Street and concentrated in the Reserve Association as a "Central Reservoir" shows that by its plan the Commission intentionally or otherwise is playing directly into the hands of Wall Street. Will the proposed investigation by the Banking and Currency Committee be genuine or a farce? The country soon will know.

Mr. Vreeland's second letter is as follows:

WASHINGTON, Feb. 9, 1912.

MR. ALFRED O. CROZIER,
The Romaine, Middleton Ave., Cincinnati, Ohio.
My Dear Sir: My answer to your former letter, saying that so far as the Government is concerned the notes issued by the National Reserve Association would have the same relation to the Government that our bank notes do, is not

clear because it has never been definitely decided what the relation of the Government is to the existing bank note circulation.

You indicate in your letter that the Government stands behind the present bank note circulation, but does it? National banks are now permitted to issue their notes against certain bonds of the United States, mostly the 2 per cent bonds. These bonds are now barely above par. If they should fall below par it would be the duty of the Comptroller of the Currency to call upon the national banks to put up additional security. But suppose a bank should fail before the additional security was deposited and suppose its assets were insufficient to pay the bank notes outstanding; then there is no law upon the statute books which require the Government to make up the difference. Many people believe that these notes being issued against United States bonds under the authority of the Government, that in equity the Government should make up any loss which occurs. That would be entirely for Congress to determine, whether to make good or not. So I say that the notes of the new association stand in the same relation to the Government that the present bank note circulation does.

I think notes issued by the Reserve Association would be, and would be considered to be absolutely safe by the people of the country. They would have behind them more than the present bank notes have. The Reserve Association would take over the seven hundred million 2 per cent bonds against which national bank notes are now issued. The Reserve Association could issue seven hundred millions of its own notes against these bonds, but it would also have to keep 50 per cent gold in its vaults in addition to the bonds of the United States. Also the notes are made a first lien against all assets of the association.

We have more security by law behind them than France and Germany have behind their notes, which have been good under all circumstances for half a century. The notes of the Bank of France were at a discount of only 3 per cent when Prussian armies were marching in the streets of Paris and a communal mob was in possession of the Government.

Our bank notes, resting upon bonds, were below par for sixteen years—1863 to 1879.

Very truly yours,

EDWARD B. VREELAND.

Following is writer's reply:

THE ROMAINE, MIDDLETON AVENUE,
CINCINNATI, O., Feb. 20, 1912.

HONORABLE EDWARD B. VREELAND,
　　Washington, D. C.

Dear Sir: Please accept my thanks for your valuable reply of February 9 to my former letter.

I quite agree that present bank note currency is not ideal and should be replaced with an elastic currency that will be more practicable. But it is imperative to avoid currency depreciation. You say bank currency was depreciated from 1863 to 1879. Was that depreciation equal with greenbacks? Bank notes I believe are not legal tender lawful money. Nor were the $450,000,000 of depreciated greenbacks a full legal tender. They could not be used to pay duties on imports or interest on the public debt, but the $60,000,000 of greenbacks issued before the $450,000,000 were as I recall made a legal tender and never depreciated, but always were equal with gold in value. Is this correct? If so, then was not absence of legal tender quality the chief thing that caused depreciation of the $450,000,000 of greenbacks and also the bank note currency of which you speak? If the $450,000,000 of greenbacks had been full legal tender and redeemable in gold, do you think they would have depreciated?

You say there is no law upon the statute books obligating the Government for bank note currency. Did you overlook section 5414, as codified in section 148 of the Penal Code of the United States, March 4, 1909 (35 Stat. L. 1115), or is it your view that it does not apply? If this does apply, the currency should be safe against depreciation. Would not the Reserve Association be a national bank and its currency national bank currency, legally speaking? Certainly it would not be a State bank or its issues State currency. If so, and the above cited statute applies and obligates the Government to maintain at par the Reserve Association's currency, there would seem to be no danger of it ever depreciating and inflicting the very grave evils any currency depreciation always imposes upon business and the people.

Trusting it may be convenient for you to further advise as to the above matter, and thanking you, I remain,

　　　　　Very respectfully yours,
　　　　　　　ALFRED O. CROZIER.

Mr. Vreeland, we believe, is a banker, congressman, member of the House Banking and Currency Committee and vice president of the National Monetary Commission. Excepting Aldrich, he has been the most active person behind the Aldrich private central bank plan. He should be thoroughly informed. He states that the Government will occupy the same relation to the corporate currency of the Reserve Association as it now does to bank note currency. If this be true, the Government will be directly obligated for every one of the billions of dollars of corporate currency such private corporation may care to print and issue during the next fifty years. Mr. Vreeland, we believe, is in error when he says the Government is not liable for bank note currency. Evidence of this fact is given later in this chapter.

Even if the Government was not directly liable for the corporate currency, if it ever depreciated Congress would be importuned to make it good to protect the people from loss, the same argument given above by Congressman Vreeland as to why Congress should stand behind bank note currency would be used. The Government by law authorized the issuance of the corporate currency by the Reserve Association. By law it compelled its acceptance for certain purposes, and it would be considered in honor morally obligated, and later by act of Congress no doubt would be legally bound to guarantee and maintain at par all such currency even if it has to issue a billion dollars more bonds to get gold with which to do it.

If Mr. Vreeland will read sections 41 and 42 of his bill he will find erroneous his assertion that the Reserve Association must keep in its vaults 50 per cent ($350,000,000) of actual gold to secure its $700,000,000 currency issued against the $700,000,000 U. S. bonds to be taken over from the banks. No actual gold is required, and under section 42 no reserve of any kind need be held behind half of such $700,000,000 of currency. And it is not true that corporate currency will have behind it more than present bank currency. It is unfair to take bank currency as a standard for comparison. Bank note currency is wrong and should be abolished, but not to make room for a worse currency. He says that the corporate currency is made "a first lien against all assets of the association." The association may issue $1,000,000,000 currency with only $100,000,000 actual net assets, except the assets bought with the billion of currency.

So the "lien" would not be much security. It is important, however, to note that the Government is compelled to turn over all of its revenues to this private corporation to be at once mortgaged with a lien to secure this vast private corporate currency. The Treasury balance on June 30, 1911, was $140,176,926, and sometimes it is double that sum. The whole scheme is rigged to give the benefits all to the banks and put the burden on the Government.

His reference to France and Germany does not apply because in those countries the business and financial conditions are entirely different. They have no "Wall Street," or its evils. He says bank note currency from 1863 to 1879 depreciated. He holds that the Government obligation was not behind bank currency. If that is true then the obligation of all the banks, plus 100 per cent U. S. bonds, securing 90 per cent of bank currency was insufficient to keep bank currency at par.

In 1879 there was only $329,691,697 bank note currency. If that small amount depreciated when fully secured by U. S. bonds, how can this private corporation keep a billion dollars of its currency from depreciating, without any Government guarantee or U. S. bonds behind it, even if it should have 33⅓ per cent or even 50 per cent of gold as a reserve? But no actual gold is required. Paper money can be used. And if no reserve of any kind is kept, there is no penalty to punish the directors.

Aldrich's Inflation Bubble.

Under Sec. 41 of the bill no actual gold need be held as a reserve to secure the corporate currency. There may be used "other money of the United States which the national banks are now authorized to hold as part of their legal reserve." This includes gold certificates, greenbacks, silver dollars and silver certificates. It will be lawful to have a reserve consisting wholly of silver and no gold. The Government by law is prohibited from issuing paper currency based on silver, but this bill authorizes a corporation to do it. The law prevents the Government issuing more U. S. Treasury notes, or greenbacks, but this bill authorizes the corporation to issue three dollars of its paper currency for each dollar of Government greenbacks it holds to "secure" such currency, even if it has no actual gold.

The Secretary of the Treasury reports as outstanding $1,809,296,685 of Government paper money. By gathering this all up and holding it as a "reserve" the corporation legally could issue and float $5,427,890,055 of corporate currency, more than five billions of dollars of wildcat paper currency, three times as much as the Government ever issued, and this without one single dollar of actual gold or even silver held by the Reserve Association to secure or insure the redemption of such currency in gold. The banks now hold $623,583,300 gold certificates, $194,474,846 silver certificates and $248,334,727 greenbacks, total $1,066,392,873. In one week this all could be turned over by the banks to their central corporation and immediately $3,199,178,619 of corporate currency could be issued and loaned out to the people through the banks at say 6 per cent, a sum about equal to all the money of all kinds now in the United States, and all this without the corporation owning an ounce of gold or silver.

This corporate currency, unlike bank note currency, is made available to be held by the banks as "legal cash reserve." If the corporation should gather up and hold as its "33⅓ per cent reserve" the $1,809,296,685 of outstanding Government paper money, and then print the $5,427,890,055 of corporate currency based thereon and hand it over to its banks to be by them held as their "legal cash reserve," the banks lawfully could inflate their loans of credit from 15 to more than 54 billions of dollars. And if, as they can under this bill, the banks convert half of their "demand deposits" into "time deposits" that will require no reserves at all, the banks will be able to inflate their credit loans to 108 billions of dollars. In other words, without one cent of extra investment or a dollar of gold or silver security, the banks lawfully could swell their loans of "credit" from about 15 to over 108 billions of dollars put out at 6 per cent interest. This is seventeen times the total gold of all nations. It nearly equals the entire wealth of the United States. The figures stagger human comprehension.

Never in all the history of government has there been such a crazy, wide-open, wild-cat scheme for currency and credit inflation as Congress now is solemnly asked to legalize under the guise of "elasticity" and turn over without reserve and beyond recall for fifty years to a private corporation that is required to have but 100 million dollars cash capital, the power to be exercised by just five men, a majority of the corporation's executive committee. Such inflation of bank credit would increase prices of stocks and property and decrease the relative purchasing power of wages 100 to 500 per cent. It would cheapen the dollar to about 30 cents, measured by its present purchasing power.

Suppose the Federal Government was legally liable for every dollar of that five billions of corporate currency? The 100 or 200 million dollars of capital of the corporation would not go far towards paying 5 billion dollars of depreciated corporation currency.

To at least the extent of the Government currency held by the association to secure its corporate currency the Government credit is used by the corporation. And by this plan $1,809,296,685 of good Government money can be taken away from the people. For all practicable purposes it is the same as destroyed, put permanently beyond the reach of the people. Every dollar of their legal-tender paper currency thus can be taken away. In its place the people must accept the doubtful optional corporate paper currency, because they could get nothing else. The corporation never will let go of any of the Government currency because if it did it must call in and cancel two or three dollars of its corporate currency for each dollar of shrinkage in its reserve of Government money. Congress might better openly vote at once to call in and burn up the whole $1,809,296,685 of Government paper money. Then this money and the Government credit it represents could not be used as the legally authorized basis for five billions of wild-cat corporate currency. That would force the corporation to provide its own capital and actual gold to create a reserve to sustain its issues of corporate currency. This would limit somewhat the wild inflation and modify the intensity of the explosion when this Aldrich inflation bubble finally bursts.

But is not the Government to be liable, legally bound for every dollar of corporate currency the Reserve Association, or the five men in control, may see fit to print?

Have we not at last discovered the "Joker," the reason for the apparent mystery, the seeming reluctance of the sponsors of the Aldrich plan to answer writer's direct and oft-repeated question as to whether the Government in any way would be obligated?

When writer was less than one year old, June 30, 1864, Congress, to help the banks float bank note currency and as a "war measure," added section 13 at the end of "an Act to provide ways and means for the support of the Government, and for other purposes." This law is in force today, and reads as follows:

"Sec. 13. *And be it further enacted,* That the words 'obligation or other security of the United States,' used in this Act, shall be held to include and mean all bonds, coupons, national currency, United States notes, Treasury notes, fractional notes, checks for money of authorized officers of the United States, certificates of indebtedness, certificates of deposit, stamps, and other representatives of value of whatever denomination, which have been or may be issued under any act of Congress."

This was reënacted, and is now law, being Sec. 5413, as codified in Sec. 147 of the Penal Code of the United States, March 4, 1909 (35 Stat. L., 1115), as follows:

"The words 'obligation or other security of the United States' shall be held to mean all bonds, certificates of indebtedness, national-bank currency, coupons, United States notes, Treasury notes, gold certificates, silver certificates, fractional notes, certificates of deposit, bills, checks, or drafts for money, drawn by or upon authorized officers of the United States, stamps and other representatives of value, of whatever denomination, which have been or may be issued under any act of Congress."

In future years, after a billion or more corporate currency has been issued and badly depreciated, is it not certain that this 48-year-old statute would be dug up and invoked by the banks as a moral and legal obligation on the Government to protect the people by maintaining at par such "national currency" and "representatives of value of whatever denomination which have been or may be issued under any act of Congress ?"

Will not the National Reserve Association in law be a national bank and its currency "National bank currency"? Surely it is not a state bank. It will legally be a bank, because the pending bill gives it the powers and functions of a bank.

This corporate currency surely will not be "state currency" issued by state banks under authority of state law. It will be "National currency" issued under authority of the Congress of the Nation. If this be true, the Government will be liable for every dollar issued. Even if it was not "National currency," or "National bank currency," it would no

doubt be held to be "other representatives of value" * * *
"which have been or may be issued under any act of
Congress."

If this is a correct interpretation of that law, and it seems
to be, it is a startling discovery. The law is printed in full
in "Document No. 580, Laws of the United States Concerning Money, Banking and Loans, 1778-1909," issued by the
Monetary Commission.

Some if not all of the members of the Commission must
have known of this law. Probably all of them did, for they
have been receiving $7,500 per year for about three years,
and presumably have read the documents and data they have
prepared and issued. If they knew that this law obligated
the Government for all currency issued by the Reserve
Association and concealed the fact or even failed to make
Congress and the people aware of that condition, they were
false to their oaths of office and should be driven from
public life in disgrace.

*It is significant, the fact that nowhere in the pending bill is
there any provision expressly stating that the Government in
no way shall be obligated or made liable by the acts of this
private corporation.* Why did not these sworn and paid
public servants discuss this important matter in their report?
Why did they not include in their bill a provision that would
protect the Government they pretend to be serving against a
possible and probable liability of more than a billion dollars?
Congressman Vreeland's letter shows that he thinks the
Government might be liable. It is impossible to believe that
a matter so important was not discussed by the entire commission, yet their report is silent on the subject, and their
bill contains nothing to protect the Government and the
people for fifty years against a possible liability that may
amount even to five billion dollars, and from which there
will be no way of escape after Congress passes the pending
Aldrich bill that then will be a contract, a "vested right."
Was the Commission working for the Government, the
People, or for the Banks and Wall Street?

These conditions, if as here stated, tend to stamp the
whole scheme as a colossal fraud on Congress and the
people. The National City Bank and the National Bank of
Commerce of New York and the Continental and Commercial National Bank of Chicago, should now explain their letters, printed in another chapter, wherein they say that in
no way will the Government be obligated if the Aldrich

plan becomes law. Mr. Reynolds of the latter bank, a former president of the American Bankers' Association, and Mr. Vanderlip, president of the National City Bank, are said to be in the confidence of Aldrich and are alleged to have been most active in originating and promoting the Aldrich private central bank plan.

It is also up to the Monetary Commission to explain!

CHAPTER V.

INFLATION AND CONTRACTION.

Cost of Living and Prices Go Up. Why?

The chief purpose of government is to establish and maintain conditions that will confer the highest good on the greatest number of its inhabitants. Every executive act, law of Congress and court decision should be with that end in view. With such conditions prevailing, the road to success will be open to every man and the general welfare conserved and advanced. "Life, liberty and the pursuit of happiness" then will be easily attainable by everybody. But these priceless blessings are available in the highest degree only when all who desire can obtain steady employment at good wages and the products of labor and the farm find ready market at profitable prices. When everybody is prosperous all are happy and contented. This tends to increase the stability and permanence of government. It causes civilization to advance and the human race to take a step nearer to its divine goal.

Business prosperity, however, depends for its very existence largely upon the supply of money and bank credit being always adequate in quantity and reasonable in price. By bank credit is meant bank loans. Ninety per cent of all business is done with bank credit and less than 10 per cent with cash. Therefore the volume of general business very much depends upon the quantity of credit that the 24,392 banks can loan to borrowers. And the volume of this credit directly and absolutely depends upon the amount of lawful money available for bank reserves; the banks on the average by law being allowed to loan about ten times as much "credit" as they have "lawful money" in their reserves.

Therefore, the prime question, the very basic foundation on which rests all bank credit, business prosperity, individual happiness and the general welfare, is an adequate supply of sound government money. An excessive inflation of the volume of money breeds certain evils and an excessive con-

97

traction of the supply of money causes still greater evils. Increase of the quantity of money tends immediately to stimulate business activity and increase prices. It increases the cash reserves of banks and puts each bank at work to find profitable chances to loan its resulting ten-fold increase of available bank credit. With more cash and credit among the people with which to buy, under the law of supply and demand prices must advance. As prices increase, profits multiply and tend to stimulate production. This increases the demand for labor and in time will advance wages, under the same law of supply and demand. But it is history that while the prices of commodities quickly advance with any material increase in the supply of money or bank credit, the wages of workmen respond slowly and usually only when the men combine in unions and demand increase. During the interim, before wages are advanced, everybody on a fixed salary or wage loses, because the fixed income will buy less at the higher prices. Those with their wealth invested in securities bearing a fixed income interest also lose because their fixed incomes will buy less property and labor at the higher prices. But farmers, manufacturers and other producers are immediately and directly benefited by an increase in the quantity of money, because the resulting increase of prices gives them greater profit from the same output of products. In fact, the general increase in the purchasing power of the people due to increase in their supply of money and credit tends to improve the demand and consumption of products. This still further increases the profits of farm and factory. It also helps those in debt, because it takes less products at the higher price to pay a debt.

For the same reasons, expansion of the currency operates to increase the prices of stocks and securities other than fixed—income notes, mortgages and bonds—and stimulates speculation. But it lowers the prices or value of investments bearing a fixed rate of interest, such as bonds.

Inflation, therefore, enhances the prices of things and cheapens the value of money. It also lowers the price of money and credit, the interest rate. It decreases the purchasing power, the value, of the dollar as measured in property or labor. If the quantity of money and bank credit was doubled without any increase in the amount of property or available labor the price of all property and labor practically would be doubled. It would take two dollars to buy the same amount of property and labor that could be obtained before for one dollar. It is the law of supply and demand, relative quantities of Dollars versus Property and Labor, operating. Doubling of prices is only another way of stating that money, the dollar, has depreciated 50 per cent, measured in property and labor and judged by its purchasing power. There is and ever will be an eternal struggle between the great incorporated and individual interests that traffic in money and bank credit for interest profits on the one side and the masses of the people who own the property and do the world's work on the other, over the value or purchasing power of the dollar measured in property and quantity of labor. The monied interests always naturally will seek to create conditions tending to keep down the prices of everything but the things they sell, money and bank credit, and to increase the price of money and credit, the interest rate. On the other hand, the producers will try to keep up the prices of property and labor and down the rate of interest paid for the use of money and bank credit.

Those who own or represent large quantities of money or bank credit seeking investment at interest are on one side and the balance of the people are on the other. These two elements are not necessarily antagonistic, but their interests are diametrically opposed. One side always loses what the other gains. If the profit and power of one side by legislation or otherwise is increased, that of the other is correspondingly decreased. The people always pay the interest that money gets. Their profits diminish when interest rates advance and swell the profits of banks and money lenders.

Much has been said about the increase in prices being due to the increase in the world's output of gold. Part of the advance of prices is due to elimination of competition by trust consolidations and other causes and part to increase in the quantity of gold. It is not increase in the ounces of metal as metal that raises prices but because gold is money and increase of the output of gold increases the quantity of money. The same increase in the quantity of paper money would produce the same effect on prices if such money was a full legal tender and had to be accepted by everybody. Any increase in the number of available debt-paying dollars always will tend to increase the prices of everything but money. That is the law of supply and demand.

On the other hand any material decrease in the quantity of available money or bank credit tends immediately to lower the prices of property and labor. It lessens the demand. The people have less money with which to buy things or to deposit in banks. This soon reduces bank cash reserves and the banks immediately must call in and cancel credit loans equal to ten times such shrinkage of reserves. To pay these loans business borrowers must at once reduce expenses and sacrifice products and property. This increases the volume of commodities seeking immediate sale, with no increase in the demand. Under the law of supply and demand prices of such commodities must fall. In fact there is an actual decrease in the demand due to decrease in the purchasing power of the people, and this further depresses prices.

In cutting expenses, salaried employees and wage workmen are laid off, which further reduces the buying ability of the public. These idle men and their wives and children get hungry. For this reason they quickly begin to bid for the jobs still held by those employed. Under the law of supply and demand for labor, this soon lowers the general wages of everybody. An idle tenth thus can reduce the wages of the employed nine-tenths. It is a fight for existence and they will not split hairs over the amount of the wages. And as a rule employers pay no higher wages than they are actually compelled to grant. It is human nature, always will be, and the weak are at the mercy of the strong who have the money. A dollar can wait, can exist without food, but a man can not. Oh, what a constant and fearful struggle by the masses for every existence, millions of women and helpless little children, with nothing between them and actual starvation except the week's small wage! With prices increasing faster than wages, they must skimp and pinch and deny themselves pleasures and even many necessaries of life.

On the other hand the excessively rich are getting richer, often through special legislative privileges improperly obtained. Incorporated wealth sometimes swells with arrogance and impudently demands for itself greater profits and power at the expense of all the people. Which will the Government serve, who will it protect?

Contraction of the currency, if excessive, is the deadly enemy of prosperity. It forces an immediate ten-fold contraction of bank credit. This sudden and unexpected demand for payment of bank loans cramps and demoralizes business. If it follows an excessive inflation of the currency that has caused undue expansion of business and wild speculation it will wreck prices and values and bring disaster, panic and general ruin. It reduces the demand for farm and factory products by decreasing the people's buying power and thus lowers prices. The man in debt must work 'onger and harder to produce more products with which to pay off his debt. Any serious reduction in the supply of money or credit or increase in the interest rate creates conditions that immediately begin to lower the general wages paid labor and lengthen the hours of work. It also demoralizes the prices of all property and all securities, except bonds bearing a fixed interest rate, by reducing dividends. Mortgages and bonds bearing a fixed interest are increased in value by contracting the supply of money because the fixed income then will buy more property and labor at the lower prices. The bulk of the vast bond or fixed income wealth of the world is owned by the banks and by other incorporated and individual holders here and abroad.

The banks of this country own bonds exceeding in value the total of all the money in circulation in the United States. This vast bond wealth would be greatly enhanced in value if contraction of the currency should make money scarce.

The Aldrich plan would put the ownership, control and management of the National Reserve Association, with power to inflate and contract the quantity of money without limit, in the hands of the very private interests that would most profit by an abuse of that dangerous power. And every dollar gained by those interests through excessive inflation and contraction of the volume of currency would come out of the pockets of the people of the United States.

Labor is immediately harmed by either excessive inflation or contraction of the quantity of money, or of bank credit used in business as a substitute for money. Excessive and rapid inflation robs labor by increasing the prices of products faster than the wages of men. Excessive and rapid contraction of the supply of money or of bank credit also robs labor by demoralizing prices and business, destroying prosperity, throwing many workmen into idleness and lowering the general scale of wages by decreasing the demand for labor. Wages go down faster than the prices of products on a falling market and go up slower than the prices of commodities on a rising market. For this reason the best thing for labor is general and steady prosperity and a constant and moderate quantity of currency and bank credit always available at reasonable rates of interest, the volume to be elastic but regulated to increase and decrease with the volume of legitimate business and healthy activities of the country, but not with reckless speculation.

When business is depressed, ill, a moderate currency inflation will be a tonic, a stimulant to restore it to normal. When the country is afflicted with the fever of wild speculation, a carefully measured dose of currency and credit contraction will reduce the fever and bring health to the business world. But it is a matter of absolute life and death that the financial doctor who prescribes and administers these two powerful remedies for those two diseases have the wisdom and skill always to give the right medicine in exactly the correct quantity for the particular disease then afflicting the country. The Chinese are said to pay their physician a regular sum while the patient is well and nothing while ill. This removes all temptation to keep the patient in bed to increase the pay of the doctor. Instead of allowing the banks, that profit most when conditions are not normal, to act as our financial doctor and administer inflation and contraction, we should put this life and death power into the hands of those who will be disintrested or will profit most by stable conditions certain to confer upon all the blessings of general and steady prosperity.

It is for the best interests of the country, legitimate business, and particularly of labor, that both extreme inflation and excessive contraction of the volume of money be avoided. The general welfare requires a steady, uniform and moderate supply of sound currency, the quantity rising and falling with the ebb and flow of the volume of ordinary business.

There is no way by which this desirable elasticity, this increase and decrease, can be made automatic and natural, because money is not endowed with human intelligence.

Human judgment must be depended upon to gauge from day to day the fluctuating volume of business and to measure and supply for the country the proper quantity of money. Also to stimulate business depression by increasing the volume of money and credit and lowering the discount or interest rate, and to put the brakes on excessive speculation when necessary by contracting the supply of available currency and credit and by raising the discount rate.

In Great Britain this imperial financial power is wielded by the Bank of England, and always wisely and patriotically.

As the directors of that great institution are all merchants and business men and no banker is allowed to serve on the board, it shows that that very practical people realize that it is not wise to put such vast power in the hands of the banks that would greatly profit at the expense of the people by an abuse of such power.

By excessive inflation of bank credit billions of dollars beyond safety and sound business principles the banks have put the country upon a false and fictitious basis with the range of prices high above true values. These prices must be lowered. It can be easily done by contracting the quantity of available money and bank credit. But to avoid this causing panic and general demoralization of business it must be done gradually and cautiously. And in justice to the people the price of money and bank credit, the rate of interest, must be reduced in proportion to the reduction of other prices. If Congress gives the banks through their Aldrich Central Bank this power to force readjustment and lowering of prices by contraction, we must expect that interest rates, the price of money and credit sold by banks, will be kept high and the price of securities, property and labor reduced. This will automatically increase the value of money and cheapen property and labor. This readjustment of prices must not be left to the banks that would profit most by an improper readjustment, and that by inflation have caused most of our present financial and industrial evils.

By expanding and contracting the volume of the public currency and by raising and lowering the general discount or interest rate, those exercising such power could be a perfect governor on the engine driving all American business and perfectly regulate it so that prosperity will be constant, steady, healthy and general. On the other hand with this same power they could wreck the machine, smash everything, destroy a nation's prosperity and happiness and inaugurate a financial and industrial "reign of terror."

The power is an arbitrary one. It must be so. It is autocratic. It is of supreme national importance, then, that this life and death power be exercised only and exclusively by disinterested and unselfish men of the highest skill, knowledge, courage, character and patriotism.

Even then their exercise of this absolute and constant control over the very heart-beats of the business of 94,000,-000 Americans must be hedged about by every reasonable

legal safeguard.   Positively, there is no other practicable
way to bring the 24,392 banks and their power of inflation
and contraction under such effective and centralized control
as will protect the country against the dangers of panic and
the evils of excessively high and extremely low prices and
insure the steady employment of labor at living wages. We
never shall have a sound and genuine prosperity and be free
from recurring periods of reckless speculation followed by
panic depressions until the volume of money and the discount rate each day is raised or lowered to increase or check
the volume of bank credit and of general business done with
bank credit. But it would be insanity, positive madness, for
Congress to put this power to regulate all business into
the hands of the very private interests that most need regulating.   Instead of granting it to a private corporation
owned by the banks, it must be delegated to a great, deliberative public institution, a part of the Government of the
United States.

To create a dignified and deliberate body of men worthy
of the entire confidence of the people, to whom safely could
be entrusted a power more vast and potent in its daily effect
on the business and activities of the whole country than the
power exercised by Congress, the executive or the courts,
is the reason for venturing in another chapter the suggestion for a *United States Monetary Council.*

Cost of Living and Prices Go Up.

From 1896 to 1911 the quantity of money in the United
States outside the treasury increased from $1,506,400,000
to $3,214,000,000 or over 100 per cent. It increased from
$21.44 in 1896 to $34.20 in 1911 per capita. This shows an
inflation in the quantity of money 60 per cent greater than
the 33 per cent growth of population. The increase in prices
of a large number of commodities and of the cost of living
has been about 60 per cent. It must, therefore, be clear that
inflation of the currency and the resulting ten-fold inflation
of bank credit are the chief causes for the rapid and large
increase in prices and the cost of living.

Coin, including bullion in the treasury (gold and silver),
increased 1896 to 1911 from $1,097,610,190 to $2,477,-
837,453, or about 144 per cent. As there has been no increase in the volume of Government greenbacks since 1896,
Providence and the banks must be held responsible for the
entire advance in the cost of living or increase of prices due

to inflation of the quantity of money. Providence increased the quantity of coin 144 per cent, while the banks inflated bank currency over 300 per cent. Providence did not do it for personal profit, but the banks did.

Gold certificates based on 100 per cent of gold held in the Treasury have increased from $154,048,552 in 1896 to $930,-367,929 in 1911. Of this total the banks on June 7, 1911, held $623,583,300 or nearly two-thirds, and such certificates were legal basis on which the banks could loan over six billion dollars of bank credit. The U. S. gold certificates held by National Banks alone increased 1896 to 1911 from $20,336,400 to $300,201,210, enabling such banks to inflate their loans of credit based on gold certificates in their reserves from $200,000,000 to $3,000,000,000.

Attention to the following facts will enable us to locate and definitely fix the chief responsibility for the rapid increase in prices and the cost of living without hunting in distant lands or holding an international conference. Foreign delegates to such a conference would be certain to send us back home with the admonition that the best way to stop increasing the cost of living and prices throughout the whole world is to stop the wild and dangerous inflation of credit that in recent years has been practiced by the banks of the United States.

And above all that Congress should not by passing the Aldrich Central Bank bill enable the banks to still further dangerously inflate the currency, credit, prices and the cost of living, practically without limit or restraint.

The statement that increase and decrease of the volume of bank credit or loans has the same effect on prices that is caused by increasing and decreasing the quantity of money is a sound economic principle. In fact the effect is more marked and sudden. When a bank discounts a $10,000 note it simply loans or grants its customer the right to draw checks on the bank for that sum. That is a loan of bank credit, not cash. The customer gets no money and desires none. But he can buy $10,000 worth of goods and pay for same with bank credit by drawing checks, the same as if he had $10,000 cash. For this reason inflation of bank credit has exactly the same effect as an equal inflation of gold or other money. It increases the demand for things and raises prices. And contraction produces the opposite effect.

Bank resources practically are all available one way or

another for use by the people. The banks may discount paper, loan on mortgage or buy bonds and other securities, their profits being the interest received. All these uses of bank resources tend to increase the buying power of the people, thus improving the demand for property and labor and enhancing prices. More than three-fourths of all bank resources are mere loans of bank credit that cost the bank nothing to supply, like a man charging 6 per cent for in-, dorsing the note of another responsible person. But it enables bank customers to go on doing business, buying and paying for goods and labor, the same as if they had actual money. Bank credit is a substitute for money in 90 per cent of all transactions. One hundred sixty billion dollars of business was done last year by check and without use of a dollar of money, while the total business done with actual cash totaled but a few billion dollars.

The entire gold production of the United States since 1896 was less than $1,300,000,000, a little more than $1,000,-000,000. But the actual increase of bank resources since 1896 is the enormous sum of $16,077,200,000, or over $16,000,000,000. This inflation of bank credit during the past fifteen years is two and one-half times more than the $6,604,100,000 that comprises all the gold held by the forty-six countries of the world. It exceeds by $3,000,000,000 the $12,936,397,600 that comprises the total of all the gold mined in the whole world since Columbus discovered America in 1492, and greatly exceeds the $12,331,200,000 (gold $6,604,100,000, silver $2,599,500,000, paper currency $3,127,600,000) that constitutes the entire present money supply of the whole forty-six nations of the earth.

While the quantity of gold has more than doubled, the present total gold stock of all countries is less than 7 billions. Should an increase of less than 4 billion dollars in the monetary gold of the whole world be held responsible for the world-wide increase of prices? Should not the increase of over 16 billion dollars in the volume of available bank credit in the United States, and the increase of bank credit in all other countries be taken into account in apportioning the responsibility for the vast increase in prices and the cost of living?

A considerable portion of the monetary gold is hoarded in the reserves of governments and does not materially effect prices, because it is not available for use as money by the people. But every dollar of outstanding bank credit is doing

business and therefore has a direct effect upon the prices of
all property and labor. Whatever advance in prices and the
cost of living is due to increase in the quantity of gold,
money and credit, a fair estimate would seem to be about 10
per cent due to increase in the world's output of gold and 90
per cent to the inflation of the world's volume of bank
credit.

According to the table on page 804 of U. S. Comptroller's
1911 report, bank currency increased 1896 to 1911, $199,-
200,000 to $681,700,000, or 342 per cent; bank credit loans,
$4,251,100,000 to $13,046,400,000, or 307 per cent; while
during the same period the population of the United States
increased only 33 per cent. During that time the number
of banks increased from 9,469 to 24,392, their capital $1,051,-
900,000 to $1,952,400,000, surplus and undivided profits
$694,400,000 to $2,065,000,000, total resources $7,553,900,-
000 to $23,631,100,000, individual deposits (largely the pro-
ceeds of discounted notes) $4,945,100,000 to $15,906,300,000,
and cash in bank $531,800,000 to $1,554,200,000, and amount
due from banks to other banks $645,000,000 to $2,788,-
800,000.

While the total population of the country increased 1896
to 1911 from 70,254,000 to 93,983,000, or 33 per cent, and
the total money in circulation from $1,506,434,966 to $3,214,-
002,596, or 113 per cent, the volume of bank credit in the
form of bank loans and discounts increased from $4,251,-
100,000 to $13,046,400,000, or 307 per cent. The astonish-
ing inflation of bank credit has gone on nearly ten times as
fast as the growth of population. We should stop blaming
Providence for increasing the gold output 100 per cent and
put a brake on the banks that have dangerously inflated
credit more than 300 per cent. Keeping in mind that increase in the volume of bank credit (bank loans to individuals and corporations) increases the purchasing power of
the people the same as an increase in the volume of money,
thereby increasing the demand for commodities, securities
and other property, causing an advance of prices and stimu-
lating speculation, have we not discovered in the tremendous inflation of bank credit the true cause of most of the
advance in prices and increase in the cost of living? If so,
then the banks, in order vastly to increase their already
swollen profits by increasing their loans of credit an amount
aggregating nearly three times the total of all money in circulation have deranged all the conditions of American life

CAUSE OF HIGH PRICES

INFLATION OF BANK CREDIT LOANS TENDS TO INCREASE PRICES AND THE COST OF LIVING THE SAME AS INCREASE OF THE SUPPLY OF GOLD AND CURRENCY. IT STIMULATES THE DEMAND BY INCREASING THE BUYING POWER OF THE PEOPLE.

and business, nearly doubled the cost of living for every family, inflated listed securities above value countless millions and made possible the wild speculation and trust consolidations since 1896 that have staggered the imagination of the entire world and thrust American finance and industry helplessly into the crater of a seething speculative volcano that perpetually endangers the country with the menace of frequent and desolating panics.

This dangerous condition has come upon us because unlike England we have left the regulation of all currency and finance to Wall Street and the banks. Congress at the instance of the financiers has passed laws that tend to concentrate financial power and profits in the hands of the very interests that profit most from exploitation of the people by abuse of such power. If the country is kept always on the edge of dangerous and devastating panic it is due to the inordinate greed that has induced the big banks and Wall Street to cause a vast and reckless inflation of the volume of bank credit billions of dollars beyond the needs of sound legitimate business and chiefly to artificially inflate the quotation prices far above value of the nearly thirty billion dollars of listed securities, a large portion of which represent no actual assets, but are sustained at fictitious prices with bank credit loaned in enormous volume at nominal rates to inside favored operators.

Notwithstanding this bank record, the Aldrich bill would shackle the hands of the people and their government for fifty years and unreservedly grant to a private corporation owned by these same banks absolute power still further to inflate the currency, bank credit, prices and the cost of living untold billions without any effective restrictions or restraint, thereby robbing the producers by further advance of prices while keeping wages down and by higher interest rates made possible by the monopoly of the supply of money and credit the National Reserve Association is designed to create.

If that private central bank, the National Reserve Association, becomes a fact, the machinery for an endless chain inflation of currency and bank credit will be complete. The banks have discounted about 15 billion dollars of commercial paper or notes based on 1½ billions of cash in their reserves. Under the Aldrich plan the banks would rediscount with the central bank, say one-tenth, or 1½ billions, of their 15 billions of commercial paper, getting therefor

1½ billions of the association's corporate currency. This currency when deposited in the bank reserves will enable the banks to double their credit loans, inflating same from 15 to 30 billion dollars. Then they could take a tenth of the 15 billions of new commercial paper and rediscount same for association currency, increasing "cash reserves" to 4½ billions and credit loans to 45 billions. And so on over and over without any effective restriction or limit. Every billion of commercial paper rediscounted for corporate currency or for a "credit balance" at the National Reserve Association increases the possible loaning power and profits of the banks ten fold. It puts a premium on wild inflation and reckless banking. It may further increase prices and the cost of living beyond all human experience.

If Congress yields and authorizes a private central bank as proposed by the pending bill, the end when the bubble bursts will be universal ruin and national bankruptcy.

CHAPTER VI.

FRENZIED FINANCING.

A Corporation With a Billion of Good Assets to be Formed Without the Investment of a Dollar. Greatest Feat of Financial Legerdemain in All History. The Mystic Power Explained.

If Congress passes the pending Aldrich private central bank bill, the financing will be accomplished substantially as follows:

The three parties interested—the Government, the National Reserve Association and the banks—sit around a table prepared to close the deal.

The Government delivers to the association (Sec. 1) its fifty-year charter—the Aldrich law. The banks hand to the association a $100,000,000 check drawn on themselves to "pay in" 50 per cent of their $200,000,000 subscription (Secs. 1 and 2) to association stock. The association being now ready to "do business," the Government "deposits" with the association (Sec. 23) its "general fund," its entire treasury balance, say $150,000,000. To facilitate matters, $1,030,000,000 (Sec. 51) National Reserve Association "currency" has been printed in advance. This now is handed over to the banks by the association for $744,000,000 U. S. 2 per cent bonds (Sec. 49), $186,000,000 of "gold or other lawful money" to put into the association's reserves (Secs. 41 and 42), and $100,000,000 as a "loan" to enable the banks to meet their $100,000,000 check given to "pay in" 50 per cent of their subscription to $200,000,000 association stock. The association then hands to the banks their $100,000,000 check and takes back $100,000,000 of corporate currency to pay same.

This completes the deal. The association now owns $744,-000,000 U. S. bonds, a cash reserve of $336,000,000 of "gold or other United States money" (being the Government $150,000,000 and $186,000,000 obtained from the banks in exchange for corporate currency), and the promissory note of the banks for $100,000,000, and $100,000,000 of its corporate currency, total resources $1,280,000,000.

It has as debts, or liabilities, paid in capital stock, $100,-000,000; Government deposits $150,000,000; corporate currency $1,030,000,000; total $1,280,000,000.

The association at once exchanges (Sec. 55) the $744,-000,000 of U. S. 2 per cent bonds for 3 per cent bonds running fifty years. It pays (Sec. 56) thereon 1½ per cent tax, 1 per cent representing the difference between 2 per cent and 3 per cent interest and the other ½ per cent being the same as now is paid (U. S. Act of May 30, 1908) on the $744,000,000 of outstanding bank note currency to be cancelled and replaced by corporate currency. Government gets and association pays nothing extra. But the Government loses the 1 per cent banks now must pay (law of May 30, 1908) for Government deposits and the association gets the benefit. The association also gets the 3 per cent interest on $744,000,000 bonds, less the 1½ per cent tax, or 1½ per cent net, a total net profit of $11,160,000 annually. This is enough to pay to the banks yearly 5 per cent dividends (Sec. 19) on the amount paid in on their association stock and to carry $6,160,000 to surplus annually, thus increasing the "book value" (Sec. 12) of association stock, for the benefit of the banks. Although the association has not from any source really received and retained one dollar of actual money, other than the Government's $150,-000,000 deposit, except the currency it has run off on its own printing press, yet already it has a permanent annual net income of more than 11 per cent on its entire $100,-000,000 of "paid in" capital stock. The banks, of course, get the benefit because (Sec. 3) they own all of the association's stock.

The $336,000,000 is (Sec. 41) a 50 per cent "reserve" covering $672,000,000 of the $1,030,000,000 issued corporate currency; the other $372,000,000 of association currency used to pay for half of the $744,000,000 of bonds (Sec. 42) requires no reserve behind it. By paying a special tax (Sec. 41) the association can issue $336,000,000 more corporate currency on this same $336,000,000 of reserve, thus reducing the reserve basis from 50 per cent to 33⅓ per cent of the volume of corporate currency. And the law permits the association (Secs. 41 and 51) to issue corporate currency without limit as to quantity.

The Aldrich bill authorizes the central bank to issue at

least two dollars of corporate currency against every dollar of Government money held in its reserves. With just one dollar and no more to start with, the association could corner and take out of circulation the entire three billion dollars of Government money and put into circulation six billions of corporate currency and never use any capital in accomplishing the deal except the original one dollar and the currency produced on its own printing press. As an "endless chain," it could buy one and issue two over and over until it has every dollar of U. S. money locked up in the vaults permanently.

The $100,000,000 of its corporate currency handed back to take up the $100,000,000 check given by the banks to "pay in" 50 per cent on the $200,000,000 association stock, can be kept by the association in its "central reservoir" to protect the banks against "runs," to "extinguish a financial conflagration in any part of the country," and to (Secs. 26, 27 and 28) rediscount for the banks. If the association needs more currency for these purposes, it can get it in any quantity in an hour's time any day practically without expense simply by starting its currency printing press going. It all will be money because (Sec. 53) the Aldrich bill makes it so. This plan makes it unnecessary for the banks to withdraw from Wall Street, and put into its "central reservoir" any of their (Sec. 39) ordinary legal reserves that now draw profitable interest steadily, being used by high finance in its speculative ventures.

It is seen that the association has emerged prosperous from the deal and that the Government has gained nothing, but it has lost the 1 per cent interest now paid by the banks for the use of Government deposits. How have the banks fared by the transaction?

The banks formerly got from the people 6 per cent for use of $744,000,000 of bank-note currency and the 2 per cent interest on the bonds securing same, less ½ per cent Government tax, or 1½ per cent ($11,160,000) annually over and above 6 per cent on their investment. The bank-note currency being now cancelled, this income is cut off. But they get precisely the same profit through their ownership of association stock, being the 3 per cent interest paid to the association by the Government as interest on the $744,000,000 of new fifty-year 3 per cent bonds, less 1½ per cent tax, or $11,160,000 net profit annually. So the banks lost nothing by parting with the bonds and the bank-note currency privilege. And through their association they get the use of the Government's $150,000,000 without (Sec. 25) paying the 1 per cent interest formerly required by law. Theoretically, the banks put $100,000,000 into association stock, and $186,000,000 into the association's reserves. Practically, they did not put up one cent; for before the ink was dry the banks without cost obtained from their association enough corporate currency usable as money, to replace the $100,000,000 and the $186,000,000, besides the $744,-000,000 of currency given them to pay for the bonds they sold. And it should be remembered that whatever the association owns belongs to the banks, for they own all the association's stock. Neither the bonds or the $744,000,000 of bank-note currency was usable by the banks as "lawful cash reserve" (See National Bank Act) on which to make credit loans. The banks only could get 6 per cent for use of the bank-note currency and 2 per cent interest on the bonds. But this new corporate currency by the Aldrich law (Sec. 39) is made usable by the banks as "legal cash reserve," against which the banks lawfully may loan about ten times the total of such reserves in the shape of credit, ordinary bank loans to business borrowers. Deducting the $100,000,000 used to replace the amount "paid in" for association stock and $186,000,000 to offset the lawful money supplied for the association's reserves, the banks still have left $744,000,000 of the $1,030,000,000 corporate currency. This put into the bank reserves increases the loaning power of the banks $7,440,000,000, an inflation about equal to half the $15,000,000,000 that comprises the present total credit loans of the 24,392 banks of the United States. When this increase of loans is accomplished at 6 per cent the bank will receive an extra yearly net profit of $446,000,000, or sufficient to pay over 20 per cent extra annual dividends on the $2,000,000,000 capital stock of all the banks of the country. That is the rich prize for which the big banks are strenuously striving. And it should be borne in mind that every dollar of profit made by the association and the banks comes out of the pockets of the people of the United States.

In passing the Aldrich bill Congress makes possible this bewildering and amazing financial transaction in every detail precisely as above stated. The National Reserve Association thus literally lifts itself financially over a billion-dollar fence by its own boot straps—its own paper currency—by grace of the law of Congress.

Without investing a dollar the confederated banks will completely finance and exclusively own a private corporation that will have a billion of assets and a billion of corporate currency made money by the law and increase the loaning power of the banks over seven billion dollars, and their possible annual profits nearly a half billion. This all can be accomplished almost immediately, when the Aldrich bill becomes law. And that is only the first round. It represents but a small portion of the overwhelming power and possible profits to be conferred by act of Congress upon Wall Street and the banks through their association—the coming great Central Money Trust. The people of the United States get not the slightest benefit. And yet it is the law of their Congress, conferring the quality of money upon the paper emissions of a mere private corporation for the exclusive profit of such corporation and its beneficiary banks, that is the magic power which in one minute makes $1,000,000,000 of actual value out of nothing, without the investment of a single dollar or one hour's human labor. This actual accomplishment will excel in daring and magnitude the wild dream of the ages by which the alchemists have sought to convert the baser metals of the world into gold.

CHAPTER VII.

CONFESSIONS OF WALL STREET.

Letters From Banks and Financiers. Political Conspiracy? Documentary Proof.

The Central Bank plan was originated by Wall Street and now is being actively promoted by the big banks and financiers of that center of high finance. Of that pregnant fact there is not the slightest doubt. Overwhelming evidence of the most convincing character is given in this volume.

The people have a right to know the truth before their Congress acts. They are entitled to information disclosing just who started the movement, what interests are promoting or financing it, the benefits such interests expect to derive therefrom and the effect its success will have upon the country and the welfare of its inhabitants. With that object in view, the writer recently wrote over his own signature letters similar to the one hereinafter given in full addressed to many of the biggest banks, trust companies, insurance companies and financiers of Wall Street. While those replying doubtless did not realize the purpose of the inquiry or expect publication of their replies, there should be no legitimate objection to their publicity. No deception was employed. The inquiries were pertinent to a public question of great general interest. The letters were from and the replies to a perfect stranger. The correspondence is written confession, evidence of the highest order, officially and conclusively showing for the information and enlightenment of the people of the United States the important fact that the most prominent and powerful banks and financiers of Wall Street favor and zealously are helping to promote the "Aldrich plan" for a privately owned central bank, named National Reserve Association, to monopolize the entire public currency of the republic.

The writer here publicly acknowledges his appreciation

for the courtesy of such replies, and makes no charges or deductions against those writing them, but leaves the language of each letter to speak for itself. In making the letters public, he believes he is violating no confidence, as none were marked confidential, but is performing a high duty and he hopes also rendering at least a slight public service.

National City Bank.

The National City Bank is the most prominent financial institution in Wall Street. It is the largest bank in the United States. Often it is called the "Standard Oil" institution. But now it is said that the several supremely potent financial interests or "groups" of Wall Street that once warred on each other, but now are alleged to "co-operate" in feasting off the public, all are directly or indirectly interested in the affairs or doings of this one great bank, the banking colossus of America. Its capital is $25,000,000, its surplus and undivided profits $27,475,000, total $52,475,000; which vast sum is nearly equal to the combined capital and surplus of one-third of the total 7,331 National Banks of the United States, taking the smaller banks. This bank also has individual deposits $182,709,000, deposits by banks $67,908,000, by U. S. Government $658,000, and other liabilities $6,141,000, total $311,930,000. It has resources: loans and discounts $137,954,000, U. S. bonds $9,907,000, state and municipal bonds $42,091,000, circulating notes, or bank note currency, $4,009,000, due from banks $11,874,000, cash and exchange $104,803,000, other resources $8,300,000. Its directors are:

J. P. Morgan, Jr.	P. A. Valentine.
Henry C. Frick.	Joseph P. Grace.
George W. Perkins.	H. A. C. Taylor.
J. Ogden Armour.	W. D. Sloane.
C. H. McCormick.	Wm. Rockefeller.
Moses Taylor.	F. M. Bacon.
Frank A. Vanderlip.	S. S. Palmer.
C. H. Dodge.	Edwin S. Marston.
Jacob H. Schiff.	G. H. Milliken.
James Stillman	James A. Stillman.
Samuel Sloan.	James H. Post.
John W. Sterling.	

NATIONAL CITY BANK
IN WALL STREET.

THE BANKING COLOSSUS OF AMERICA.

While this often is called the Standard Oil bank, it will be seen that the two great alleged Wall Street parties, Morgan and Standard Oil are merged in the control of this imperial bank. The steel, beef, harvester and other great trusts and railroads, and vast foreign capital all are represented on its board. The First National Bank with $10,-000,000 capital, $21,189,000 surplus, $160,090,000 resources, and the National Bank of Commerce with $25,000,000 capital, $15,532,000 surplus, and $207,130,000 resources, are companion financial giants largely controlled by the same interests, as also is the Continental and Commercial National Bank of Chicago, that has $20,000,000 capital, $10,-285,000 surplus and over $200,000,000 resources. The combined resources of these four great banks is $1,000,000,000, and indirectly they control many billions and dominate many banks in New York and elsewhere throughout the United States.

The recent organization of the "National City Company" with $10,000,000 capital, said to be owned or controlled by the National City Bank or its stockholders, was reported to have been largely accomplished out of the excess profits by an extra $10,000,000 cash dividend made by the bank for the purpose of holding or dealing in stock market and other securities and things thought to be unlawful for a National Bank to own.

The public press has said substantially that this "side partner" corporation already had acquired interest in the capital stock of nearly a hundred other banks in various parts of the United States, but that lately it has sold or parted with actual possession of such bank stocks. Whether its accumulation of stock in other banks was with the purpose of ultimately controlling or increasing its influence in the proposed National Reserve Association, the stock of which under the "Aldrich plan" would be exclusively owned by the banks, not pro rata but in proportion to size of capital of each bank, and thereby to obtain a larger hold upon the entire public currency and all the revenues of the Government to be turned over to such central bank under the "Aldrich plan," only those "on the inside" can tell.

Whether the subsequent reported shifting of the ownership or possession of such bank stocks was due to official objection or to fear that the regretted publicity of the fact of their acquisition might alarm and prejudice the public into fearing that Wall Street already was getting ready quickly to seize control of the Central Bank and the entire public currency and the public revenues to use the same for its purposes, thereby perhaps endangering the passage of the scheme by Congress, the writer does not care to say.

Was this bank or its "side partner" corporation to be the holding company for the stock of enough banks to control the National Reserve Association, so that in effect it would have as much power and control over the public currency as though Congress by law made the National City Bank direct the great Private Central Bank of the country?

This bank or its principal officers for years have been ardent and consistent advocates of the central bank plan in public addresses, circulars, letters and literature circulated at large expense. Its president, Frank A. Vanderlip, has been particularly prominent, intelligent and active in the movement. The writer does not criticise or question their right to do this. Doubtless a central bank would greatly add to the profit and power of this bank, therefore it would be only natural that they strain every nerve and sinew to bring about the passage of the act by Congress. But writer believes that the people, whose servant Congress is, should know the facts. This done, *the people must judge for themselves whether they want for their patriotic welfare just what Wall Street wants for its selfish interests.*

The following letters and replies explain themselves:

"PLANKINTON HOUSE, EUROPEAN PLAN.

H. Stanley Green, Manager.

MILWAUKEE, WIS., November 20, 1911.

National City Bank, New York City.

Gentlemen: Kindly send to me here any printed information issued by you on the Aldrich monetary plan.

Do you understand that a bank gets 4 per cent dividends only on that part of its subscription called in in cash or on the face of its subscription to National Reserve Association stock?

Will the credit of the Government be pledged to make it certain that the currency of the said association always will be maintained at par?

What are the prospects for early favorable action by Congress?

Thanking you, I am, very truly yours,
(Signed) ALFRED O. CROZIER."

"THE NATIONAL CITY BANK OF NEW YORK.

Capital $25,000,000, Surplus and Undivided Profits $25,000,-
000. Cable Address 'Citibank.'

NEW YORK, November 24, 1911.

Mr. Alfred O. Crozier, Plankinton House, Milwaukee, Wis.

Dear Sir: Replying to your favor of November 20th, we beg to send you herewith a copy of the revised plan of Senator Aldrich for monetary legislation, in which you will find the complete details of Senator Aldrich's ideas. Under separate cover we are also sending you a copy of an address made by our president, Mr. Vanderlip, before the Commercial Club of Chicago on the Aldrich plan as originally submitted, and we also send you a copy of addresses made by Mr. Vanderlip this past summer before the Chautauqua Association on Modern Banking, in which you will find material covering the general idea.

In paragraph No. 4 of the plan enclosed herewith, you will find a statement of the proposed distribution of earnings. From this you will note that after the payment of all expenses and taxes the stockholders shall receive 4 per cent. There is no definite statement as to just what principal this 4 per cent is to be paid on, but our natural assumption is that it would be paid on the amount of cash actually paid in. We do not understand that it is contemplated that dividends will be paid on anything but actual cash subscriptions.

In paragraph 71 of the plan, you will note that it is provided that the notes of the National Reserve Association shall be received at par in payment of all taxes, excises and other dues to the United States, and for all salaries and other debts and demands owing by the United States to individuals, corporations, or associations, except obligations of the Government which are by their terms specifically payable in gold, and for all debts due from or by one bank to another, and for all obligations due to a bank. It will be seen from this paragraph that the notes of the Reserve Association are to be legal tender. As to any specific pledge of the credit of the Government to make it certain that the currency of the association always will be maintained at par, however, we do not understand that such a pledge is contemplated.

It is quite impossible for us to predict what may be done along the lines of favorable action by Congress at an early date. Our only guide to this possibility is the fact that

The National City Bank
of New York.
New York.

November 24th, 1911.

Mr. Alfred O. Crozier,
Plankinton House,
Milwaukee, Wisconsin.

Dear Sir:

Replying to your favor of November 20th, we beg to send you herewith a copy of the Revised Plan of Senator Aldrich for Monetary Legislation, in which you will find the complete details of Senator Aldrich's ideas. Under separate cover, we are also sending you a copy of an Address made by our President, Mr. Vanderlip, before the Commercial Club of Chicago on the Aldrich Plan as originally submitted, and we also send you a copy of Addresses made by Mr. Vanderlip this past summer before the Chautauqua Association on Modern Banking, in which you will find material covering the general idea.

In Paragraph No. 4 of the Plan enclosed herewith, you will find a statement of the proposed distribution of earnings. From this you will note that after the payment of all expenses and taxes the stockholders shall receive 4 per cent. There is no definite statement as to just what principal this 4 per cent is to be paid on, but our natural assumption is that it would be paid on the amount of cash actually paid in. We do not understand that it is contemplated that dividends will be paid on anything but actual cash subscriptions.

In Paragraph 71 of the Plan, you will note that it is provided that the notes of the National Reserve Association shall be received at par in payment of all taxes, excises, and other dues to the United States, and for all salaries and other debts and demands owing by the United States to individuals, corporations, or associations, except obligations of the Government which are by their terms specifically payable in gold, and for all debts due from or by one bank to another, and for all obligations due to a bank.

It will be seen from this paragraph that the notes of the Reserve Association are to be legal tender. As to any specific pledge of the credit of the Government to make it certain that the currency of the Association always will be maintained at par, however, we do not understand that such a pledge is contemplated.

It is quite impossible for us to predict what may be done along the lines of favorable action by Congress at an early date. Our only guide to this possibility is the fact that there is at present a widespread movement to induce early action along this line. You will undoubtedly have noticed from the public press that there have been organized in various states branches of

Mr. Alfred O. Crozier...............   November 24th, 1911.

an organization entitled - The National Citizens League, for the dissemination of information regarding our currency and banking problems, and it is to be assured that the object of the League is to educate the people to understand the problems, and to comprehend also the necessity for prompt action by Congress. You will also have noted that practically the entire session of the American Bankers Association now in convention at New Orleans has been devoted to consideration of Senator Aldrich's Plan. It is quite likely that the favorable attitude of the members of the Association will have considerable weight with Congress. These two circumstances would seem to indicate that a good deal of pressure will be brought upon Congress to pass this legislation at an early date. Whether or not such pressure will be effective is, of course, a matter for time to determine and we could not make any prophesy along this line.

Trusting that we have covered the points you raise to your satisfaction, we are,

Very truly yours,

Enclosures

there is at present a widespread movement to induce early action along this line. You will undoubtedly have noticed from the public press that there have been organized in various states branches of an organization entitled The National Citizens' League, for the dissemination of information regarding our currency and banking problems, and it is to be assumed that the object of the league is to educate the people to understand the problems, and to comprehend also the necessity for prompt action by Congress. You will also have noted that practically the entire session of the American Bankers' Association now in convention at New Orleans has been devoted to consideration of Senator Aldrich's plan. It is quite likely that the favorable attitude of the members of the association will have considerable weight with Congress. These two circumstances would seem to indicate that a good deal of pressure will be brought upon Congress to pass this legislation at an early date. Whether or not such pressure will be effective is, of course, a matter for time to determine and we could not make any prophesy along this line.

Trusting that we have covered the points you raise to your satisfaction, we are very truly yours,

(Signed) F. A. VANDERLIP.
(By) A. H."

A. H. Enclosures.

This confession that "pressure" is to be brought on Congress and, of course, on members of Congress by the banks of the country is of the greatest significance and importance. That seems to be the bank way of getting legislation beneficial to banks, always. Further correspondence between the National City Bank and the author will be found in the chapter "The Legal Tender Joker." As the corporate currency is not made a tender for the payment of private debts, the above statement that it is to be "legal tender" is not true. Notice that the organization cited as publicly promoting the measure, "The National Citizens' League," was the outgrowth of the action taken by the New York Chamber of Commerce March 2, 1911, for the formation of such a "public" organization to corral the people and business men to support this Wall Street scheme.

National Bank of Commerce.

The National Bank of Commerce is said to be the leading Morgan bank of Wall Street, with 40 directors, $25,000,000 capital, $15,161,660 surplus and undivided profits, $95,-954,120 of individual deposits, and $80,377,170 of other deposits; its total resources being over $215,000,000. Another alleged Morgan bank, the First National, has $10,000,000 capital, $21,189,000 surplus and undivided profits, and $160,-090,000 of resources.

It is said that every important financial institution in New York, during the panic of 1907 or since, was practically forced or induced to surrender to the big Wall Street combine. And this combine in turn is known to be closely affiliated with the Rothschilds and other individual and incorporated interests that control the vast billions of liquid and invested capital of Europe.

The Boards of Directors of the National City Bank and the National Bank of Commerce, representing the two great dominating groups, Morgan and Standard Oil, are interlaced and bound together by certain powerful common directors. The same thing is true of The First National Bank of New York and The Continental and Commercial National Bank of Chicago. In fact these banks comprise "The Financial Big Four," now said to be morally bound together in an impregnable offensive and defensive alliance, with which is alleged to be directly or indirectly affiliated practically every big bank, insurance and trust company, railroad and trust in the United States. No bank anywhere now would feel that it could safely resist the demands or refuse to follow any orders if made by this *great consolidated and incorporated money power.*

This group of four banks has a billion dollars of resources, and the interests therewith are said to directly or indirectly control or dominate a large share of the $2,000,-000,000 of capital and $23,000,000,000 of resources of all the banking institutions of the country, and the $25,000,000,-000 of listed securities. And it is alleged that through these and other direct or indirect agencies this one great combine dominated by a mere handful of men to a large extent now controls practically everything worth going after in the United States.

The National City Bank has 24 directors, the Bank of Commerce 40, and The Continental and Commercial National Bank 44, total 108; but there are many duplications, so that less than 100 men with their affiliations now seem to control about everything tangible in the country. With the start they have obtained, their limitless resources, the foundation of which largely consists of the deposits savings of the people, their ability to borrow billions of bank credit, and the boundless power at their command, if they are allowed to go on unchecked soon they will virtually own the republic and all its inhabitants.

This "Big Four" is the head-center of the movement to induce Congress to create a private central bank, the National Reserve Association. And it will no doubt rule that corporation if it has to buy control of the stock of half the banks in the United States, as it has the resources to do, for with it they would get the right to print and issue without limit billions of dollars of corporate currency to be used as money, and power by manipulating the volume of the currency to permit expansion and force contraction by 24,392 banks of the $23,000,000,000 of bank loans and resources, thereby gaining life and death control over the business and activities of every borrowing individual and corporation; also power artificially and automatically to raise and lower the prices of all securities, property and labor by merely increasing and decreasing the discount rate and the supply of money. The directors of the National Bank of Commerce are:

J. P. Morgan, Jr.	E. J. Berwind
Geo. J. Gould	F. Cromwell
Brayton Ives	V. Morawetz
Allen A. Ryan	J. S. Alexander
J. F. Dryden	J. H. Parker
John Claflin	J. B. Duke
A. D. Juilliard	F. Sturges
A. W. Krech	J. N. Jarvie
A. Iselin, Jr.	Geo. F. Baker
Levi P. Morton	T. H. Hubbard
Frank A. Vanderlip	W. A. Day
D. Guggenheim	C. J. Blair
H. P. Whitney	V. P. Snyder
P. D. Cravath	W. Langdon
Jacob H. Schiff	C. A. Peabody
H. P. Davidson	W. A. Simonson
H. A. Smith	A. W. Mellon

H. W. DeForrest   Charles Lanier
A. W. Wiggins   C. H. Russell
F. L. Hine   C. H. Allen

The following letter shows the interest and activity of that bank for the Aldrich Central Bank Plan:

NATIONAL BANK OF COMMERCE
IN NEW YORK

Capital, Surplus and Undivided Profits Forty Million Dollars

January 8, 1912.

Alfred O Crosier, Esq.,
   The Romaine,
     Cincinnati, O.

Dear Sir:

  We are in receipt of your favor of December 20th, and in answer would say that we have not issued any printed matter relative to the Aldrich bill, but take pleasure in sending you under separate cover a pamphlet issued by one of our banks, showing the bill as originally submitted some time ago, and also the revised bill of recent date.

  In case the bill should pass and become operative, we do not understand that the Government would guarantee in any way currency issued by the National Reserve Association. The writer has not before him the annual message of President Taft, but his recollection is that the Aldrich bill was favorably mentioned therein.

    Yours respectfully,

      Vice-President

NATIONAL BANK OF COMMERCE IN NEW YORK.

Capital, Surplus and Undivided Profits Forty Million Dollars.

President, James S. Alexander.
Vice-Presidents, Henry A. Smith, R. G. Hutchins, Jr.
Cashier, Neilson Olcott.
Assistant Cashiers, Oliver I. Pilat, Faris R. Russell, A. J. Oxenham, Samuel Wilcox.

Manager Foreign Department, G. S. Mason.

January 3, 1912.

Alfred O. Crozier, Esq.,
The Romaine,
Cincinnati, Ohio.

Dear Sir: We are in receipt of your favor of December 20th, and in answer would say that we have not issued any printed matter relative to the Aldrich bill, but take pleasure in sending you under separate cover a pamphlet issued by one of our banks, showing the bill as originally submitted some time ago, and also the revised bill of recent date.

In case the bill should pass and become operative, we do not understand that the Government would guarantee in any way currency issued by the National Reserve Association. The writer has not before him the annual message of President Taft but his recollection is that the Aldrich bill was favorably mentioned therein. Yours respectfully,

H. A. SMITH, Vice-President.

The Continental and Commercial National Bank.

The Chicago member of the "Big Four" is The Continental and Commercial National Bank. This has been called the Standard Oil institution of the West. Financially, it is alleged to be the Siamese twin of the National City Bank of New York and brother-in-law of the Bank of Commerce and the First National. Following are its forty-four directors:

J. Ogden Armour	Edward Hines
E. H. Gary	Joseph H. Talbert
A. J. Earling	R. H. McElwee
F. E. Weyerhaeuser	T. P. Phillips
W. J. Chalmers	Alfred Cowles
Frank Hibbard	E. S. Lacey

R. C. Lake
R. Van Vechten
F. A. Hardy
W. I. Osborn
Geo. M. Reynolds
J. C. Black
B. A. Eckert
A. Robertson
Robert T. Lincoln
W. H. McDoel
Joy Morton
Darius Miller
A. F. Banks
E. J. Buffington
M. H. Wilson
R. J. Dunham

C. H. Weaver
James W. Stevens
John C. Craft
Eames MacVeagh
E. A. Cudahy
E. P. Ripley
Chas. H. Thorne
J. F. Harris
S. McRoberts
E. A. Potter
Wm. V. Kelly
E. P. Russell
D. H. Burnham
C. T. Boynton
H. F. Perkins
A. H. Milliken

The following letter from its president, who has been very prominent in his support of the Aldrich Private Central Bank plan by way of public addresses and otherwise, was written on his return from the meeting of the American Bankers' Association at New Orleans, of which association formerly he was president:

Capital, Surplus and Undivided Profits $30,000,000

CONTINENTAL & COMMERCIAL NATIONAL BANK OF CHICAGO

George M. Reynolds, President.

Edward S. Lacy, Chairman of Advisory Committee.

CHICAGO, November 29, 1911.

Alfred O. Crozier, Esq.,
   Care Plankinton House,
     Milwaukee, Wis.

My Dear Sir: Your favor of the 21st instant, received during my absence from the city, has just been handed to me and I have noted contents of same.

Under the revised plan as made by Senator Aldrich, the maximum amount of dividend to go to the banks subscribing for the stock of the National Reserve Association is 5 per cent. In addition to this, provision is made for the accumulation of a reserve or surplus fund to an amount equal to 20 per cent of the capital stock, so that the subscribing banks would get, for the present, provided the association is organized and the dividends earned, a dividend of 5 per cent; but in the event of the sale of the

Chicago, November 29th, 1911.

Alfred O. Crozier, Esq.,

    c/o Plankington House,

       Milwaukee, Wisconsin.

My dear Sir:

Your favor of the 21st instant, received during my absence from the city, has just been handed to me and I have noted contents of same.

Under the revised plan as made by Senator Aldrich, the maximum amount of dividend to go to the banks subscribing for the stock of the National Reserve Association is 5%. In addition to this, provision is made for the accumulation of a reserve or surplus fund to an amount equal to 20% of the capital stock, so that the subscribing banks would get, for the present, provided the association is organized and the dividends earned, a dividend of 5%, but in the event of the sale of the stock or withdrawal from the association, it would be paid for the same at its book value, which would include its proportionate share of the surplus or reserve.

The plan does not propose that the credit of the Government be pledged to secure the currency which will be issued by the association.

~~Continental and Commercial National Bank of Chicago~~

- 2 -

Referring to the prospect for early favorable action by Congress, I beg to say that while sentiment is rapidly crystalizing around the bill, naturally,
it is a bill concerning which most people are not familiar,
and it will probably be necessary for a campaign of education to be waged before it can finally be successful.

I enclose herein revised plan as proposed by
Senator Aldrich, and beg to remain,

Yours very truly,

G. M. Reynolds

President.

stock or withdrawal from the association, it would be paid
for the same at its book value, which would include its
proportionate share of the surplus of reserve.

The plan does not propose that the credit of the Government be pledged to secure the currency which will be
issued by the association.

Referring to the prospect for early favorable action by
Congress, I beg to say that while sentiment is rapidly
crystalizing around the bill, naturally, it is a bill concerning which most people are not familiar, and it will probably be necessary for a campaign of education to be waged
before it can finally be successful.

I enclose herein revised plan as proposed by Senator
Aldrich, and beg to remain,

Yours very truly,
G. M. REYNOLDS, President."

"J. P. MORGAN & Co., Wall St., Cor. Broad, New York. DREXEL & Co., Philadelphia. MORGAN, GRENFELL & Co., London, MORGAN, HARJES & Co., Paris.

NEW YORK, November 28, 1911.

Alfred O. Crozier, Esq.,
    Care Plankinton House,
        Milwaukee, Wisconsin.

Dear Sir: In reply to your letter of the 24th instant we would say that we do not have any copies of the "Aldrich plan," and are unable to give you the information desired.

Yours truly,

J. P. MORGAN & Co."

WILLIAM SHERER, Cashier   WILLIAM J. GILPIN, Ass't. Manager

NEW YORK CLEARING HOUSE,
77-83 CEDAR STREET.

NEW YORK, November 29th, 1911.

Alfred O. Crozier, Esq.,
    Plankinton House,
        Milwaukee, Wis.

Dear Sir:-

Referring to yours of the 24th inst.,
I would say that this institution does not issue
any printed matter in connection with the Aldrich
Plan. One of our banks, however, has issued a
copy of the Revised Edition of the Plan, which I
have pleasure in sending you under separate cover.

Very truly yours,

Manager,

The document referred to was received. It was entitled "The New Aldrich Currency System, revised edition, 1911," issued by the Fourth National Bank of the City of New York.

New York Clearing House.

"William Sherer,
    Manager.

William J. Gilpin,
    Asst. Manager.

NEW YORK CLEARING HOUSE. 77-83 Cedar Street.
    NEW YORK, November 29, 1911.

Alfred O. Crozier, Esq.,
    Care Plankinton House,
    Milwaukee, Wisconsin.

Dear Sir: Referring to yours of the 24th inst., would say that this institution does not issue any printed matter in connection with the Aldrich plan. One of our banks, however, has issued a copy of the revised edition of the

---

New York Stock Exchange

Secretary's Office   *New York* ___ Nov. 28, 1911.

Alfred O. Crozier, Esq.,

    Milwaukee, Wis.

Dear Sir:-

    Answering your letter of November 24, 1911, I regret to say that I am unable to give you any information in the matter you refer to.

          Yours truly,

          George N. Ely
              Secretary

plan, which I have pleasure in sending you under separate cover. Very truly yours,

(Signed) WM SHERER, Manager."

New York Stock Exchange.

"NEW YORK STOCK EXCHANGE.

SECRETARY'S OFFICE,

NEW YORK, November 28, 1911.

Alfred O. Crozier, Esq.,

Milwaukee, Wisconsin.

Dear Sir: Answering your letter of November 24, 1911, I regret to say that I am unable to give you any information in the matter you refer to.

Yours truly,

GEORGE M. ELY, Secretary."

Chamber of Commerce of the State of New York.

Founded April 5, 1768.

A. Barton Hepburn, President.
Vice-Presidents.

New York, Nov. 28, 1911.

Dear Sir:

I take pleasure in sending to you, in reply to your request of November 24th, the Monthly Bulletins of the New York Chamber of Commerce for March and April 1911, which contain a report from the Chamber's delegates to the Monetary Conference held in Washington in January, and also the debate upon this report.

Yours very truly,

Secretary.

Mr. Alfred O. Crozier,
Plankinton House,
Milwaukee, Wis.

New York Chamber of Commerce.

"CHAMBER OF COMMERCE OF THE STATE OF NEW YORK.
Founded April 5, 1768.

A. Barton Hepburn, President.

Sereno S. Pratt, Secretary.

Chas T. Gwynne, Asst. Secretary.

Vice Presidents.

Cleveland H. Dodge,	Otto G. Bannard,
James J. Hill,	Arthur Curtis James,
George F. Baer,	John Claflin,
William A. Nash,	A. Foster Higgins,
J. Pierpont Morgan,	James Talcott,
Jacob H. Schiff,	

William H. Porter, Treasurer.

NEW YORK, November 28, 1911.

Dear Sir: I take pleasure in sending to you in reply to your request of November 24th, the Monthly Bulletins of the New York Chamber of Commerce for March and April, 1911, which contains a report from the Chamber's delegates to the monetary conference held in Washington in January, and also the debate upon this report.

Yours very truly,

SERENO S. PRATT, Secretary."

Mr. Alfred O. Crozier,
    Care Plankinton House,
        Milwaukee, Wisconsin.

The Bulletins mentioned were received and are extensively quoted from by the author in Chapter "Wall Street's First 'Plan'."

"THE FOURTH NATIONAL BANK OF THE CITY OF NEW YORK.

James G. Gannon, President.
Samuel S. Campbell, Vice President.
Chas. H. Patterson, Vice President.
Daniel J. Rogers, Cashier.
E. W. Davenport, Asst. Cashier.
Charles E. Meek, Asst. Cashier.

NEW YORK, Friday, November 24, 1911.

Mr. Alfred O. Crozier,
    Care Plankinton House,
        Milwaukee, Wisconsin.

Dear Sir: In reply to your esteemed favor of the 21st instant, we take pleasure in forwarding you under separate cover a copy of our latest publication on the "New Aldrich Currency System," revised, on pages 6 and 7 of which you will find articles marked, which we think will answer satisfactorily inquiries made in your letter concerning dividends, etc.

Thanking you for your interest, we beg to remain,

    Yours very truly,
        S. S. CAMPBELL, Vice President."

Union Trust Company of New York.

"Edwin G. Merrill, President.
Augustus W. Kelly, Vice President.
John V. B. Thayer, Vice President and Secretary.
Edward R. Merritt, Vice President.
Carroll C. Rawlings, Trust Officer.
Henry M. Popham, T. W. Hartshorne, Henry M. Myrick,
        Asst. Secretaries.

UNION TRUST COMPANY OF NEW YORK,
        80 Broadway.

All communications should be addressed to Union Trust Company of New York, P. O. Box 1015, Cable
        Address "Unitrust."

NEW YORK, November 29, 1911.

Mr. Alfred O. Crozier,
    Care Plankinton House,
        Milwaukee, Wisconsin.

Dear Sir: Replying to your favor of the 24th instant, would say that this company has issued no printed matter explanatory of the "Aldrich plan," but I think if you will apply to the secretary of the American Bankers' Association in the Hanover National Bank Building, New York City, you will be accommodated with such literature as they may have on the subject.

        Yours respectfully,
            J. V. B. THAYER, Vice President."

American Bankers' Association.

The above letter is interesting as evidence that the American Bankers' Association has its headquarters in the Wall Street district. Thus we have the body officially representing the entire banking system and the financiers of Wall Street brought together with headquarters in Wall Street in a great common effort to promote a private central bank for mutual benefit.

The following official declaration by the American Bankers' Association that in his message of December 21, 1911, to Congress, President Taft endorsed the "Aldrich Plan," is of the highest importance as showing the Wall Street point of view, and particularly because Wall Street and the big banks generally know what they are talking about politically:

THE AMERICAN BANKERS' ASSOCIATION

11 Pine Street, New York.

President:
> William Livingstone, President Dime Savings Bank, Detroit, Mich.

First Vice-President:
> Charles H. Huttig, President Third National Bank, St. Louis, Mo.

Chairman Executive Council:
> Arthur Reynolds, President Des Moines National Bank, Des Moines, Iowa.

General Secretary:
> Fred E. Farnsworth, 11 Pine Street, New York City.

Treasurer:
> J. Fletcher Farrell, Vice-President Fort Dearborn National Bank, Chicago, Ill.

Assistant Secretary:
> William G. Fitzwilson, 11 Pine Street, New York City.

General Counsel:
> Thomas B. Paton, 11 Pine Street, New York City.

Manager Protective Department:
> L. W. Gammon, 11 Pine Street, New York City.

ELEVEN PINE STREET,
NEW YORK.

December twenty-seventh, 1911.

Mr. Alfred O. Crozier,
C/o The Romaine,
Middleton Avenue,
Cincinnati, Ohio.

Dear Sir,

    Acknowledging your favor of December twenty-second, I am sending to you, under separate cover, such literature as has been issued from time to time from this office on request. We have not published any matter in outright support of the "Aldrich plan," that is, more than is conveyed by these documents.

    Our last Convention, in New Orleans, was given largely in the discussion of the National Reserve Association. There were fourteen-fifteen addresses, all of which will be published in our Annual Proceedings. The Association is, of course, on record as favoring the National Reserve Association plan, resolutions having been passed at our Executive Council meeting last May, and also at the Convention in New Orleans.

    Referring to your inquiry about President Taft's attitude, we have no further advices than extracts from the President's message to Congress, in which it appears that he endorses the "Aldrich plan."

        Very truly yours,

            General Secretary.

DECEMBER 27, 1911.

Mr. Alfred O. Crozier,
    care The Romaine,
        Middleton Avenue, Cincinnati, O.

Dear Sir: Acknowledging your favor of December 22d, I am sending to you, under separate cover such literature as has been issued from time to time from this office on request. We have not published any matter in outright support of the "Aldrich plan"; that is, more than is conveyed by these documents.

Our last convention in New Orleans was given largely to the discussion of the National Reserve Association. There were fourteen or fifteen addresses, all of which will be published in our Annual Proceedings. The association is, of course, on record as favoring the National Reserve Association plan, resolutions having been passed at our executive council meeting last May, and also at the convention in New Orleans.

Referring to your inquiry about President Taft's attitude, we have no further advices than extracts from the President's message to Congress, in which it appears that he endorses the "Aldrich plan."

Very truly yours,
    FRED E. FARNSWORTH,
        General Secretary.

New York Life Insurance Company.

The following shows the attitude of the big Wall Street insurance companies:

NEW YORK LIFE INSURANCE COMPANY
New York, N. Y.
Darwin P. Kingsley, President.
November 28, 1911.

Mr. Alfred C. Crozier,
    Plankinton House,
        Milwaukee, Wis.

Dear Sir: Replying to your favor of the 24th inst., I send you under another cover copy of an address delivered in April last in which I referred incidentally to the Aldrich Plan of Currency Reform. As you will see by the reference, I am in favor of some such plan as Mr. Aldrich has outlined, because the present plan breeds panics instead of preventing them. Mr. Aldrich's plan is still under discussion and has been considerably modified since the first draft was published. It has just been heartily endorsed by the Bankers' convention at New Orleans after full consideration.

The provisions covering the issue of circulating notes have, so far as I have noticed, been the least questioned of any. They deserve careful study. In a general way they provide for a gradual taking over of the privilege of issuing circulating notes—the banks being allowed to retain their present bond secured circulation, if they choose to do so, but not to add to it. When taken over, the Reserve Association is to issue its own notes in place of those of the banks which have been redeemed. The Reserve Association is also to have power to issue additional notes within certain well-defined limits, and upon certain conditions as to security and taxation. These conditions are such as to provide a volume of currency that shall expand and contract according to the necessities of business.

The clause respecting the security of notes, issued by the Reserve Association in the revised draft published in October, reads as follows: "All note issues of the Reserve Association must be covered, to the extent of at least one-third by gold or other lawful money, and the remaining portion by bankable commercial paper as herein defined or obligations of the United States, but no notes shall be issued whenever the lawful money so held shall fall below one-third of the notes oustanding."

"The notes to constitute a first lien upon all the assets of the National Reserve Association, and shall be redeemable in lawful money on presentation at the head office of the National Reserve Association or any of its branches."

As the capital stock of the Reserve Association is to be approximately $300,000,000, and the national bank circulation is less than $800,000,000, the notes of the association will be covered by one-third gold or lawful money and two-thirds by commercial paper of obligations of the United States, while the capital stock of the bank will be an additional security equal to more than one-third of present issues. It would appear, therefore, that the notes of the association will be amply secured.

There is every reason to suppose that the management of a National Reserve Association, such as is outlined by

Mr. Aldrich, will be composed of men of as high character as those who will occupy high places in the Government, and that they will be even more experienced in financial affairs. There seems to be also ample provisions for preventing the association from falling under the control either of politicians, on the one hand, or of what is called "Wall Street influence," on the other. In short, the wisdom of both politicians and of financial experts will be united under a system that will make the currency and credit systems of the country available for legitimate business, and the sinister influences in both politics and finance will not be able to use them for selfish purposes.

Under the present system the currency of the country does not expand when business expands, and when a bank's funds are all loaned out its customers can borrow no more. During such times currency accumulates from taxes in the Treasury, and is deposited in banks at the discretion of the Secretary of the Treasury. It is therefore within the power of the banks and of the Secretary of the Treasury to make money scarce if they choose to do so, and when a certain limit has been reached, it becomes scarce in spite of them.

In my judgment the plan of the National Reserve Association will go a long way toward preventing stringency and panics, and in equalizing interest rates throughout the country.

As to the prospects of favorable action by Congress, no one can say, but if bankers and business men generally demand the enactment of Mr. Aldrich's plan into law, it will be done. The banks have naturally taken more interest thus far than the business men, because it is their specialty; but from now it will be up to the business men to consider the plan and express their opinions.

Very truly yours,
DARWIN P. KINGSLEY, President.

This is an interesting contribution to the subject, and a valuable one. The statement that "the bankers have naturally taken more interest thus far than the business men, because it is their specialty"—is true and highly important. The intimation in these letters from the highest financial circles of Wall Street that the Aldrich plan approved unanimously by Wall Street contains iron-clad provisions to prevent this private corporation, as Mr. Kingsley says, "from falling under the control either of politicians on the one

hand or of what is called 'Wall Street influence' on the
other" is, we believe, rather Pickwickian, and belongs to the
domain of subtle humor.

The above published correspondence, of course, will be
sufficient to establish to the satisfaction of everybody that
all the big banks, trust companies, insurance companies and
financiers of Wall Street are united and exceedingly active
supporters of the Aldrich plan for a great private central
bank, owned exclusively by the banks and controlling the
entire public currency of the United States. And there
is ample public evidence by published speeches and articles
made by railroad presidents and trust magnates that such
corporations, all largely under the control of Wall Street,
are also behind this measure. These special interests always
are "non-partisan," or rather "bipartisan," whenever they
must have both Republican and Democratic legislative votes
for a measure conferring upon themselves greatly increased
profits and power. And it is illuminating to see that such interests, and President Taft in his message to Congress on
December 21, 1911, earnestly urge that this question, which
in every sense and in the highest degree is political, shall
be made non-political and non-partisan. If this plan succeeds, it will keep the great majority of the people, the
masses, who certainly are opposed to substituting a corporation currency for Government money, and control of all
money by a private syndicate under act of Congress, divided
about equally between the Republican and Democratic parties. This will enable the relatively small number of supporters of the Aldrich plan to act as a dominating "balance
of power" and force the scheme upon the country notwithstanding it is offensive to and opposed probably by three-
fourths if not nine-tenths of all of the voters of the United
States.

These powerful Wall Street interests have the undoubted
"legal" right to want and to fight to obtain control in their
hands, or in a private corporation owned by their banks, of
a monopoly of the entire public currency, the money supply of all the people. Presumably they do not think it
would work to their disadvantage, or lessen the power and
profits of the banks and of Wall Street. We have a right
at least to suspect that a private central bank under their
direct or indirect control would increase, in fact vastly augment, their profits and power, and this at the sole expense
of the people.

Do the people for their welfare want just what Wall Street desires and is seeking for its interests? Congress must soon decide this question for the people, and the people should lose no time in making Congress fully aware of the popular will.

CHAPTER VIII.

WALL STREET'S FIRST "PLAN."

New York Chamber of Commerce in 1906 Originates Present Central Bank Scheme.

The New York Chamber of Commerce is an association for mutual interest of the brains of Wall Street. Its powerful guiding hand is seen in the provisions of every banking and monetary system and in the language of every financial statute adopted since the association was founded, on April 5, 1768. It is largely entitled to the credit and blame for all successes and failures. For in the long run it usually has had its way and forced its will upon the country and into the provisions of law.

The chronological record of its achievements in this line printed in its Monthly Bulletin for April, 1911, is its claim and boast that the above is true. That record shows: In 1819 it opposed repeal of the charter of the first central bank, the Bank of The United States, unsuccessfully. In 1841 it adopted a memorial in favor of a Central National Bank. This was in the old days when President Andrew Jackson vetoed the bill renewing the charter of the second central bank, the United States Bank, thereby destroying the institution because of its pernicious and dangerous activity in politics, the same thing that caused the downfall of the first central bank. Both were private corporations seeking to control the public currency and money supply for private profit and power.

It is said that President Biddle of the Old Central Bank called on President Andrew Jackson in the White House telling him that he had power to bring about or to prevent President Jackson's renomination, and would renominate him if he signed and defeat him if he vetoed the bill renewing the Central Bank's charter. "Old Hickory" replied: "I believe you are correct; but that is too much power for one man to have in this Republic, and *'By the Eternal I'll veto that bill!'*" And he did so.

President Jackson so thoroughly exposed the sordid duplicity of the bankers and high financiers, and their purpose
to use the imperial powers of the central bank to rule politics and the Government in the interest of Wall Street instead of the people, that it was considered useless to attempt

another central bank until the country forgot the vicious
sins of the old ones. The men of Jackson's day are all
dead. A new generation has taken their places. At last
the same old cat comes out of the same old hole, for on
October 4, 1906, the New York Chamber of Commerce
again declares for a great central bank, and this has led to
the proposal now called "Aldrich Plan." Whether Democracy can be made to forget the past as Wall Street softly
strokes its fur and soothingly whispers into its capacious

ear those clever, enticing and deceptive words "non-partisan and non-political monetary, banking and currency reform," and will swap Jackson for Aldrich, as its future Patron Saint, the country soon will know. If that great, popular and patriotic organization, with its splendid past achievements for popular government, and the undying precepts and examples of its great historic leaders, by its voluntary consent now can be thus easily chloroformed as it stands on guard to protect the people against their insidious and powerful enemies, it will be the greatest of the many mysterious miracles wrought by Wall Street.

Examination into the history of the New York Chamber of Commerce, the list of past and present members, officers and directors, induces the belief that the Chamber always is ruled and guided in its every act and resolution by the masterful minds that also rule Wall Street, and to a large extent the big banks, insurance and trust companies, railroads and trusts of the United States, and, many believe, seek to influence or dominate politics and parties that shape and administer the laws and government of the republic.

The present officers, as printed on a letter of November 28, 1911, which writer received from its secretary, are: President, A. Barton Hepburn. Secretary, Sereno S. Pratt. Treasurer, Wm. H. Porter. Asst. Sec'y, Chas. T. Gwynne.

Vice-Presidents.

Cleveland A. Dodge	Otto T. Bannard
James J. Hill	Arthur Curtis James
George F. Baer	John Claflin
William A. Nash	A. Foster Higgins
J. Pierpont Morgan	James Talcott
Jacob H. Schiff	

These officers and the Chamber's board of directors, and their *affiliations*, is "Wall Street."

New York Chamber of Commerce's 1906 Plan.

To the courtesy of The National City Bank of New York we are indebted for a printed copy of the full report of the "Special Currency Committee" of the New York Chamber of Commerce, dated October 4, 1906, which report was adopted by the Chamber.

The members of the committee were John Claflin, Frank A. Vanderlip (now president of National City Bank), Isidor Strauss, Dumont Clarke and Charles A. Conant.

The report is voluminous and illuminating. We quote substantially in full the portion advocating a central bank, as follows:

"A CENTRAL BANK OF ISSUE.

In our opinion, the best method of providing an elastic credit currency, the volume of which could never be excessive, would be the creation of *a central bank of issue under the control of the Government.* This central bank should have branches in the leading cities, and should have dealings only with banks. Although its capital stock might be privately owned or distributed among the banking institutions of the country, it should be under the direct control of a board of governors appointed, at least in part, by the President of the United States, for it should perform some of the functions now imposed upon the United States Treasury, and should at the same time be managed not exclusively for private gain but for the public good as well. This bank should have a large capital, not less than $50,000,000. It should carry a large reserve of gold and should act as custodian of the metalic reserves of the Government and is its agent in redeeming all forms of credit money. It should also be receiving and disbursing agent for the Government, doing at its branches the work now done at the sub-treasuries. It should hold the 5 per cent redemption fund now deposited in the Treasury by the national banks for the current redemption of their bond secured notes, and should redeem national bank notes both at its central office and at all of its branches.

ADVANTAGES OF A CENTRAL BANK.

The operations of central banks in Europe, especially in France, Germany, Austria-Hungary and the Netherlands, make it impossible to doubt that the existence of such a bank in this country would be of incalculable benefit to our financial and business interests. Such a bank in times of stress or emergency would be able by regulation of its note issues to prevent those sudden and great fluctuations in rates of interest which have in the past proved so disastrous. Furthermore, it would have the power to curb dangerous tendencies to speculation and undue expansion, for *by the control of its rate of interest and of its issues of notes it would be able to exert great influence upon the money market and upon public opinion. Such power is not now possessed by any institution in the United States.* Under our present system of independent banks, there is no centralization of financial responsibility, so that in times of dangerous over-expansion no united effort can be made to impose a check which will prevent reaction and depression. This is what a large central bank would be in a position to do most effectively. A central note issuing bank would supply an elastic currency varying automatically with the needs of the country. This currency could never be in excess, for notes not needed by the country would be presented for deposit or redemption.

RÉSUMÉ OF ADVANTAGES,

The advantages of such a central bank, in brief, would be as follows:

(1) It would supply the country with an elastic currency responsive to the varying needs of business.

(2) It would tend to steady the rate of interest at all seasons, and to give relief in periods of industrial and financial stress, for its large resources would enable it to meet extraordinary and sudden demands for both capital and currency.

(3) It would relieve the Federal Treasury of the duties now imposed upon the division of issue and redemption, and, on account of its intimate relations with the money market, would be in a position, as the Treasury is not, to protect itself against a prolonged drain upon its reserves.

(4) It would do away with the cumbersome sub-treasury system and keep the money of the country always at the disposal of trade and commerce, so that the Government's collections and disbursements would cause neither contraction nor inflation.

*   *   *   *   *   *   *

We, therefore, make the following recommendations:

1. That legislation be enacted which shall provide the country with a flexible and elastic bank note currency; and to this end we suggest that either one of the two following plans might wisely be adopted:

(a) Let there be created a central bank of issue similar to the Bank of Germany or the Bank of France; such bank to deal exclusively with banks; its stock to be owned in part by banking institutions and in part by the Government; *but in its management representatives of the Government shall be supreme.* This central bank shall issue currency, rediscount for other banks, hold public money, and act as agent of the Government in redeeming its paper money and making its disbursements.

Or (b) let any national bank whose bond-secured circulation equals 50 per cent of its capital have authority to issue additional notes equal in amount to 35 per cent of its capital.

Let such additional notes be subject to a graduated tax as follows: The first 5 per cent, taxed at the rate of 2 per cent per annum; the second 5 per cent, taxed at the rate of 3 per cent; the third 5 per cent, taxed at the rate of 4 per cent; then an issue equal to 10 per cent of capital, taxed at 5 per cent; then an issue equal to 10 per cent of capital, taxed at 6 per cent.

Let the proceeds of this graudated tax constitute a guaranty fund, in the custody of the Government, for the redemption of the notes of failed banks.

To insure the prompt retirement of notes when not needed, let redemption agencies be established at sub-treasuries and other convenient points.

Let all the notes of a bank be alike in form, and let it be the duty of the United States Treasury to redeem all the notes of a failed bank, as at present, in full on presentation, and to recoup itself from the assets of the failed bank and from the guaranty fund.

2. That the law restricting the retirement of nationa' bank notes to $3,000,000 per month by the deposit of lawful money be repealed.

3. That future issues of United States bonds be not made available as a basis for the issue of national bank notes.

4. That the laws regulating the operations of the United States Treasury be amended in such a manner that they shall not, as now, interfere with the money market; and to this end we suggest a law requiring that all money in the general fund of the Treasury above a reasonable working balance be deposited in national banks."

Other portions of the above quoted report concede:

1. That prices and rates of interest tend to increase and decrease with the volume of available currency and credit.

2. That the increase and decrease of a bank's cash reserve automatically operates to increase and decrease its

total loans of credit. If its loans total ten times its cash reserve, loans should be reduced $10,000 for each $1,000 shrinkage of cash in its reserve.

3. That stock market speculation always is stimulated and increases whenever the quantity of available money and credit is increased or the rate of interest is lowered, and is checked and decreased whenever the available supply of money and credit is decreased or the rate of interest is raised.

4. That the quantity of credit banks can grant in the shape of ordinary interest bearing bank loans depends wholly and absolutely upon the amount of lawful money they can get to put into their reserves. The profits of banks automatically increase and decrease with the volume of such loans. (On the average, including all state banks, and trust companies, banks issue and keep afloat a volume of loans of credit aggregating at least ten times the total cash resources in their reserves.)

The dominating importance of these four conceded axioms of finance and banking, so easily understood by everybody familiar with the "cause and effect" of the ordinary elemental "law of supply and demand," will be apparent as we proceed. Particularly so when we compare the provisions of the above "First N. Y. Chamber of Commerce Plan," adopted October 4, 1906, with the "Second N. Y. Chamber of Commerce Plan," adopted by the Chamber March 2, 1911 (see Monthly Bulletins for March and April, 1911), and with the "Aldrich plan" announced in January, 1911, and the "revised Aldrich plan" issued in October, 1911.

Note particularly that the above report says: "By the control of its rate of interest and of its issues of notes, *it would be able to exert great influence upon the money market and upon public opinion. Such power is not possessed by any institution in the United States."* Just so! That is the "power" Wall Street seeks by making it a *private* instead of a *public* institution.

Briefly, suppose there was some potential individual, or a group of men, with "axes to grind" by stock market manipulations, emitting and selling vast flotations of stock and bond issues, forming trusts, consolidating railroads into systems, maintaining low interest rates for themselves to pay and high rates for the public, and increasing their political influence to obtain legislative favors and judicial immunities. And suppose these persons were able absolutely to control the supply, and from day to day regulate the volume, of money or currency for use in the United States by the banks and the people. Under the above four axioms, would not they have absolute power, if they wanted to use it, to:

1. Increase interest rates by making available money scarce.

2. Decrease interest rates by making money over-plenty.

3. Increase the prices of all securities, property, commodities and labor by inflating the quantity of money and credit available with which to buy.

4. Decrease the prices of all securities, property, commodities and labor by contracting the quantity of money and credit available with which to buy.

5. Profit both by such artificial increase and decrease of prices, because of having exclusive advance information as to the extent of such inflations and contractions of the money supply and just when they will take place.

6. Vastly increase the interest profits of the banks by increasing the currency available for bank reserves, thereby enabling banks to inflate the volume of their loans of credit ten times such increase in cash reserves.

7. Greatly decrease the earning power and profits of banks by contracting the currency, thereby reducing bank cash reserves and forcing banks to contract the volume of their loans ten times as much.

8. Make or break the prosperity of the country, by this power to enable banks to increase their loans to commercial, industrial and business borrowers, or to force banks unexpectedly to contract loans and make such borrowers curtail their activities and reduce the volume of their business, and their profits.

9. Cause panics any time, whatever the general and natural conditions of the country may be, by suddenly contracting the currency to such an extent as quickly to rob the banks of a large portion of their cash reserves, thus forcing banks to demand payment of their loans in such vast volumes that borrowers would be compelled instantly to slaughter prices and make forced sales of securities, properties, and commodities at ruinous figures for money to pay such bank loans, thus causing general demoralization and universal panic.

10. Take advantage of panic so caused, to acquire cheap

the stricken and crippled enterprises and industries, turning them over to their trusts, thus removing competition and enabling trusts to increase profits by increasing prices against consumers and by reducing the wages of labor.

11. Force labor wholesale into idleness by such panics or semi-panics, or terrify it with the fear of general lack of employment, thereby enabling reduction in wages and increase in the hours of labor, "teaching labor a lesson," so that unresistingly and unprotestingly it will forever submit to the demands and the conditions imposed by the Wall Street masters of the great employing corporations.

12. So control the supply of money and credit as to make it forever impossible to finance or start any important enterprise or undertaking until control and most of the profits are surrendered to them.

13. Master and control the banks in their every act, because of the power to control the volume of their profits, cash reserves and loans of credit, making them

(a) Buy securities, perhaps undesirable, at high prices;

(b) Make loans to certain parties and corporations;

(c) Call loans of business men generally;

(d) Call loans to punish certain parties;

(e) Call certain loans to force the dumping upon the market of the particular securities up as collateral;

(f) Call loans, generally, to help force upon the market in vast quantities the securities held as collateral, thus aiding to wreck prices during a "bear" raid when insiders want to buy cheap;

(g) Make undesired loans to the secret "pools" on stock exchange collateral, thus causing refusal of applications for legitimate business purposes during a "bull" campaign when insiders are driving prices to high levels to unload upon the public;

(h) Induce granting loans to trusts and refusal of accommodations to the competitors of trusts;

(i) Loaning on call to trusts and stock gamblers at 2 per cent and charging ordinary business borrowers 6 per cent;

(j) Reducing bank's ability properly to care for regular customers by inducing loans as favors to individuals or corporations in position to give preferences in the purchase of supplies and by way of transportation rates or advantages to favored trusts or individuals;

(k) Crowding for favors to the extent that banks to

N.Y. CHAMBER OF COMMERCE

THE CHAMBER OF COMMERCE 1901

PLACE WHERE PRIVATE CENTRAL BANK SCHEME WAS HATCHED.

avoid offending will overloan, or violate other provisions of the laws, perhaps involving bankers in criminal prosecution.

14. Permanently increase interest rates paid by borrowers for bank accommodations.

15. Permanently reduce the rate of interest paid by banks to depositors.

16. Extort from the political party in power special legislative, executive and judicial privileges and immunities under threat or fear that if not granted, panic will be caused at the right moment to discredit the administration, the party in power and its political leaders, and cause its defeat in approaching National or State elections.

17. Increase alarmingly the prevalence of graft and corruption and betrayal of public trust by officials by insiduous methods of moral if not legal bribery and opportunities to "participate" in flotations and "deals" where profits will be certain and tempting.

18. Complete mastery of politics and parties and of the Government itself, through 24,000 influential and widely distributed banks as a vast and invincible political machine that by means of bank loans granted for bribes or called in for punishment will have life and death power over the business of almost every individual and corporation throughout the United States.

The above 18 things are a few of the many potential possibilities if those few Wall Street men had private control of the public currency. And does anybody doubt that they will obtain control and be able to do these things if Congress commits the folly of taking control of the public currency away from the Government and grants it to a mere private corporation?

Second New York Chamber of Commerce Plan.

The first plan, adopted by the chamber on October 4, 1906, in its language was sound, honest and patriotic. It proposed a central bank under the absolute control of the Federal Government. It said "in its management representatives of the Government shall be supreme." Under the "Aldrich Plan," of the 46 directors of the National Reserve Association the banking fraternity will name 42 and the Government of the United States 4.

On March 2, 1911, the "Second New York Chamber of

Commerce Plan" for a central bank was formally adopted by the chamber.

This plan, hereinafter given, was printed in the chamber's "Monthly Bulletins" for March and April, 1911. Author has copies of these bulletins, obtained from the chamber's secretary. This plan and the "Revised Aldrich Plan" are practically identical. This is conceded, and both seem to claim priority. Under these later "plans" the central bank is to be a private corporation, exclusively owned by the banks, instead of a public institution controlled by the Government, as the chamber's "First Plan" demanded. If Congress adopts this "revised version," those few Wall Street men soon will own enough banks to control the central association. Then they can do all of the things above enumerated, because they will absolutely control the entire money supply of the United States.

Why did the New York Chamber of Commerce radically change from one extreme to the other, from a central bank controlled by the Government of 94,000,000 people to a central bank with governmental powers controlled by Wall Street?

Was its original action, in 1906, insincere? Did it resort to the trick of pretending to favor a Government central bank, thereby disarming criticism and allaying suspicion and opposition while an irresistible demand for "elasticity," a central bank and monetary "reform" was being worked up, secretly intending at the opportune moment to "shift the cards" and hastily push through Congress under whip and spur a scheme for a private central bank with a complete monopoly of the entire public currency?

The representatives of the New York Chamber of Commerce to the currency conference organized by the National Board of Trade, held in Washington, D. C., January 18, 1911, were Paul M. Warburg, chairman, Welding Ring, Algernon S. Frissell, Samuel Sachs and Maurice L. Muhleman. They persuaded the conference to adopt the views of the New York Chamber of Commerce. The delegation reported their success to the Chamber on February 2, 1911, their report in full in its March Bulletin was laid over until the March 2, 1911, meeting, when it was discussed and formally adopted. The report was made by Paul M. Warburg, of the Wall Street International Banking House of Kuhn, Loeb & Co., chairman, and reputed author of the private central bank scheme, the "second

New York Chamber of Commerce plan," now known officially as the "Aldrich plan."

Leaving out the long preamble, following is all that portion of said report comprising in full the resolutions adopted advocating a private central bank:

"Resolved, That this convention unequivocally declares in favor of the creation for the United States of a central banking organization, based upon the following general principles:

1. That such central organization be a corporation endowed with a large stock capital and not merely an association of banks.

2. That its stock capital be owned by incorporated banking institutions, including trust companies, whether under national or state charter, willing to assume equal duties as a basis for equal privileges.

3. That its administration be divided between the Government, the member-banks and the commercial classes, in a manner which will safeguard against individual, sectional or political domination.

4. That its business be limited to transactions with the Government and with the incorporated banking institutions which become stockholders, i. e., member-banks, except as provided in paragraph 9, clause b.

5. That dividends on its stock be limited to a fixed moderate return and profits in excess of such dividends, after providing for a reasonable surplus and emergency fund, be turned over to the Government.

6. That its business be conducted through branches, to be established in the banking districts into which the country shall be divided, the member-banks of the several districts constituting joint associations, and sharing in the administration of the branches.

7. That it shall, free of charge, receive and disburse all moneys of the United States Government in places where it shall have offices.

8. That it shall not allow interest on deposits.

9. That it shall have power:

(a) To issue circulating notes payable in gold, to be secured by gold and negotiable paper, and, if necessary, eventually to retire the present bond-secured bank notes to a limited amount by Government bonds;

(b) For the regulation of its gold reserve to buy and sell bullion, and to contract for loans of gold, and under proper restrictions to deal and invest in foreign bills of exchange;

(c)   To require the member-banks to keep with it a portion of their reserves prescribed by law;

(d)   To rediscount, only for member-banks, commercial paper under regulations prescribing the limit of amount for each member-bank, the maximum time to run, and determining the degree of guarantee to be provided by the joint associations of member-banks of each district;

(e)   Under careful and proper restrictions to discount approved American bank acceptances;

(f)   To transfer funds standing to the credit of a member-bank, to the credit of any other member-bank at any of its branches;

(g)   To buy and sell the bonds and treasury notes of the United States.

10.   That the central organization is ultimately to become the sole note-issuing power.

Resolved, furthermore, that copies of this resolution be sent to the President of the United States, to the members of the National Monetary Commission and to each senator and representative in Congress.

On the day preceding the meeting of the conference Senator Aldrich had published his plan for banking and currency reform, and copies thereof were in the hands of the members of the conference.   The general provisions of the plan were explained in an instructive address by Assistant Secretary of the Treasury A. Piatt Andrew.

Your delegates are greatly pleased to report that this plan, barring a few comparatively unimportant details, complied so fully with the principles established in the foregoing resolution that subsequent resolutions endorsing the broad principles of the Aldrich plan, without committing the conference as to every detail of the same, and advocating the creation of a business men's league to assist in a campaign of propaganda and education, were unanimously adopted by the Committee on Resolutions read as follows:

Resolved, that there be appointed by the chairman of this conference a committee of seven to organize a Business Men's Monetary Reform League, which shall have its main office in Chicago, with branches in the various centers of the United States, where local committees shall constitute the management.   The object of this league shall be to carry on an active campaign of education and propaganda for monetary reform, on the principles, without endorsing every detail, of reserve association with branches in the business centers of the country as outlined in Senator Aldrich's plan.

Resolved, that the delegations here present be requested to use their influence in the commercial bodies they represent to gain the active coöperation of these bodies and of their individual members in the work of the league as defined.

Resolved, that the Business Men's Monetary Reform League be requested when organized to provide for a committee on propaganda and education, and also for a committee on legislation, whose duty shall be to further monetary legislation on the principles adopted by the league.

Resolved, furthermore, that the committee on organization be requested to bring about the coöperation and, if possible, a consolidation between this league and the National Currency League, already organized about a year ago by the Merchants' Association of New York.

All of these resolutions were presented to the conference at its afternoon session by the chairman of the Committee on Resolutions (Paul M. Warburg), and after instructive debate they were carried by an overwhelming majority."

Another portion of the above-quoted report says that of the eleven members of the Committee on Resolutions three, Mr. Warburg, Mr. Ring and Mr. Sachs, were members of the delegation from the New York Chamber of Commerce, and that Paul M. Warburg was chairman of the committee and presented, and presumably prepared, the above-quoted resolutions. It is said that the National Citizens' League, now actively promoting the Aldrich plan all over the country, with headquarters at Chicago, was the outgrowth of this plan originated by the New York Chamber of Commerce, the "Business Men's Monetary Reform League" having been merged into the same. It will be remembered that this new organization is the one spoken of by the National City Bank of New York in its herein before quoted letters as doing such valuable work promoting the Aldrich plan in many states.

The Chamber's April, 1911, Bulletin shows that upon April 2, 1911, the report was taken up, discussed and adopted, thus becoming officially the "New York Chamber of Commerce Second Plan." Following is a portion of the discussion published in said Bulletin:

"Paul M. Warburg, chairman of the delegation to the

monetary conference held in Washington, January 18th, called up the report of the delegation presented at the last meeting and laid over for action at this meeting.

Mr. Warburg.—Mr. Chairman and members of the Chamber: The report of the delegation to the monetary conference at Washington was placed before you in printed form at the last meeting and sent to every member since that meeting. I shall not, therefore, take time to read the report, but will simply move its adoption. In doing so, I would like to say a few words.

I think you could not fail to have been impressed, upon the reading of our report, with the remarkable degree of unanimity with which the proposed Central Reserve Association was approved. The delegates met, and aften ten minutes they knew that they all agreed on that question. We then met with the delegates of the New York Produce Exchange and the Merchants' Association. It took us about half an hour to agree. We went to Washington to the conference. At that conference there were representatives from all over the country and from Canada. After discussion the Central Reserve Association was agreed on with but one dissenting voice.

Meanwhile, Senator Aldrich's plan had been brought forward, and it recommended the same plan that had been recommended by our resolution. Since then a body of bankers had met in Atlanta, over twenty, representing all parts of the country, and they again after going over this plan most thoroughly and giving it searching criticism, unanimously adopted it, with some amendments as to details. They adopted the underlying principles of the report. So there can be no doubt that the country is ready for this plan and for its adopt n. There is no doubt. at the same time, that the prospect of getting this plan through in the next session of Congress will depend upon the chances of making it a non-partisan measure. As a party measure, the plan cannot succeed. If it is a plan that comes forward in a non-partisan form, there can be no doubt of its success; as Mr. MacVeigh has said, there is no difference between a Republican and Democratic depositor. Everybody alike looked miserable during the panic, and it is more to the interest of the people of small means than it is to people of larger means that this plan should be carried out.

The Monetary Reform League, with which our report

deals, will meet by the end of this month in Chicago. Very important men have been addressed, and have signified their willingness to serve. It is strongly hoped that the Chamber of Commerce will co-operate in this matter when the time comes, and will strongly join in this effort. On behalf of the delegates, I move the adoption of this report.

J. Howard Coperthwait.—* * * Now, the idea I have that this will become a political question is this: Senator Aldrich is no longer a senator, he has no more power in the Republican party, but a letter that I received from Washington intimates that he will still retain the position as head of the Monetary Commission. I suppose he can do that or not as he sees fit. Now, if any bill is to be gotten through Congress in the next two years it must be gotten through a Democratic Congress, and if this appears to be a proposition by Senator Aldrich alone, it is not likely to receive a great deal of favor; but, if it is proposed by the Monetary Commission, why then it will meet with a different sort of reception, and the Monetary Commission is the one to decide this question.

Maurice L. Muhleman.—Mr. President, and members of the Chamber, I hesitate, as a member of the delegation that went to Washington, to oppose Mr. Coperthwait's motion, but there are several things that I believe we have a right to differ upon in the statement that was made by him. In the first place, the report of the delegates to Washington does not indorse Senator Aldrich's proposition as such. It states its own proposition first, and then says that Senator Aldrich's proposition is in harmony in general principles, and in essentials, with its own proposition. The proposition which the delegates put before the conference in Washington was absolutely in harmony with the action which this Chamber took in 1906, and absolutely in harmony with the policy of this Chamber dating back to 1840. Mr. Coperthwait is afraid that we are going too far in this report in even suggesting that Senator Aldrich's plan has some essential features which are similar to the plan which we have elaborated, which was embodied in the resolutions which we took to Washington, and which met the support of the representatives of every commercial body in the National Conference except one. Mr. Coperthwait seems to be afraid that this subject is going to become the football of politics. Gentlemen, unless the commercial bodies of this country take up this question as they should, it may become

the football of politics; and it is up to the commercial
bodies to take hold of the question, and see to it that it is
kept out of politics and handled as it should be handled by
the business interests and not by the politicians.

Mr. Coperthwait says that there seems to be no need for
haste. The only reason why Mr. Warburg presses for
immediate action is this:

This report was presented at the last meeting of the
Chamber, and by special request it was laid over to be acted
upon today. The movement of the commercial bodies of
the country, which is instigated through the instrumentality
of the National Board of Trade, under whose direction a
national committee has been appointed, proposes to meet in
Chicago before the end of the month, as Mr. Warburg has
stated. If the action of this Chamber goes over another
month, this Chamber has failed to place itself upon record
upon this most important question. If it is postponed, the
Chamber has adopted a shifting policy. Should the Chamber
be afraid again to announce its policy upon this question,
which it definitely stated in 1906, as the leading important
body of the country? It is for this reason, Mr. Chairman,
that I rise to oppose the motion of Mr. Coperthwait, and I
hope that the Chamber will accord to the delegation that
went to Washington the indorsement of adopting its own
report.

Samuel Sachs.—* * * As New York speaks, so the
rest of the country speak, and if the Chamber of Commerce
of New York should not support this resolution, the whole
question of banking reform and currency reform will die
out, and will not again come up until we are face to face
with the next panic, whenever that may occur. Now, I
earnestly hope that the gentlemen here assembled in this
Chamber will give their support to the work of Senator
Aldrich, and that they will indorse the report of Mr.
Warburg.

Mr. Warburg's motion that the report of the delegation
be adopted was then carried.

CHAPTER IX.

A CONFIDENCE GAME.

Ninety Per Cent of All Banks the Victims. State Banks and Trust Companies Hard Hit.

Judged by the cold facts plainly stated in the "Revised Aldrich Plan," Wall Street is playing upon the banks of the country wholesale a successful and clever confidence game. As in "three-card monte," "green goods," and other "sure thing" games, it is made to appear a cinch for the banks; but, as usual, the victims will get nothing but "experience" for their pains and money.

What Banks Will Get.

Under the "Aldrich Plan" a given bank will get:

1. National Reserve Association stock equal to 20 per cent of its own capital stock. It must pay par. Dividends, if earned, will be 4 per cent, or at most 5 per cent. If there are no profits it gets no dividends. There is no guaranty by anybody.

2. A supply of currency by paying for it dollar for dollar. This currency, like any lawful money, can be put into bank's reserve. A bank could buy gold or treasury notes just as cheap.

3. A "mere hope" that the bank can "rediscount" some of its commercial paper at the Central Bank. But this will not be an enforcible legal right. It is entirely within the discretion of the Central Bank whether it will take any certain piece of commercial paper or rediscount at all for a particular bank. It is a one-sided option. A bank can only hope, and pray—and beg.

4. Consolidation of all bank reserves in one financial "jack-pot" under the absolute control of a mere private corporation? No, but perhaps later by its "regulations" the association will require this to be done. It may at times then be as impossible for banks to get their reserve money

A CONFIDENCE GAME

WALL STREET:— THIS IS THE FAMOUS "SHELL GAME" UNDER WHICH SHELL IS HE PEA? YOU CATCH THE PEOPLE AND I'LL SKIN 'EM AND THEN WE'LL WHACK UP. — PERHAPS.

COUNTRY BANKER:— BUT THE PEOPLE YOU WANT TO SKIN ARE MY NEIGHBORS AND FRIENDS. EXCUSE ME!

out of this "one reservoir" as it was during the panic of 1907 from New York banks that repudiated their obligations and loaned the money to insiders to buy securities cheap from the public.

5. *A mere promise* that the Central Bank will perform a miracle and stop panics, or at least perhaps help the bank save itself in case of a "run." But the bank cannot compel the Central Bank to do so. And as was done when the big New York trust companies were put in a hole by "runs" purposely started or stimulated, permanent control of the bank may be demanded by the interests behind the Central Bank as the price of Central Bank aid, even in a panic.

6. Participation in the boasted "town-meeting-republican-form-of-government" monarchy control of one of the local twigs of one of the branches of the big Central Bank tree, to the extent of the proportion of the total $300,000,000 National Reserve Association stock held by the local bank.

In round figures, the capital of 24,392 reporting national and state banks is $2,000,000,000. The pending bill makes the association's authorized capital 20 per cent of the combined capital stock of the "eligible" banks, say $400,000,000. But to be safe call it $300,000,000.

The following shows the per cent of the total control enjoyed by any given bank having the capital indicated, the smallest outside national or state bank or trust company, with $25,000 capital, would own $5,000 of the $300,000.000 Central Bank stock and have the magnificent although indirect and remote power over the management and operations of the National Reserve Association obtained by owning and voting one and two-thirds one-thousandths of one per cent of the total three hundred million stock!

Just one Wall Street institution, the National City Bank, with $25,000,000,000 capital will own one thousand times as much Central Bank stock, or as much as a thousand such sized banks.

Size of Bank.	Central Stock.	Per Cent of Control.
$25,000,000	$5,000,000	.0166⅔
1,000,000	200,000	.0066⅔
500,000	100,000	.0033½
200,000	40,000	.0013⅓
100,000	20,000	.0006⅔
50,000	10,000	.0003⅓
25,000	5,000	.0001⅔

Don't laugh! It's the truth. Figure it out yourself—
then get someone to kick you for consenting to be a mere
pimple on the face of the other fellow's moon.

What Banks Must Give.

The "revised version" of Aldrich's New Testament plays
up as an afterthought and a generous "concession" the
proposal to "allow" state banks and trust companies to
"participate in and enjoy" the manifold blessing vouchsafed
to those financial institutions contritely approaching the
Wall Street "Mercy Seat" and espousing "out-of-sight-and-
unseen" the cleansing Aldrich plan.

The records, however, of the New York Chamber of
Commerce show that that program was decided on long
before the Aldrich tag was tied on to the predetermined
"plan." It may have been left out of the "original Aldrich
plan" so it could be made to appear "a concession to
popular demand."

But there is no more danger of state banks and trust
companies being "left out in the cold" when Wall Street
sets out to form for its use a universal money trust than
there is chance for a lone 'possum to escape from a hungry
colored camp-meeting crowd.

All banks and trust companies look alike to "high finance."
They are all "Jonahs" and Wall Street is the "whale."
Aldrich was only trawling, with his "plan" as the "spoon."
Every state bank and trust company making a grab for the
shining, whirling "spoon," too late will discover that all it
has got is a hook in its jaw, the other end of the line being
firmly and permanently attached to the reel on Wall Street
great Central Bank pleasure yacht.

When high finance sets out to promote a trust it takes in
enough concerns to stifle all serious competition. A successful Central Bank trust for eliminating all vexatious
competition that might increase the rate of interest paid
depositors or decrease the rate charged borrowers, and for
combining under one central control the entire money supply
of the people, could not be formed if state banks and trust
companies are left out. Such state institutions hardly would
allow Congress to grant to a private confederation of
national banks a monopoly of the entire public currency
that they might win away the deposits of state institutions
by publicly boasting that only national banks had been made

fish the people and the outside bankers must seem to the "insiders" who plan the "sport" and will feast on the "catch"!

Under the Aldrich plan a bank must give:

1. Twenty per cent of its capital to be permanently employed at not over 5 per cent, invested in Central Bank stock that it can never sell.

2. Ultimately it will lose its present currency issuing power.

3. It assumes its share of a serious and increasing burden of maintaining the gold standard and reserve and of keeping at par an enormous and increasing volume of currency without the aid of the Government credit now behind the public currency and gold standard. The Reserve Association will have power and means by which it could financially wreck any or all banks if it so desires; and this may happen in spite of the association because of a wild inflation of its currency and injudicious rediscounting.

4. By joining this private association, it incurs an indefinite and almost unlimited liability by staking everything on a new experiment that it cannot guide or control and from which it never can escape. It takes the chance of the most reckless of gamblers.

5. Voluntarily it surrenders to the power of a single corporation that vital and large portion of its resources represented by its deposited reserves (the association having legal power to require this by "regulations"), without getting for its use even the customary 2 per cent now allowed by reserve banks. In return, there is no legally enforcible obligation on the central bank to grant currency in time of need or re-discount a single dollar of paper. Everything done by the central bank legally is only a "favor." Such favors may be granted to the big banks that will control the central bank and be withheld from the unimportant small banks and trust companies.

6. Morally and legally it becomes responsible for the policy and every act of a private institution in which it has but an insignificant interest and over which it can exercise not the slightest effective control. It will have responsibility without power.

7. It is surrendering its independence by irrevocably joining a financial combine or trust absolutely controlled by outsiders and strangers having nothing in common with

interests and the welfare of the local people may be over-looked or ignored in the shuffle of "big business," by "big business" for "big business."

It must legally and irrevocably bind itself to obey all "regulations" hereafter adopted, whatever they may be, thus making itself a firm but helpless part and servant of a great central bank trust.

8. It is agreeing to pay any discount rate and interest hereafter fixed from time to time by a private corporation for the exclusive profit of such corporation.

9. It repays the people for enacting laws granting special privileges and immunities that have made banking the most powerful and profitable of all business, by joining with Wall Street in a conspiracy to create a dangerous money monopoly to enormously swell the already inordinate profits of Wall Street and the big banks, the entire extra burden falling upon the people of the United States.

10. For the hope of unneeded extra profits, it would cause its officers, directors and stockholders to forget their higher obligation as citizens of the republic by joining in the demand that Congress adopt the "Aldrich plan" that forces the Government without a cent of compensation to turn over into the hands of a private corporation, for its use and profit, as loanable deposits every dollar of the billions of future revenues to be collected by taxation and otherwise by the Federal Government for the next fifty years.

11. It joins in the plan that by law would forever prohibit the Government paying out a dollar for any purpose whatever, except through such private corporation, thus in effect creating a guardian for the Government.

12. In the hope of gain, it supports the movement for taking from the Federal Government, where under the constitution it always has remained, control of the issuance and volume of the currency that a private monopoly of the entire public currency may be granted to an irresponsible private corporation to be forever used and loaned out at the cost of the people of the United States for the profit of such corporation.

13. It does this fully realizing that such private syndicate, simply by raising and lowering the discount rate or by expanding and contracting the volume of currency, or both, can to a large extent automatically increase and decrease the prices of all securities, property and human

labor to the loss of the public and the profit of the insiders.

14. It favors granting to such corporation absolute power to force such bank against its will or desire to contract its loans to an unlimited extent, to require its own solvent and responsible customers suddenly and unexpectedly to pay up their loans even if it entails the ruinous sacrifice of securities and property, closing down of industries, general idleness and distress, panic and financial chaos. Such corporation can do all this and more in the name of that high-sounding slogan, "elasticity," in the most easy and quick manner by calling in and canceling a portion of its "currency," thereby automatically depleting the cash reserves of the banks and under the law forcing them to call in loans aggregating at least ten times such shrinkage of reserves.

This voluntary surrender of the bank's interest and honor and that of its customers and friends to possible and probable defilement by the libertines of "high finance" who may have seized control of the central bank, if induced by the lust for greater profits, would be an exhibition of business prostitution and brutality unexampled in the lowest red light district of a metropolitan city.

15. It is deceiving itself and its business customers into believing, or at least claiming, that the "Aldrich plan" will stop panics, where in fact it is an express grant by Congress to a private syndicate of power quickly and easily to *cause panics* by suddenly making money scarce and dangerously contracting bank credits whenever the manipulators desire to increase interest rates and the purchasing power of their money and "credit" by wrecking prices while like wild beasts they shop for bargains at the expense of the stricken people in the ruins they themselves have made.

16. The American Bankers' Association by recently indorsing the "Aldrich plan," after its Currency Committee had obtained the changes it desired, has officially (on November 24, 1911) committed the banking fraternity to the plan as now urged and to each of the provisions thereof. But no individual bank is bound by that action, and many banks resent such action.

Thus the banks have deliberately made themselves an issue, a political issue, by demanding that Congress take from the Government and turn over free to a private corporation, to be exclusively owned and controlled by the banks, a billion dollars or more of currency or money to be forever used for the profit of private interests, same to be put into the reserves of the confederated banks, thereby enabling such banks with relatively no extra investment to swell their ordinary loans of bank credit nearly ten billion dollars and annually collect interest on this huge extra total from the people of the United States.

Now that the banking system, by action of the banks themselves, has been brought under the spotlight, the public no doubt will insist upon the complete elimination of every harmful practice that careful and thorough investigation may show exists in the monetary and banking systems of the United States. And they will require that all disclosures be made on oath in a public congressional investigation.

There are among bankers thousands of honest, high-minded, law-abiding, patriotic gentlemen. When these questions come to be understood, most of such men will refuse to follow Wall Street and the big bankers in their raid upon the Government, but will stand shoulder to shoulder with their neighbors and friends and in the interest of the common good demand that any institution controlling the public currency must be a public institution under absolute public control.

State and Savings Banks—Trust Companies.

By changing present law and granting national banks authority to make loans on real estate and requiring no cash reserve held against "time deposits," the Aldrich bill lays the foundation for national banks ultimately to monopolize the entire business of banking. Already they are starting savings departments generally. National banks thus are to be powerfully equipped by the law to invade the exclusive field of state and savings banks and trust companies and take away their deposits, business and profits. And inasmuch as national banks divert the use of their resources to such new channels they take away from trade and commerce the money and credit that the present law intended should be used exclusively for the accommodation of commercial business. Why should national banks cease being mere banks of discount? Why should they become real estate loan agencies, trust companies and savings banks? Surely they do not need the extra profits, or deposits, for their present profits are excessive and increasing rapidly. There are plenty of state and savings banks and trust companies to adequately serve the public needs in those lines.

It is only the Wall Street mania for monopoly, the desire to grab all business anywhere that will yield a profit. And as it is out to organize a real money trust, with the National Reserve Association as the directing head and currency "holding company," they propose that their national banks shall be granted such power that all state and savings banks and trust companies can be forced to surrender to the Wall Street combine or have their deposits, business and profits taken away and diverted to national banks.

It will be easy for national banks to entice away the deposits of other banks and trust companies by the claim that only members of the National Reserve Association have been made "panic proof" by the Government. If necessary, a little panic "object lesson" can be started to frighten depositors of state institutions into hurriedly transferring their deposits to national banks. With an artificial panic in 1907 about $50,000,000 of deposits were scared out of trust companies and into national banks in New York City in a few days.

If the Aldrich bill passes, state institutions can survive only by joining the Reserve Association. And if they join that money trust they will be ruined. They will surrender their independence, will be exploited and squeezed and their present influential and independent officers and directors will in effect become mere errand boys to execute the orders of the men of big business, who will be masters of the ruling central association. There is only one way of escape for state and savings banks and trust companies. They must help defeat the private central bank scheme and induce Congress to create the public institution for the protection of banks and business described in a later chapter.

The aggregate capital and resources of all reporting financial institutions June 7, 1911, were:

Number.	Kind of Bank.	Capital.	Resources.
7,277	National Bank....................	$1,019,633,152	$10,383,048,694
12,864	State Banks.......................	452,944,684	3,747,786,296
635	Mutual Savings Bank...........	(None)	3,762,401,625
1,249	Stock Savings Bank.............	72,177,899	889,911,677
1,251	Loan & Trust Co's..............	385,782,933	4,665,110,868
1,116	Private Banks....................	21,872,416	182,824,220
24,392	Total	$1,952,411,084	$23,631,083,380

The 7,277 national banks with 10 billion dollars of resources are expected ultimately to swallow or rule the 17,115 other financial institutions that have 13 billion dollars of resources. The job will be easy if the Aldrich bill becomes law. Its provision that no reserve need be held by a bank to secure "time deposits" is the bait expected to induce state banks and trust companies blindly to grab the concealed barbed hook. That is wildcat banking. No state bank or trust company can afford to jeopardize its solvency and the safety of depositors. And if they become reckless of the interests of depositors and the public, state laws will be passed to restrain them. Then to escape even present state laws they must become national banks and jump into the arms of Wall Street. No state bank can afford the sacrifice, and yet all will be sand-bagged into submission if the Aldrich bill ever becomes law. Wall Street is determined to control every institution in the United States receiving the people's deposits or loaning credit. If it can not accomplish it one way it will try another. Big business has discovered that the easiest and most profitable way to dominate and gradually absorb all business and wealth and rule the republic and its 94,000,000 inhabitants is to obtain physical control of the country's entire supply of money and bank credit. It thus will gain the same power over the life of all business that a private monopoly of the supply of all air and water would have over all human life. To accomplish this it is only necessary to stop the Government issuing money and then be in position, not necessarily to own all the banks, but to control their policy and actions, to force them to obey in concert the orders from the central association that will be ruled by Big Business.

The Aldrich Bill grants to the National Reserve Association power to master and direct the policy and acts of every one of the 24,392 financial institutions of the country, once they join the association and in writing legally bind themselves to obey its present and future "regulations." And the association will have power indirectly to force them all to surrender and join this universal combine—this huge incorporated money trust.

Every state institution and national bank must turn itself inside-out and expose to the agents of the central association all facts about its condition and business, including its confidential information and data as to the financial standing, resources and business operations of all its customers. And because the association is a mere private corporation and its agents not sworn public officials, all this sacred in-

The trusts thus easily can learn the true condition and operations of competitors, and ultimately drive them out of business. The 24,392 financial institutions will in effect be spies to discover and record the business secrets of every borrowing individual and corporation, placing the information thus gained at the disposal of Big Business through the central association. It is said that Wall Street now has a complete card index showing in minute detail the exact condition of hundreds of thousands of business men scattered in every state who do not even suspect that they are being constantly watched and trailed by high finance. The Aldrich bill enables this system to be made general and uses the banks to pry the secrets out of their customers under threat of refusal of bank accommodations. This one scheme will greatly facilitate Wall Street's financial, industrial and political conquest of the United States.

In New York City it is said that a central agency, a trust company, has been established by the banks to which customers of all banks are expected to go and disclose every fact about their financial condition and present and proposed business operations. It is like being physically examined by a doctor before obtaining life insurance. This information is at the disposal of all the coöperating banks and trust companies, and the customer is charged by the agency for the privilege of thus disclosing his most confidential business secrets. The tendency of the times is to make mere human beings and their welfare subservient to the will and profit-interest of the banks, to put the dollar above the man. The American people should reverse this. In the law and in business they must put the man above the dollar.

It is said that the big Wall Street banks have established a sort of financial "rogues' gallery," using a modified Bertillon system, thumb or finger prints, for identification. But it is the depositors who must submit to this new scheme, instead of the big rogues of "high finance" who use the depositors' money.

This plan of appraising everybody for bank purposes no doubt will be extended to all cities and the process of consolidating little banks into big ones will go on until in each town every business man will depend for money and credit upon the will and pleasure of just one central agency; and the operations of these city agencies will be under the direc-

Street. This is the ultimate program and will be carried out as soon as Congress passes the Aldrich bill. It is part of the process of forming one great centralized combine under the sway of high finance to monopolize and direct the use of the entire supply of money and bank credit for the whole country. The head agency no doubt will have a copy in ready reference form of the data possessed by every city agency. This business beaurocracy will be the climax of the Russianizing of all American business by Wall Street. It will be an easy matter then for those directing this machine to ruin any business man or corporation by shutting off its supply of money and credit, dogging its business operations, and diverting its business by pressure on its customers exerted through this underground bank channel. When one central agency comes into possession of accurate knowledge of the details of every man's affairs, the few men who control and use that agency for their purposes soon will own absolute and permanent control of the business of every man and corporation. This system will restrain trade, suppress competition, raise prices to consumers and foster and increase every evil and danger of the present, and yet these acts cannot be reached by the anti-trust law, because in passing the Aldrich bill Congress will legalize a trust of the trusts and make lawful the practices above described.

A trust company surely has nothing to gain by tying up a fifth of its capital in association stock, and it has much to lose by legally shackling itself to the big central machine. And private banks get no advantage by incorporating and doing the same.

Savings banks with a capital stock would get no benefit. Instead they should be fighting the growing practice of national banks of starting savings departments. This must eventually injure savings banks, as will the proposed making of real estate loans by national banks.

The 635 mutual savings banks cannot join the Reserve Association if they would. They have no capital stock. They are owned absolutely by their depositors. They are co-operative institutions and as such have been wonderfully successful. The average interest received on deposits by mutual savings banks is 50 to 100 per cent higher than the average interest paid on all deposits by all national banks. And yet the mutual institutions receive and loan only cash. They do not loan and get interest on mere credit to a volume ten times their aggregate cash, as do national banks.

If their cash deposits are diverted to national banks it will cause excessive and dangerous inflation of bank credit. It will unsettle prices, and values, and stimulate reckless gambling speculation at the expense of sound, legitimate business. A firm brake must now be put on the 10 for 1 multiplication of fictitious credit by the banks or the financial air-castle soon will go to smash and with it the prosperity of the country.

The only net assets of the 7,277 national banks are their capital, surplus and undivided profits, $1,933,134,055. Practically the entire resources of the 635 mutual savings banks of the country, aggregating $3,762,401,625, are cash savings deposits, net assets. Possessing nearly double the net assets of the 7,277 national banks, these 635 mutual savings banks, owned by their 7,690,973 depositors, who with their families represent nearly one-third of the 94,000,000 population of the United States, are utterly ignored by the Aldrich Central Bank plan. If these three billions of cash savings deposits were transferred to national banks it would increase the loaning power and profits of national banks 200 per cent, inflate their credit loans over thirty billions of dollars!

Panic endangers these mutual banks the same as other banks and fills with anxiety or terror the hearts of these millions of hard-working American citizens and their wives and children, and yet no protection is to be given to them or the banks that contain the savings of a lifetime. In fact, the plan is to entice the deposits away from mutual savings banks and into the national banks. These are the very people who most need the protecting care of the Government. The more wealthy depositors of national banks usually can look out for themselves. No provision at all is made in the Aldrich bill for these mutual banks.

In the New England states (Maine, New Hampshire, Vermont, Massachusetts, Rhode Island and Connecticut) there are 466 national banks. They have net assets (capital, surplus and undivided profits) $192,096,507. The capital stock of these banks is all owned by a few thousand people.

But the same states have 413 mutual savings banks with no capital stock, but with $175,462,872 of accumulated surplus and undivided profits and $1,366,710,866 of savings deposits, a total of $1,542,173,738 net assets owned by their 3,377,546 depositors. In fact, the aggregate resources of all national banks in those states are but $848,000,503, the larger portion of which are not net assets but the result of loans of credit. Even such inflated total resources are only about half the amount of the actual net assets of the mutual savings banks. Will the senators and congressmen from those states go in for Wall Street and the national banks and ignore the rights and welfare of 3,377,546 savings depositors who are residents of those six states?

In Ohio the three mutual savings banks have 112,935 depositors who own the $62,512,536 of net assets, the savings and accumulated profits. This is more than half of the entire net assets (capital, surplus and undivided profits), $103,175,186, of the 380 national banks of that state, the entire capital stock of such national banks being owned by relatively few persons. If Congress is to legislate for people instead of for dollars it never will pass the Aldrich bill to increase the excessive profits of a few hundred thousand national bank stockholders and ignore nearly eight million humble savings depositors and their families, or nearly one-third of the population of the United States.

National banks take the profit made with the people's deposits away from the millions of depositors and give most of it to the relatively small number of stockholders. If the facts showing the aggregate losses sustained and charged off by national banks could be revealed it would astonish the country. Hundreds of millions if not billions have been so lost and the facts concealed from depositors and the public. Some losses are unavoidable, but many are due to reckless, unbusinesslike or dishonest loans made on the "you scratch my back and I'll scratch yours" basis by conspirators who often acquire control of a bank to obtain the deposits of the people or credit based thereon for use in outside speculations or business ventures. The United States has no real banking system, such as is found in leading European countries. Over there, those who manage a bank are bankers and nothing else. All loans are made on a strict business basis. Here in too large a degree bank directors have only a nominal interest in the stock of the bank, their chief business being other than banking. They only became directors to obtain adequate credit for their regular business. They can not be blamed. It was the only way they could get sufficient credit, because others were doing the same thing and would utilize all the bank credit available unless forced to divide.

and divide use of the bank's credit between themselves instead of running the institution in a way to safeguard depositors and impartially serve the community that supplies the deposits and the law that created and protects the bank. In a sense, American banking to a considerable extent has degenerated into a scramble for control of money and bank credit, a sort of buccaneering adventure, a fight to gain the rich fruits obtained by controlling and using for personal profit the deposit savings of the public. This by no means can be said of all banks or bankers or of every town. But in another chapter will be found conclusive evidence that more than half of all national banks have been guilty of deliberate acts that would cause them to forfeit their charters if the laws were properly enforced.

The whole system is wrong and scientifically rotten and it is getting worse constantly.

Almost every crime short of deliberate murder is believed to have been committed in this fierce fight for control (particularly in New York) of these big quasi-public institutions that exist at all only because the law created and maintains them. It may not become necessary for the Government actually to seize and administer the banks impartially and honestly for the benefit of depositors and the general welfare. But drastic laws rigidly regulating the banks and their practices are imperative, or soon the whole system will go to smash. Only inordinate profits have enabled them to charge off and conceal staggering losses and survive. If the banking system was properly managed and all favoritism and graft and discriminations eliminated, the reduction in the volume of losses and increase of business would enable banks to pay 4 per cent or 5 per cent for cash deposits and charge only 4 per cent for credit loans and commercial discounts, and still realize greater net profits for the banks. Every banker knows this, and many deeply regret the fact, but so many are interlaced and bound together by mutual interest and inside investments, few seem to have the courage or feel that it would be safe to take a positive independent stand for the correction of the acknowledged abuses and dangerous defects of the system. So any remedy must come from without instead of from within. Law is the only power that can reach and remedy the evils and Congress alone can act. Because these conditions exist, the entire banking system quakes with fear and influential even talks about a genuine investigation of the banking system. The bankers fully realize the danger of having the curtain raised, for they know what is behind the scenes.

A bank with $1,000 cash can loan $10,000 "credit," while an individual with $1,000 of money can loan only $1,000. As increasing wealth sharpens the competition between individual investors and the banks for desirable mortgage and other loans, this law-made advantage may enable banks to monopolize investments by cutting interest rates. This would tend to force individuals to leave their funds on deposits in banks at nominal interest, largely because they could not safely and profitably invest the same. Each $1,000 so deposited enables the banks to increase credit loans $10,000, which increases the power and advantage of the banks in their competition for loans against those who actually own the deposits. As the income that individuals can derive from their capital thus grows less annually and the cost of living and general prices go up because of this resulting inflation of the volume of bank credit loans, the individual more and more will be sacrificed for the benefit and profit of incorporated wealth. The effect if not the chief object of the Aldrich plan will be vastly to increase the already over-swollen power and profits of the banks at the expense of individual investors. That is the whole tendency of modern banking, finance and legislation. It is an alarming symptom. This course should be reversed. The law must place the welfare of the individual above that of incorporated dollars.

CHAPTER X.

A CENTRAL BANK TO BE BOUGHT?

$1,000,000 "Promotion Fund" Raised.

Testifying in November, 1911, at the public hearing before the Senate Interstate Commerce Committee, Wharton Barker, a prominent, respected and wealthy retired banker and capitalist of Philadelphia, is reported to have positively affirmed that at that very time an enormous $1,000,000 cash fund was being raised by Wall Street and the big banks of the country as a "promotion fund" to put the Central Bank scheme through Congress.

He said that banks of Philadelphia were expected to supply or raise $100,000, or one-tenth of the amount, and were then engaged in doing so. A prominent Wall Street banker has admitted the raising of the fund, but claims it is only $500,000.

No one acquainted with Mr. Barker and his high reputation and unblemished character will for a moment doubt that he believed what he said and had ample evidence to prove its truth. And if it be true, it is a fact of grave significance. Everybody knows that Wall Street puts money into a mere gamble only on the basis of what it believes to be a 100 to 1 or 1,000 to 1 shot. That when it gambles with a million, it at least thinks it has a cinch to win a hundred million or a billion. When the "special interests" put up in cold cash to promote just one bill through one Congress a greater sum than sometimes is required by all parties to conduct an entire national campaign throughout the whole United States, it is pertinent and wise for the people to ask what such "special interests" expect to make as the result of the passing of such bill, and who is to pay them their expected profit. What will Wall Street and the big banks gain if their conspiracy to "put over" a great private Central Bank is successful?

Big Banker—Corporations can not legally pay money for "political" purposes. So this $1,000,000 fund is subscribed to "educate" the people and to lobby the private central bank bill through Congress. Why can't we use this money to "educate" the people to nominate for the presidency and Congress in both parties candidates who secretly will pledge themselves to support our central bank scheme?

Wall Street—Sure thing! "Educate," that's the proper word, pard. Havemeyer had the right idea. The sugar trust contributed to the democrats in democratic states, and to the republicans in republican states. In doubtful states it financed both parties.

It's cheaper and much safer to buy a man before he is nominated or elected, or buy the party boss or machine that will control him. We must stir up the tariff issue to divert public attention from our bank scheme. If we can keep those pesky progressives divided between the two parties we always can elect the men we want. Barnum was right—the people want to be humbugged!

Former Secretary of the Treasury of the United States Leslie M. Shaw is reported to have publicly stated that "a private corporation could well afford to pay the entire debt of the United States, which on October 31, 1911, amounted to nearly one billion dollars (or, to be exact, $963,349,390) for the power and opportunities for profit which the "Aldrich plan" for a great central bank would have Congress confer free upon just one private corporation, the National Reserve Association.

If this be so, and in fact it is a very moderate estimate, "high finance" can well afford to put up $1,000,000 or $10,000,000, or even $100,000,000, to lobby the bill through Congress, and to bring about the nomination for President in 1912 a candidate of one or each party who will not veto the bill, and of congressmen and senators who will support the measure if it happens to fail in this Congress and must go over to the next. And "high finance" generally knows what it wants, the surest way to get it and is not stingy or slow about putting up any required amount of money needed when the game is big and the reward large and certain; nor has it a burdensome and inconvenient excess of moral scruples to interfere with the spending of its "legitimate campaign fund" where and in ways to insure winning what it is after—not simply an election, but rich legislative, executive and judicial favors and immunities *after election*.

With the giant trusts fighting for their very lives, and their officials to keep out of prison and demanding from Congress legislation to that end; with 235,000 miles of railroad dependent more or less for profits upon the will of an interstate commerce commission appointed by the President; with 24,392 banks and trust companies scattered over the country hoping that their power and profits soon will be vastly augmented by act of Congress; and with Wall Street organizing and financing a nation wide campaign to induce Congress to grant for fifty years to a private corporation it will manipulate a complete monopoly of the entire money supply of the people and power to rule the banks and through the banks the business of every individual and corporation, by inflating and contracting the supply of currency and $15,000,000,000 of bank credit; the true friends of the people and of poular Government may well stand aghast with anxiety if not fear as the ravenous flock of financial vultures assembles above the campaign of 1912 ready to devour the expected feast to follow.

Unless conditions now apparent change or all signs fail, the national campaign of 1912 and the preliminary struggle for control of the nominating conventions, presidential and congressional, will be full of intrigue, secret deals, selfish compacts, unpatriotic, political and financial bargains, and the most venal and corrupt and degrading of all American history. It is an approaching climax. Will it destroy one or both of the great political parties? At last, will it break the corrupt and dominating small "balance of power" that so long has terrorized and controlled many of the acts and the destinies of both parties because, though small in numbers, it has ruled by keeping the great majority, composed of patriotic citizens politically divided? Will it force a union somewhere of the unselfish, law-abiding and patriotic of all parties? The present air is surcharged with potential possibilities likely to lead, under the unseen guidance of an all-wise and merciful Providence, to a grander republic and greater hope and happiness for the people.

"High finance" cares little for the fate of parties or of statesmen after it has gotten away with the legislative spoils. As a certain insect invariably destroys its life in giving birth to its young, so Wall Street would gladly welcome the political death of a President or a party first serving its purposes by giving birth and perpetual corporate life to its private central bank financial monstrosity.

The "interests" consider this a republic in name only. They doubt the intelligence and capacity of the people to rule themselves. They hold that money should be master. And they own the money. Therefore, that from its throne in Wall Street the "special interests" as an imperious monarch must and shall rule the republic.

They are mistaken! This is a republic in fact. The people can and will rule. Their wonderful patience spoken of by the immortal Lincoln that makes them conservative and cautious soon will be exhausted. Then their turn at the wheel of events will come. They have the power, for as yet the constitution and the laws have not been abolished, even if often they have been ignored. And these are effective instruments for the protection of the people and the execution of their will.

Already there are laws prohibiting corporations using corporate funds for political purposes. Banks are corporations. Such acts are ultra vires, beyond the corporate powers. There are criminal penalties. It is said to have been reported at the recent American Bankers' Association meeting that that body last year spent about $200,000, much of it for missionary work, presumably for a private central bank. Since the insurance investigation "yellow dog funds" have been under the ban of the law. Is the Albany "house of mirth" now to be moved to Washington? Are the banks of the country to join Wall Street in financing their corrupt and criminal orgies that will make the Albany exploits that so shocked the whole country mere Sunday-school picnics in comparison? We soon will know.

But beware! The people sometime will have their "in-ning." There will follow public congressional investigation that will lay bare the entire conspiracy and every corrupt or criminal act, even if every denizen of Wall Street and every American banker is summoned and on oath forced to reveal to the committee or to a grand jury "the truth, the whole truth and nothing but the truth." It is passing strange what some big men will do for money—for a little more money that they do not need!

"Mene, mene, Tekel; Upharsin." (Daniel 5-25.)

CHAPTER XI.

WALL STREET STOCK "MARKET."

A "Fixed" Monte Carlo. The Game in Detail Exposed. United States Attorney General's Strange Opinion.

A banking or currency reform plan that does not take into account the constantly daily monetary, financial and banking practices of Wall Street will be ineffective and useless. There conditions constantly prevail that decisively influence the supply and flow of currency and credit, the rates of interest on both time and call loans, the making and calling of bank loans in vast volume, the international ebb and flow of the tides of gold that now measure all values, and the quotation prices of twenty to thirty billion dollars of listed securities, a total three times the value of all annual crops of the soil and eight times all the money of the United States.

If these forces were moved only by natural causes—"natural supply and demand"—values would be relatively accurate and stable, fluctuations and changes comparatively moderate and harmless, monetary conditions would be sound and financial institutions safe; and Wall Street as a barometer of the nation's prosperity and a "governor" on the financial engine moving the wheels of all American activities would be an accurate and useful indicator and regulator of steady and inestimable value to the entire country and all of its inhabitants. There would be no dangerous extremes and consequently no possibility of panics.

But, unfortunately, in Wall Street everything is artificial. Nothing is natural or logical; therefore the unexpected always is happening. Every effect is the result of a planned and purposeful cause. Whatever is done usually was intended, procured.

If prices soar to the swallows' nests, they were put up there. If they slump to the coal cellar, they were dumped there. And only the few big inside operators know which will be done on any particular day. Consequently every-

TALE OF THE TAPE.

FOUND IN EVERY WALL ST. BANK

AUTHOR HAS A PIECE OF "TICKER" TAPE
SHOWING $20,000,000 SHRINKAGE
IN 20 MINUTES IN THE "MARKET PRICE"
OF THE "LISTED" STOCK OF ONE COMPANY;
WHICH DROP HE SAW TAKE PLACE.
THE LOSS RUINED THOUSANDS
AND IT WAS A CROOKED DEAL.

body else in the United States who either speculates or invests in "listed" securities is merely gambling blindly, recklessly, without the slightest knowledge or chance of knowledge. A mere guess as to whether that day the masters of the machine will decide to lift the lever up or push it down. And he will not and can not know, or have the slightest idea or inkling until after, figuratively, he has dropped his money in the slot, made his bet, heard the whirl of the unseen wheel behind the impenetrable curtain, and the attendant, "the broker," opens the little peek-hole and, as usual, calls out: "You lose! Try your luck again."

The fact is the putting up or down of the price of a given stock or bond is simple and easy. The shares of the company are limited. It is not like speculating in wheat or corn against every bushel in the world. A large portion of a corporation's shares of stock never change hands, howevermuch the price may fluctuate. The proportion of shares "on the market" usually is relatively small. It is only necessary to organize a syndicate or "pool" with sufficient available means or *borrowing power* to put up as a margin a sum equal to 10 per cent of the quotation price of whatever shares of that particular stock may be offered. Usually but 10 per cent to 25 per cent of the stock of the smallest or largest railroads or trusts will appear on the market, even if prices are forced far above conceded value. Most holders want steady investments, dividends, not to gamble on stimulated changes in prices. And the manipulators must furnish only 10 per cent of the value of the relatively small amount offered. Another 10 per cent is furnished by the brokers and the balance 80 per cent by the banks, loaned on the securities as collateral. Thus the banks are the chief factor in every stock-market manipulation.

While the great Wall Street insurance companies, controlling in their reserves hundreds of millions of the accumulated savings held for "the widows and orphans," are prohibited by law from investing in stocks, the law does not say that they can not, to help out their stock-market masters, deposit a hundred million of money in the banks and thus enable such banks during a great market manipulating campaign to loan to inside operators four hundred million dollars additional credit to aid them in running the gamble against the public, the living fathers, husbands and brothers of such future "widows and orphans." Whatever the amount, they certainly deposit many millions in the big banks.

Such a pool always is formed and operates in absolute secrecy. Often its members do not know the plays to be made from day to day with the common funds for mutual benefit. That is a "blind pool," only the manager, usually one of the pool members, knows the moves made or to be made. A pool of that character has the price of that stock, the welfare of the corporation, its stockholders, officers, employees, and the public absolutely at its mercy, and yet no one outside of the pool itself even can know of that fact. Sometimes it is a long, exhausting, wearing, heartbreaking, strangling struggle. Often it is just a quick, deep stab in the dark, always from behind, and all is over. The guilty never are caught or detected or even suspected, for the stock exchange is created and operates to hide the identity and completely screen the actions of the bandits of high finance.

Very often the different pools manipulating the various stock and bond issues of the many trusts, railroads and other corporations quietly put their heads together and coöperate, or conspire. The whole list of price quotations goes up, a "bull" movement, or down, a "bear" movement, according as has been predetermined. The public that owns most of the securities but does not know until too late which way prices are to be put is, of course, always fleeced, the profits going to the insiders. In fact, it is the regular practice of the manipulators to put out hints and "tips" through the daily press and otherwise to cleverly induce the uninformed public always to take the wrong side of the market, and lose. Sometimes dividends are increased and decreased for the purpose of manipulating quotations for the speculative profit of "insiders."

An honest, legitimate trading market for securities would be a useful national blessing. But the Wall Street Monte Carlo, in its practice and results, is the most colossal, crooked and financially dangerous den of gamblers and robbers the world ever has seen or dreamed of.

Quotation prices sometimes are pushed up or down 10 to 50 per cent. The overwhelming consequences of these fluctuations can be realized from the fact that an average fall of but 10 per cent means a total loss to holders of the nearly $30,000,000,000 of securities amounting to $3,000,-000,000, a sum exceeding all the money in actual circulation in the United States. A few such "swings" each year and the losses will equal eight or nine billion, the yearly value of all the crops.

In this and other ways "high finance" silently and constantly and irresistibly harvests an ever increasing portion of the fruits of all human toil and effort. Yet the methods and means employed are so secret and mysterious, the victims may not even realize they have been intentionally victimized, and never would suspect the right parties in any event. Indirectly most of the losses fall on the people who never buy stocks at all.

It is "high finance" against people, with the cards always "stacked," the game always "fixed." It is hard for the people to figure out just how it is worked, but a large portion of the prevailing high prices is due to the machinations in one way or another of "high finance." The inflation of the volume of securities out of all proportion to assets, increase in interest rates on billions upon billions of dollars of municipal and corporation bonds and upon the loans of bank credit, are some of the agencies used, the extra burden falling always and only upon the people.

Mr. Carnegie is said to own about $300,000,000 first mortgage bonds of the steel trust. Writer heard him testify a few years ago before the House Ways and Means Committee to the effect that he refused to accept as a gift with his bonds an enormous quantity of steel trust common stock because it was all "water" and worthless. The issued common stock amounts to $508,302,500. Its market value now is about 70. If Carnegie told the truth, the stock is worthless today, except as unlawful use of the power of monopoly temporarily gives it a fictitious "earning power" that creates an illegal value by extorting illegal prices and profits from the public. But stock quotations do not depend upon or register intrinsic values. The will of the secret manipulating pools determines the quotation prices of listed securities. These pools can advance and maintain quotations far above values because they control the banks and can borrow as much as needed of the country's entire supply of money and credit, and they also can prevent the public, against which the pools are playing the game, from borrowing from the banks relatively a dollar of credit or money.

"Money makes the mare go." This old saying is particularly true in Wall Street. Those who control the cash supply, rule and dominate everything else. A few men of giant wealth own a large share of the available cash. They put it in the banks and thereafter are masters of the banks; for upon every million cash put into bank reserves, the banks build up and loan for interest profits four to ten millions of bank credit. The banks are at the mercy of and dependent upon the owners of the cash, because every million withdrawn forces contraction of bank loans four to ten millions.

A financier with $10,000,000 cash can get the interest only on $10,000,000 if he loans or invests the money. But if he owns a bank and puts the $10,000,000 in its "cash reserve," the bank for his profit can, based thereon, increase its credit loans $40,000,000 to $100,000,000 without the investment of one additional dollar.

The banks serve Wall Street and devote their limitless resources to further stock gambling (and 75 per cent of all stock exchange transactions are conceded to be fictitious gambling deals), for the reason that the owners of the cash, who are masters of the banks, and the organizers of the secret price-manipulating pools often are identical. And by a succession of consolidations, mergers, arrangements, "gentlemen's agreements," interrelationships, pools, and combines for mutual profit and advantage, practically all of the large banks, insurance and trust companies, containing the deposit savings of the people and the reserves of outside banks and controlling all important loanable funds, together with the trusts, railroads and other large corporations, generally have fallen under the absolute power of the same few Wall Street men, who are the big operators of the stock market, the masters of "high finance," the architects and beneficiaries of vast tidal-wave flotations, and the instigators and originators of the pending Private Central Bank plan, by which they expect to corner and control and manipulate and turn to personal profit the entire public currency and all the revenues of the republic.

The outside individual, whatever his wealth may be, who either invests or speculates in any stock or bond dealt in on the stock exchange, is blindly playing the game single-handed against the combined power of all these coöperating pools. And because of the control exercised by these pools over the financial institutions, and their ability to borrow without limit the money and credit of the Wall Street banks and the reserves of outside banks deposited in New

York banks, the outsider, to a large extent, is playing against the invincible power of the marshalled and intelligently manipulated combined banking capital of the entire United States. And if the Aldrich Central Bank plan is adopted, he must also play against the weight of the entire public currency and the total revenues of the Federal Government. What chance has any individual outsider in such a game?

The Central Bank "plan" is a dazzling, daring scheme. If it succeeds, the Government, the people and the banks forever will be chained helpless to the Wall Street machine like the conquered and abject slaves to the wheels of the chariots of the returning and victorious Roman generals.

Money is the supreme magnet. It is the sun that attracts and holds in place and regulates a universe of credit.

The interest rate, like the moon, is a lesser magnet; performing, however, an important office in the world of finance.

It is unlawful in New York to charge more than 6 per cent on time loans. That would be usury. It once was the same as to "call loans." But years ago, "when the people were not looking," Wall Street stole up to Albany and had the law changed. Now it is lawful to demand the "pound of flesh," and to cut it out close to the heart, for any interest rate from 1 to 1,000 per cent may be agreed upon and enforced in the courts of "justice" of that state and in the federal courts respecting deals made in New York, provided the loan is always left payable "on demand." And in recent years it is a common thing to see interest on "call" loans bid up into the clouds—10, 20, 50, 100, 200 per cent many times have been the ruling rates for call loans, and once, during the cornering of the stock of the Northern Pacific Railroad, and the resulting panic, the interest rate actually was run up on the New York Stock Exchange to 1,000 per cent.

It has been admitted that after the instigated brokers have run the call loan rate up to ruinous figures, over and over big banks have called the loans of customers at one window for the sole purpose of forcing them to go to another window of the same bank, or to another of the co-operating banks, and submit to an interest extortion and robbery that would be a crime in another state and once was in New York.

The great Empire State will not right this glaring and

growing wrong to the whole country. For about four million dollars annually in stock transfer fees, three-fourths of which is exclusively from mere gambling transactions, it has sold its independence and honor and licensed the gamblers to prey upon and plunder on its own soil the citizens of that state and the people of the whole United States.

It is common knowledge that big Wall Street banks daily ignore and break both the spirit and plain letter of the National Banking Law, illegally loaning sums aggregating untold millions to further stock market operations of the Wall Street masters of such banks. "High finance" knows no law, human or divine. It is a bold and daring outlaw on the highway of commerce, making frequent raids to "hold up" honest business and plunder American prosperity.

The practice of high interest extortion falls heavily upon legitimate business, for commerce and industry must compete with the gamblers for the banks' favors or get along without money or credit. This is because many banks ignore their obligations to the public whose deposits they use, and to the law to which they owe their existence, immunities, and special privileges. They are only "out for the coin," every last dollar, and they often auction off their "credit" to the highest bidder. And the gamblers can afford of course to outbid honest business.

High interest on call loans is advertised in the daily press and made to entice away from outside banks their deposits and to induce country banks all over the land to deny the legitimate and necessary demands of local business that the funds of the institution may be sent hunting for usury in the deadly quicksands of Wall Street's great paradise of gamblers.

And when this enticed money reaches the metropolis, call loan rates suddenly are put down to 2 per cent. By that time the fierce stock market struggle is over. The high rates demanded prevented the public borrowing so as to hold on to its securities until the artificially disturbed condition again becomes normal, the banks forcing the public to sell to insiders at bottom prices by "calling" the loans to secure which such securities are up as collateral. But the high rate as a magnet attracted into the reserves of Wall Street banks enough extra of the country's cash to enable such banks to loan hundreds of millions of additional bank credit to "insiders" to enable them to carry the securities the public thus was forced to sell cheap, until quotations can be manipulated and again marked up and the operators unload at a profit on the confiding public. And during these long periods of "rest," while the public is getting ready to "forgive and forget," the banks charge the "insiders" on such call loans only the nominal rate of 2 per cent per annum, while everybody else must pay at least 6 per cent. In this way the monetary balances and currency streams of the whole country are altered and deranged, causing distressful and dangerous conditions tending toward panic.

And the "interests" and the banks that repeatedly work these giant wrongs upon the country are the identical interests upon whom the Aldrich plan would confer a thousand fold greater power for evil and unearned and unjust profits, by means of a great Private Central Bank under their control.

The banks of the United States foolishly may be anxious to become the willing concubines of Wall Street in the mere hope of increasing their profits that they may wear finer clothes. But the business interests of the country depend constantly on the banks for an adequate supply of bank credit in order to make any money, or even keep their business alive. Surely they are not going to commit business and financial suicide by helping to persuade Congress to create a Private Central Bank that in Wall Street's hands will enable it, by contracting the currency, to force the banks, even against their will, to call in and cancel bank loans to business borrowers, suddenly and unexpectedly to the extent of billions of dollars!

No important deal now can be financed in New York or in fact anywhere without the consent of the few ruling high financiers. Their consent usually can be obtained only by surrendering to them control and most of the profits of the enterprise. Many a deal is financially sandbagged because it does not first get the O. K. of the masters of finance; and no matter how attractive and sound it may be. All our banking laws play directly into the hands of these few men. They tend to force everybody in the United States to go to New York for money. This monopoly of American cash and credit by Wall Street is due chiefly and directly to the natural operation of federal laws pertaining to bank reserves. These laws should be changed so that every city in the country will be on an equality with New York, with an equal chance for business.

David H. Moffat, multimillionaire president of the great First National Bank of Denver, a man of character, integrity and influence, recently died disappointed because for fifteen years and to the last the money-masters of Wall Street blocked in this country and Europe the sale of his gilt-edge bonds on the new railroad from Denver to Salt Lake that is half completed with money Moffat personally advanced. The road would open up a vast new territory that has no railroad, but between the terminal cities it would compete with the Union Pacific on the north and on the south with the Denver and Rio Grande, a railroad also built by Moffat. It is reported that the bankers who first considered financing the splendid independent electric railway scheme between Philadelphia and Atlantic City gave as a reason for dropping the project that they had been ordered to do so by financial interests behind the Pennsylvania Railroad, such interests intimating that if they went ahead every scheme they tried to put through in the future would be fought and blocked. The bankers said that it was one of the most sound and profitable deals they ever had considered but that they could not afford permanently to antagonize the powerful men behind the Pennsylvania Railroad. So Wall Street has its "Black Hand."

In 1908 writer suggested to the General Assembly of New York a legislative investigation of Wall Street and drafted the bill introduced for that purpose. He urged the plan at a public hearing in Albany at which John G. Milburn as counsel for the Stock Exchange publicly consented to such investigation. Evidently he was not serious, because agents of Wall Street blocked the measure notwithstanding Gov. Hughes twice urged its passage in special messages.

Mr. Milburn said the members of the Stock Exchange were all honorable men, had nothing to hide. In reply writer read from the 1908 official report of the state comptroller the direct charge that each year the members of the Stock Exchange swindle the state out of more than $2,-000,000 of stamp-transfer taxes on deals they do not report. As brokers always collect this tax from customers, instead of paying it themselves as was intended, it would appear that the offending brokers steal the $2,000,000 from either the state or their customers or both and pocket it.

The Stock Exchange has 1,100 members. The franchise

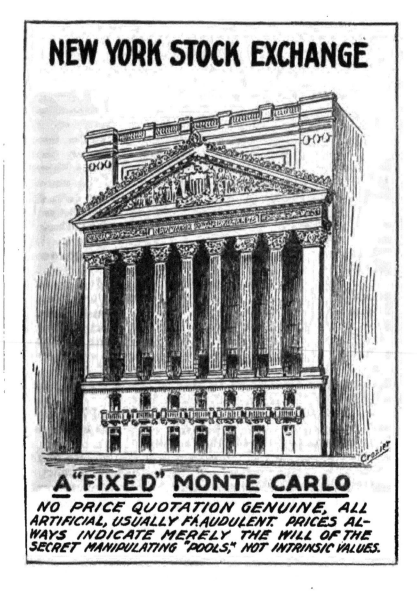

NEW YORK STOCK EXCHANGE

A "FIXED" MONTE CARLO

NO PRICE QUOTATION GENUINE, ALL ARTIFICIAL, USUALLY FRAUDULENT. PRICES ALWAYS INDICATE MERELY THE WILL OF THE SECRET MANIPULATING "POOLS", NOT INTRINSIC VALUES.

value of a "seat," or membership, increased from $35,000 in 1900 to $96,000 in 1909, a total value of $105,600,000 for the 1,100 "seats" and actual property, its building, worth perhaps $3,000,000. It is the right to participate in the rich fruits of the vast gambling operations that makes men pay $96,000 to join that "club." The rules allow the brokers to charge customers ⅛ per cent commission. In margin deals this is figured on the 100 per cent face value of the stock bet on. It is 1¼ per cent on the actual cash involved, the 10 per cent margin put up. And it costs another 1¼ per cent to let go, to close a trade, 2½ per cent for the "round trip." Brokers also can charge 6 per cent "interest" on the 90 per cent of wind or imagination, the difference between the 10 per cent margin and the face value of the phantom stock. Figuring his margin money worth 6 per cent, customer pays 60 per cent "interest" on the actual money he puts into the deal. Broker will soon get all of his customer's money even if quotation prices remain the same. The interest, commissions and state tax speedily rob customer of all his cash.

The Stock Exchange is not incorporated. It is an irresponsible, unregulated, unrestrained private club. Yet its transactions total twenty to thirty billions annually, several times the value of all crops, and daily affect vitally all American life and business. No law of state or nation exercises the slightest effective public control over the exchange, its members or their transactions, yet every panic was caused or intensified by this body and its dangerous manipulations.

As the Stock Exchange regulates the state of New York and dictates its legislative policy, it is folly to expect that state effectively to regulate the exchange.

Have we 48 little despotisms within the borders of the republic, each with supreme power permanently to inflict on the other states and the nation the grossest wrongs and most dangerous evils? Can one state that gets a big share of the profits forever maintain in spite of all the others the greatest gambling institution in the world and plunder the citizens of all states by crooked means out of more than a billion dollars every year? Is there no defense, no way of escape, for outraged people?

Congress surely has power under the Constitution to regulate any exchange dealing in the securities of interstate railroads, and probably of any corporation engaged in interstate commerce.

It can and should prohibit margin gambling in the shares of such corporations because that practice interferes with their business and tends to increase their expenses and the rates they must charge. That margin gambling is the most dangerous panic-inciting practice is evidenced by the reported fact that during the panic of 1907 Morgan's first imperial order when he took command of the situation was, "Stop all margin trading!" He was obeyed, and instantly the strain relaxed and the danger grew less. If there was no margin gambling, there never would be any real panics. The gambling or fictitious deals, largely "wash sales," total between ten and twenty billion dollars every year.

Congress at once should prohibit the pretended selling of shares of corporations engaged in interstate commerce that vendor does not own. This would abolish the 75 per cent of gambling deals without harm to legitimate business. It would make the exchange a genuine securities market instead of a gambling institution. Quotations then would be a true index of value. Severe criminal penalties for violators should be provided. Congress has power and should make it unlawful for national banks directly or indirectly to charge more than 6 per cent interest or discount on either call or time loans. This would force state legislation imposing the same restriction on state banks, trust companies and individuals. Congress should also forbid any usurious loans being made on any such stock exchange.

These two things would do much toward settling the monetary problem, increase the elasticity of the currency, and the volume of bank credit available for legitimate business, remove the cause of panics and save the people a billion dollars of losses annually. It would be the greatest blessing conferred on the country by any act of Congress in forty years.

Evidently no help from the present administration can be expected. In an interview in the New York World May 27, 1908, Attorney General Wickersham is reported as saying that margin trading, as carried on by the New York Stock Exchange, is perfectly legal and not gambling. He adds:

"Actual deliveries of stock are made. It is not simply betting that a stock will go up or down. The men are actually buying and selling stock."

As the Attorney General is an able lawyer, is reported as

saying that he has been counsel for a very large number of the biggest financiers and interests in Wall Street, it seems impossible that he is ignorant of the fact that a large majority of the hundreds of thousands of people who play the stock game on margin never get or even see or expect to get one share of the stocks on the quotation prices of which they merely bet. The Attorney General as well might justify horse-race betting and claim that there is an actual delivery of horses to the bettors. There may be mentally, but not legally.

Billions of dollars of "margin" deals are made every year in which the customers never receive into their possession a certificate for even one share of actual stock or have title to any stock legally transferred to them on the books of the several corporations, and no one knows better than the Attorney General that this is true.

A wonderfully clever scheme has been evolved to confuse and hide the true character of margin deals. But everybody in Wall Street realizes that it is gambling and nothing more.

To illustrate: In one day say a hundred purchases and sales on margin are made, each for 1,000 shares New York Central Railroad stock at par by 100 brokers for 100 customers, one deal each. The price of 1,000 shares at par ($100) is $100,000. Each of the 100 buying customers puts up $10,000 as a 10 per cent "margin" with his broker, a total of $1,000,000 margin money in the hands of the 100 brokers, or $10,000 apiece. Each broker goes on the floor of the exchange and "buys" the 1,000 shares, the transaction being entered on the exchange clearing-house sheet as a "purchase" by one and a "sale" by another broker. Stock never is delivered on the floor but at the broker's office by messenger next morning. Each of the 100 buying brokers "bought" in one deal and "sold" in another. At the end of the day in the clearing-house these deals are "matched" or off-set. The whole hundred deals are settled by the last selling broker handing the first buying broker one certificate for 1,000 shares of that stock.

A hundred "sales" of 1,000 shares each, total 100,000 shares, worth $10,000,000, is settled by the delivery of one certificate for 1,000 shares in just one of the 100 deals, and $10,000 instead of $10,000,000 is all the money paid by the only one to whom any sort of actual delivery is made. The other 99 got no stock at all. Yet behind each of the 99 brokers is a customer betting that the price of New York

TREASURY DEPARTMENT

WASHINGTON

December 12, 1911.

Mr. Alfred O. Crosier,
  Plankinton House,
    Milwaukee, Wisconsin.

Sir:

In reply to your letter of the 11th inst. you are advised that a table showing the percentage of banks violating the law in regard to real estate loans, reserve, excessive loans and borrowed money, appears on page 22 of the Comptroller's report for this year, a copy of which is being mailed to you, under separate cover, as requested.

A copy is also being sent to F. W. Crosier, c/o The Romaine, Middleton Avenue, Cincinnati, Ohio.

Respectfully,

Deputy Comptroller.

(See Page 283)

Central will advance, ready to take his winning if it does, and with $10,000 up in the hands of the broker as a security wager to cover commissions and pay the "loss" to the customer behind some "selling" broker, who took the other side and bet that New York Central would go down. Neither wants to bother with any certificate of stock. The customer who "sold" had no actual stock to sell or deliver. The customer who "bought" got no stock and did not want any. Both are interested only in the shifting quotation figures on the blackboard or tape as the game goes on. If there was any sort of real delivery by the last to the first man, there certainly was none to the 99 between, not even mental delivery, for they did not expect or want any actual stock. Each just bet the price would advance. If these had been genuine sales, it would have required 100,000 shares and $10,000,000 money to make the deliveries. As it was a gamble, 1,000 shares was enough to make the sham "delivery" for the whole 100 "deals" and $1,000,000 to protect the 100 brokers in case quotations happened to go down instead of up. But even the first buyer did not actually get any stock. The certificate never was legally transferred to him on the books of the company. There was no stock actually delivered to him. He never saw any stock, or expected to. His broker got the 1,000 share certificate. It was indorsed in blank and thus transferable by mere delivery to "bearer." Without any consent or action by the customer, the broker takes this certificate to his own bank and pledges it as collateral security for his own note for $80,000, or 80 per cent of its market value. If broker defaults, the bank hands the certificate to a different broker who sells same to anybody desiring it. The bank pays itself and the expenses from the proceeds and gives the balance, if any, to the defaulting broker.

Unless the legal title to the 1,000 shares vested in the customer, clearly there was no "delivery" and the deal was a mere gamble, a wager or bet on the quotation price, and as such illegal and a violation of the New York state constitution which prohibits gambling.

On the other hand, if there was delivery, and title vested in the customer, then the broker has committed a felony and violated the statutes of New York by converting to his own use the property of another, pledging his customer's stock at the bank as security for his own personal debt. Margin dealing in either case is an illegal, criminal proceeding, and the distinguished and able Attorney General should know of that fact. If he does, why is he apologizing for what is conceded to be the greatest of the many Wall Street evils, defending the stock exchange in its lawless course?

In the above situation only 1,000 shares of actual stock worth $100,000 is involved, and yet $1,000,000 cash is up as a security wager with 100 brokers who charge their customers ⅛ per cent commission on $10,000,000 for "buying" and another ⅛ per cent on $10,000,000 for "selling" and also 6 per cent "interest" on an imaginary $9,000,000 while the deal is pending; also the state transfer tax. And the Attorney General is said to see nothing improper in this proceeding. Likewise he seems to see nothing improper in over half the national bankers violating the United States laws that he took an oath to enforce, for he takes no action in the matter.

It is believed that in a United States Court money lost in a margin deal can be recovered by the victim in a suit against the broker. This view should be tested in the courts.

Congress is the only power that can throttle or curb this most deadly of Wall Street's instruments for the spoilation of all the people. If Congress had acted twenty-five years ago, more than 10 billion dollars of wealth now dangerously concentrated would have remained scattered in the pockets of a large portion of the 94,000,000 people of the United States.

CHAPTER XII.

PANICS NATURAL OR ARTIFICIAL?

Inside Facts About 1907 Panic.

The "Aldrich Plan" is loudly advertised as a sure "cure all" for every panic. The country needs a "preventive" rather than "cure." This can be provided only if we discover and disclose the cause or causes of these repeated calamities. Are panics natural and therefore inevitable, or artificial, and for that reason unnecessary and avoidable? Do they just "happen" or are they "sent"? Are they the work of Providence or of Man? If panics are not a visitation of Divine Wrath, if they are man-made, who does it and for what reason?

Investigation leads us first to ascertain *where panics start*. History and common knowledge answer as to that. It is conceded that every American panic began in Wall Street. Why? Are they accidental or incendiary? If accidental, due to financial conditions likely to produce panic, we can avoid panics only by removing these panic-inciting conditions. To do that we must go where they exist, to Wall Street. We must learn why these conditions prevail, who creates them, and for what purpose.

On the other hand, if panic is incendiary, deliberately started, we must find out just who does it, how it is done, and for what object or objects. This done, it will be relatively easy to find and apply an effective remedy.

The first overt act at the beginning of every financial panic is the violent and sudden contraction of bank credit, the wholesale and imperative calling in of bank loans. This always will cause panic instantly. This panic-inciting step by the banks may be involuntary or voluntary. If deposits are withdrawn by depositors through fear or otherwise, cash reserves shrink and banks must contract loans about ten times such withdrawals. This is involuntary and not the fault of the banks. Big Business thus can force the banks to cause panic through violent contraction of bank

201

loans caused by the simultaneous withdrawal by the "inter-ests" of bank deposits in large volume. If panic results from unnecessary and general coöperative contraction of bank loans voluntarily done by the banks to put pressure upon business men generally for the purpose of inducing them to influence Congress to pass legislation beneficial to the banks, or for the purpose of steering the course of poli-tics and influencing a national or state election, it is a deliberate crime for which the banks and guilty bankers should be severely punished.

In seeking to prove the guilt of a prisoner against whom there is circumstantial and no direct evidence, the first thing is to establish that the accused had a guilty motive, that he got some profit or advantage as the result of the crime committed. Circumstantial evidence often is as un-erring and convincing as direct, pointing irresistibly and logically to the guilty party. Many a man has been justly convicted and hung for murder exclusively on circumstan-tial proof.

Once the prosecution conclusively shows that the accused benefited by the crime, the prisoner is more than half con-victed. Practically he must then prove an alibi or produce other evidence of innocence.

By this legal standard let us test and judge Wall Street, accused and indicted as the criminal author of panics, and now arraigned on trial in the Court of Public Opinion. The specific count, under present consideration, is the one charg-ing that Wall Street caused the panic of 1907.

Seeking a motive, let us first show what that panic accomplished and who profited thereby.

The N. Y., N. H. & Hartford R. R. obtained control of the Portchester Railroad that soon would have been a com-pleted competing line between New York and Boston if the panic of 1907 had not forced the promoters to sell when banks and trust companies called their loans secured by Portchester R. R. securities.

The Morse coastwise shipping trust that had become a serious and successful competitor of that same railroad by cheap water route was wrecked and ruined by such panic and sold out for a nominal price to interests said to be affiliated with that railroad.

The Georgia Central R. R. had a similar experience with like results.

Morse committed the unpardonable Wall Street sin of

quietly buying up control on his own hook of a string of the smaller New York banks, with the alleged object of using their deposits and credit to manipulate his ice company and other "high finance" flotations. He had seen others do the same thing, men higher in finance than he, why should he not do it? He tried it, and was sentenced to serve a fifteen-year term in Atlanta prison. And the financial world now knows it is not wise for any individual to try to corral any New York banks and build up a financial power independent of certain well known "powers that be."

Of course Morse broke the law and deserved his fate. But the woods are full of others guilty of all the same crimes —except the crime of trying to avoid "playing second-fiddle" to the great masters of Wall Street.

For years the big trust companies of New York paid higher interest rates for deposits than were paid by national banks. The trust companies, such as the Knickerbocker, the Lincoln, and the Trust Company of America, were state institutions and not subject to the reserve and other restrictions of the National Bank Act. Millions of dollars of deposits thus were enticed away from the banks and into the trust companies. These companies had many sources of profit denied to banks. They were rapidly growing large, rich and powerful. They were handling underwriting, financing many profitable flotations. They were largely owned and run by different men than those all powerful in the big banks. The banks increasingly became jealous, envious, sore at the trust companies. They would not allow trust companies to join the Clearing House, forcing each to clear its checks in the Clearing House every day through some bank member. But the trust companies refused to lower the rate enjoyed by depositors and their deposits kept climbing. All at once something happened, and "presto change!" The deposits of the trust companies shrunk and the deposits of the banks increased some fifty million dollars in a few days, or enough to decrease the credit loaning power of the trust companies and increase that of the banks more than a half billion dollars. What did it? Panic! The panic of October, 1907. How did it happen? Let us see.

Times were fine. Prosperity was in the air, everywhere. Business was expanding, demand increasing, prices high, profits big. Everybody was making money and happy.

Factories were running full time or overtime. Everybody had a job at good wages. Surely the people had followed "the pursuit of happiness," had caught it, and all, men, women and children were enjoying it to the full.

It is alleged that one night a quiet conference of some of the "big ones" interested in the banks was held in New York to devise "ways and means." Writer has it on the word of the editor of one of the great New York dailies that late one night an official of one of the big financial institutions came personally to the newspaper offices with an article for publication, stating that a certain big bank, named, had decided to refuse to further clear for a certain big trust company, named, because it considered the trust company shaky and unsound.

The news was sensational, and when published with big, black scare-head-lines, of course it frightened trust company depositors into "runs" not only on that but on other trust companies. Most of the vast withdrawals went into the banks. Very grave and ugly charges against very high financiers and big banks have been privately made, and some things have become public.

For instance, Oakleigh Thorne, president of the Trust Company of America, one of the large institutions made to grossly suffer, is reported to have publicly testified at the steel trust congressional hearing that the panic of 1907 was artificial, deliberately caused or stimulated, and named the high "interests" responsible.

Wharton Barker, a very prominent, respected and wealthy retired banker and capitalist of Philadelphia, is reported as testifying in November, 1911, at the hearing of the Senate Interstate Commerce Committee that he had definite information and proof that the panic of 1907 was deliberately planned in advance and purposely caused, naming the parties, the time and the place.

The trust companies begged for mercy and help. "Mercy" is free, but "help" in Wall Street only comes in exchange for "quid pro quo." The runs continued, it is alleged, until control of part or all of the stock of big trust companies was surrendered to the powerful interests behind the big banks, and until the trust companies gave up possession of certain stocks held as collateral by the trust companies to secure large loans that the "runs" and the panic forced the trust companies to call in, then the runs are said to have stopped and the panic soon was over.

It is alleged that control of the Tennessee Coal & Iron Co., the most powerful and dangerous competitor and rival of the steel trust, was obtained during the shuffle in the midst of the panic of 1907.

Why should not Wall Street have panics once in a while when they shower upon the great masters of "high finance" so many rich and glorious blessings obtainable in no other way? And if Providence won't send a panic, why not make one, when it is so easy and will be so useful and profitable?

If insiders caused the panic, of course they knew when it would happen. Did they first "sell short" and thus reap the billions of dollars the public lost by shrinkage of quotation prices on the twenty to thirty billion dollars of listed securities?

Wall Street banks flatly repudiated their obligations during the panic, refusing to give up demand deposits comprising cash reserves of banks all over the country, keeping the money so that they could supply cash or credit to the big operators who were buying at half their value securities the panic forced the public to sell. "Possession is nine points of law," when it comes to money in a panic and the insiders need it.

Panics often go further than intended, and may endanger even insiders; 1907 did so. Even the big operators became frightened when the people kept withdrawing, hoarding and hiding deposits. They appealed to the Government to help the people by helping relieve and save the banks of the country. The Treasury responded by turning over about $120,000,000 of public moneys to the Wall Street banks. It is alleged that instead of properly helping country banks by immediately releasing reserve money arbitrarily and illegally detained, much of the Government's money was "salted" and kept by the Wall Street banks and their loans to insiders for stock speculations greatly increased.

But the most important advantage expected to be derived by Wall Street and its banks from the panic of 1907, is a great privately owned central bank—a huge private money trust to monopolize and forever control the entire public currency and the deposited revenues of the United States. The people always have been jealous of their money supply. They never have taken kindly to control of the entire monetary circulation, the life-blood of all trade, by private parties for private profit. Nothing but extreme emergency and the most urgent necessity could possibly induce the people to consent to that course by Congress. As Wall Street was bound to get control of the public currency, what more natural thing than that it should cause a panic to inflict upon the people distressful conditions that comprise "extreme emergency" and thus induce them to consent to a private central bank and surrender to it of a billion of public currency as an "urgent necessity" and the only possible way of avoiding future panics? *That's the big game!* If the "interests" caused the panic of 1907, the chief object was to make it serve as an "object lesson" to the people and induce them blindly to drive Congress into granting a private monopoly of the entire money supply of the people to a central bank corporation owned by banks controlled by Wall Street.

And if it is necessary to have another panic as a new "object lesson" to pinch and drive the public into hurrying favorable congressional action on the "Aldrich plan," there is not the slightest doubt that Wall Street can cause it on short notice, and those who know or realize the daring and desperation of "high finance" and its determination to put the central bank through Congress at all hazard and whatever the cost, do not doubt that it will cause another panic if necessary to force its will upon the country.

For this reason business men no doubt will think it the part of wisdom not to expand but to keep near shore with their financial sails snugly furled until Wall Street no longer has so much reason and temptation to start another panic.

The panic of October, 1907, immediately preceded the introduction into Congress, in December, 1907, of a central bank bill based on the plan adopted by the New York Chamber of Commerce long before the panic or any public signs of panic were visible, the bill being practically identical with what now is called the "Aldrich plan."

When the greatest of all Wall Street organizations, that combine of the brains and power of the financial metropolis, the New York Chamber of Commerce, formulated its demand in 1906 for a central bank, it was not to "stop" or "cure" a panic. There was then no panic in sight and no natural conditions to cause one. Was the panic later worked up and staged after the insiders had put their own financial house in order and just before the session of Congress in which the central bank bill actually was first introduced, in December, 1907? Right after the panic, in November, 1907, and just before Congress convened in December, 1907, a meeting was held in Philadelphia at which prominent Wall Street bankers urged Congress to authorize a great private central bank as the only cure for panics.

Was the panic of 1893 also deliberately caused by the same interests to help induce Congress to repeal the Sherman silver purchasing act and adopt a gold standard, as has been charged?

Was the panic of 1873 also artificial, caused to compel Congress to pass measures for resumption of specie payments and destruction of the "greenbacks," that they might be replaced by bank note currency yielding regular profits to the banks, as demanded by Wall Street?

Was the panic before the Civil War deliberately caused by high finance in its fierce struggle with President Andrew Jackson over the private central bank of that day?

As each panic in history was coincident with some great contemplated raid by Wall Street upon Congress to obtain legislative privileges and special advantages of priceless value and limitless power, is not panic, planned panic, the one great, invincible and final instrument of torture applied on great occasions by Wall Street to the country in its continuous campaign of conquest?

In a later chapter inside facts about the bank-made panic of 1893 are given. Panics cause privation, poverty, sorrow, suffering, bankruptcy, embezzlement, larceny, suicide and murder. Everybody knows this fact. Therefore, any man deliberately co-operating in acts that he knows will or may cause panic is both morally and legally guilty of causing every crime induced by such panic. If all or any one of past panics was deliberately caused or intensified by Wall Street interests, the most important work ahead for the people of the United States is to either shackle or exterminate the bandits of "high finance." The "Aldrich Plan" would give such bandits power for fifty years to shackle the people and exterminate their business and prosperity. It grants to them by act of Congress a hunger hold over the people, their business and welfare, that in effect will enable the soulless incorporated money power to establish in this country a condition of human slavery as real and more terrible and merciless than the black slavery abolished by Lincoln after the sacrifice of about a million lives; but instead of enslaving a few million negroes, this may plunge permanently into direct or indirect bondage the larger portion of the 94,000,000 inhabitants of the United States, white and black.

CHAPTER XIII.

MONEY IS THE POWER.

Secrets of High Finance Exposed. Steel Trust's $75,000,000 Cash. The Real Money Trust. Heart of the Trust Problem.

"We, the United States Steel Corporation, keep about $75,000,000 on deposit in the banks of the country, which we can shift about where it is needed by our business."

The above is from the published report of the testimony of Judge Elbert H. Gary, executive head of the Steel Trust before the Senate Committee on Interstate Commerce in Washington on December 7, 1911.

Without intending hereby to make any specific charges against Judge Gary or that corporation, we hope to evolve a short, useful hypothetical sermon with the above quotation for a text. Readers may draw their own moral conclusions.

At times, say before dividend periods, no doubt this cash fund is much greater, perhaps double, $150,000,000 or more.

Remember, this is not "bank credit," or "deposits" merely offsetting "loans." It is cold cash. As such, when deposited, it instantly becomes part of the cash reserves of the favored banks. Such banks under the law, on the average, are permitted to inflate their ordinary loans of "credit" an amount aggregating about ten times such increase in cash reserves.

In "reserve cities" banks must keep a cash reserve on hand equal to 25 per cent of their "deposits"; in other places 15 per cent. But three-fifths of the 15 per cent can be kept in reserve city banks and therefore is twice used as the basis of credit loans. This is the reason the volume of loans of all the banks happens to aggregate at least ten times the total money in their cash reserves. Ninety per cent of all bank deposits are mere checks or discounted notes, not actual money.

In other words, the Steel Trust, by depositing seventy-five million dollars cash in banks, substantially enables such banks immediately to swell their loans of "credit," and to collect interest on about three-quarters of a billion dollars extra without investment by the banks of one additional dollar.

Likewise, if the Steel Trust suddenly should withdraw the $75,000,000 from the banks it would force such banks immediately to contract their total "loans" three-fourths of a billion dollars—that is, require borrowers from banks to pay up loans aggregating $750,000,000—and the banks would lose the chance to get 6 per cent per annum, or other going rate on that vast sum.

There will be some reduction of these figures (not more than say 25 per cent) if the money should be deposited in banks in "reserve cities" where a cash reserve equal to 25 per cent of total deposits is required. These figures in relative proportion and size are substantially correct, but any ultra-captious critic is welcome to reduce the figures 50 per cent and still we will have the same grave dangers modified slightly only in degree.

Bank Inflation and Huge Profits.

According to the United States comptroller's report of December 4, 1911, the 24,392 reporting national and state banks and trust companies of the United States on June 7, 1911, all combined owned and possessed just $1,554,147,-169.28 of money, in round figures a billion and a half in cash. With only this amount of cash in their reserves to use for all purposes the banks and trust companies have piled up liabilities that total the enormous sum of $23,-631,083,382.67, more than twenty-three and one-half billions of dollars, the larger portion of which represents loans of credit, on which they get regular interest and which costs the banks relatively nothing. It is similar to getting pay for indorsing another man's note. In other words, they have fifteen times more liabilities than cash.

All that a bank really owns net is its capital, surplus and undivided profits. The balance of its assets merely represent and offset its debts or liabilities made in buying such extra assets. So to be fair, we should take the combined capital stock, $1,952,411,085.56, and the combined surplus and undivided profits, $2,065,574,839.70, add them and we find all banks and trust companies have combined net assets amounting to $4,017,985,925.26, a little over four billion

dollars. And over half of this is excess profits earned over and above profits paid out as dividends.

According to the United States comptroller's said report, the total net earnings of all the national banks in 42 years is $3,107,185,441; practically equal to the $3,214,000,000 that represents the total money in circulation, all the gold and currency of the United States in the hands of the people, banks and federal treasury. And such national banks have actually paid out as dividends $2,236,815,679. While some national banks earn 20, 30, 50 and even 100 per cent, the average earnings of all, last year, exceeded 15 per cent on their capital stock, and their dividends averaged 11.38 per cent. And yet they are not satisfied and now seek to have Congress vastly increase their profits by law.

In 1907 there were only 418,057 stockholders of national banks, including duplications. So most of the vast profits go to a few persons. The bulk of the profit was made by relatively few of these stockholders and in recent years, because while now there are 7,331 national banks, more than half of them were organized since 1900; and since that date 3,086 small banks with average capital of $26,060 and aggregate capital of $80,425,500 have been organized. Just one New York bank, The National City Bank, has $25,000,000 capital and $27,733,860 surplus and undivided profits, total $52,733,860; and under the Aldrich plan this one Wall Street bank will own nearly one-third as much National Reserve Association stock as these entire 3,086 (of the total 7,331) national banks scattered in every state.

Returning now to the summary of all banks and trust companies, deduct $4,017,985,925.26, their combined net assets (capital, surplus and undivided profits) from their $23,631,083,382.67 of total liabilities and we have $19,613,097,457.41 as the total amount they owe in excess of what they own net. And this nineteen and one-half billion dollars of excess liabilities is twelve and one-half times as much as the billion and one-half cash they possess. So the basis herein used of ten times as much credit liabilities as they have in cash was far below the average. And these figures are from the official Government report available without cost for everyone on request to the United States Comptroller of the Currency, Washington, D. C., his December 4, 1911, report, or through a congressman or senator.

This inflation of credit out of all proportion to cash reserves is the danger point in the banking system. It has been getting worse and worse, banks taking greater chances grabbing for more profits. Banks loan their credit usually for thirty, sixty or ninety days, and can not require payment until the time matures and the discounted note falls due. Usually banks do not loan actual money. They give borrower a bank book with the proceeds of the discounted note entered therein as a checkable credit. He then is a "depositor" and his "credit" is payable "on demand" and can all be at once checked out. This seldom is done and the bank profits accordingly. But to be in debt $19,000,000,000 or even $15,000,000,000, most of it in shape of credit "deposits" payable "on demand," and to have all combined only $1,500,000,000 cash to pay with if the avalanche starts, would get on the nerves of an ordinary mortal.

Whether the fact that most of the money belongs to and is risked by the stockholders and the people, and relatively little by the men actually managing the institutions on salaries and sometimes "indirect" profits, acts as a nerve tonic, and perhaps often as a daring narcotic, bankers can best answer.

It is a serious defect in a banking system that puts most of the power and profits in the hands of those who will lose the least by any calamity. The people who have deposited actual cash savings and business men whose loans unexpectedly are called in are the greatest sufferers when panic occurs. The banker can get "his" out quick, if he has any in. To borrowers he can shrug his shoulders and say, "Very sorry, sir, but the panic is the work of Providence. Business is business. Go sell your property for any price you can get. We must have our money." The bank loaned the business man $10,000 *credit* and no *cash*. He sent checks right and left to pay bills for goods in stock and unsold. Now the bank instead of renewing as expected, demands $10,000 in *actual money* to settle a debt that was for credit. And at a time when two or three dollars of property must be sold to get one dollar of cash. And the humble depositor whose deposit was not *credit* but actual *cash* may be told that he must wait for his money, perhaps thirty days, and take the intervening risks. In the 1907 panic most big banks were legally insolvent, refused to pay deposits in cash, repudiated. They were saved only by the patience and good nature of the people. And now, in return, they swell up with lordly air and join Wall Street

BIG BANKER.

RETURNS EVIL FOR GOOD.

This banker REPUDIATED during the 1907 Panic. His bank became legally insolvent by refusing to pay in cash on request its demand obligations. Only the patience and generosity of its depositors—the people—saved it from permanent bankruptcy and ruin.

In return, this big banker now swells with lordly arrogance, claims to be the "whole thing" in America, and has joined the great Wall Street-Bank conspiracy to rob the people and their government of all control over the issuance and volume of the public currency for fifty years.

in a conspiracy to take away from the people and the Government for nothing, just appropriate by act of Congress, $1,000,000,000 of public currency, money, to put in their vaults as "cash reserves" to enable banks to increase their loans and make the people pay regular interest on $10,000,-000,000 more credit that they might not need if the banks would allow Congress to increase Government currency so more business could be done on a cash basis.

Owners of Cash Rule All Banks.

Returning now to the steel trusts $75,000,000,000 of cash. If the banks had made the $750,000,000 of extra loans, based on this $75,000,000 of money, payable in say thirty, sixty or ninety days, and the steel trust suddenly should exercise its legal rights by demanding immediate payment in money of its $75,000,000 of cash deposits that are payable "on demand," the banks might be utterly helpless and fail and close their doors unless they could get other banks to come to their rescue and save them from ruin. And a bank thus asking for help to save its life often must give control of its stock to the interests furnishing such "help."

And if the banks thus were forced to close and liquidate, the losses to small depositors who had put in actual cash savings and had no timely warning would be a real calamity.

Take a single country bank for example—say its capital stock and surplus (all that it really owns net) is $200,000, its total "deposits" say $2,000,000, 10 per cent "cash deposits" and 90 per cent "credit deposits." Suppose a man should deposit $200,000 additional cash in that bank. Perhaps he would be paid interest thereon at 2 per cent or 4 per cent per annum. The bank could, based on such $200,-000 cash deposit, swell its loans of "credit," and its nominal "deposits" two million ($2,000,000) dollars, making its totals "loans" and "deposits" $4,000,000. On such extra $2,000,000 of loans it would collect interest at perhaps 5 per cent or 6 per cent per annum. The $200,000 cash deposit enables the bank practically to double its "loans," its "deposits" and its income. And obviously the owner of that $200,000 has power any time simply by withdrawing the money to decrease the total "loans" and "deposits" of the bank one-half, or $2,000,000, and to take away at least 50 per cent of the earning power of such bank. These figures are strictly accurate, and will be varied only in localities or in degree, according as a bank may keep relatively a greater or less cash reserve.

The $75,000,000 cash divided and deposited in the 3,086 smaller banks that have $80,425,500 aggregate capital would practically double the loaning power and profits of them all. This accomplished, and the aggregate loans of such banks expanded say $750,000,000, put out for thirty, sixty and ninety days, every bank would be in the absolute power of the owner of that $75,000,000 cash on deposit payable on demand. Is there any action political or otherwise in any or all of those 3,086 cities and hamlets in every part of the country that the owner of that $75,000,000 could not get for the mere asking? Could there be a greater or more dangerous political machine? It is the power to control the actual cash that is the evil, the danger.

Suppose, now, that the real object in depositing that $200,000 cash in that bank was ultimately to acquire actual ownership of a majority of the shares of the capital stock of such bank—say $101,000 thereof. How could the bank safely refuse to induce its stockholders to part with 51 per cent of their stock holdings, even if the price offered was low, if the alternative was the possible sudden withdrawal of the $200,000 cash deposit and forced contraction of loans $2,000,000, and possibly the closing of the banks' doors because it might be unable to collect in its loans fast enough? Often in such cases no threat or demand for stock control is necessary. The mere intimation that "tomorrow" the owner probably will withdraw the $200,000, "because he will need it to invest in some securities" he thinks of buying, is sufficient to make the bank suggest and finally to beg that he invest in the stock of such bank, instead of something else, which he permits himself to be "persuaded" to do in case enough stock to control the bank is turned over to him. And of course he gets control.

Control of more than one great financial institution in New York City and elsewhere, containing millions upon millions of the deposit savings of the people have been obtained by big business in this or other questionable ways, or in the midst of "runs" or "panics" deliberately caused or stimulated by "high finance" adventures for sinister purposes.

Again, suppose what the owner of this $200,000 rapid fire cash gun is "gunning for" is control of some big local industry, situated in the small town where such bank is located, such industry being a successful and troublesome competitor of a big trust. It is easily discovered that the industry is a large borrower at the local bank, necessarily so at times to carry an adequate supply of suitable raw materials and large quantities of finished product up to marketing time, and the accounts of customers until due.

Gradually and secretly the net is spread. The $200,000 is deposited in the bank, not by the trust, but in the name of some individual or several persons. The bank is thus encouraged to expand the volume of its loans. The industry in question being perfectly solvent and sound is persuaded by the bank to borrow greater sums, which it does to effect a saving by larger purchases of raw materials.

All now is ready. The trap is sprung. The money suddenly or gradually is withdrawn from the bank under one pretext or another. The bank hastily presses for the repayment of its loans. The local industry is importuned to help. It turns over its cash balance. It crowds its customers, urging, begging, demanding payment. These proceeds are handed over to the bank. But the amount relatively is insignificant. The bank demands, even threatens. It can do nothing else, and comply with the cash reserve law. The industry slaughters prices and sells large quantities of its products at a loss. It reduces expenses by "laying off" large numbers of its workmen, although the market demand would justify an increase rather than decrease of output. It discharges some of its office help and traveling men, and even reduces the salaries of its officers and managers. Every dollar the bank insists on having, for a bank in distress usually thinks only of itself.

All this is done quietly, even secretly, the public knows nothing of it. If it did, local depositors might take alarm, withdraw more deposits and increase the peril of the bank. There is no "panic," no "hard times;" in fact there is general prosperity. This transaction has nothing to do with "general conditions." It is just a quiet little game of "freeze-out" and the bank and the industry do not even know they are sitting in a "game." They think "Providence" is the architect of their misfortunes. Superstitiously, they consider themselves the victims of fate.

But the trust and the manipulators of that $200,000 know differently.

At the "psychological moment," the darkest hour, some entirely different party just casually "happens" to ask one

of the officers of the industry if any of its capital stock is
for sale, or could be bought at a reasonable price. Or perhaps the inquiry is made of the distressed local banker.

Wonder of wonders! The miracle of the ravens dropping manna from the sky to save the life of the famishing
prophet of old lost in the wilderness was nothing compared
with this modern miracle.

A chance to sell out for real money, and the buyer does
not even know the financial hole the industry is in!

The rest is simple and easy. The bank, for its own benefit, helps induce the stockholders of the industry to accept
a low price and part with control or all of the stock. And
lo and behold! The bank is saved, the former owners of
the industry fleeced or ruined, and another competitor has
been "benevolently assassinated" by the trust in the interest
of "co-operation" and "the logical and inevitable development of natural and immutable economic laws!"

Bosh! It was just a common, low-down bunco game.
And the present banking methods, and control and use by
the selfish few of a dangerous quantity of the actual money
of the country, were the agencies employed. Or, more
likely, the pinched and terrified officers of the local industry, perhaps under pressure from the bank, themselves rush
to the trust with an offer to sell out, and the trust kindly
consents to buy, of course, "against its interest and desire," solely for the benefit of suffering humanity and to
prevent the possible spread of public fear and alarm that
might perhaps cause failures and general panic, or what
not. Oh, fiddlesticks!

The real trust problem is not merely high prices and a
way to lower them a little, but it is to regulate or destroy
trust power over money and banks and railroads and politics, that deadly conspiracy of all the interests of Wall
Street for mutual power and profit. If we must have
monopolies the law should effectively and permanently deprive and take away from such corporations every extra
profit, power and advantage obtained by use of the power
conferred by monopoly. And should not all excess profits
due to monopoly be confiscated by law and be returned to
the people through the Federal Treasury?

Once more, suppose the owner of the $200,000 wanted
to borrow, say $2,000,000 for himself and associates in some
stock market "secret pool," organized like the "Hocking
Railroad Pool," to manipulate up and down 50 per cent

the entire stock of some particular corporation. Say, artificially to force the stock up to twice its value, unload at the top and after "selling short," knock the props from under the market by withdrawing "pool support," profiting again by letting the quotation prices go to smash, the public as usual being caught both ways and left to "hold the bag."

He proceeds by putting the $200,000 cash in the bank. The bank under the law then can increase its "loans" about two million dollars. The man is to get the backing of the bank, and the use of its "credit" in the shape of ordinary "loans" for $2,000,000, in his stock market campaign, and the bank will get 6 per cent, or perhaps only 2 per cent, on $2,000,000 of extra "loans," less say 2 per cent or 4 per cent the bank will pay on the $200,000 cash deposit. No doubt the man and the bank between them can devise a way to get the entire $2,000,000 into the hands of the "pool" by loans to various of its members, or to their office boys or colored porters as "dummies," or otherwise. For there are forty ways to "skin a skunk" when black fur brings high enough prices.

The utter fallacy of the old saying, "A man cannot lift himself over the fence by his own bootstraps," may begin to dawn upon the reader as we study the bank methods of inflation of "credit,"—or financial wind. "Wind" is cheaper than "water," so banks just pump "wind" into their holdings. And the secret of the enormous profits and rapid rise in stock value enjoyed by many banks now can be better understood.

If all this could be accomplished, or only a fraction of these things, by use of a paltry $200,000 of cash, what is impossible to those possessing $75,000,000 or perhaps $750,000,000 of actual money ever ready for instant use, and which can be "shifted about to further their business."

We are not saying the trust would do it. Our present purpose is to show the *power* to do so. The people must judge as to the safety or danger of lodging such unlimited, unrestrained and unregulated power in private hands.

Is it not mere child's play to put the quotation price of the $508,302,500 of steel trust common stock up to 70, or any other price, so long as the trust with its $75,000,000 cash can increase the loaning power of the banks enough to supply sufficient credit to the pool sustaining that stock to buy every share in existence? What chance has any one trying to "buck" such an omnipotent financial power?

Power of the Money Combine.

So far we have shown but a fraction of the evil, the danger. We must multiply the $75,000,000 of the steel trust by the cash controlled by every trust, railroad, insurance company, bank, trust company or other corporation directly or indirectly dominated by the small group of men in Wall Street, who usually act as a unit for mutual profit and private advantage.

The Northern Pacific Railroad alone has over $60,000,-000 cash or cash assets, the Tobacco Trust $20,000,000, Express companies $70,000,000, or nearly as much as the Steel Trust, and every other system a greater or less sum. Three of the many Wall Street banks have on hand nearly $300,-000,000 of actual cash. They have three-fourths of a billion dollars of resources. And they control directly or indirectly other banks with vastly greater resources.

The Standard Oil interests are said to directly or indirectly control many times as much ready cash as the $75,-000,000 of the Steel Trust. And two or three Wall Street firms are believed to be in position to command when needed, to be "shifted about to further the business" of the money combine, unlimited portions of the billions of dollars of ready wealth said to be owned by the four European branches of the great banking Rothschild family, and other individual and corporate foreign capital in unlimited amounts.

Those who control the depositing and disposition of the vast cash funds of corporations have within their reach rich and sure opportunities for personal profit. They are in position often to swap favors with the banks. It is not their own money, but that makes no difference. Money is power, and control of large money is both power and opportunity.

Directly or indirectly, this one financial Wall Street group is believed thus absolutely to control much more than half and perhaps a sum equal to all, of the $1,500,-000,000 comprising the total cash reserves of all of the 24,392 banks and trust companies of the United States. If this be true, that group has power, simply by withdrawing this money from banks, to easily and quickly force the financial institutions to contract by calling in and canceling more than one-half if not all of their entire $15,000,000,000 or more of outstanding loans. By thus extinguishing or forcing the banks to require the repayment of at least $8,000,000,000 of bank loans made to industrial, mercantile, commercial and other business borrowers, an amount nearly three times the total of all money actually in circulation in this country, those few men could if they would thus deprive the financial institutions of at least half if not all of their entire gross income, plunge such institutions into grave peril if not into bankruptcy, cripple if not ruin a large per cent of active business men and corporations, close factories, mills and mines wholesale, cramp the operations of agriculture, drive millions of toilers into idleness and their helpless dependents into distress and poverty, and in fact to easily inaugurate the greatest and most devastating financial and industrial panic in the world's history.

These few men possess absolutely the power of life and death over every bank and through the banks over the business of every individual and corporation in the United States, because they control the money, the life blood of all business and the source of the credit oxygen necessary to the lungs of commerce to sustain its life and vitality. If the country enjoys prosperity, it is because these few men grant it and have loosened their purse strings. If the Republic is plunged into the horrors of panic it is because these few men so willed and have locked their guarded steel vaults with much of the needed cash of the nation on the inside.

Think of the nation-wide and powerful political machine this creates! Wall Street turns the switch and the current, its order, flashes over the wires to a distant bank. The bank tightens the screws on its customers by calling loans or threatening to do so, of course "as a matter of prudence for the safety of the bank, made necessary by fear of a possible panic if Congress does not quickly pass the Aldrich plan," etc., etc. Thus the bank's customers, all influential constituents of the local congressman, are "sicked onto" the representative and the senators until they are made to believe that the measure is popular and a great public necessity, and against their better judgment reluctantly they join those supporting the scheme in Congress. Wall Street from the first realized that its only possible chance of passing the bill was to so tempt and enlist or coerce the banks of the country that they would go to the limit in helping to force the congressmen of both parties to support the measure as "a non-partisan affair" under pressure of constituents inspired to action by the local banks. It has been charged that the panic of 1893, which also came suddenly in the midst of general prosperity, was largely caused or accelerated in just this way, the object being to stop the Government issuing more silver money in particular and more money of any kind in general, because the banks desired for profit to supply all of the money as well as the credit that the people use.

There are, as we have seen, different and equally effective ways to control a bank and its actions other than by owning a majority of its capital stock. And also to control the making of its loans and the purchasing of securities and even the political actions of its officers, directors and customers. It has been said that interests friendly or affiliated with Standard Oil long maintained a cash deposit sufficient to increase by over $1,000,000 the loaning power of a certain financial institution outside of New York City of which institution a well known and very high public official is an officer. How could that public servant oppose the "special interests" even under his oath of office?

As the curtain now is drawn back, we behold the majestic and imperial power of Wall Street, and the easy and invincible methods of employing that power for the ever increasing enrichment of the few at the expense of the many by the great Masters of Finance! We discover just how the rapid concentration of banking capital and control and the consolidation of industries and railroads can be forced. We find the banking system willing or unwilling slaves chained to the wheels of the Wall Street machine, helpless to resist and afraid to protest. And through the banks Wall Street has a strong, strangling rope around the neck of every borrowing individual and corporation in the United States. It is the physical control over the actual money that is the power. For actual cash is and must be the foundation upon which rests that vast inverted and inflated pyramid of bank "credit" that is at least ten times larger than the volume of money. Many of the evils of the present system are directly caused by improper state and federal banking laws, particularly as to bank reserves.

When now the combined wealth of just two living Americans, if turned into cash and withdrawn from the banks and hoarded, would rob every bank and trust company in the country of practically all their cash reserves and force them to call in most, if not all, of the fifteen or more billion

dollars of credit loans legally resting on such cash reserves, the power of such men will be understood and we may well be gravely concerned about the future, as this concentration continues at compound ratio.

The banks in the country have a greater need of legislation to remove the possibility and danger of frequent "silent raids" on the cash reserve of the banks by powerful manipulating "special interests" than to protect against infrequent panic-inspired "runs" by small depositors, for usually the "runs" are only the effect of the panic which the "raids" cause. If the causes of panics are removed, the effects automatically will disappear. In the panic of 1907, the first important withdrawals and the major part of all of the cash taken out of menaced trust companies was owned or controlled by the big interests of Wall Street. And it was such withdrawals by these very interests in 1907 that caused or helped to cause or stimulate that dangerous and far-reaching panic that involved the whole country and all its business, and was only stopped when, at the earnest pleadings of Wall Street, the vaults of the Federal Treasury were opened and millions upon millions of public money was dumped into the financial institutions of New York City as an advertized bluff to quiet the general alarm and restore confidence in the banks.

Money is power, control of money. Growth of this power must be checked now or never, and there is no time to be lost. Law, backed by the strong arm of the Federal Government, supported by the popular will, is the only force that can resist, regulate and effectively control the overswollen power of money.

Will all this insane lust for profit and power end in general confiscation as the one alternative to financial, industrial and political serfdom to some one uncontrolled, irresponsible, insatiable, imperious, man-master, who has all power and no responsibility, and whose only virtue is that he has "got the coin"? All lovers of orderly government hope not. Will the "interests" madly drive on over the cliffs to destruction?

If the banks dared to do so, instead of joining with Wall Street in a private central bank conspiracy to help corner every other dollar of real money not already controlled by "high finance," such banks would be on their knees in fervent prayer to Congress to rescue the financial institutions from the greedy and every tightening grip of Wall

Street. The one remaining chance of salvation for the banks and the business interests dependent in any way upon the banks is the creation of an independent financial power bigger and stronger than Wall Street and its allies, a Government central bank or institution absolutely owned and controlled by the Federal Government, to supply banks direct and the people through the banks an adequate quantity of public currency to keep the cash reserves up to standard and thus maintain an ample volume of bank "credit" based on such reserves always available and ready at reasonable cost and on fair conditions for the legitimate and fluctuating needs of business. This done, the $75,000,000 or the $750,000,000 can be withdrawn from banks if Wall Street and its foreign allies so desire. It will do no harm because as fast as it is withdrawn its place will be taken by Government currency supplied on fair and reasonable terms by such public institution issuing the currency. This plan absolutely protects the banks and the entire business community, takes all excessive and dangerous power away from Wall Street, makes future panics impossible, and does not harm or endanger the banks, the Government or the people. And this or some similar plan is the only way of escape for the people and the country from present evils and dangers. Wall Street then would not withdraw its funds because it could gain no advantage by so doing. The banks will find the Government, the people, a better friend and a more generous and safe master than Wall Street. Their rights and privileges will be clearly defined and enforced by law, and not left subject to the greedy will and pleasure of interests that will promise and not perform, help only that they may the better rule and exploit. The welfare of the banks and the people are or should be mutual, and Wall Street is the deadly enemy of both.

The sharp claws of "high finance" can be clipped in no other way. It is the only way to emancipate the banks, individual and corporate business, the people and the Government from the intolerable and increasing financial despotism of Wall Street.

CHAPTER XIV.

THE SLAVERY OF DEBT.

Mortgage on Human Race 39 Billions.

The official mortgage on the human race now is $39,-343,079,476. That is the bonded debt of all nations. It is nearly 10 per cent of the wealth of all the countries on the globe. It is about $22.00 per head for every man, woman and child in all Christendom. The aggregate interest on this world's debt is approximately $2,300,000,000.

Since Columbus plucked the American continent from the unknown in 1492, down to date, the whole world has produced for all purposes $12,935,042,800 of gold and $13,-214,956,600 of silver. If every dollar of this gold and silver output of the entire earth for the last four hundred years was applied upon the principal of the world's debt there would remain unpaid $13,193,080,076, a sum exceeding half the value of all the precious metals mined since 1492.

Portions of these debts are constantly falling due by maturity. The issues are refunded over and over. Every year, on the average, the total debt is increased, the debt burden on the human race is made heavier. In 1908 all nations expended $10,177,280,993 for all purposes and raised from all sources $9,969,519,433. The deficit was $207,761,560. This was borrowed and swelled by that amount the principal of the world's mortgage debt, and the yearly interest proportionately. Thus interest compounds and humanity constantly sinks deeper and deeper into the quicksands of hopeless debt.

If one-tenth of the world's debt falls due each year it would require $3,900,000,000 annually to meet payments on principal and $2,300,000,000 to pay the yearly interest, a total of $6,200,000,000. This is double the total of all money of the United States. The interest must be paid, but the principal falling due usually can be extended, re-

WORLD'S BONDED DEBT
CONSTANTLY INCREASING.

funded, if the owners of the bonds consent, and on the terms and conditions which they dictate.

The Gold "Joker."

Practically every dollar, principal and interest, is payable in gold coin. The entire stock of gold for all purposes held by all the nations, 46 of them, aggregates $6,604,-100,000. This would pay just one year's interest and one installment of 10 per cent on principal and leave $204,-000,000. If we use this $204,000,000 on next year's payments, principal and interest, of $6,200,000,000, where will we get the other six billion dollars of gold with which to meet our payments? There is only one place to get it because last year the owners of the bonds got all there was in the world except the two hundred million balance. We must buy it of the money changers at whatever price they may exact. Now, Shylock may not actually demand and cut out the pound of flesh next to the heart and carry it away this year, or next, or the next. But when he demanded such condition in the bond he showed that he had the disposition that sometime will cause him to take advantage to use the power he undoubtedly has, and augment his profits by tightening the screws on all humanity.

The above computation is based on the assumption that the whole $6,604,000,000 comprising the world's stock of gold is available for such use. The fact is the larger portion of all gold is hoarded by the different governments and could not be obtained for any purpose or at any price. There probably is little more than one billion dollars of actual gold free for ready current use, or not enough to meet half of one year's interest, not mentioning principal.

Providence is coming to the rescue of the race, but not fast enough to overtake the usurers. The gold output of the world has doubled in recent years. In 1908 the world produced $441,932,000 of gold; $113,996,000 was used in the arts, leaving $327,936,000 for monetary purposes. It took two-thirds of this to meet the deficits of governments of that year. Hunting for gold is precarious, hazardous. No one can see into the ground. It is a big gamble. "Gold is where you find it," is the old saying. If you get it today, it may "pinch out" tomorrow. No one positively knows but what this year will practically exhaust the available gold ore and the gold output fall to nothing after that. Probably it will not, but it is a possibility. Yet all principal nations have been cajoled or driven to take the plunge, the giddy gamble, and we have made 39 billion dollars of Government debts payable at a future time in a commodity that may not exist in any available form when that time arrives.

We are not complaining, nor advocating abandonment of the gold standard, nor a law prohibiting the making of contracts payable in gold coin. We'll cross that bridge when we get to it. We are in a boat easier to get into than to get out of. We'll probably have to stay in it, and do the rowing for the owner of the boat, even if he keeps piling a bigger and heavier load on the craft. We are only speaking plainly now so that the facts may be known and understood clearly as we prepare to work harder to earn more to meet the increasing burden we are sure to have to bear because voluntarily we have given the usurers the legal right to increase our financial burdens for their profit.

The great international battle of the future may not be with guns or tariffs. It will be a huge and fierce struggle between the giant governments for physical possession of the relatively small quantity of available gold, that they may be in position to comply with the possible demand of the usurers for gold payments in some future national crisis when financial panic or actual war has made the opportunity by reducing the Government to a condition of helplessness so that it cannot resist or refuse the demand. It is imperative, more now than ever, that the Government of the United States keep absolute and exclusive control over its monetary system and every branch thereof. If it surrenders this power to the usurers it is lost, it will commit financial if not political suicide.

We cannot refrain from asking another question in passing. Suppose after March 14, 1900, the date on which Congress passed the gold standard act, the output of gold had fallen off half instead of doubled, what would have measured in property and labor? The President and the been the result? The promoters of the gold standard internationally expected that the production of gold would decline, and it is almost a miracle that it went the other way. If it had fallen off half, would not the value of all property and labor have fallen 50 per cent in value? Would not gold and bonds payable in gold have doubled in value, financiers have publicly attributed the advance in prices to the increase in the output of gold. If this be true, it must also be true that if the gold output had fallen off instead of increased the prices of everything else would have gone down proportionately. So we have put ourselves where we can only bet on the mysterious and uncertain future gold supply, trusting the Lord and "hoping for the best." What a pickle that is for the whole human race to be in!

The world will find a way out of the hole if the hole ever gets hot enough, but meantime we must expect that the usurers will get away with most of our belongings before the race gets mad enough to climb out of the hole and throw the Shylocks into it.

This is not an argument for free coinage of silver. That might have relieved a little or postponed the inevitable day of settlement slightly, but it was not the remedy. We now have the gold standard and must adjust ourselves to the inevitable and govern ourselves accordingly.

So far but half the tale has been told. Only government

debts have been mentioned. While the interest-bearing
United States bonded debt on October 31, 1911, was $963,-
349,390, the debt of all states, cities, counties and school districts is more than double that amount. In 1906 the aggregate debt of the states was $234,314,190 and of counties,
cities and districts $1,629,881,636, total $1,864,195,826. In
fact, New York City alone has a debt that is crowding the
national debt in size. It is $750,245,583.

It is possible that debts of this kind in different countries at least will equal the aggregate debts of all governments. If so, the total of all public debts would be 78
billions of dollars, or 20 per cent of all the wealth of the
world. And the rates of interest on municipal debts average much higher. Compound interest that owners cannot
spend may in one generation increase the debt to nearly
50 per cent of the world's wealth.

Then we must add the vast issues of corporation bonds,
also payable in gold, with interest rates averaging at least
50 per cent higher than on Government bonds.

Every share of stock is a title deed of ownership of an
interest in the corporate property; every bond is a mortgage on such corporate property.

The railroads alone of the United States in 1910 had a
bonded debt of $9,600,634,906, and an unfunded debt of
$269,887,378, a total about equal to one-fourth of the aggre-
gate Government debts of all the countries in the world.
In 1900 the railroad debt was only $5,758,592,754. In
ten years railroad mileage increased 25 per cent, but the
bonded debt was swelled 66 per cent. From 1900 to 1910
railroad capitalization (stock and bonds) increased from
$11,517,185,508 to $17,981,454,096, or 56 per cent. The big
trusts have billions upon billions of bonds outstanding. The
street railways, telephone, electric light, gas, telegraph and
hundreds of other kinds of corporate enterprises have
bonded debts that approximate if they do not exceed the
entire actual cash investment, the stock being largely fictitious. If such bonds in all countries were totalized and
added to the Government, state, city, county and school-
bonds the grand total might reach 150 billion dollars, or
about 50 per cent of the wealth of the world.

Bonds we believe are included in the inventory of the
world's wealth. If bonds now do, or soon will, equal half
of the world's wealth, then all the wealth other than bonds
of the entire human race already is mortgaged to the

usurers for 100 per cent of its value, and the debt is all payable in gold!

But assuming 100 billions as a conservative estimate, the yearly interest that must be paid by the peoples of the world on bonds will exceed five billions of dollars, or five-sixths of all the gold in the hands of all nations, available and unavailable. This would make the debt $60.00 for every human being on the globe. Leaving out the Orient, the debt would be nearly $100.00 per capita.

Every dollar of this awful tax directly or indirectly must come out of the people, out of those who toil, those least able to bear the burden. If raised by tariff, tax on corporations, personal property, real estate or otherwise, it usually is passed along and saddled upon producers. The adjustment is made by raising rents, transportation charges, prices of food and clothing. Capital knows the game, but labor does not, and cannot dodge the blow.

And everybody who does anything with head and hands, who owns any kind of securities or property other than gold bonds is here included among the producers and must help pay this ever-increasing mortgage interest burden. And to get a sufficient income from their modest fortune most people must invest in securities yielding larger income than Government bonds, and in property and factories, all of which is mortgaged to the great international individual and incorporated usurers who have billions night and day yielding compound interest. At the present rate of progress it will be only a matter of time, and relatively a short time, when one man or one family will own and rule the entire earth and all the people on it.

In the broad sense, the frightful load of the cost of royalty, vast standing armies, huge navies, excessive transportation charges, monopoly prices, and a thousand other big and little profits and grafts all rests upon the calloused and jaded back of helpless human labor. And all this is borne chiefly for the sake of yielding $5,000,000,000 of annual income to a few smug owners of the vast fixed income or bond wealth of the world whose principal labor is cutting coupons and scheming to devise a way to double by law or license their mortgage on the human race without increasing their investment. This they will do by doubling the interest rate as soon as their international money combine is complete and has eliminated all important competition for such bonds. And the National Reserve

Association is to do that very thing here, as similar institutions largely have already done in England, France, Germany and Austria. It is to confederate all American banks and financiers, the individual and incorporated usurers, and be the United States branch of the world-wide money trust.

Debt Slavery.

This is human slavery; slavery of the toiling millions to the usurers, their masters. The interest burden is the lash that forever goads and drives. It is worse than the "black-snake" because it is constantly plyed night as well as daytime. It never stops. It is constant as the flight of time. It is as merciless as fate.

The one object of ordinary involuntary servitude is to get the fruit of other's toil without paying for it. That is the object of interest slavery. The old way was individual, debt enslaves the race wholesale. In ordinary slavery the master is obligated to feed, clothe and preserve the life and health of his human asset. It pays him to do so. The invisible foreign masters who profit from the grinding system of slavery through debt acknowledge no responsibility for the welfare, health or even the lives of their victims. The driven men, women and children all must shift for themselves; they must hustle or starve and die. Ordinary slavery could know just who was responsible for its wrongs, abuses. It could appeal in the name of humanity to the masters direct. As time goes on and the human burden is steadily increased by multiplication of national, state, county, city and district debts, and the seas of corporate debts are funded into oceans of interest bearing gold bonds, and interest rates are compounded and advanced throughout the world, humanity can only feel the pinch as it groans and staggers under the cumulating load. It never can know just how the mysterious game is worked or just who tightens down the screws. It is all so easy, simple, subtle. But it is real, very real, terrible. The pressure is applied on every living soul at the cradle and ends only at the grave. Every child is born with a mortgage on its back that dooms it to life-long toil. Unborn generations are mortgaged into involuntary, life-long, helpless debt slavery years before the Almighty breathes into them the breath of life. Their immortal souls are predestined by the universal debt system to be coined into additional dollars to gratify the insatiable greed and avarice and profit-lust of the usurers.

This is not a new or original system. It is the identical plan always in use in the red-light district of any large city. White slavery would be impossible but for the system of debt slavery that holds the unhappy daughters of the race in its sharp and merciless talons. It is the common practice of every dive keeper cleverly to plunge every new girl quickly into such hopeless debt under one pretext or another that she never can get the debt paid and escape until the deadly pace and life of shame robs her at last of good looks and health, if not of life, then she is kicked out to shift for herself, or die, or become a permanent burden on the community as an object of charity. The great money changers of the world, the few big ones, who really dominate in the finances of all countries, those who shape international monetary systems and policies, have borrowed this simple but effective device from the slums. They are rapidly applying it to the successful and permanent enslavement of the entire human race, white, black, brown, red and yellow, male and female, adults and children, in a universal bondage of hopeless debt.

Warning to American Jews.

Author has no prejudice against the Jewish race. Some of his best friends are Hebrews. He greatly admires many racial traits, the marvelous history of that people and its triumph over obstacles and adverse environment in various countries during the past two thousand years.

And author earnestly hopes that American civilization may ever proceed on the original plan, the Gentile and Jew, protestant and catholic, all enjoying equally and impartially liberty of conscience and equality of opportunity.

But right now action is being taken by certain powerful leaders of the Hebrew race that may start in free America that dreaded European cry "Down with the Jews!" In the hope of helping to avoid the establishing of conditions here that may become for the Hebrew race as unhappy and intolerable as in other countries, even Russia, this word of warning to the Jews is sounded.

Rothschild was a Jew. His descendants comprise the four great banking houses of that name in Europe—in London, Paris, Berlin and Vienna. In 1863 the wealth of this one family was conservatively estimated at $3,200,000,-000, over three billions of dollars. This huge total compounded during the past fifty years and increased by incidental investments in mines, timber and many other things, may now amount to fifty or one hundred billions. No one outside knows the amount. With alliances controlled by this family it surely directly or indirectly controls a large portion of all government bonds and at least one-third of the world's estimated total wealth of $377,000,000,000.

But suppose the Rothschilds themselves only own $39,-000,000,000, an amount equal to the bonded debt of all the governments of the world, with an annual income of $2,300,-000,000 or two-thirds what their total wealth was in 1863. Any change either way in these figures will be a variation only in degree. In no way does it materially change the acknowledged potent fact that in all great national and international monetary and financial affairs the Rothschilds always play the ruling hand. They possess masterful genius and financial intellect. But it is the sheer weight of liquid or ready wealth held in such large quantity that all the nations of the world must go to the Rothschilds for financial assistance in time of peace, or before they can go to war whatever the provocation or emergency, that gives them supreme power in the world's affairs. No war can be waged without money, and no large nation can get adequate money to finance a war from any one but the Rothschilds. Therefore it is reasonable to assume that whenever any war is begun the Rothschilds have consented thereto. They may finance both sides, because it is immaterial whether the interest profits they crave come from one or both countries. In fact the war furnishes an excuse recognized as legitimate for charging both nations higher interest rates not only on the new debts but on old obligations maturing and being refunded. Increase to 4 per cent from 3 per cent is a 25 per cent increase in the total income and in the value of bonds, measured by their earning power.

It is known, of course, that after the nations have fought for a while and murdered tens of thousands and wounded and permanently maimed hundreds of thousands of human beings on both sides, pressure exerted by other governments instigated by the financiers will force a quick compromise, leaving the nations both in approximately the same condition as before except that each has vastly increased its debt and the annual interest burden on its people while the financiers have gotten rid of accumulated capital in exchange for high interest gold bonds that cannot be paid for perhaps thirty or fifty years. This surely is the result if not the deliberate plan.

Then again, the debt of the principal European countries has been doubled or vastly increased during the long period of "armed peace."

Frequent rumors of war or warlike preparations each year have been ping-ponged back and forth between the countries in the public press. These have tended to excite popular fear, hate and patriotism and cause the people to consent and even to urge the governments to swell vastly the mortgage burden upon the peoples for funds to increase and equip still larger standing armies and to build greater and more expensive navies. By withdrawing millions of men into armies and idleness it reduces production and the earning power of the people, increases the burden on those employed, and makes it more certain that existing bonds will not be paid but will be refunded and increased. Why not have bigger armies, navies, forts, guns, idleness of millions of soldiers, rumors of war or even occasional war, when such things are so fruitful, so necessary to cause the issuance of more bonds to provide profitable investment for the $5,000,000,000 of excess income derived yearly from interest paid on existing issues of gold bonds?

These conditions explain at least a substantial portion of the bonded debt and yearly interest of these countries:

Country.	Bonded Debt.	Yearly Interest.
United Kingdom	$3,869,931,360	$152,759,411
British Colonies	699,198,319	29,040,837
British India	1,346,997,187	41,687,212
Russia	4,558,152,565	204,766,421
France	5,898,675,451	186,802,380
German Empire	1,094,790,575	40,856,044
German States	3,175,698,141	132,942,135
Italy	2,602,299,757	96,941,138
Austria Hungary	1,063,795,105	60,467,407
Austria	960,997,758	35,392,309
Hungary	1,146,500,658	37,136,118
Spain	1,817,614,397	78,709,000
Portugal	864,561,212	29,907,983
Belgium	663,325,145	27,022,108
Belgium Congo	20,089,409	1,260,306
Egypt	463,854,243	17,904,885
Greece	157,877,067	5,940,304

Turkey	527,985,636	36,494,817
Netherlands	451,309,208	14,608,371
Canada	323,930,279	11,931,537
Japan	1,287,604,201	76,283,836
China	601,916,605	92,375,017
United States	1,023,801,531	21,803,836

Peaceful and quiet little Netherlands (the home of the dove of peace, the Hague) and Belgium together have a larger debt than the United States, although their aggregate wealth is but $13,000,000,000, as against $125,000,000,000 for this country. Belgium has 7,074,910 population and a debt of $93.77 per capita. Evidently they have been frightened into hopeless, permanent debt by the menacing actions of their neighbors towards each other. Poor exploited Congo, whose ignorant natives do not know a bond from a hole in the ground or interest and the gold standard from the milky way and the Aurora Borealis, has been given a hot dose of the "blessings of Christian civilization" by being saddled with a debt of $20,000,000 on which annually they must pay $1,260,306 interest profits to the exploiters. Unwelcome British rule has imposed upon India a yoke of mortgage debt 40 per cent larger than the total bonded debt of the United States.

Portugal with $2,500,000,000 wealth has a government debt of $864,561,212, or 35 per cent. No wonder it tired of royalty and sought relief as a republic. The tombs of Pharaohs of Egypt now groan under a public debt half that of the United States. China may be the next debt victim.

Is hopeless debt and perpetual interest slavery forever to be the price of Christian civilization and civil liberty?

Large portions of most of these vast bond issues are in the strong boxes of the Rothschilds. No doubt they are satisfied with their clever work in Europe, their manipulation of Governmental policies, their control of state and private finances through great private central banks dominated by them in the principal countries, and their mastery, through the purse, over kings, czars and emperors. They have seen the average government debt of European nations grow until it has become about equal to one-tenth of the entire wealth of those countries.

But they must be sorely disappointed and dissatisfied with the work and progress of their direct personal representatives in the United States. Here we have the richest and most substantial country, the best security, on the globe and the financiers have succeeded in keeping it in debt only about three-fourths of 1 per cent of its $125,000,000,000 of wealth. And worse than that, the Government has kept control of its monetary system and currency supply and so conducted its finances that most of the bonds bear only 2 per cent interest, or 40 to 60 per cent less interest annually than is paid by other governments that have turned monetary control over to the same private interests that buy and own the bonds issued by themselves for the Government to themselves for their individual profit.

Then no doubt they have been worried over another serious problem. Their financial ascendency and control over governments and maintenance of relatively high interest rates is possible only so long as they own or at least control all large loanable funds seeking such investments; only while there is no important competition.

The wonderful natural resources of the United States and the boundless energy of its people has greatly increased the liquid capital of the country. Hundreds of millions of American debts to European investors have been paid off or bought up by Americans. This has tended to increase the supply of idle capital in Europe. And now the United States has invaded Rothschild's exclusive melon patch by bidding for large issues of the new or of refunding bonds of various governments. This is a serious situation. If this competition goes on it is certain to lower the rates of interest not only on new issues but ultimately on the entire 39 billion dollars of present bonds, to say nothing of state, county, city, district and corporation bonds. Genuine competition, such as the United States could furnish with the available investment capital it now commands or soon will have, might easily lower the average bond interest of other governments to the 2 per cent basis enjoyed by our Government. This would cut down by one-half the annual income of the owners of the fixed income or bond wealth of the world. They would lose thereby $2,500,000,000 annually. This in effect would be the equivalent of a direct shrinkage of 50 per cent in the value of the 39 billions of bonds, an immediate loss of nearly 20 billion dollars, for the value of bonds is measured by their rate of interest, the annual income they yield, their earning power.

And we now see the stealthy hand of these foreign bondholders in one of the most clever and far-reaching schemes

ROTHSCHILDS

ROTHSCHILD: FOR BILLIONS A YEAR AS INTEREST ON BONDS, I RENT THE HUMAN RACE THE PRIVILEGE OF EXISTING ON **MY EARTH.** THROUGH THE PRIVATE CENTRAL BANK SCHEME, I'LL SOON GRAB THE UNITED STATES — THEN I'LL **OWN** ALL CHRISTENDOM. CZARS, EMPERORS KINGS AND THE PEOPLE ALL MUST OBEY MY ORDERS, SUBMIT TO MY EXACTIONS, OR **GET OFF MY EARTH!**

ever devised by the mind of man, driving American sentiment and politics rapidly toward the adoption of a plan that will instantly remove the one menace to the supremacy and profits of the Rothschilds, viz.: competition for bonds.

It is believed that the scheme now called "Aldrich plan" was originally conceived and worked out in Europe by the Rothschild interests, and that it was put out here or pushed by Jacob H. Schiff and Paul M. Warburg of the firm of Kuhn, Loeb & Co., said to represent here or do business with the Rothschilds of Europe. It is at least certain that Mr. Schiff of that firm was actively advocating a central bank as far back as 1906, when the New York Chamber of Commerce on October 4, 1906, officially adopted the plan after sending its representatives to Europe for several months to meet and personally discuss the matter with the big financiers of Europe.

The official records of the Chamber, printed elsewhere in this volume, show these facts.

Since then Mr. Warburg has been the most active of the Wall Street financiers in promoting the central bank or National Reserve Association plan by way of articles, speeches, conferences, and in persuading bankers and the American Bankers' Association to join in promoting the scheme through Congress, and in thereafter participating in its benefits. He has been greatly aided from the outset by the Standard Oil interests, officials of the National Bank of Commerce and National City Bank of New York (Mr. Schiff being a director of both of these banks), and affiliated banks in that and other cities and by many of the powerful financiers of Wall Street. We show elsewhere conclusive documentary proof that the Aldrich plan is identical with what we could call the Rothschilds' plan, but have named "New York Chamber of Commerce's first plan," adopted in 1906, except that the original plan at least made a pretense of Government control, while the Aldrich plan is strictly for a private corporation.

At the currency conference of the National Civic Federation in New York on December 16, 1907, Mr. Spyer presided, and Mr. Seligman introduced the prepared resolutions. Both are Hebrew Wall Street international bankers said to do business for or with the great financiers of Europe. August Belmont, who then was president of the National Civic Federation, is said also to represent or do business with the Rothschilds.

Jacob H. Schiff seems to have led the movement that has caused the abrogation of the commercial treaty with Russia. The action taken was right, for obedience to the provisions of all treaties must be enforced. But we wonder if the only object was to punish Russia for denying passports to a mere handful of American Jews?

Was there back of it in Europe a Rothschild scheme to embroil the two nations so that each would increase its bonded debt, sell more bonds, to be prepared for possible complications if not actual hostilities?

Several attempts looking to a vast increase of the bonded debt of the United States have been made, other attempts will be made. But this Government should pay every dollar of its bonded debt and then stay out of debt. It would be a wholesome example to the world. It would show to all nations the advantages of self-government and human liberty.

With the Standard Oil, the Morgan and the Kuhn, Loeb & Co. groups linked by ties of mutual interest and profit with the Rothschilds and their affiliations abroad, there would be complete harmony and co-operation and practically no competition between America and Europe for big government loans. All danger of lowering interest rates has been removed and an effective plan adopted that will enable substantial increases from time to time in the bond interest rate the world over. There will be no adequate market for such bonds except with this international money combine. Truly, the United States proposes to become a "financial world power" by this merger, but it will be controlled from the other side because Europe, the Rothschilds, will furnish 90 per cent of the cash. Wall Street seems to be willing to play second fiddle and permanently sell out the interests of the United States and the welfare of all the people for the mere hope that by thus getting near the money throne of the Rothschilds some crumbs from their table will fall within the reach of our high financiers.

This Rothschild scheme if adopted will ultimately plunge the United States into the slavery of debt like the European nations. They do not want 2 per cent bonds. So it is proposed to increase the interest 30 to 50 per cent, make the rate 3 per cent, refund the present United States debt and make it payable in fifty years. That is the Aldrich plan, the provisions of the pending bill. Then it will be proposed to so change the tariff and increase expenditures that each year will show a deficit that can be converted into long time bonds. No doubt it is expected that in time the mortgage debt of this country will be increased to $2,000,000,-000, or even more, which with interest at 3 per cent instead of 2 per cent would be the equivalent of a bonded debt of $3,000,000,000 so far as the yearly interest burden is concerned.

The only way the human race can get the benefit, or its due because of the rapid increase of the world's wealth, is to have free and unrestricted competition for loans maintained, so that as wealth increases the rate of interest will decrease.

A billion of public currency now is to be taken away from the Government and given outright and free to a private corporation owned by the banks, and ultimately the National Reserve Association is to control the entire three billions of money heretofore issued by the United States Government. The association will gather up the United States money, hold it as a "reserve" and issue thereon two or three times its amount in corporation currency. Then by contraction and expansion of the money supply it will rule every bank and manipulate the supply of $20,000,000,-000 of business credit and all prices and dominate everything in America for the profit of the world-wide money trust of which the National Reserve Association will be the American branch. This is the game, the program. If it succeeds the republic and all its people will find themselves permanently enslaved by the bondage of debt, chained helplessly to a system that takes everything and gives nothing, the victims of a soulless and sordid conspiracy that is moral if not legal treason against the welfare and perhaps the life of the nation.

When this hour comes, and the people find that they have been tricked and betrayed and are helpless, the country may become as inhospitable as Russia to the Hebrew race, if unfortunately the cry goes up "Down with the Jews!"

Many of the American people will believe that the instigators of their troubles and the chief beneficiaries are those greatest of all world-owning Hebrews—the Rothschilds.

It will be to the interest of every American Hebrew outside of Wall Street to have the Aldrich plan defeated, and every loyal citizen of this race will demand that the Government of the Republic retain control of the people's money supply and avoid permanently plunging this great republic into the bondage of hopeless debt.

CHAPTER XV.

NATIONAL BANKING SYSTEM.

Origin—History. Banks Against Government Money. Want Bank Currency. Gold Standard-Free Silver Campaign. Law-Made Bank Profits. Astonishing Political and Legislative Intrigue. Official Record Revealed. Investigation Imperative. Was 1893 Panic Caused by the Banks?

The American Bankers' Association officially representing all banks, by resolution in November, 1911, indorsed and urged Congress to adopt the Aldrich National Reserve Association plan. It is actively helping to promote the scheme. It is alleged to be spending money for that purpose, furnished by the banks. It is said to be helping to create and steer public sentiment through the press or with special literature prepared or distributed by various banks, at the cost of the banks, or to organize or encourage the organization of so-called "citizens'" associations and monetary reform leagues to entice and marshal business men to support this movement. Presumably this united effort and expenditure of money is expected by the banks to yield benefit to the banks.

It is conceded that the bill prepared and advocated by the National Monetary Commission and now pending in Congress would create a mere private corporation named National Reserve Association, and that every share of the stock will be owned and voted by banks. And that as the management of such corporation, or forty-two of the forty-six directors, will be chosen by the banks, the institution will absolutely and permanently be controlled by the banks, the banks exclusively wielding the powers and getting the profits of the National Reserve Association. There will be no dispute as to these facts.

It is proposed that Congress take away from the Government and delegate to such private corporation certain governmental powers heretofore exercised under the Constitution by the Federal Government exclusively. And it would prohibit the Government and everybody except such corporation from hereafter exercising such powers. In other words, it confers an exclusive monopoly by law of Congress upon such private corporation for the sole profit of the banks owning the stock of such corporation. It is a syndicate of banks, a central money trust.

The chief grant is the exclusive right of issuing public currency for use as money by the people. It will thus regulate the volume and supply of the money the people must have as a medium of exchange and to put into bank reserves as a cash basis on which banks loan credit to borrowing customers.

In a collective capacity, acting through their subsidiary corporation, the National Reserve Association, the banks hereafter will manufacture with the printing press their own "cash reserves" on which the huge volume of bank credit is based. What is the use of the banks going to the expense of providing actual cash capital when its central corporation can print and supply currency, money, to the banks without legal restraint or limit? It's all in the bank family. They can do as they please. The Government and the people henceforth are to have nothing to say about the public currency or the quantity to be furnished for their use.

It is also proposed that the Government shall turn over to this corporation as received all money raised for every purpose from any source, amounting to nearly three-fourths of a billion dollars annually and that such corporation shall not pay the Government anything for the use of this vast sum while on deposit. Also, that all disbursements hereafter made by the Government shall be through such corporation. There are many other powers and privileges that the measure would confer upon such corporation beneficial to the owning banks, but the above is sufficient to show that the power and profits of the banks would be enormously increased and their political influence and control over all business vastly augmented if Congress should pass the measure.

Investigate the Banking System.

This makes it wise and highly proper and important that before passing the measure it be definitely ascertained whether the banks and those managing banks have in the past so conducted themselves that it is reasonably safe and wise thus to so greatly increase their profits and powers.

It could hardly be expected that any sane man would favor increasing the power and pay of a trusted employee or trustee clearly shown to have deliberately and repeatedly violated his trust obligation and the laws of the land as well. If it can be clearly shown that the banks have been faithful to their trust, their express and implied obligation to the public, always furthered the interests of the Government in return for the rich, valuable and exclusive privileges and immunities conferred upon them by law, and have rigidly complied with the provisions of their charters and the laws regulating their conduct, then they can come with clean hands asking for the greater benefits and powers proposed. But if it shall appear from undisputed sworn evidence that a large portion of all national banks have been faithless, have ignored their charters and for profit have continuously, knowingly, flagrantly violated the laws of the land, the acts of Congress, have blocked good and promoted bad legislation in their own interest, who would seriously advocate increasing the profits and augmenting a hundred fold the power of these very lawless banks and bankers by putting the National Reserve Association into their hands instead of under the control of the Government?

Origin of National Banking System.

The national banking system originated during the Civil War. It was a war measure. The facts are set forth in detail in "The Origin of the National Banking System" and a "Supplement" thereof issued by the National Monetary Commission.

A careful study of the facts tends to impress the reader that the adoption of that banking system was largely due to the belief by Congress, Secretary of the Treasury Salmon P. Chase and President Lincoln that in order to market Government bonds and get money with which to carry on the war and save the life of the nation it was absolutely necessary to buy co-operation of the bankers and Wall Street financiers with profits. Their patriotism seemed to have been in proportion to the size of the profits they realized at public expense from bond transactions and issuance of currency.

Orlando B. Potter, of New York, on August 19, 1861, in a letter to Secretary Chase first suggested and in detail outlined the national banking system afterwards recommended by Secretary Chase on December 1, 1861 and

BANKERS FIGHT
PRESIDENT LINCOLN

THE UNION MUST BE PRESERVED

WALL BANKER

ORIGIN OF·NATIONAL BANKING·SYSTEM. (1863).

PRESIDENT LINCOLN AND SECRETARY CHASE (1863) YIELD TO THE
CLAMOROUS AND GREEDY BANKERS FIGHTING IN THE REAR
TO SHUT OFF THE GOVERNMENT'S CREDIT AND THUS SELL BONDS
AT RUINOUS PRICES FOR MONEY TO SUSTAIN THE LOYAL ARMY
FIGHTING THE CONFEDERATES AT THE FRONT. THE UNION WAS
SAVED ONLY BY GIVING DOUBLE PROFITS TO WALL STREET AND
THE BANKS.

1862, and later adopted by Congress. One of Mr. Potter's chief arguments was: "This would make Government and the capital mutually dependent on each other, and every bank and banker would feel a daily interest in supporting and keeping the Government credit above suspicion." Stating it the other way, they would not support the Government that sheltered and protected their business or do anything to keep its credit above suspicion, even during its life and death struggle, unless they could make a big and steady money profit doing so. Isidor Bush, of St. Louis, a leading German citizen, on December 28, 1861, wrote Secretary Chase favoring his national bank currency plan, saying: "It makes it for the interest of capitalists, of the money power, and of banking institutions to uphold and sustain the credit of the Government. It would increase the common interest for the preservation and safety of the Union."

Silas M. Stillwell, of New York, who at Secretary Chase's request aided in drafting a bill for the purpose, prepared a pamphlet on the subject that was issued in December, 1861, 30,000 copies being printed and circulated by the Treasury Department; and another, called "Explanatory Notes," on January 6, 1862, in which he said: "The object to be obtained by this system of banking is to provide a plan that will create a demand for bonds and thus fund in this way as many demand notes as possible." In other words, convert the Government non-interest bearing "demand notes," or greenbacks, into interest bearing 6 per cent bonds to be deposited by the bankers with the Government in exchange for 90 per cent of bank-note currency to be loaned out by the bankers at 6 to 10 per cent, the bankers getting and keeping this interest for use of the currency and also the 6 per cent on the deposited bonds, a total of 12 to 15 per cent less a currency tax of 1 per cent. That was the price that seems to have been necessary for the people and the Government to pay to insure the loyalty of the bankers and Wall Street financiers at a time when a million patriots were at the front risking their lives in defense of the Union for $13.00 per month in Government money depreciated below 50 cents on the dollar by these same financiers for their own profit.

On February 9, 1862, Enoch F. Carson of Cincinnati wrote Secretary Chase that the people were with him, believing that it was a fight between the Government and the banks, and that Mr. Chase represented the people in the struggle. Secretary Chase on October 7, 1862, in a letter to John Bigelow, expressed the belief that his national bank currency plan would "bring to the support of the public credit the whole banking interest of the country." It would open "a gradually enlarged market for the securities of the Government, and thus sustain their credit at the highest point." Evidently the Government had not been getting the support "of the whole banking interest of the country," but Secretary Chase expected that the big double profits the Government thus was forced to offer the banks, that is 6 per cent on bonds and 6 per cent or more for the currency obtained by deposit of such bonds, would "bring to the support of the public credit the whole banking interest of the country."

December 23, 1862, Secretary Chase wrote Thaddeus Stevens, chairman of the Committee of Ways and Means, saying: "I see no ground for belief that the funds necessary for the pay of the army and the prosecution of the war can be in any way provided without the support to public credit expected from that measure."

The Government of the republic was in a desperate financial hole. Without money the war must fail and the Union be destroyed. The bankers could easily help it out and thus save the nation's life, but would not do it until they got an immediate 12 per cent to 15 per cent profit and a permanent system that has largely supplanted Government currency with bank-note currency, a bank system that in forty-eight years has cleared more than three billion dollars of net profits ($3,107,185,441), over three times the amount of the present Government debt and equal to all the money in circulation in the United States. Surely the bankers drove a good bargain, and each year for over forty years have received millions from the people as a sort of pension to keep the bankers patriotic and from backsliding in their loyalty to the republic. By frequent Congressional intrigues this pension has been steadily increased, until the yearly cost to the people of bank patriotism now in time of peace is about ten times as much as it was in time of war. And under the Aldrich plan reported by the monetary commission, it is now proposed to vastly increase the profits and power of the banks without the slightest benefit to the Government or the people.

Senator Sherman finally came to the aid of Secretary

Chase and the bill, the "Sherman Act" was passed on February 25, 1863, and approved, he declaring that it would "promote a sentiment of nationality," evidently among bankers.

The volume from which the above quotations are made, issued by the monetary commission, says on page 84: "The Senate was the stronghold of the banks. It would have been impossible to have secured the passage of any bill in that body which seemed in any way to be unjust toward state banks." All banks then were state banks, so it must be clear that the provisions of the law creating the national banking system are such as the bankers approved or dictated. This may explain why the law did not contain a single personal penalty on bankers for violating the law as to matters pertaining to the safety of depositors and the general welfare and yet it imposes upon any public official who should countersign and deliver bank notes to any but the right bank a fine not exceeding double the amount of such notes, and imprisonment not exceeding fifteen years!

The Sherman Act of February 25, 1863, "An act to provide a national currency secured by a pledge of United States stock, and to provide for the circulation and redemption thereof," was supplemented by the law of June 3, 1864, entitled "An act to provide a national currency secured by a pledge of United States bonds, and to provide for the circulation and redemption thereof." The new law of course was more liberal to the banks, and practically every change made since has been to increase the immunities, powers and profits of the banks, while every proposal during the past forty-eight years having for its object increasing the soundness of banks or the safety of depositors and the public, has been defeated in Congress by the lobbying of the banks. This was the fate of the recommendations of eleven different U. S. comptrollers of the currency designed to strengthen the national banking system in the interest of depositors and the public. There were about sixteen hundred state banks scattered throughout the country. They were turning out corporation currency as fast as their printing presses could supply it. Most of this was depreciated and much worthless. December 13, 1861, the Chicago Tribune called it "the ragged and doubtful issues of 1,600 corporations." There was about $200,000,000 of this currency. The inconvenience and loss to the people was frightful. There were 10,000 different kinds of bank

notes in circulation. Counterfeiters added enormously to
the volume, danger and losses. All was confusion. Business was more or less paralyzed.

To improve this desperate condition as well as to aid
the Government in carrying on the war Congress by acts of
July 17 and August 5, 1861, authorized the first national
Government currency, money, $50,000,000, of "demand
notes" backed by the Government. These by act of March
17, 1862, were made legal tender for all debts. It was the
best paper money in existence, good everywhere, and never
depreciated but always was equal with gold. The bankers
were furious. They saw that this kind of national currency, Government money that all must accept at par because it was full legal tender, soon would supplant and
drive out of circulation the doubtful or worthless state bank
note currency. So the banks began to fight the Government.
While the confederates were fighting in front with guns
the bankers were fighting behind choking off the Government's credit and supply of money. With an enemy both
sides the Union was doomed. So the Government yielded
to the bankers. It adopted the national banking system as
a means of buying the support of the bankers and to provide a way by which banks could keep the issuing of currency in their private hands and stop the issuance of full
legal tender Government money. The history of bank intrigue and influence in Congress and opposition to the Government during the Civil War is the most sordid and for
the banks the most despicable chapter in American annals.
The bank selfishness shown then has increased with time
and with the enormous growth of bank wealth and power
until in 1912 we see them actually grasping for all power,
for mastery over everything through a private monopoly
of the supply of money.

On March 3, 1865, Congress destroyed all state bank
circulation with a 10 per cent annual tax that remains to
this day. But with destruction of the $200,000,000 of state
bank issues, the national bank note currency grew. In
1864 it was $31,235,270; 1865, $146,406,725; 1866, $281,-
583,365; 1867, $298,759,436. There was not enough bank
note currency before the war ended to do much good. It
was the $450,000,000 of Government money, greenbacks,
that carried the Government through that great struggle,
crippled as they were at the demand of the banks by being
made only a limited legal tender, after the first $60,000,000.

Banks Fight Government Currency.

From 1861 to 1912 the irrepressible and constant aim of the banks has been to prevent the issuance of Government paper money in order to increase bank currency that yields steady profit to the banks. And the present Aldrich National Reserve Association plan is the same fight carried to a most audacious and daring extreme.

Besides the first $50,000,000, an additional $10,000,000 of full legal tender "demand notes" were issued under act of February 12, 1862. The Government was authorized to reissue these as they came back, but not after December 31, 1862. Thirty thousand dollars was so reissued. These "demand notes," or first greenbacks, legal tenders, were paid in gold as presented. They never depreciated.

The act of February 25, 1862, authorized $150,000,000 "United States notes," $50,000,000 thereof to be used to take up and cancel the balance of the $60,000,000 "demand notes" outstanding, and by July 1, 1863, all but $3,350,000 of the $60,000,000 had been paid and cancelled, the balance being retired during the next year.

But the $150,000,000 U. S. notes (greenbacks), at the insistent demand of the financiers and gold gamblers of Wall Street, were not made a full legal tender. They were by law made "legal tender for all debts, public and private, except duties on imports and interest on the public debt." They were thus only a "limited legal tender." This "exception" made them unequal and less valuable than gold because they could not be used wherever gold could. Such exception caused their depreciation as measured in gold. Or in other words it caused appreciation of the price of gold measured in this Government currency.

Specie payments were suspended from January 1, 1862, to January 1, 1879. While at times the gold price of greenbacks went much lower, once to about 35, the average price per year was: 1862, 88.3; 1863, 68.9; 1864, 49.2; 1865, 63.6; 1866, 71; 1867, 72.4; 1868, 71.6; 1869, 75.2; 1870, 87; 1871, 89.5; 1872, 89; 1873, 87.9; 1874, 89.9; 1875, 87; 1876, 89.8; 1877, 95.4; 1878, 99.2. And the yearly average currency prices of gold were: 1862, 113.3; 1863, 145.2; 1864, 203.3; 1865, 157.3; 1866, 140.9; 1867, 138.2; 1868, 139.7; 1869, 133; 1870, 114.9; 1871, 111.7; 1872, 112.4; 1873, 113.8; 1874, 111.2; 1875, 114.9; 1876, 111.5; 1877, 104.8; 1878, 100.8

The act of July 11, 1862, authorized another $150,000,-
000, greenbacks, of which $50,000,000 was used to pay a
"temporary loan," and a third $150,000,000 issue was au-
thorized March 3, 1863, a total of $450,000,000 of green-
backs. The highest amount outstanding at any time was
$449,338,902 on January 30, 1864. There are still out-
standing $346,681,016 of these U. S. notes, commonly called
"greenbacks," or "legal tenders." Most of them are tightly
held by the banks in their cash reserves. A gold reserve of
$100,000,000 in later years was held in the Treasury to
"secure" these notes, until the gold standard act of March
14, 1900, increased this gold reserve to $150,000,000.

In other words, *to discredit government paper money,* or
greenbacks, in 1900, when every dollar out was worth dollar for dollar with gold and had been for over twenty years,
the gold standard law forced the Government always to
keep on hand $150,000,000 gold to "secure" the $346,681,-
016 of greenbacks that are as much an obligation of the
Government as U. S. bonds. Thus the banks caused the
Government to actually raise by taxation and the selling
of long-time interest-bearing bonds payable in gold, the
enormous sum of $150,000,000 and pile it up idle in the
public Treasury permanently without one cent of advantage
or benefit to the Government or the people and when it was
wholly unnecessary. And this was done to head off the
possible issuance of any additional Government currency
and to insure that all future currency would be issued by
banks for the profit of the banks.

In contrast, it is interesting to note that by the comptroller's report there was on October 31, 1911, $744,071,715
of bank note currency outstanding in the hands of the
people, five times as much as when the Civil War ended,
without one dollar of gold held by the Government or the
banks to secure same; and it is all mere optional currency,
not legal tender, and no one can use it to pay even an ordinary debt if the other party cares to refuse to accept it.
Of course the currency is sound because the Government
holds an equal amount of U. S. bonds to secure it and also
by law has expressly guaranteed such currency. But what
is behind the bonds? Only the faith and credit of the
United States, the same identical thing that was back of
the greenbacks before any gold reserve was provided.

Surely the credit of the banks behind bank note currency
does not make such money more sound than if only the

Government, with all its unlimited taxing power, guaranteed the same. *If every dollar of currency was issued and guaranteed by the Government, made full legal tender by law for all purposes, and secured by whatever reserve of gold is considered ample, we would have the most simple, sound and practical monetary system in the world.* It would be the cheapest for the people because the Government charges nothing for issuing it. It costs the Government but a small fraction of 1 per cent. But the banks always have, and always will oppose it, for two reasons:

1. It would not yield the banks a steady profit, as bank note currency does.
2. Banks are afraid that the quantity might be so increased that the people would do more business on a cash basis and less on credit bought from banks.

These are the chief reasons actuating the banks and Wall Street in their continuous legislative and political struggle to discredit and destroy all Government paper currency and bring about a complete monopoly in the banks, or in a corporation owned by the banks, of the currency issuing privilege, as now proposed by the National Monetary Commission in the most bold form ever suggested.

The banks won't trust the people and the Government not to overinflate the currency, but by the Aldrich plan they ask the Government and the people to trust the banks with unlimited power to both inflate and contract the entire currency. And if the plan is adopted it is certain that the volume of currency at all times will be either too big or too little, for the banks will profit most when the supply is not normal, when it is unduly inflated or unfairly contracted.

Banks continually warn against the danger of increasing the prices of property and stocks by overinflation of the currency, but they themselves have inflated bank currency 400 per cent in twenty years, and they have inflated bank credit, which produces the same effect, billions of dollars. The banks want to do all the inflating that is to be done, and for their own profit.

By the act of April 12, 1866, instigated by the banks, $10,000,000 of greenbacks were retired and burned the first six months and not more than $4,000,000 per month thereafter. This was stopped by the protest of the people and the act of Congress February 4, 1868, after $44,000,000 of the people's "war money" had thus been burned up. The bank note circulation of course increased as Government currency was destroyed. June 30, 1864, there was $146,-406,725 bank note currency outstanding, having increased from $31,235,270 the previous year; the first being issued on December 21, 1863. But on June 30, 1868, there was $300,545,392 of bank note currency.

Government currency remained the same until after the panic of 1873 when popular demand forced the Government to reissue $26,000,000 of the cancelled greenbacks, making the total outstanding $328,000,000. Growth of business increased bank note circulation (while Government currency remained stationary) from $300,545,392 in 1868 to $354,-408,008 in 1875. The reissue of $26,000,000 Government currency helped reduce the demand for bank note currency and in 1877 bank note currency fell to $317,048,872. Bank currency fluctuated slightly during the next eight years (Government currency remaining the same), to $319,069,-932 in 1885. In 1886 an era of great general prosperity set in and continued until the panic of 1893. The demand for bank *credit* grew amazingly. Banks could by law sell credit for four to ten times the volume of the "lawful money," gold, silver or Government currency, in their reserves. Bank note currency cannot be counted as part of bank cash reserves. Banks began to contract bank note currency, selling their Government bonds for "lawful money" to put in their cash reserves to enable them to increase their credit loans four to ten times such increase of cash reserves.

A bank, for example, could make more charging 6 per cent for $10,000 bank "credit" issued based on $1,000 of "lawful money," Government money, held in its reserve than it could by investing that $1,000 in a $1,000 U. S. bond, depositing it with the Government and getting $1,000 bank note currency that it could not hold as "cash reserve" because not "lawful money" and could not use as a basis for increasing its loans of "credit."

It got the 2 per cent interest on the U. S. bond deposited as security, and say 6 per cent for use of the $1,000 bank note currency needed by some customer to meet a pay roll in cash, less 1 per cent tax on the currency paid to the Government.

But by selling the bond for "lawful money" and holding

the $1,000 in its "cash reserve" it could increase its loans
of credit $10,000 at 6 per cent without investing an extra
dollar.

This contracting of bank currency was further accelerated during this period by the decrease in the supply of
bonds by payment of large portions of the public debt, the
whole bank currency system proving then, as it always has
been, inelastic and unresponsive to the fluctuating demands
of business.   In fact, the bank currency system should have
been abolished after the Civil War and a system of elastic
sound Government currency put it its place.   Congress in
1888 authorized use of a large surplus for buying at a
premium unmatured Government bonds.   This premium
tempted banks to sell bonds and contract bank currency
based thereon because it was temporarily more profitable.

By June 30, 1890, bank-note currency had been thus contracted to $185,970,775 from $252,362,321 in 1888, $309,-
010,460 in 1886, $319,069,932 in 1885, and $358,742,034 in
1882, the highest year between 1864 and 1902.   In 1891,
bank-note currency had been contracted to $167,921,574.
Thus as business and the demand for currency increased
the banks actually decreased the supply, *because they could
make more profit doing so.*

This shrinkage in the quantity of available currency
tended to force people to do business less on a cash basis
and more by check, bank credit, which further increased
bank profits.

Senator John Sherman, that great Ohio statesman and
financial authority, undertook to relieve the people of their
increasing shortage of currency.   If the banks would not
supply bank-note currency because it was more profitable
to do otherwise just then, it was necessary to increase
the quantity of Government currency.

Sherman saw that the banks would not allow Congress
to increase the volume of greenbacks because for twenty-
five years the banks had been trying to get all greenbacks
destroyed.

The banks for their own greater profit had contracted
bank currency, and the volume of available money, over
$150,000,000.   If the banks had not objected, this shrink-
age could have been replaced with United States notes,
greenbacks, with a total cost to the Government of but
perhaps $1,000, the cost of printing the money, and the
notes, being the obligation of the Government, would have

been as sound as Government bonds, which are nothing more than the obligation of the Government.

But the banks objected to any increase of the greenbacks, so the Sherman silver purchasing act of July 14, 1890, was passed. This authorized the Government to buy 4,500,000 ounces of fine silver at the market price each month and to issue "Treasury notes" redeemable on demand in "coin" to pay for the same. These notes were made full legal-tender, "lawful money." At a cost to the Government of $155,-931,002, for which Treasury notes were issued, 168,674,-682.53 fine ounces of silver were purchased.

The banks did not at first object because they needed for themselves more "lawful money," legal-tender money, to put in their reserves so they could inflate their loans of credit tenfold. And if the banks got hold of the whole $155,-931,002 of these silver "Treasury notes" and held same in their cash reserves it would increase the loaning power of the banks $1,500,000,000, on which they would get 6 per cent, or other going rate, and the entire extra investment of the banks would be the $155,000,000 paid for such "lawful money," Government currency.

Gold Standard and Free Silver Campaigns.

The banks make their money chiefly selling or loaning *credit*. They are interested in having as *much credit* and as *little money* used as possible. Therefore they do not want the Government to issue money that they can neither profit from or control the supply of. It is largely immaterial to banks whether the country has a double monetary standard or a single gold standard, for they know either would be sound so long as the Government guarantees every dollar issued.

The big Wall Street men, on the other hand, usually do not sell credit. They are private bankers, not national or state bankers, although in recent years they have become more largely interested in such banks. But their chief business is selling bonds, the bonds of governments, states, counties, cities, districts, railroads and other corporations. Their best clients are the individual and corporate owners of the great fixed income or bond wealth of the world, largely in Europe, such as the Rothschilds.

The owners of such wealth for a half century have been striving to get every nation to adopt the single gold standard. They expected that in time the reserves of gold ore in the mines and the new discoveries would grow less.

They realized that with their wealth invested in bonds payable in gold coin, if the output of gold should decrease half, automatically that would double the value of their bonds and wealth measured in other securities, property or labor. Or if the gold output remained the same but growth of the world's business should double the demand for gold for Government reserves, and other uses, likewise that would double their fortunes without any extra investment. Of course they did not expect that Providence would turn their success into defeat by doubling the world's gold production. The world's gold output was, in ounces: 6,250,-000 in 1870, 5,540,000 in 1880, 5,470,000 in 1890, 12,315,-000 in 1900, 18,268,000 in 1905, 22,058,000 in 1910. United States gold production, ounces: 2,418,000 in 1870, 1,741,-000 in 1880, 1,588,000 in 1890, 3,829,000 in 1900, 4,265,000 in 1905, 4,646,000 in 1910.

The world's silver production, ounces: 43,000,000 in 1870, 78,600,000 in 1880, 109,000,000 in 1890, 173,591,-873 in 1900, 217,838,695 in 1910. United States silver, ounces: 12,375,000 in 1870, 30,318,000 in 1880, 54,516,000 in 1890, 56,647,000 in 1900, 56,438,695 in 1910.

Because of the unexpected doubling of the world's gold production, the bondholders failed to double the value of their bonds as they expected, either through shrinkage in the supply or increase in the demand for gold, but by demonetizing silver and reducing by half the basic metallic standard, making gold alone the measure of value, the bondholders prevented the purchasing power of their incomes from gold bonds decreasing, or the value of securities, property and labor measured in gold increasing to the extent that would have taken place if silver as well as gold had remained standard or a legal measure of value.

The high financiers of Wall Street, at the instance of their best foreign customers, the Rothschilds and others, in 1892 undertook to demonetize silver and get Congress to establish permanently in the law the single gold standard. It was rumored that the job complete cost the "interests" about $40,000,000. The resulting panic, however, cost the people many billions of dollars by way of losses. The first thing (as usual, and as now has been done to promote the central bank scheme) was to form a great offensive and defensive alliance with the banks of the country. The banks comprised an invincible political machine with branches in every community throughout the country, with influential and shrewd men in control, and with unlimited power due to ability to apply financial pressure upon the business of every man and corporation in the United States. Considering the object, it was not an alliance but *a conspiracy*. And if the exact truth ever could be revealed, just what was done behind the scenes from 1892 to 1900, it would cause the country to stand aghast and shudder that such things could be done in this "Year of Our Lord," in the midst of civilization, by such men and so many of them, and solely for sordid gain, for profit.

It was easy for Wall Street to show the banks that to continue issuing Treasury notes to pay for silver bought at the rate of $2,000,000 to $4,000,000 per month, under the "Sherman law" of July 14, 1890, in time would put afloat so much Government money that it might cause the permanent retirement of all bank-note currency and give the people so much actual money that they would do business more upon *a cash basis,* thus reducing the demand for *bank loans of credit.* And it also was easy to show that while the gold standard might not directly benefit the banks in any way it in no way would harm them.

The banks needed the wonderful political and legislative skill and liberal campaign contributions of Wall Street to stop the increasing of the volume of *Government currency.* So the alliance, the conspiracy formed was natural, logical, each having a different end to attain through action by Congress and approval by the President, and both Wall Street and the banks would share in the advantages and profits realized by their joint political raid.

The first successful undertaking of the allies was to defeat President Harrison and the Republican party in 1892 for paying instead of extending United States bonds and for passing the Sherman act in 1890, and elect Grover Cleveland president and a Congress containing enough representatives and senators, Republicans and Democrats, of a kind that could be steered by the banks and Wall Street to insure the repeal of the purchasing clause of the Sherman silver act of 1890 and the passage of a law establishing the single gold standard. The tariff was a sham issue used to hide the real issue in 1892 and will be in 1912 if the people will allow themselves to be again fooled by the same old game. The banks decided the election in 1892 and expect to do the same in 1912.

Cleveland was inaugurated March 4, 1893. Up to that

time there was not a single threatening cloud in the financial or business sky. There was no panic, or thought of panic by anyone outside of Wall Street and the very few big banks "on the inside" and "wise" to the moves contemplated. Business conditions never had been better or more sound, or general prosperity more real and justified in the entire history of the United States. Bank clearings had increased between 1883 and 1891 from thirty-six to fifty-six billions of dollars. Cleveland called a special session of Congress and demanded repeal of the Sherman act. He of course knew that the panic or financial disaster that came in the midst of prevailing prosperity was not due to the Sherman act increasing the supply of Government money, but to the deliberate and wicked act of Wall Street and the banks inflicting upon the country an awful panic to frighten and drive the distressed and terrified people like cattle into hastily forcing Congress to do the will of the criminal conspirators who caused the panic of 1893.

1893 Panic Was Bank-Made?

An article in Pearson's Magazine for March, 1912, by Allan L. Benson, makes public alleged important additional data designed to further prove that the banks deliberately caused the panic of 1893 for legislative purposes. It gives the following as a mandatory circular letter to all the banks alleged to have been sent by the National Bankers' Association on March 12, 1893, eight days after Cleveland was inaugurated:

"Dear Sir:—The interests of national bankers require immediate financial legislation by Congress. Silver, silver certificates and Treasury notes must be retired and the national bank notes, upon a gold basis, made the only money. This requires the authorization of $500,000,000 to $1,000,-000,000 of new bonds as a basis of circulation. *You will at once retire one-third of your circulation and call in one-half of your loans.* Be careful to make a money stringency felt among your patrons, especially among influential business men. Advocate an extra session of Congress for the repeal of the purchase clause of the Sherman law; and act with other banks of your city in securing a large petition to Congress for its unconditional repeal, as per accompanying form. Use personal influence with congressmen, and particularly let your wishes be known to your senators. The future life of national banks as fixed and safe investments depends upon immediate action, as there is an increasing sentiment in favor of governmental legal tender notes and silver coinage."

Such a "round robin" circular would cause a panic any time. Every banker knows that fact. Nothing could be more heartless and criminal. Any man who would send out or follow the instructions of such an order deserves to be court-martialed and shot as a public enemy. The panic of 1893 caused every kind of crime to be committed by thousands who but for the panic would have remained good and useful citizens.

Congress should immediately pass a penal statute making it a felony punishable by both fine and imprisonment any co-operative contracting of loans by national banks for the purpose of influencing legislation or the political actions of borrowers or causing panic or financial stringency.

In his message to the special session of Congress President Cleveland said:

"Our unfortunate financial plight is not the result of untoward events, or of conditions related to our national resources; nor is it traceable to any of the afflictions which frequently check national growth and prosperity. With plenteous crops, with abundant promise of remunerative production and manufacture, with unusual invitation to safe investment, and with satisfactory assurance of business enterprise, suddenly financial distress and fear have sprung up on every side."

Thus we have the highest evidence that there was no natural reason for panic, and that, therefore, the panic was wholly artificial, created.

With several thousand banks alleged to be secretly contracting their bank-note currency, robbing the people of their daily money supply, and putting the screws on business men everywhere by forcing them unexpectedly to slaughter securities, commodities and other property to pay up bank loans to an amount aggregating billions of dollars, of course "suddenly financial distrust and fear have sprung up on every side." And co-operative calling of loans is the only thing under the conditions then prevailing that could have caused the "financial distrust and fear," and the resulting panic.

Later in this chapter is shown just how the banks tried to execute the alleged order to increase the bonded debt of the Government another billion dollars.

Mr. Benson quotes an alleged article in the July, 1895, Forum, by William Solomon, a member of the great Wall Street international banking house of Speyer & Co. to the effect that Cleveland was elected by the "special interests" on tariff reform as a sham issue, the concealed but real issue being the stopping of the issuing of Government currency and repeal of the Sherman silver law, and that the panic was to be an "object lesson" to force the people to make Congress repeal that law, and that a special session was called and did the job according to the prearranged program. Congress was overwhelmingly against repeal, but the awful pressure of the panic and the banks on the people compelled them at last to drive Congress into surrendering to the banks and Wall Street. And right now it is believed that the banks and Wall Street are preparing to do the same thing in the same way to drive through Congress the Aldrich scheme that is a thousand times more important to Wall Street and the banks than was the repeal of the silver-purchasing act. In the campaign of 1912 the tariff is to be the nominal, the sham issue, the real but concealed issue being the Aldrich plan, which is to be forced through Congress before March 4, 1913, if the President is defeated in this convention or election.

If panic comes, the banks will cause it. If they do, the people will make short work of the banks. They may organize a general depositors' "strike" and all transfer their deposits from the national to the state banks and trust companies. If national banks conspire to inflict upon the country the horrors of general panic, Congress is likely to seriously consider a repeal of the National-Bank act, forfeiting the charters of every bank shown to have violated the law (and 59 per cent of the entire 7,331 banks are guilty), and the creation of a genuine Government bank with branches in every city to receive the deposits of the people, issue the currency and supply bank credit for business. Such a course is not desirable, but it is preferable to a continuance of the present Bank-Wall Street despotism and the fiendish panics they cause for their selfish purposes.

Co-operative calling of bank loans operates directly to restrain trade and interstate commerce. It is a violation of the anti-trust law, a crime with fine and imprisonment as the penalty. If the banks in concert contract loans and cause panic, or even a stringency, the people will not stop until the jails are filled with bankers in prison stripes. Artificial panic is war, and hereafter if the banks again declare panic the fighting may not all be on one side.

Senator David B. Hill of New York, a conservative but courageous patriot, in a speech in the United States Senate on August 25, 1893, said:

"They (the bankers) inaugurated the policy of refusing loans to the people, even upon the best security, and attempted in every way to spread disaster throughout the land. These disturbers—these `promoters of the public peril—represent largely the creditor class, the men who desire to appreciate the gold dollar in order to subserve their own selfish interests; men who revel in hard times; men who drive harsh bargains with their fellow men regardless of financial distress, and men wholly unfamiliar with the principles of monetary science."

This indictment was true in 1893 and it is true in 1912. If the banks by circular letter were now ordered to "at once retire one-third of your circulation (bank currency) and call in one-half of your loans," and did so, it would take out of circulation among the people $250,000,000 of currency and force business borrowers to immediately pay up bank loans to a total of more than ten billion dollars. It would put almost every business man and 95 per cent of all corporations into bankruptcy.

One of the chief objects of the Aldrich plan is to be able to avoid the dangerous practice of sending broadcast to all the banks even a secret circular letter ordering general contraction of currency and loans.

The National Reserve Association will be able to force banks to contract bank loans, say $5,000,000,000, simply by secretly contracting its corporate currency $500,000,000, thus shrinking the legal reserves of the banks and forcing the reduction of loans ten times as much. If $500,000,000 of corporate currency is taken away from the people and cancelled, the people will withdraw $500,000,000 from the banks for their daily pocket use. This reduces the legal cash reserves of the banks $500,000,000 and forces the banks to call in $5,000,000,000 of credit loans. That will cause panic, wreck prices and raise interest rates, the chief objects sought by Wall Street through the Aldrich plan.

There is reason to believe that the panic of 1873 was caused by the same interests to force through Congress the bills for the resumption of specie payments and the de-

struction of the remaining greenbacks. And that the panic
of President Jackson's day was caused to punish him and
the country for abolishing the central bank.

There is increasing general belief that the panic of 1907
was wholly artificial. It also came in the midst of the
greatest industrial and financial prosperity the nation ever
experienced. It is conceded that there was no natural reason for a panic. Yet it came out of a clear sky, and caught
everybody but the big insiders, who months before had
quietly unloaded hundreds of millions of securities on the
people at high prices and kept the proceeds as ready cash
which they later used in the midst of the panic they themselves had helped to create or intensify to buy back from
the stricken public the same securities at half price.

The panic came in October, 1907, after Wall Street, on
October 4, 1906, at a meeting of bankers and others, had
decided to put through Congress a measure creating a central bank to issue and control the entire public currency,
and just before the opening of the session of Congress in
December, 1907, in which the central bank bill was promptly
introduced.

It is American history, the fact that every great panic
has immediately preceded a very great joint effort by Wall
Street and the big banks to put through Congress legislation vastly increasing the profits and power of the banks
and Wall Street. This historic fact, and knowledge that
the interests, if they desire, easily can cause a serious panic
through the Stock Exchange and by instigating runs on
banks any day on an hour's notice, whatever the general
conditions may be, and belief that they will not hesitate to
do so if necessary to drive the people into forcing Congress
to hastily adopt the Aldrich plan for the creation of a huge
private money trust, impells this warning to the country
to "keep near shore" financially and out of the clutches
of the banks until Wall Street and the banks get what they
want or are completely beaten in the impending struggle
by the people. It is likely to be a finish fight with no quarter asked or granted by either side.

Right now every natural condition would justify expansion and steady increase of business. Banks have an abun-
dance of money and rates are low. Yet things drag. Every-
one knows something is the matter, but most people at-
tribute it to the wrong causes. The fact is that Wall Street
and the banks are holding things back by main force. They

are beginning to tighten the financial screws. There is plenty of money and credit but banks arbitrarily refuse to loan it generally to the extent necessary to cause proper resumption of business. So long as they can keep people grumbling, complaining, they have a better chance to steer them into supporting the new and revolutionary Aldrich plan, when they are told that such plan adopted by Congress positively is the only way to "reform" the situation and revive business. Then the banks may think, possibly, that it may be necessary to cause another panic or semi-panic to force the Aldrich plan through Congress, and no doubt they consider it best not to be too much spread out.

Before March 4, 1893, the big interests were quietly getting ready for the coming panic that no one else even dreamed of. Soon after that date in different parts of the country, certain banks are said to have begun to apply the pressure on customers. They are alleged to have explained as the reason that the existence of the Sherman act of July 14, 1890, on the statute books threatened the stability of the entire financial system and that if Congress did not quickly repeal it there might be runs on banks, bank failures and possibly a great panic, or words to that effect. This was enough to send customers who needed new bank accommodations or to renew maturing paper post-haste to the local congressman or the senator with the imperative demand that such "public servant" at once get to work to avert the impending panic by repealing the silver purchasing clause of the Sherman act. The scheme seems to have worked, Cleveland called an extra session of Congress and the bill was passed and on November 1, 1893, was approved.

The banks perhaps did not intend to have a real panic, at least not one so severe. They probably intended only to threaten panic and force action by Congress and then let things quiet down and go on as before. Wall Street, however, knew from its experience with the panic of 1873 and before the Civil War that they were playing with fire; that when influential bankers and financiers predict panic the people are likely to take them seriously and do the very things certain to cause a real panic; that is, they withdraw and hoard deposits, which forces banks to call in their loans quickly in large volume, and this in turn causes business men to slaughter goods and prices to get money to pay up bank loans, wrecking all prices and values, closing factories, plunging workmen by thousands into idleness and their families into distress and poverty, in fact causing general demoralization, panic, ruin.

That is just what happened in 1893. Wall Street expected it and was ready with actual cash to buy in at nominal prices what the public was forced by the panic to sacrifice.

The banks got their share of the plunder, the repeal of the silver purchasing clause, and increase of Government currency was stopped. But Wall Street had to wait for its share, the gold standard. The banks, however, were loyal to the conspiracy. They stood with Wall Street in the campaign of 1896, and on March 14, 1900, Wall Street and its foreign bond-holding clients got their share of the plunder, the adoption by Congress of the single gold standard.

Writer is not hereby attacking the gold standard or advocating its repeal. That law is an accomplished fact. Nor is he favoring free and unlimited coinage of silver at sixteen to one. He is a republican, and never believed free silver coinage to be the proper remedy. But he is trying plainly to state without political bias certain historic facts and seemingly fair deductions of great significance because such facts have a most important bearing tending to reveal the true character and methods of the national banking system and Wall Street and throw a flood of needed light upon the present attempt of these interests to still further increase their profits and power at the expense of the people.

"Joker" in Law Gives Millions to Banks.

To pay the banks full measure for their truly great and unanimous political and lobbying efforts, some additional "good things" were slipped into that gold standard act of March 14, 1900. For instance, banks thereafter were allowed to take out 100 per cent instead of 90 per cent of bank note currency on the U. S. bonds deposited with the Government as security for bank note circulation. Thus, without investing a dollar or putting up any additional security, the banks were given 10 per cent more currency that they could loan to the people at 6 per cent. The next year, on June 30, 1901, the bank currency increased to $353,742,186. Ten per cent of this, representing the increase from 90 per cent to 100 per cent (currency equal to the face of the bonds), is $35,374,218. This the banks loaned to the people at 6 per cent per annum. After paying the 1 per cent Government tax on the currency, to cover expense of printing same, etc., the banks realized say 5 per cent, or an extra net profit that year of $1,768,710. The bank currency doubled in ten years, and there was outstanding October 31, 1911, $744,071,715. Ten per cent of this (the difference between 90 per cent and 100 per cent) is $74,407,171. Five per cent on this 10 per cent of excess currency yielded the banks last year without $1 of extra investment, or additional deposit of securities, increased net profits amounting to $3,720,358. This was enough to pay an extra annual dividend of one-third of 1 per cent on the entire capital stock ($1,032,632,135) of all the national banks in the United States. Adding the extra profit of 1901, $1,768,710, to that of 1911, $3,720,358, and dividing the total, $5,489,069, by two we find that $2,744,534 is the average yearly extra net profit derived by the banks from that simple little "Joker" inserted in the gold standard act of March 14, 1900, handled with his usual cleverness by that renowned "reformer," Senator Aldrich, as chairman of the Senate Finance Committee. Therefore, in the ten years, 1901 to 1911, the confederated banks have received as a free gift by act of Congress $27,445,340. That was a quid pro quo and a half, for the banks. No wonder the campaign funds of 1896 and 1900 were ample and the patriotic zeal of the banks sufficient to insure a political result that would make it possible for the banks to harvest these manifest blessings by means of a grant in due form passed by Congress and signed by the president. If the banks subscribed to campaign funds with the understanding that this law would be passed, in effect it was a grant from the public Treasury for political purposes.

Before 1900, after getting 2 per cent interest on the U. S. bonds deposited as security and 6 per cent for the use of the 90 per cent of currency obtained thereon, and deducting the 1 per cent Government tax on the currency and other expenses, the banks realized an extra net profit beyond 6 per cent for their money of between ¾ and 1 per cent. Under the old law they would have realized a profit of $6,200,588 from issuing $744,071,710 of bank currency. But, according to the comptroller's report, they realized, because of the change by the law of 1900, about $9,920,946, or 1⅓ per cent profit, an increase of $3,720,358, or 60 per cent in the net profits of the associated national banks from issuing bank note currency, and this without any extra cost or investment by the banks or the slightest benefit to the people or the Government.

The above $27,445,340 shows only the extra profit of the banks in ten years without extra investment. But the extra inducement of 100 per cent instead of 90 per cent of currency given on deposited U. S. bonds caused the banks to increase bank currency from $353,742,186 in 1901 to $744,071,715 in 1911, a gain of $390,390,529. The ordinary profit above 6 per cent on this gain in ten years was about $14,637,360. This added to the $27,445,340, the extra profit in the ten years due to increase from 90 per cent to 100 per cent of currency, makes a total of $42,082,700 extra profit realized in ten years by the banks over and above 6 per cent for their money, as the direct result of the law of 1900, or an average of $4,208,270 each year.

But that was not all of the "good things" for the banks in the "gold standard" act of March 14, 1900.

United States notes, and Treasury notes, were handicapped as against bank currency by the requirement that the Government should spend $150,000,000 for gold to be held permanently to "secure" or redeem such Government currency. To maintain such gold reserve the Secretary of the Treasury was authorized, and when necessary required, to issue Government bonds bearing interest not more than 3 per cent and payable, principal and interest, in gold coin, to buy gold to replenish such gold reserve. No limit as to the amount of such bonds that can be issued was fixed, and the Government has no option but must issue bonds whenever the gold reserve falls below $100,000,000 and cannot be otherwise replenished. The famous Government *bond trap* is now set. In Cleveland's time the Government was run in debt arbitrarily more than a quarter of a billion dollars by the gold gamblers of Wall Street with the aid of the banks by use of the "endless chain" employed to repeatedly abstract the gold from the reserves of the Federal Treasury. By the act of 1900 the proceeding is made lawful and issuance of bonds made mandatory on the Government.

At the right future time we shall see a renewal of raids on the Treasury gold reserves for the purpose of again forcing the issuance of Government bonds. This will be done whenever the banks need more bonds to deposit to enable them to still further increase their bank currency. And to prepare for this coming event, the act of 1900 repealed the old restrictions on the banks and they now can issue bank currency equal to their total capital stock, or more than one billion of dollars.

There have been many times since the Civil War when it was a problem to dispose of vast surplus revenues accumulated in excess of expenditures by the Government. It would have been possible long ago to have paid off with such excess revenues the entire balance of the oustanding bonds of the United States, amounting on October 31, 1911, to $963,349,390, only the banks would not permit this to be done. The banks now own about 90 per cent of all these Government bonds. If the Government had thus paid all its bonds and got out of debt, and stopped all annual interest expenses, as it could and should have done, that would have forced the retirement of the entire bank-note currency based on such bonds deposited as security, amounting on October 31, 1911, to $744,071,710, and the substitution in its place of a Government currency that would not yield rich profits to the banks every year as does the bank currency. So the Government is kept in debt nearly a billion dollars and forced to pay over $20,000,000 bond interest each year, a total unnecessary interest cost since the civil war about equal to the entire present bonded indebtedness of the United States, for no other reason than to enable the national banks to make a currency graft off the people amounting to less than ten million dollars annually. And to enable this bank grab, Congress all these years has had to resort to all manner of reckless extravagance to spend the surplus revenues; so much so that Senator Aldrich himself publicly declared that a proper and business-like administration of the Government would reduce expenditures $300,000,000 annually. This would have been done years ago but for the intrigue in Congress by the banks and the manipulations of Senator Aldrich. Four years of such saving would have wiped out the entire national debt and enough over to create a permanent fund which, invested at 5 per cent, would have provided a continuous annual pension of $10,000,000 for the banks, or more than they realize from the currency privilege. And it would save the Government every year more than $20,000,000 now paid out for interest on bonds.

The U. S. bonded debt was reduced from $1,797,643,700 in 1879 to $1,021,693,350 in 1887 and $585,029,330 in 1892. From 1888 to 1892 $235,000,000 surplus was expended buying up bonds not yet due, the price going as high as 130 on the market. This was during Harrison's administration. It was business-like to use surplus revenues to extinguish the interest bearing debt, thus returning vast sums of money to the channels of trade. It then looked as though Uncle Sam soon would be out of debt. But the big banks ran the price up and forced the Government to pay a bonus of about $300,000 for each $1,000,000 of bonds to get the surplus back into circulation. March 1, 1889, the surplus, over and above the $100,000,000 gold reserve, was $230,348,-916.12. Payments for bonds and other things reduced this to $62,450,575.18 on March 4, 1893, when Cleveland was inaugurated. The gold raid began immediately. The banks gathered up greenbacks and presented them to the Treasury, demanding gold. In sixty days they had reduced the gold reserve below the $100,000,000 minimum. The Government issued $50,000,000 of bonds, dated February 1, 1894, and thus got back this withdrawn gold. The banks then gathered up more greenbacks and again took that same gold away from the Government, forcing the issuance of another $50,000,000 of bonds in November, 1894, to get it back into the treasury. These were 5 per cent 10-year bonds. The banks kept on raiding the Government's gold, forcing two more bond issues, $62,315,400 in February, 1895, and $100,000,000 in January, 1896. Thus the banks forced the Government to increase its bonded debt $262,-315,400, and at the end the Government had but little more gold than at the beginning, but it had an unneeded and injurious surplus (on March 1, 1897) of $157,213,632.08, besides the $100,000,000 gold reserve. The banks would have kept right on, only Secretary Manning got disgusted and told the banks if they kept raiding for gold he would give them silver. That stopped the gold raid and the issuing of bonds.

The banks forced the Government to pay several million dollars as a bonus in buying unmatured Government bonds between 1889 and 1893 to get rid of an injurious surplus of (1889) $230,348,916, and between 1893 and 1896 by raiding the gold reserve the banks forced the Government to accumulate an injurious surplus (1897) of $157,313,632 by selling $262,315,400 of high-interest, long-time U. S. bonds.

The act of March 14, 1900, provided for the refunding, instead of payment, of maturing U. S. bonds, the new bonds to be payable in not less than thirty years. This reversed the regular policy of the Government, which had been to either pay maturing bonds or to issue bonds redeemable at the pleasure of the Government after some short period. Thus the 5-20 bonds issued during the war were made redeemable at any time after five years, but payable at the end of twenty years. Under this system the Treasury could use its surplus revenues to pay off bonds at par instead of buying them in the market at a ruinous premium, and the money would thus be restored to the channels of business as promptly as though deposited in the banks without interest, although the banks would not make so much profit. As the chief object of maintaining Government, according to the above official facts, seems to be to legislate profits out of the pockets of the people and into the banks the plan least advantageous to the Government and most profitable to the banks, of course, was adopted by the "public servants," republicans and democrats, in Congress who were trained to sneeze every time Aldrich took snuff.

March 1, 1901, the net surplus was $229,196,327.90. Much of this could and should have been used to pay maturing bonds. But the bonds were refunded into thirty-year bonds and the surplus turned over to the banks for their use absolutely free, increasing their loaning power more than a billion dollars and their possible annual profits $60,000,000, without one cent of cost to the banks.

The maturing bonds were to be due in 1904, 1907 and 1908. The law of 1900 voted a bonus of about one-fourth of 1 per cent per annum from 1900 until due on these bonds. That sounds small, but on the nearly $550,000,000 of public debt quickly refunded the Government paid out of the public treasury a bonus of nearly $50,000,000 on the old bonds and received less than $2,000,000 as a premium on the new bonds. This enormous sum was a direct gift to the banks, as they owned about 90 per cent of the bonds.

The Treasury report of 1904 shows this refunding operation and claims a net profit of $14,245,851 for the Government. But in making the computation $257,837,642 of interest the Government must pay on the new bonds before their maturity and after the expiration of the old bonds is ignored. Deducting the $14,245,851 of apparent profit from the $257,837,642 interest to become due and we get some idea of the net loss to the Government. When the panic of 1907 occurred the Government had a surplus of

$240,000,000, or nearly enough to have paid half of the principal of the bonds so coming due and refunded.

The unrefunded portion of the bonds maturing July 1, 1907, instead of being paid, $50,000,000 of the bonds were extended for twenty-three years at 2 per cent, and the money in the big surplus that might easily have been employed in paying the public debt was deposited in the banks without interest. This $50,000,000 left in the cash reserves of the banks enabled the banks to increase their loans of credit nearly a half billion dollars on which the banks got 6 per cent, or other going rate. To enable the banks to use that public money the Government was obligated to pay $23,000,000 interest before another opportunity to pay those $50,000,000 of bonds would arrive. July 1, 1907, was a time of great prosperity, with no panic in sight or expected. Fifty million dollars to pay those matured bonds would have only slightly reduced the great $240,000,000 surplus, but it would have saved the Government $23,000,000 of future interest expense.

The only excuse offered was that if the bonds were paid the banks would not have enough bonds to keep their bank currency up to the profitable volume then enjoyed by the banks. Since the Act of 1900 the Government through refunding operations has actually been saddled with interest obligations from which it cannot escape, and which was unnecessary, amounting to nearly $300,000,000, for no other reason than to enable the national banks to keep afloat about $700,000,000 of bank-note currency from which the banks derive a net profit of about $10,000,000 annually.

Is it not high time to drive the national banks out of the Government's business, pay off our national debt, abolish the bank currency and issue in its place full legal tender Government currency, backed by the Government and an adequate reserve of gold?

No wonder the banks are anxious always to have a friendly Secretary of the Treasury as well as Comptroller appointed by the President. Do they sometimes bargain for this in advance in exchange for their political support? The origin and history of the national banking system impels the belief that if such a political bargain is not made it is not the fault of the profit-grabbing, legislation-promoting banks.

The act of March 14, 1900, was indeed a "gold mine" for the banks. It contained another provision highly valuable for banks. It legalized counting of "gold certificates" as part of the cash reserves of banks. Gold certificates are not "lawful money" because not legal-tender. Therefore, up to 1900 they could not be counted as "cash reserve of lawful money." There is no reason why they should not be considered "cash reserve." Every dollar of gold certificates is secured by a dollar's worth of gold held in the Treasury. But likewise there is no reason why gold certificates should not be made full legal tender so they could be used by the people for paying any debt. Now, gold certificates are mere optional currency that anybody can refuse who cares to do so. October 31, 1911, $903,367,929 of gold certificates were in circulation. The law of 1900 made this good money for the banks to hold in their reserves so they could loan seven to ten times as much credit based thereon, but it did not make it legal-tender so the people could force its acceptance when tendered in payment of a debt. The reason was that banks want to discredit Government currency as much as possible to increase the use of bank currency and credit that yields profits to the banks. This act of 1900 has increased the supply of money available for bank reserves nearly a billion dollars and thus has increased the possible loaning power of the banks about ten billion dollars. Six per cent on the net gain of nine billion dollars shows the possible annual extra net profit for banks under this "joker."

The act of March 14, 1900, was amended by the act of March 4, 1907. This authorized a contraction of bank currency at the rate of $9,000,000 per month. It also reduced the tax on bank currency one-half, to half of 1 per cent per annum, when secured by 2 per cent U. S. bonds; and under the refunding clause of the act of 1900 most of the bonds already had been converted into 2 per cent bonds by the banks. So this was a direct gift to the banks and not to induce a lower interest rate on U. S. bonds.

Assuming that the entire $744,071,710 of bank-note currency out October 31, 1911, was based on 2 per cent bonds, this reduction of the tax was another outright gift to the banks by act of Congress amounting to an additional net profit of $3,720,358 per year without one dollar of extra cost, investment or security by the banks and without a cent of benefit to the people or the Government. The banks found that the steal of 1900, increasing by 10 per cent the volume of bank currency and by 60 per cent the net profits of the banks from currency, worked so well that in 1907 they tried it again, that time by having their tax to the Government on such currency reduced half, or to ½ per cent, and their extra profits so won under the law of 1907 were about the same in amount as those obtained under the act of 1900 by the increase from 90 per cent to 100 per cent in the quantity of currency obtainable on deposited bonds.

The act of 1907 also made national banks depositories and required the Government to deposit public moneys in national banks without requiring banks to pay a cent of interest on such deposits. Millions upon millions of public funds were thus obtained by the banks, and each million of lawful money so deposited enabled the banks with no extra investment or cost to increase their loans of credit ten million dollars.

During the panic of 1907, which was caused by these interests seven months after the act of March 4, 1907, had given them the rich extra profits described above, most of the banks repudiated their deposit obligations, refused to pay on demand. Frightened by the increasing danger to their own institutions, they appealed to the Government, begging it to save them from threatening ruin, which the Government generously did.

The Secretary of the Treasury dumped into the banks nearly all of the $240,000,000 cash balance in the treasury. In fact, at one time the Government had in its own hands only a cash balance of $2,000,000, and would not have had a dollar if certain vouchers executed and due had not been held up arbitrarily. About $120,000,000 was turned over to New York City banks by the Government, increasing the loaning power of such banks more than a half billion dollars. Yet the banks never paid the Government one cent for use of this money, for actual salvation, but used much of it to increase the financial ability of inside operators so they could acquire cheap the securities the artificial panic forced the public to sacrifice. If the Government had not possessed that large sum of ready money, or had refused to surrender it to the banks, it is likely a majority of all national banks would have shut their doors or become legally bankrupt.

And now in return for thus rescuing the entire banking system from danger if not from destruction, and for all these rich privileges conferred by the laws of the land, the banks have joined Wall Street in a selfish conspiracy to rob the

Government of its constitutional power to issue the public currency, that a monopoly of all money and credit may be gained by the banks through a single private corporation owned by the banks, the National Reserve Association.

We now come to the Aldrich emergency currency act of May 30, 1908. Senator Aldrich in that bill tried to remove the prohibition against contracting bank currency more than $9,000,000 per month so as to allow sudden and unlimited contraction. He only struck out that provision of his bill after it had been exposed by the reading in open Senate of a petition signed by writer denouncing the scheme as a "joker." If Aldrich had not withdrawn that provision it would have been possible suddenly to contract and destroy the $700,000,000 bank currency as well as $500,000,000 emergency currency, a total of $1,200,000,000, or more than a third of all money and over half of all in circulation. This wide and sudden contraction would force the calling of loans by the banks wholesale, demoralize business, wreck prices and cause general panic. The present Aldrich plan contains this power of unlimited contraction in even more dangerous form.

Aldrich was also forced to eliminate the plan designed to make a market for hundreds of millions of railroad bonds, specifically, which Wall Street desired to unload on the banks at high prices after buying them from the public during the panic at low prices. This was to be the entering wedge looking to the ultimate substitution of Wall Street-made bonds in place of Government bonds as security for bank-note currency, which again would have increased the net profits of the banks. Said act did authorize the banks, affiliated in currency associations, to issue $500,000,000 additional currency on security other than Government bonds for the benefit of banks in emergencies. In fact any kind of securities, including commercial paper, could be used by a bank to obtain emergency circulation for 75 per cent of the "market value" of such securities, and 90 per cent of the value of municipal bonds. This act allows banks to issue currency equal to both the capital and surplus instead of the capital only. This more than doubled the currency issuing power of the banks, for their aggregate surplus exceeds their aggregate capital.

This emergency measure allows a bank to convert so large a portion of its securities and paper into currency that it makes banks reasonably safe, protects them against injury during panics. But does not this very fact make it likely that panics will be more frequent if now banks are made immune, because the interests in a panic can buy back securities from the public at half price? So long as panics to a certainty will harm or endanger the banks the giant power of the banks will be exerted to prevent panics, except when panics may be necessary to force through Congress legislation desired by the banks. Once fix it, as proposed by the National Reserve Association, so that banks always can quickly and completely protect themselves against danger due to withdrawals of deposits by panic-frightened depositors, by enabling them instantly to convert their assets into practically an unlimited amount of currency supplied by law, with which to meet "runs" and pay off depositors on demand, and we may expect to find the banks thereafter more indifferent about panics. Will not the big banks desire panics occasionally so that they can raise interest rates and buy securities at "cut rates"?

What the country needs is legislation not to make banks safe and sound during panics, but to remove altogether the practices in Wall Street and the conditions in the banking system that always tend to cause financial disturbances and panics. The Aldrich plan seeks only to protect the banks, to make banks panic-proof. It does not make the country proof against panics. In fact it grants to the National Reserve Association power to cause panic any time by contracting the currency, which in turn instantly forces contraction of bank credit, or loans, ten times as much. This may be ruinous to borrowing business men and corporations, force slaughter of securities and commodities, smash prices, close factories and cause distress and panic.

Unless the causes of panics and the means used to create them can be abolished, Congress surely should leave the laws so that banks will have just as much to lose by panics as individuals. Leave the banks in the same boat with the people and corporations. Banks can somewhat restrain Wall Street, the people cannot. This is the very best insurance against panics possible to obtain, until the country is ready resolutely to grapple with Wall Street and the banks to remove for all time the well-known panic-inciting evils.

It was reported that in an address before the Merchants' and Manufacturers' Association at Milwaukee on January

30, 1912, Robert W. Boynge, a member of the National Monetary Commission, said:

"The United States has 40 per cent of the banking wealth of the world, and yet it is the only country that has a banking system that collapses at the first sign of a panic.

We have a system of banks, which as soon as they see a speck upon the horizon, draw within themselves, and we have a situation similar to that of 1907. In 1907 we had more than $1,000,000,000 of gold actually on hand, but we were forced to go to the Bank of England to beg it to come to our rescue. We had the resources, but we had no affiliations of our banks to co-operate to meet the situation.

Our present system of bond security currency is most unscientific. The time may come when the national debt is paid off, and then there will be no issue of currency, regardless of the business conditions of the country. Then again, we might become involved in a big international war, when we would have a big issue whether we need it or not. The time has come when we must change our entire monetary system."

This severe indictment of the national banking system is true. But he should have said that the bankers alone are to blame, because they framed and have jealously kept the system in force for 48 years. When the banks have so signally failed, shall we now allow Congress to turn the whole thing over to the discretion of the banks, public currency and all? The system must be changed. But the new should be a public institution, not a private bank trust. We should not "jump out of the frying pan into the fire."

The national banking system in its provisions was dictated by bankers for the benefit of bankers. Since 1864 the banks have caused the defeat of every bill designed to strengthen and improve the system. It has blocked in Congress changes recommended in the interest of depositors and the public made by every United States Comptroller of the Currency during 40 years. Every material amendment of the law has been at the demand of the banks for their own benefit. They have fought steadily to maintain that system and increase its profits and power by acts of Congress. But now with one voice the bankers condemn their system as inelastic, inefficient, panic-inspiring and dangerous. Why? Just because the Aldrich scheme will greatly increase the power and profit of the banks, and therefore they are trying to

frighten the people into forcing Congress to adopt this new experiment.

Depositing Government funds in banks has largely been a matter at the discretion of Secretaries of the Treasury. If the trail was followed and all facts laid bare it would be a welcome thing if during some administrations a condition was not uncovered reeking with favoritism, bank intrigue, political bargaining, official delinquency if not graft and crime. During the past forty years hundreds of millions of dollars have been handed over to the banks for their use absolutely free, and even now (since 1908) only a nominal 1 per cent per annum is paid for the use of Government deposits that enable the banks to increase their credit loans 4 to 10 times such deposits. It would be worth the cost of an investigation if it could be shown that such deposits have not been used for political purposes and their disposal had no connection with the well known fact that so many treasury officials and their subordinates leave the public service to accept highly profitable bank positions. It would be a splendid tribute to official honesty if the record proved clear, for evidence is abundant that there is no length to which some big banks would not go to increase profits. The whole system of dealing between the banks and the Government during 48 years has been of a character that no sane business man would employ in his private business. In 1864 national banks were an "infant industry." The Government was generous to its offspring from the start. But as the infant has grown in size it refuses even at forty-eight years of age to be weaned, and it has attained such strength on the profits it has nursed from the Government that it is a question whether the parent now has power to wean this profit-hungry corporate monster.

The biggest congressional bank graft has yet to be described. By the act of June 3, 1864, national banks were charged a duty or tax of 1 per cent per annum on such bank-note currency as they issued. This was nominal because they got the 6 per cent interest on the deposited bonds and also 6 per cent to 10 per cent for the currency loaned to the people. That law also required national banks to pay each year ½ per cent on their total average deposits and on the portion of their capital in excess of their holdings of Government bonds. This was a franchise tax paid for the monopoly and the rich privileges granted by law under which banks receive the deposits of the people, advertise their institutions as United States depositories, and make loans of credit at 6 per cent or other going rate aggregating 4 to 10 times their cash assets, or reserves.

From 1864 to 1882 the national banks paid Government taxes: on circulation $52,253,518, on deposits $60,940,067, on capital $7,855,887, total $121,049,473. For 1881 the tax on deposits was $4,940,945 and on capital $431,233. For 1882 and to June 1, 1883, on deposits $8,295,717, on capital $707,751. This was besides the internal revenue stamp tax on bank checks and drafts put on as a war measure, and which the banks forced their customers to pay.

By act of March 3, 1883, the war stamp tax was abolished. But that was not all. The banks got a provision in the same act abolishing their ordinary tax on deposits and on capital. This absolutely exempted national banks and bank assets from all federal taxation. They only had to pay the special 1 per cent on such currency as they might issue.

The loss to the Government and gain to the banks by this one little legislative act was enormous, and the Government and the people did not get one penny of benefit.

If that law had not been repealed the Government would have received from the banks in 1911, $33,424,000 as ½ per cent tax on $6,684,800,000 deposits and $5,040,000 on $1,008,180,225 capital, total tax for 1911, $38,464,901.

During the 29 years, 1883 to 1911, deposits averaged each year $3,024,000,000, a taxable total of $87,690,400,000, and capital averaged $680,000,000, a taxable total of $19,719,-000,000. Thus a grand total of $107,409,400,000 escaped the ½ per cent tax, a direct saving to the banks and a direct loss to the Government of $537,047,000, more than a half billion dollars, or enough to pay off and cancel about 60 per cent of the entire bonded debt of the United States. That prodigious sum was voted by Congress out of the pockets of the people and into the pockets of the associated national banks without the slightest justice, reason, necessity or benefit to the people or the Government, a direct gift by law to the banks obtained either by skillful lobbying or political and legislative corruption and crime.

And so long as Congress continues to allow the banks to shape the banking and currency legislation of the United States so that the 7,331 national banks can go on collecting interest on ten billions of dollars with but one billion of cash capital invested, paying the Government not one dollar for the privilege and protection granted, just so long the banks will save and the Government and people will lose the 38 million or more dollars of taxes the banks would be paying annually if they had not put through Congress that sinister legislation. Why should national banks be exempt while other corporations and individuals must pay heavy taxes? There is no higher duty upon Congress than to end this half-century of bank graft and crime. It must be expected that the banks will threaten panic and ruin, and they may even inflict it on the country. If any panic comes the banks will cause it. If they do it, the people will break every bank and fill every prison with lawless bankers. The people will fight fire with fire. The tyranny of the banks must be broken right now or the people forever will be mere abject slaves of a merciless, cruel and criminal incorporated bank combine. There can be no compromise. The campaign of 1912 will for all time determine whether the people, or Wall Street and the banks, are to rule this republic.

Is there anything in this history of the national banking system that will justify Congress in now taking away from Government and granting for 50 years to a corporation owned by the banks a monopoly of the issuing and control of the volume of the entire public currency, absolute control of the life-blood of all business?

We wonder how long the people are going to remain asleep to the fact that for fifty years in one way or another the confederated banks and Wall Street, as a great and greedy incubus on the Government, have been constantly grafting and plundering the nation and the people under acts of Congress of their own creation, every year in greater degree and all the time treating with utter contempt the Government and its laws by violating every restriction and every civil and criminal statute made to regulate banks in the interest of the public. How long are the people going to tolerate such things? No wonder these special privilege interests have such contempt for the people!

We hear a great deal about "too much politics in business." These striking facts from the official records and statutes seem clearly to show that since 1864 there always has been too much "business" in politics. Any impartial student must see that the national banking system has been the great organized source of political corruption and legislative wrong-doing; that by clever and subtle means it has continuously robbed the public treasury and the people of untold millions under forms of law procured through their

improper influence and activity; that uniformly during
nearly half a century it has sought and usually obtained
legislation vastly increasing the powers and profits of the
banks and has successfully blocked all legislation proposed
for the benefit of the public imposing restriction or regulation upon the banks to increase their soundness and
efficiency.

CHAPTER XVI.

BANK GRAFT AND CRIME.

Bankers Accused Wholesale by United States Comptroller of the Currency.

If Christ should reappear in 1912, no doubt His first work would be to again scourge the dishonest "money changers" and drive them from the banks.

There are honest, upright, conscientious bankers, very many of them. But not so many as we had supposed until the United States Comptroller of the Currency, a fearless, courageous and honest public officer, with the reports of the banks and his bank examiners before him wrote, and on December 4, 1911, filed, his recent official annual report to Congress.

In that report, covering the current year to October 31, 1911, he officially makes the most shocking indictment and grave charges against an actual majority of all the national banks and bankers of the United States.

In 1910 author came into possession of definite information showing that a large per cent of all national banks repeatedly and intentionally violate the spirit and plain letter of the law. The estimate then made was 40 per cent. This seemed so astounding, and struck the few persons spoken to about the matter as being so incredible and impossible, author hesitated to jeopardize his own reputation for veracity by publicity of the facts he knew to be true. It was only when these very lawless banks publicly sought to greatly augment their profits and power by urging Congress to adopt the Aldrich central bank plan that author ventured to disclose his information about the astonishing prevalence of lawlessness among national banks.

Writer alluded to the subject in his written analysis of the "Aldrich plan" made on November 10, 1911, and personally handed to President Taft at the White House on November 16, 1911, which statement in full appears in the appendix of this volume, together with other surprising information as to the attitude of the present administration on this grave question.

Subsequently, on December 4, 1911, official confirmation of these alarming conditions was made by the U. S. Comptroller of the Currency in his report to Congress filed on that date.

"MILWAUKEE, WIS., Dec. 8, 1911.

Hon. Lawrence O. Murray,
 U. S. Comptroller of the Currency,
  Washington, D. C.

Dear Sir: A published Washington dispatch quotes from your annual report to Congress as follows:

'The dishonest practice by officers of national banks of receiving personal compensation for loans made by the bank is a growing evil and has already reached such proportions as to call for criminal legislation on the subject. In this manner either the bank is defrauded of lawful interest, which it would otherwise receive, or usurious interest is exacted of a borrower by the corrupt officer. A secret reward to the officers is sometimes a deliberate bribe for obtaining a loan on insufficient security.'

Is this a correct quotation? If so, I most heartily congratulate you for your courage in thus rendering a great and timely public service.

A few years ago two personal acquaintances, prominent and active field representatives of two of the larger bond houses, amazed me by stating that in their work, that for years has chiefly been selling securities to national, state and savings banks and trust companies, it was the exception when they found a bank official who would not demand or receive a secret commission for himself on securities that he purchased for his own institution. As legally this was a felony, larceny or embezzlement, it seemed unbelievable. But they insisted that this was true of their own personal knowledge, and my relation to them is such that I know they would not deceive me. And now your astonishing official charges against the honesty and character of many bank officials is additional confirmation.

You of course realize that any such commission is added to the price of securities and really is paid by the bank and not by the bond house. In institutions having a capital stock the stockholders are robbed by their own paid and trusted official. In mutual savings banks the loss would fall upon savings depositors.

These two sources of graft may help to explain the mystery as to how some bank officials with no personal capital and only a living salary in a few years have accumulated great fortunes. And it also illuminates the motives actuating the fierce scramble for control of every financial institution or insurance company holding for investment any considerable accumulation of the deposits or savings of the people.

Your disclosures are especially timely and important in view of the pending proposal that Congress actually turn over to a private syndicate of bankers a billion dollars of public currency and the entire revenues of the Federal Government to be forever held and invested for the exclusive profit of such private syndicate.

I have it on seemingly good authority that the sworn reports of the banks on file in your office show that a large per cent of all national banks have violated the law. If not inconsistent with your duties, I would be glad to learn whether in whole or in part this report is true.

Thanking and again earnestly congratulating you, I am,
Very respectfully yours,
ALFRED O. CROZIER."

"W L E   TREASURY DEPARTMENT.
WASHINGTON.
Office of
Comptroller of the Currency.
Address reply to
'Comptroller of the Currency.'

December 12, 1911.

MR. ALFRED O. CROZIER,
Plankinton House,
Milwaukee, Wis.

Sir: In reply to your letter of the 11th inst., you are advised that a table showing the percentage of banks violating the law in regard to real estate loans, reserve, excessive loans and borrowed money, appears on page 22 of the Comptroller's report for this year, a copy of which is being mailed to you, under separate cover, as requested. A copy is also being sent to F. W. Crozier, care The Romaine, Middleton Avenue, Cincinnati, Ohio.

Respectfully,
T. P. KANE,
Deputy Comptroller."

Page 87 of said report shows that the above quotation was accurate. On the same page the Comptroller also says:

"An amendment forbidding any officer of a national bank to directly or indirectly receive or accept money or other valuable thing from any borrower from the bank as a reward, inducement, or consideration for obtaining the loan from the bank of which he is such officer should also be enacted.

It is recommended that the taking or accepting of money, or other valuable thing from a borrower by any officer of a national bank for his own personal use as a reward, inducement, or consideration for obtaining the loan from the bank of which he is such officer shall be made an offence and punished by imprisonment in the penitentiary.

A law should be enacted determining the period during which any person can be prosecuted, tried, or punished for offences under the National Bank Act.

Many criminal offenders against the national banking laws have escaped just punishment by reason of the statute of limitations."

Such crimes are secretly done and usually easily concealed for a long time. Yet after three years no prosecution can be started. This is an inducement to commit crime, for the guilty always think they can conceal the crime at least three years. The Comptroller recommends the period be ten years within which action by the Government may be started in such cases.

The following exact quotation from page 22 of said report, including the table given in full, not only confirms author's information and statement to the President made three weeks before such report was filed, but it shows that instead of only 40 per cent being lawbreakers, the sworn official reports filed by the bankers themselves contain the amazing confession that more than half of all the national banks of the United States persistently, continuously, knowingly and wilfully violate several different plain provisions of the law. Th report says:

"*Violations of the Provisions of the National-Bank Act.*

A record is made, subsequent to the abstracting of the reports of condition of the national banks for each call, of the number of banks violating the restrictions and limitations of the national bank act for the purpose of ascertaining the percentage of offending banks. Deficiency in reserve represents the greatest number of violations and during the past report year has varied from 21.38 per cent on June 7, 1911, to 25.54 per cent on September 1. The percentage of banks making excessive loans and granting accommodations on the security of mortgages or other lien on realty is very nearly the same, varying in the former case from a minimum of 14.10 per cent on June 7 to a maximum of 19.21 per cent on November 10, 1910, whereas the violations in relation to loans on realty vary from a minimum of 14.73 per cent on November 10, 1910, to a maximum of 16.10 per cent on June 7 last. The number of banks violating the provision of law relating to liabilities for borrowed money, etc., in excess of their capital stock is relatively very small, ranging during the past year from a minimum of 0.51 per cent on January 7 to a maximum of 2.91 per cent on September 1.

The percentage of violations of the provisions of law in question at date of each call, from January 31, 1910, to September 1, 1911, is shown in the following table:

Date.	Sec. 5187 real estate loans Per cent.	Sec. 5191 reserve Per cent.	Sec. 5200 excessive loans Per cent.	Sec. 5202 borrowed money Per cent.	Total. Per cent.
Jan. 31, 1910......	15.03	19.91	16.03	0.24	51.20
March 29, 1910...	10.52	25.87	16.04	.32	52.75
June 30, 1910.....	11.40	17.68	14.56	.95	44.59
Sept. 1, 1910......	12.42	22.46	16.40	1.78	53.06
Nov. 10, 1910.....	14.73	22.97	19.20	.58	57.49
Jan. 7, 1911......	16.04	23.72	17.47	.51	57.74
March 7, 1911....	15.37	23.69	16.56	.79	56.41
June 7, 1911......	16.10	21.38	14.10	1.49	53.07
Sept. 1, 1911......	15.86	25.54	15.56	2.91	59.87"

The most recent report of the banks, September 1, 1911, shows that 59.87 per cent, or about 4,400 of the 7,331 national banks of the United States, were deliberate law-breakers, only 2,931 complying with the statutes of the United States. As time goes on it seems to be getting worse, for on September 1, 1911, nearly 700 more banks were violating the law than on January 31, 1910. If the same per cent of all the people were law-breakers there would be 54,000,600 criminals in the United States.

Breaking law is crime. Why did half the banks knowingly commit crime? For profit, nothing but profit! It was always by making loans illegally or on unlawful security for the sake of the interest profits they received.

That is the motive, the only motive, actuating the thief,

embezzier, burglar and highwayman. But such criminals have at least an excuse that lawless bankers do not have, they are homeless, friendless, penniless and hungry.

Isn't there a bit of terrible humor in the national association of bankers employing that distinguished detective to discover and punish those stealing *from* the banks, when crime against the interests of depositors and the community is constantly being committed wholesale *by* banks, *yes by a majority of all national banks?*

The Federal Government now is devoting its giant strength to discover, expose and punish labor union men alleged to be guilty of unlawfully transporting dynamite in interstate commerce and using it to destroy property involved in controversies between capital and labor. This action is right, and necessary. Law breaking of every kind must stop or soon there will be no government.

No honest man can or will justify, excuse or condone criminal violence and destruction of property to advance the cause of labor or any other cause. And the moral sense of everybody is shocked when such crimes even unintentionally cause loss of human life.

But the relatively few labor men accused (less than 1 to each 100,000) at least claim that they did not break law for personal profit but to advance the cause of labor and improve the condition in life of their brother workingmen. But the banks by affidavits attached to their official reports to the Government coolly confess that all the time half of them are breaking the law for no other reason than to get extra personal profit that they do not need.

We have shown in a former chapter that the comparatively few national banks, because law has prohibited individuals doing what banks are granted authority to do, in 42 years actually have cleaned up net profits aggregating about as much as the total of all the money of the United States in the hands of the people, the banks and the Government. The relatively larger portion of these wonderful profits have been made since about 1900.

If the American Bankers' Association was thus "caught with the goods on it" the comparison with the International Iron Workers' Union might just now be more exact. But while the Federal Government seems to have conclusive evidence of the guilt of a majority of all of the local national banks federated in such national banking association, there has been no charge and no suspicion of guilt against the hundreds of local unions and their thousands of members federated in the national iron workers' organization, the officers of which, or some of them, seem to have been lawless and unfaithful to the highest interests of labor. Out of several million union men only a few dozen are even accused; but over half of all national bankers confess their guilt on oath.

How can the Federal Government justly and safely pursue and punish lawless workingmen unless it as relentlessly prosecutes and brings to justice the guilty bankers of the United States against whom already it has ample and conclusive evidence in the shape of sworn confessions now on file in the office of the United States Comptroller of the Currency.

Why has not prosecution against even one of the thousands of rich and powerful bankers conclusively shown by the Government records to be law-breakers been started by the Department of Justice?

If the laws and penalties have been made inadequate at the instigation of the offending but politically influential men and banks now shown by the United States Comptroller to have been all along violating law, why did not the President indorse, in his financial message to Congress on December 21, 1911, the earnest and urgent recommendation of the Comptroller in his December 4, 1911, report that the laws be amended to reach the high grafting bank criminals, instead of endorsing the Aldrich plan for a private central bank multiplying a hundred times the profits and power of these very lawless bankers?

The law requires banks always to have a cash reserve equal at least to a certain specified per cent of its total loans of bank "credit," varying from 15 to 25 per cent according to locality. Loans of credit average at least ten times the cash in reserves. This is because three-fifths of the reserve of a "country bank" can be deposited in a central reserve city bank where it becomes the basis for another volume of credit loans. To say that the cash reserve of a bank is below the legal requirement is merely another way of saying that the bank has illegally and dangerously inflated its loans of credit out of all lawful proportion to its cash reserve. The larger the volume of such loans of credit the greater the profit that the bank gets with the same investment. So usually it is done deliberately, and solely for extra profit. There might be some moral excuse during a panic for reserves being below the legal limit, but there has been no panic now for over four years.

On page 22 of said report it is shown that in the 42 years since the present system started the national banks have actually earned net $3,107,185,441, and have paid $2,336,-815,679 as dividends. The average dividends of all the banks, good and bad, during 42 years was 9.07 per cent, and for the year to June 30, 1911, it was 11.38 per cent, and net earnings 15.57 per cent, on their capital stock. Of course many individual banks earn 20, 30 and some even 50 to 100 per cent. So their violation of law to gain more profits was unnecessary as a reasonable business matter and seem to put the majority of the bankers of the country and many of the great leaders of finance in the unenviable position of mere reckless, gambling financial adventurers, willing to ignore and break the laws of the land and endanger the safety of the deposits of the people for the chance of getting just a little bigger profits for themselves.

Does the business of banking tend to make good men narrow, selfish, sordid and criminal, or do men of that natural stripe seek control of banks to gratify their inordinate lust for profit and power?

Truly the banking system needs "reform," but not the kind the bankers now are seeking and always seek. Does it not morally need fumigating? Whatever delinquency there is in the present system and law the financiers are responsible for it. Usually they have framed most monetary and banking legislation and induced Congress to adopt it. Some provisions of the law are as harmless to malefactors as the "ten commandments," because intentionally or unintentionally the law was framed to provide no way of enforcing it—no criminal penalty for its violation.

The showing of bank violations made by the present Comptroller in his report must have existed at least to a greater or less extent during the terms of former U. S. Comptrollers. Why was not the law enforced against the offending banks? Why were not those dangerous conditions that so gravely affect the interests of depositors and the soundness of banks and the strength and stability of the country's financial and banking system exposed and correction of the evils and abuses demanded by former U. S. Comptrollers? We do not know that there was any connection between this seeming neglect by some of the highest public duty, which conferred such rich and valued immuni-

ties upon lawless banks and bankers, and the well-known fact that many Treasury officials almost immediately after leaving the public service have obtained high and permanent official positions with banks at salaries said to be many times what they received from the Federal Government.

On page 31 of his report the present Comptroller says: "Sixty per cent of the failures of national banks have been caused by violations of the national banking laws." The management often is reckless and rotten as well as criminal. Concealed losses because of improper loans to favorites and otherwise are "charged off" amounting to hundreds of millions of dollars. Inordinate profits alone have prevented general ruin of banks. Just consider what it means, the fact that most of the deposit savings of all the people of the United States are in the custody of these criminal "guardians"!

If the Aldrich central bank plan is adopted by Congress, an absolute majority of the shares and control of the National Reserve Association will be owned and forever held by banks officially shown by the Federal Government and admitted under oath to be guilty of repeatedly, knowingly and wilfully violating their charters and the laws of the land just for the profits there was in it.

Is Congress ready to turn over for fifty years the entire public currency and all the revenues of the Government and the other imperial powers demanded to a private corporation so owned and controlled?

The people soon will know.

CHAPTER XVII.

CRIME OF CONSPIRACY.

40,000 Bank Officers and Directors Each Liable to $10,000 Fine and Two Years' Imprisonment.

The reason the Ten Commandments announced by Moses, or some of them, are constantly violated by so many people is because the penalty prescribed will be inflicted in the next world—perhaps—instead of in this. The chances of punishment are too slim and remote.

That is the precise reason why so many distinguished bankers break the laws of the land over and over day after day, week after week, month after month, year after year.

For instance, in his official report of December 4, 1911, the U. S. Comptroller on page 22 (quoted in the preceding chapter), charges that on September 1, 1911, 59.87 per cent of all national banks were violating four separate provisions of the national bank law, viz., Secs. 5137, 5191, 5200 and 5202, prohibiting loans on real estate, inadequate cash reserves, excessive loans to borrowers and excessive indebtedness by banks, respectively. No penalty whatever against bank officers and directors committing such offenses against the law is prescribed in the "National Bank Act." These restrictions were imposed by law for the protection of depositors and the good of the community, to make banks more sound. Every time these provisions of law are broken it is a menace to the safety of depositors and the public welfare and every offense is committed knowingly by officers and directors for profit.

There are severe penalties, fine and imprisonment for offenses like embezzlement by subordinates against the interest of banks, but no penalties are imposed upon officers and directors who ignore and violate practically every provision of law enacted to protect depositors and the public. As the system was devised and framed by the financiers this condition of course was not accidental. For almost fifty years bank influence and intrigue has prevented Congress enacting amendments in the public interest recommended by Comptrollers of the Currency who had full sworn information showing criminal conduct and contempt for law by a large per cent of banks and bankers. On the other hand, the National Bank Act again and again has been amended at the instance of banks to increase their immunities, profits and power. Deputy Comptroller of the Currency Kane has been retained in office for years by different administrations because of his high ability and integrity, expert knowledge and skill. In a public interview reported in the Washington Post of March 21, 1908 (cited by Senator La Follette in his speech of March 24, 1908, in the U. S. Senate), Mr. Kane said:

"While numerous have been the recommendations of the eleven Comptrollers who have presided over the affairs of the Currency Bureau since its establishment, which, in the judgment of each, would have increased the security of the depositors and creditors of the banks, practically none has been enacted into law or has received the serious consideration of the legislative branch of the Government. No one has had better opportunities to observe from an impartial and disinterested standpoint the practical operation of the banking laws and to note their weak features in regard to the security of creditors than the respective Comptrollers of Currency. Notwithstanding this indisputable fact and the many recommendations made by the several Comptrollers, there has been practically no amendment of the law since the passage of the original bank act of February 25, 1863, which can be said to have had for its object the particular welfare of the depositor.

Of the fifty-four acts amendatory of the original enactment which have been adopted since that date, practically all have been in the interest of greater latitude or privileges to the banks.

The remedies suggested for the many unsatisfactory conditions for which the national banking laws are primarily responsible may be found in the recommendations made from time to time by the Comptrollers of the Currency in the forty-five annual reports submitted to Congress since the establishment of the Currency Bureau, and until supplied by legislative enactment the responsibility should rest where it properly belongs—upon the law and the lawmakers, and not upon the administrative officials."

This is a terrible indictment of the political and legislative activity of the Bank-Wall Street political combine made

by the one man in the United States who best knows the
facts and has daily access to the confidential records of the
Comptroller's office that startlingly show the duplicity,
graft and crime of the bankers.

During much of this long period of nearly fifty years one
individual, posing as a public servant, has been the pliant
tool of the interests. That man, as chairman of the Senate
Finance Committee, has come into official possession of
practically every bill to strengthen and improve the banking
system. He seems to have suppressed them all. Now that
man, former Senator Aldrich, is posing as the great apostle
of "reform" to improve the banking and currency systems.

"A leopard cannot change its spots, or an Ethiopian his
skin," and Aldrich cannot and has not changed. He is still
betraying the people and the public welfare into the hands
of banks and Wall Street.

The pending central bank bill he wants passed as a "monu-
ment" to his name and public record. It would be appropriate; for it is by far the most crafty, selfish, subtle, unpatriotic, evil, daring and dangerous measure introduced into
Congress since the republic was created. It is a fitting end
and climax of such a treasonable career.

The only remedy the National Bank Act provides is the
possible forfeiture of charter by the bank for violation of
the provisions of the law.

Sec. 5239 reads: "If the directors of any national banking association shall knowingly violate, or knowingly permit
any of the officers, agents, or servants of the association to
violate any of the provisions of this title, all the rights,
privileges and franchises of the association shall be thereby
forfeited. Such violation shall, however, be determined and
adjudged by a proper circuit, district, or territorial court
of the United States, in a suit brought for that purpose by
the Comptroller of the Currency, in his own name, before
the association shall be declared dissolved. And in cases of
such violation every director who participated in or assented
to the same shall be held liable in his personal and individual
capacity for all damages which the association, its shareholders, or any other person shall have sustained in consequence of such violation."

The Comptroller's report clearly shows that on September
1, 1911, just 4,389 of the 7,331 national banks under said
Sec. 5239 legally had forfeited their charters, only 2,942
banks being then within the law. But the clever genius who

drafted that section carefully provided that no bank should
be declared dissolved until the Comptroller *personally in his
own name* had instituted suit in court and prosecuted same
to judgment. If the Comptroller refuses or neglects to act
all the banks are safe and immune under that act even if
all such banks (as they do) daily violate every such provision of law. There is no power in the law or under the
Government to punish or bring to justice or to forfeit the
charter of a bank if the Comptroller will not proceed. He
is the autocrat over all banks and above the law. The very
life of over half of the banks is in his hands and each justly
merits the *death penalty*. Yet year after year passes, Comptroller after Comptroller comes and goes, the banks, a majority of them, laugh at the penaltyless laws and go on violating for gain the statutes of the United States, and nothing is done to remedy the rotten condition or to bring the
offenders to justice. Why?

Is the explanation partly in the fact that many comptrollers go from their faithless public service and immediately become president or an officer of some bank at a
salary many times greater than that paid them by the Government? What paralyzed their official conduct? Were
some of them bribed in office by the promise or hope of subsequent high position in private life, or were they bribed
with office before they were appointed on the understanding
that they would enforce the law against employees of banks,
but not against bankers? Does it go still higher? Is it
possible that sometimes the lawless banks in advance have
bargained for immunity, in exchange for nation-wide bank
political support, with a candidate or prospective candidate
for President or with his political managers, the banks to
name the Comptroller and perhaps the Secretary of the
Treasury? It is a serious thing even to think about, but
there is some reason why banks and bankers are always
exempt while all other people must obey the law or be
pursued by the entire power of the Government and brought
to justice.

This is not intended to reflect on the present Comptroller.
Writer has means of knowing that he is honest and fearless
and has been making an almost desperate effort to induce or
force the banks to keep within the law. And this apparently
without the proper support of the present administration.
And his brave and courageous public denunciation of bank
graft and crime and criminals in his official report, and his

showing from the record the extent of violations, is almost Providential, coming at this time when the banks brazenly are trying to induce Congress to turn over to them some of the greatest functions of Government; practically giving to the lawless banks power to "regulate" themselves for the next fifty years.

It is a hard place to put a Comptroller, for better than anyone else he knows the imperial political and legislative power of the banks and their ability to punish any Comptroller who may refuse to do the will of the banks instead of his sworn public duty.

Sec. 5147 reads: "Each director, when appointed or elected, shall take an oath that he will, so far as the duty devolves on him, diligently and honestly administer the affairs of such association, and will not knowingly violate any of the provisions of this title, and that he is the owner in good faith, and in his own right, of the number of shares of stock required by this title, subscribed by him, or standing in his name on the books of the association, and that the same is not hypothecated, or in any way pledged, as security for any loan or debt. Such oath, subscribed by the director making it, and certified by the officer before whom it is taken, shall be immediately transmitted to the Comptroller of the Currency, and shall be filed and preserved in his office."

This clever bank act was put through Congress when the attention of the public and Congress was absorbed by the daily events of the civil war. It was moral if not legal treason to take advantage of the Government at such a time.

The "joker" in the above quoted oath is this: A prosecution for perjury can be maintained only for false swearing as to a past or present fact, not future official conduct. If the director did not own the shares he swore he did he could be sent to jail for perjury. But if he continuously violates his oath of office, commits treason to his sacred trust, as a majority of bank officers and directors do, the penalty for perjury cannot be inflicted. The President of the United States might be impeached, but could not be punished for perjury if he violated his oath of office. But there is no one in the bank to move impeachment of an offending director, for all are particeps criminis, coöperate in the violations, are guilty of the same offenses. And impeachment of bank officers is not authorized by law. Exces-

sive loans, illegal real estate loans, inadequate cash reserves
and excessive indebtedness by the bank usually are impossible except with the knowledge and consent of practically
all of the officers and often the directors of the bank. Particularly so when it goes on continuously year after year.
The fact is, such matters are deliberately done or winked
at because most directors have become such solely to obtain
favors from the bank for enterprises or corporations in
which they are financially interested. That almost universal
condition is the curse and greatest evil and danger of the
present banking system. In a broad sense they are *conspirators*, not bankers.

With no penalties against bankers in the National Bank
Act and friendly Comptrollers to protect the banks against
forfeiture of their charters, and with a statute of limitations
outlawing offenses after three years, the national banking
system, steeped in lawlessness, graft and crime, has gone
on for nearly a half century scott free and immune. The
law defying beneficiaries are constantly seeking richer legislative exemptions and privileges as they grow inordinately
rich, often by the fruits of graft and crime. In their fan-
cied security, shielded by the significant omission of the
usual penalties from the bank statute, they have overlooked
another statute that may cause them a rude awakening and
at last bring them to justice.

Crime of Conspiracy.

Section 5440 of the United States Revised Statutes in
the New Code is as follows:

"SECTION 37. IF TWO OR MORE PERSONS CONSPIRE EITHER
TO COMMIT ANY OFFENSE AGAINST THE UNITED STATES, OR
TO DEFRAUD THE UNITED STATES IN ANY MANNER OR FOR
ANY PURPOSE, AND ONE OR MORE OF SUCH PARTIES DO NOT
ACT TO EFFECT THE OBJECT OF THE CONSPIRACY, EACH OF
THE PARTIES TO SUCH CONSPIRACY SHALL BE FINED NOT
MORE THAN TEN THOUSAND DOLLARS, OR IMPRISONED NOT
MORE THAN TWO YEARS, OR BOTH." ·

Under this section and the court decisions there is not the
slightest doubt that *every participating officer and director of
the 4,389 offending national banks is legally guilty of the
crime of conspiracy,* and that there is in the Comptroller's
office and elsewhere ample evidence to indict, arrest, convict
and *punish by a fine not exceeding $10,000 or imprisonment*

not more than two years, or both, more than 40,000 bank officers and directors. Nor will the statute of limitations aid them to escape justice. The courts have decided that in a *continuing conspiracy* of this character the three years begins to run only from the last act by any one of the conspirators pertaining to the subject matter of the conspiracy.

It is clearly *an "offense against the United States" to violate any law of the United States whether there is a prescribed penalty for such violation or not.* And "two or more persons conspire to commit an offense against the United States" every time bank officers or directors violate the National Bank Act. The Supreme Court decisions make this fact clear.

"Ignorance of the law excuses no man." Even if the offending bankers have overlooked this drastic statute imposing severe penalties for the crime of conspiracy, they are entitled to no sympathy or mercy. They admit under oath that they have repeatedly treated the authority of the Government with contempt and they violated the laws of the land because they thought there was no effective punishment provided.

"Atwell on Federal Criminal Law," on page 219, says: "A conspiracy as commonly understood is a corrupt agreeing together of two or more persons to do, by concerted action, something unlawful, either as a means or an end. The word "corrupt," as used, means unlawful. The intendment of this definition is that to conspire to do an unlawful act; or to conspire to accomplish a result which may in itself be lawful, but to do it in an unlawful manner; or an unlawful agreement to accomplish an unlawful result, are conspiracies. The unlawful combination may be expressly proven, or it may be provable from concerted action in itself unlawful. If one join the conspiracy at any time after the formation of the conspiracy, he becomes a conspirator, and the acts of the others become his, by adoption.

That there is, or may be, a difference between the punishment prescribed in this section, and that prescribed in the statute that the conspiracy was formed to violate, is immaterial. Congress has the power, says the Supreme Court of the United States, in Clune vs. United States, 159 U. S. 590, to enact a statute making a conspiracy to do an act punishable more severely than the doing of the act itself. The power exists to separate the offenses, and to affix distinct and independent penalties to each.

As above indicated, there need be no proof of the express agreement. The full measure of the law is met if the facts and circumstances indicate with the requisite lawful certainty the existence of a preconcerted plan. Reilly vs. United States, 106 Federal, 896; U. S. vs. Cassidy, 67 Federal, 698; U. S. vs. Barrett, 65 Federal, 62; U. S. vs. Wilson, 60 Federal, 890; U. S. vs. Newton, 52 Federal, 275; U. S. vs. Sacia, 2 Federal, 754. So, under the same authorities, it need only be shown that one or more of the overt acts charged in the indictment have been committed, and that they were done in furtherance of the conspiracy. Federal Statutes Annotated, Volume 2, page 250.

Text-books and courts unite in the proposition that where there is *prima facie* showing of conspiracy, all of the acts done, and all of the declarations made in pursuance of the originally concerted plan, and with reference to the common object, by any one of the conspirators, are admissible against all."

The above is a verbatim quotation from the leading text-book on federal criminal law and is an authority reorganized by the courts. And the definition of conspiracy given and the matters incidental thereto above described are all fully sustained by the Supreme Court of the United States in the cases cited and by many other cases.

Every national bank must have at least five directors. Some have as high as 20 or more. The National City Bank of New York has 23, and the National Bank of Commerce 40. The average number of directors of each of the various national banks, no doubt, is at least 10. This would seem to indicate that there are at least 43,890 directors of the 4,389 national banks officially accused by the United States Comptroller in his report of December 4, 1911, of violating the laws of the United States. Besides, many officers not directors are also involved. The total number of bankers and directors implicated and thus officially charged with the crime of conspiracy by a high federal official must exceed 40,000. No doubt a large portion of these offending directors have participated in these acts either ignorantly or thoughtlessly, trusting the bank officers and blindly doing what they are directed. Unfortunately for them, this does not relieve such persons from legal guilt and liability. If they have as directors aided or consented to the making of just one illegal loan or the doing of just one illegal act or omission by the bank, they are under the law guilty of the crime of conspiracy and liable to indictment, arrest, conviction and a fine not exceeding $10,000 or not more than two years' imprisonment, or both. And each separate violation may be considered a separate and distinct conspiracy carrying the same penalty. As some banks are committing such offenses almost daily, every participating officer and director is accumulating penalties that if exacted, as sometime surely they will be if the lawless practices continue, it may ruin him financially and even force him to spend much of the balance of his life in prison as a condemned criminal. Does it pay to be mixed up in such a dangerous mess?

This accurate and plain statement of the law and the liability can be verified by any director who will consult his legal adviser on the subject. It is here put forward as a friendly and timely warning to the thousands of honorable and patriotic business men who have been induced by bankers to accept directorships and thus give the bank the benefit of their influence and the profit of their accounts and business, and who have put implicit but mistaken faith and confidence in the honor and wisdom of the bankers managing the institutions, carelessly and unquestioningly complying with their requests and blindly acquiescing in their decisions.

They have been misled and put in a position of grave personal danger by the bankers whom they trusted and who knew the law and the fact that it was being violated. There are no extenuating circumstances excusing most offending bank officials, because they know the condition of the bank at all times and make frequent sworn reports to the Comptroller of the Currency; and from such reports that official shows that over half of all national banks are guilty. For a director who is really honest and patriotic at heart and desires in fact to be a law-abiding citizen instead of a confessed criminal there is but two honorable courses:

1. Tell the bank officers who have deceived and led him into danger just what he thinks of their conduct and then resign from the board.

2. Purge the bank of all criminal lawlessness by forcing the immediate resignation of every official whose past conduct has shown a willingness to ignore and violate the provisions of the law and thereby subjected directors to the danger of successful criminal prosecution and brought the

institution and the banking system into contempt and public disgrace.

Every honest director owes it to the community, the Government, the depositors who have trusted him, and to himself and his family, to act promptly and courageously, and thus so far as possible cure the grave evils that have grown up largely because of his carelessness and lack of thought and attention about important matters for which he voluntarily became morally and legally responsible.

As the comptroller has made his sweeping charges without naming the particular offending banks, the 2,942 honestly conducted banks should insist on the guilty banks being named if not punished so that unjust suspicion may not cause the innocent banks to suffer because of these lawless acts of the guilty. That would be simple justice. A public congressional investigation of the national banking system is now justified and necessary and the best means for acquitting innocent banks and fixing the blame upon the guilty. Honest and upright bankers should join in the demand for such a public investigation.

As more than half of all national banks are officially shown to be guilty of intentional lawlessness, and their officers and directors guilty of criminal conspiracy under the statutes of the United States, it will be patriotic and the part of wisdom for all honest and honorable bankers and directors to oppose the Aldrich plan for now increasing the profits and power of the banks by giving them ownership of the proposed National Reserve Association that is to control the public currency and entire money supply of the country. They should promptly and vigorously join with the people in demanding that the institution be absolutely owned and controlled by the Government of the United States.

This course alone will prevent their neighbors and friends and the people generally believing that they are willing parties to the conspiracy of the big banks and Wall Street to rob the people and the Government of their rights and powers for the graft, profit and advantage of lawless and selfish private interests.

If state banks and trust companies are wise they will oppose this "will you come into my parlor, said a spider to a fly" Aldrich proposition. They have nothing to gain and everything to lose by this lion and lamb merger, for they must play the part of the lamb. They will not desire to join this National Bank-Wall Street Conspiracy and cause the people to believe that they are as selfish and criminal and unpatriotic as the majority of national banks.

And state banks and trust companies cannot afford to allow national banks thus to increase their profit and power and their advantage over state institutions. National banks would entice away the deposits of state institutions by

advertising that national banks alone are "panic-proof." On the other hand it would be a great benefit and advantage, and no disadvantage, to state banks and trust companies to be allied with a great central reserve association or currency issuing body provided same was a public institution owned and controlled by the Government and strictly regulated by law.

The crime of conspiracy statute above quoted, that has been violated by about 40,000 bank officers and directors, is the identical statute under which 54 labor union members recently were indicted and arrested or prosecuted by the United States Government under direction of the President. In one case it was conspiracy to violate the federal law regulating banks, and in the other it was conspiracy to violate the federal law against transporting dynamite on railway trains. Justice must be impartial. Can the Government justly or safely put the stripes on the few misguided working men and let the many offending bankers go free?

CHAPTER XVIII.

BANK CREDITS VS. GOVERNMENT CURRENCY.

Banks Increase Cost of Living — Business Done Too Much on Credit and Too Little on Cash Basis.

There are two ways of doing business. One is to pay in cash, the other with credit—bank checks, notes and drafts. In *cash transactions* it costs the people nothing for *use* of the "medium of exchange" employed—the money, or currency—because the Government coins or prints and issues it without charge. In *credit transactions* (and by "credit" we do not mean trusting, or selling on time) settled by check, note or draft, the *banks always receive a profit* for the agency used as a substitute for money. They either get "interest" at 6 per cent, or other going rate, on the promissory note discounted to create a book account against which the "checks" are drawn, or "exchange" to pay for New York or other drafts used in place of cash.

In New York City and some other places banks profit double. They get interest on the note discounted to create a checking account, then they charge for all outside checks drawn on similar accounts in other banks when receiving such checks for deposit. This plan gradually is being extended throughout the country. And when customer checks out say but half the proceeds of the discounted note, the bank receives the equivalent of double interest, or 12 per cent. Offsetting this is the 2 per cent, 3 per cent or 4 per cent interest paid by banks on deposits, but usually this is only on cash or time deposits represented by "certificates of deposit." Few banks pay any interest on "checking accounts" created by discounting notes or depositing the checks of other people. They can well afford to pay that small rate on deposits of cash, because the cash becomes part of their "cash reserves" and enables them immediately to swell their loans of credit an amount equal to about ten times such cash. For example, a bank may pay 3 per cent per annum on a cash deposit of $1,000 because it at once then can charge and receive 6 per cent yearly on $10,000 of extra loans of "credit." This is the "inside" mysterious and Crœsus-like "Holy of Holies" of the banking business.

Two things must be obvious:

1.　It is for the financial interest of the banks to have the people do as little business on a cash basis and as much on a credit basis as possible, because banks supply all of the "credit mediums of exchange" and receive a good profit for doing so.

2.　It is for the financial interest of the people to do as much business on a cash basis and as little on a credit basis as possible, because the Government charges the people nothing for producing the cash for them and banks always charge for the use of credit.

The development of business methods and practices have grown, or been so engineered by the banking system that the relative proportion of cash transactions has steadily decreased and credit transactions increased until now it is conceded that of all business at least 95 per cent is done with credit and but 5 per cent with cash. This is partly due to the convenience of checks instead of cash, less bother in some transactions, but more to the constant temptation and encouragement by banks to solvent customers to overexpand their business by using credit instead of actual capital; for it is easier to go in debt to a bank than to provide cash capital to carry on a given business.

Some idea of the size and weight of this bank burden upon the people and their business activities, because of the use of bank credit instead of cash almost exclusively in all of the business transactions of life, may be gathered from the official report of the 140 clearing houses of the United States for the year to September 30, 1911.

According to the U. S. Comptroller's report of December 4, 1911, in one year the volume of business settled by bank checks and drafts that went through clearing houses (not including checks cashed by banks on which they were drawn) was the colossal total of $159,373,450,000, almost one hundred and sixty billions of dollars. All of the annual crops of the soil are worth only seven to nine billion. All of the money in the United States (June 30, 1911), coin and currency, in circulation, in bank reserves and in the treasury, was only $3,555,900,000. The total capital (known and estimated on June 7, 1911) of the 28,551 banks and trust companies of the United States (national, 7,277; other reporting banks and trust companies, 17,115) was but $2,032,-411,351, their surplus and undivided profits (being mostly excess profits earned but not divided and paid out as dividends) $2,105,574,839; deposits, $16,514,730,351; circulation (bank note currency), $681,740,513; making the total banking power of the United States (by Comptroller's report) $21,334,456,790, an increase during the year of $285,-212,407, or over 13 per cent.

So the banking power, entire money supply, and total value of all crops, combined amount only to less than $34,-000,000,000, or 21 per cent of the nearly $160,000,000,000 of credit represented by reported bank checks. In one way or another this entire business is made to yield such profits to the banks that they have been enabled to accumulate, chiefly from excess net profits, $2,105,574,839 of surplus and undivided profits, or more than their total $2,032,411,351 capital, besides steadily paying unusually large dividends. While many banks annually earn 10, 20, 50 and some 100 per cent net on their capital stock, for the year ending June 30, 1911, the average dividends paid by all of the national banks was 11.38 per cent on their capital stock, and their average net earnings was 15.57 per cent.

Cost of Living Increased.

It would be interesting to know, and highly illuminating, just how much higher the cost of living has been made by this use of 160 billion dollars of bank checks as a substitute for Government currency as the chief medium of exchange in American business. Every dollar paid by a business man to the banks for such "credit" is added as an item of cost and increases correspondingly the price of commodities to consumers. Therefore all of these rich and increasing profits made by banks are saddled directly upon the people. There is no way for them to escape this burden. It increases the prices of food, clothing, everything they buy. Advocates of a protective tariff claim that it tends to bar out the products of cheap foreign labor that if admitted free might tend somewhat to beat down prices and benefit consumers, but that it would thereby injure labor and agriculture by requiring less of the products of American factories and farms. And of course working men and farmers comprise the larger portion of the consumers of the country. Also, that if local industries do not combine into trusts or otherwise conspire to eliminate all genuine competition in order to keep prices high the tariff, by keeping out foreign products, may encourage the starting of so many industries in this country employing American labor that prices to consumers actually will be lowered instead of increased. This notwithstanding the tariff, because such local industries in competing with each other, if competition is real and unrestricted, in order to get the business naturally will make low prices yielding only reasonable profits. At least this is the theory of protection.

But a tariff not fixed by Congress, levied upon 95 per cent of all business by the banks in the form of charges for "credit," can in no way be avoided by the people unless the volume of Government currency is increased and the people do business more upon a cash basis. It should be remembered that the entire foreign commerce on which tariff is collected is less than one-tenth of the volume of domestic commerce on which the banks levy their credit tariff.

The foreign commerce of the United States in 1911 was: Exports, $2,013,549,000; imports, $1,527,945,000 (balance of trade, $485,604,000); total, $3,541,494,000. The entire foreign commerce (exports and imports) of the twenty-nine leading nations was thirty billion dollars, or less than 20 per cent of the 160 billion dollars of checks that went through the clearing houses of the United States last year. The total value of all manufactures of this country in 1909 was but twenty billion dollars.

And this bank-levied tariff may be duplicated many times on the same article. If the expense of producing the raw material, the selling price of same, the freight on it to the factory, the cost of working it into a finished article, the labor cost, the expense of administration and selling, the freight to the wholesaler, the price paid by wholesaler, the freight to retailer, the price paid by retailer and the price paid by the ultimate consumer, are all settled by bank checks it will be seen that to a greater or less extent the banks get the chance to make ten assessments for use of their "credit" against that one article. Perhaps it is a common everyday household necessity and the whole ten assessments are added to the price and paid unknowingly but invariably by the consumer. The consumer pays it all and the banks get it all. No one else profits a dollar from the sale of bank credit. And whatever decrease of the use of bank credit may occur by reason of increase of the volume of business done on a cash basis the whole loss will fall upon the banks and the entire benefit will go to the people in the shape of lowered prices on all the things they must purchase.

Have we not now smoked out the "Senigambian in the woodpile" that always has and always will cause banks to fight the issuance of currency by the Government, and particularly any serious increase of that currency whether it be uncovered "greenbacks" or treasury notes secured amply by a gold reserve? And the true although concealed reason why now they are trying to get Congress to prohibit the Government issuing any currency at all and to grant a monopoly of the issuance of all currency to a private corporation owned by the banks? Then they could make the people pay for the use of the pocket money they own as well as for use of bank credit, and the banks would get the other 5 per cent for which so long they have hungered. Then they would get a rake-off on 100 per cent instead of 95 per cent of all business transactions carried on by the people, with power in the banks to increase at will the size of such rake-off.

Right now the banks by clearing house agreements are extending throughout the country the new plan of charging "'exchange" on outside checks deposited by their regular customers. If this becomes general (as it will if business men submit), if the rates charged were applied to the whole 160 billion it and other new charges would increase the bank tax on business (and commerce) an amount nearly equal to half of the annual cost of running the Government of the United States.

It is not proposed or desired to abolish bank credit or arbitrarily curtail or unduly or unfairly restrict its supply or use. Nor is it intended to diminish or limit the legitimate profits of banks by law so long as they deal justly by the people, giving them good service at reasonable cost and exercise their law-given privileges and powers honestly and impartially for the general welfare.

But it is proposed and demanded that banks shall keep their restraining hand off the people's supply of public currency; that they shall stop every attempt and action that tends to compel the people against their will and interest to buy more bank credit and use less Government currency. Laws should not be framed, as at the instigation of the banks they have been, to force the people to do more business on a credit and less on a cash basis solely to increase the profits of the banks at the cost of the people.

On October 31, 1911, $744,071,715 of bank-note currency was in circulation. Not a dollar of gold secures this

SQUARE DEAL BANKING.

UNCLE SAM:—(TO BANKER):—BY CRACKY, THE TIME HAS COME WHEN I'M GOING TO ESTABLISH THE "SQUARE DEAL" BETWEEN THE BANKS AND THE PEOPLE!

vast bank currency. Banks want a gold reserve only behind Government currency. Banks pay this out over and over because it is not lawful money, is no good in their cash reserves, and because upon every dollar they are making a steady profit so long and only while it is out of their hands and in the hands of the people. The people do not have to accept bank-note currency because it is not a legal tender. Since December 21, 1863, the date of the first issue of national bank circulation, bank-note currency of the value of $5,460,186,435 has been issued by national banks that have received therefrom while it was out and unredeemed steady profits that were paid by the people. If this had all been Government currency the banks would have made less and the people would have paid less because the Government would have asked no profit for supplying such currency.

It is thus seen that banks do not object to paper currency. They only object to the Government issuing it without profit, or at all, because whatever Government currency is issued reduces the quantity of bank currency and credit used, and this decreases the profits of the banks.

All that is now asked is to lift the bank embargo on the free play of currency so that the people can use just as much or just as little such Government currency and purchased bank credit as they desire. Let the law of supply and demand be the sole regulator, the will and preference of the people determining the proportion of business to be conducted with bank credit and the amount to be done on a cash basis.

Let the Monetary Council, hereinafter suggested, establish and enforce a square deal between the banks and the people, the Government issuing all of the currency and the banks all of the credit, the people to use as much of each as they desire. Is not this right, business-like and just?

Every dollar of currency so issued will be made sound, guaranteed by the Government, redeemable in gold, backed by an adequate gold reserve and always kept equal in value with gold. The banks can not question the soundness of such a currency, or frighten the people with the old cry of "irredeemable paper money," "inflated unsecured greenbacks," "rag-baby," etc., for it will have all the security proposed for the "Aldrich plan" currency and the direct guarantee of the Government besides.

CHAPTER XIX.

THE LEGAL TENDER "JOKER."

A New Progressive Party?—"Lawful Money" and "Legal-Tender" Defined—Government Money vs. Corporate Currency.

The next great American monetary struggle is to be around the issue, Government Money vs. Corporate Currency. The report of the Monetary Commission has launched that issue in politics. The character and contents of its bill introduced in Congress on January 8, 1912, precipitates the fight. A vital political question of the most grave importance can not be kept out of politics just to accommodate and aid its bank and Wall Street promoters. The sly suggestion of Aldrich or the fiat of a President can not prevent the greatest political question since the civil war becoming a party question. No doubt the promoters of the Aldrich scheme desire in Congress and among the people to keep the 90 per cent who are opposed to the measure divided between the parties until the 10 per cent that never had any political principles, but plenty of legislative profits, as a balance of power can dicker and drive the bill through Congress.

This is likely to be the leading issue in the campaign of 1912. It should be made so. We believe one and probably both parties ultimately will declare against the Aldrich scheme. If one party indorses the plan the other party will win if it courageously fights the measure and the whole pack of ravenous wolves concealed behind it. If the special interests succeed in their attempt to bully or buy the nomination of reactionary candidates by both parties the great masses of the people will believe that those parties are mere bought and paid for concubines of Wall Street and no doubt will organize the National Progressive Party. Forced to form by such considerations of the highest duty and patriotism such a party should attract to its standard the 90 per cent of good men from both parties, north, south, east and west, and in a whirlwind campaign of popular indignation and aroused sentiment overwhelm Wall Street and all its allies and win victory in the first contest. Such a union of all unselfish citizens would be a great national blessing and the best guarantee of a safe, conservative, orderly Government for the republic for all future time. The only alternative, the only hope for the people, the only way to preserve popular government in the republic, if neither republican or democratic parties will resist the all-devouring interests and champion the people's cause in the impending struggle to keep their money free and preserve their financial liberty will be for the patriots of all parties to unite and form a new party that will serve the people. Because the people politically are so evenly divided a very small number as a gipsy balance of power swung back and forth often has decided the fate of national elections and really ruled the republic.

In 1884 a change of less than 1,000 votes in New York defeated Blaine and elected Cleveland. Think of 1,000 thus ruling 10,000,000 voters! President Harrison offended the banks and Wall Street by signing the Sherman silver purchasing law of 1890 and by paying Government bonds out of the enormous treasury surplus instead of depositing the surplus in the banks without interest and extending the bonds so the banks could use them as a basis for bank-note currency. Therefore he was defeated and Cleveland was elected in 1892 relatively by a few thousand votes in close states turned by the influence and political activity of the banks. The people do not realize that the national banking system always has been a vast, powerful and alert nation-wide political machine managed by Wall Street. Wall Street knows the value of thus throwing the election to one side and then to the other. It shows both parties the vital power of the "interests" under the electoral college system of choosing Presidents (which should be abolished for the public good) and terrifies them into naming candidates acceptable to the "interests" and tends to induce subsequent legislative and executive, if not judicial, subserviency to the will and pleasure of high finance. To a large extent the people do not count. This is because politically they always play the game "tug of war," one-half pulling on one end and the rest on the other end. Wall Street and the big banks in the middle give a little push one way or the other and thus decide the contest. Just how long the people will continue thus to be victimized is a question. This great

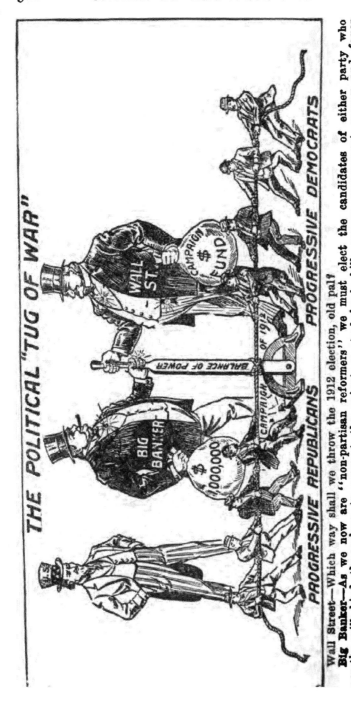

THE POLITICAL "TUG OF WAR"

PROGRESSIVE REPUBLICANS   PROGRESSIVE DEMOCRATS

Wall Street—Which way shall we throw the 1912 election, old pal?

Big Banker—As we now are "non-partisan reformers" we must elect the candidates of either party who secretly will bind themselves to support the private central bank bill, oppose government money and favor corporation currency.

Uncle Sam (to himself)—Why don't them goldarn fool progressives all get hold of the same end of that rope, or lock by themselves and form the National Progressive Party?

money issue on which their happiness and pocket-interest so largely depends may be the means of their political emancipation and cause party reorganization. The shadows cast by coming events already are in sight. The campaign of 1912 will be memorable and momentous. It may be the most sinister, corrupt and desperate in all history, for the "interests" are desperately playing for big stakes.

Legal-Tender Quality of Money.

Part of Sec. 8, Art. I, of the United States Constitution, defining the powers of Congress, says:

"To coin money, regulate the value thereof, and of foreign coin and fix the standard of weights and measures:

To provide for the punishment of counterfeiting the securities and current coin of the United States":

"Sec. 10. No state shall * * *coin money, emit bills of credit; make anything but gold and silver coin a tender in payment of debts; * * *"

On page 24 of "U. S. Treasury Circular No. 52" issued July 1, 1910, by the Treasury Department, it says:

"LEGAL-TENDER QUALITIES OF UNITED STATES MONEY.—There are ten different kinds of money in circulation in the United States, namely, gold coin, standard silver dollars, subsidiary silver, gold certificates, silver certificates, treasury notes issued under the act of July 14, 1890, United States notes (also called greenbacks and legal-tenders), national-bank notes, and nickel and bronze coins. These forms of money are all available as circulation. While they do not all possess the full legal-tender quality, each kind has such attributes as to give it currency. The status of each kind is as follows:

Gold coin is legal-tender at its nominal or face value for all debts, public and private, when not below standard weight and limit of tolerance prescribed by law; and when below such standard and limit of tolerance it is legal tender in proportion to its weight.

Standard silver dollars are legal tender at their nominal or face value in payment of all debts, public and private, without regard to amount, except where otherwise expressly stipulated in the contract.

Subsidiary silver is legal tender for amount not exceeding $10 in any one payment.

Treasury notes of the act of July 14, 1890, are legal tender for all debts, public and private, except where otherwise expressly stipulated in the contract.

United States notes ('greenbacks or legal tenders') are legal tender for all debts, public and private, except duties on imports and interest on the public debt. (Note—(a) United States notes upon resumption of specie payments, January 1, 1879, became acceptable in payment of duties on imports and have been freely received on that account since the above date, but the law has not been changed.)

Gold certificates, silver certificates and *national-bank notes* are *not* legal tender, but both classes of certificates are receivable for all public dues, while national-bank notes are receivable for all public dues except duties on imports, and may be paid out by the government for all salaries and other debts and demands owing by the United States to individuals, corporations and associations within the United States, except interest on the public debt and in redemption of the national currency. All national banks are required by law to receive the notes of other national banks at par.

The minor coins of nickel and copper are legal tender to the extent of 25 cents.

Foreign coins are not legal tender—Section 3584 of the Revised Statutes of the United States provides that no foreign coins shall be legal tender in the United States."

"Legal tender" money is the only "lawful money." It is the kind everybody must under the law accept when tendered in payment of any debt or purchase. There may be non-legal tender currency like bank notes and gold certificates, mere optional currency, used as a substitute for money. But this is good only so long as the other party does not care to refuse it.

Gold is not money. If it was, then wedding rings, ear rings, spoons and other articles of gold would be money. Gold hidden by nature in the bowels of the earth is not money. Nor is silver, copper, nickel, paper or ink. These commodities all are used as substances on which to print or stamp the evidence of money. The parchment or paper is not a man's will. His will is his formed ideas or wishes. For convenience, safety, record, these wishes are written with ink on paper in due form. The document is called a will. So we call the paper or coin evidence, money. The will of the man is his act of formal decision. And the will of Congress expressed in form of law is the thing that creates money. It is an act of sovereignty. It is the statute forcing its acceptance by the people, making it legal tender for the payment of debts, that breathes into those inanimate pieces of metal and paper the breath of life and vitalizes them into money. Without the statute they would remain mere commodities worth only their market price by weight. Gold has been enhanced above iron in value largely because law has singled it out and made it the standard or measure of value by weight, thus giving it special value by creating a fictitious artificial demand. If every Government should demonetize gold by repealing their laws making gold the monetary standard the price of gold would go down to what the metal is worth in the arts as a mere commodity. The price would be very low because so small a portion is required in the arts. And less would be used if gold should cease to be a "precious" metal.

Because creating money is an act of sovereignty, a function of government exercised only by means of the will of the people as expressed in the law, the issuance of money should not be farmed out or delegated by the Government to any private individual or corporation for private profit or advantage. And for the same reasons this is true of any currency based on or issued under authority of law to be used in place of or as a substitute for money. Law and all benefits thereunder must be impartial and general for the good of all the people without special favor or discrimination. To by law of Congress grant to a private corporation owned by the banks a monopoly of issuing the currency, and by law forcing the people to use such corporate currency and to pay to get it whatever the corporation and the banks may exact, is a dangerous departure in government likely to open the door to the granting of all kinds of special legislative profits and immunities to politically powerful special interests while denying such privileges to the rest of the people. We are at "the parting of the ways." This bill if passed will be the entering wedge opening the political pandora box and will permanently release a thousand evils and dangers that since 1776 have been kept securely imprisoned by the Constitution and the law through the wonderful foresight of the fathers or the kindly oversight of Providence.

Under the law the only "lawful money" is that which is a legal tender for the payment of all debts public and private. It will never depreciate but always remain equal in value with gold because it can be used equally with gold in doing all of the things for which money is required. This is reason and it is history. Under acts of July 17 and August 5, 1861, the government issued $50,000,000 of paper currency called "demand notes" and $10,000,000 additional under act of February 12, 1862, the first paper national currency ever issued by the Government. The act of March 17, 1862, made this currency full legal tender for all debts public and private except interest on the public debt. This provision kept these original greenbacks from depreciating and they never were worth less than gold. But the banks and Wall Street financiers, as shown in another chapter, made such a fuss and brought such pressure on Congress that the $150,-000,000 greenbacks, U. S. notes issued under act of February 25, 1862, $150,000,000 under act of July 11, 1862, and $150,000,000 March 3, 1863, a total of $450,000,000, were by law made only a "limited legal tender." The act of February 25, 1862, said: "And such notes herein authorized shall be receivable in payment of all taxes, internal duties, excises, debts, and demands of every kind due to the United States, except duties on imports, and of all claims and demands against the United States of every kind whatsoever, except for interest upon bonds or notes, which shall be paid in coin, and shall also be lawful money and a legal tender in payment of all debts public and private within the United States, except duties on imports and interest as aforesaid."

The *"exception"* refusing their use to pay interest on Government bonds and notes did little harm because such interest then was relatively small. But when the Government by law, this "exception," refused to accept its own money in payment of duties in imports, the principal source of revenue to the Government, it denied the greenbacks the largest active market and was official notice to the world that the currency was to be discriminated against even by the Government issuing it. This "exception," discrimination, and the use made thereof by Wall Street and the big banks in their manipulations by which the Government was forced to sell hundreds of millions of dollars of bonds for greenbacks at less than 50 cents on the dollar measured in gold, caused the rapid depreciation of this currency. And because the *law* required the Government to accept the first $60,000,000 of full legal tender greenbacks for duties on imports (not to pay interest on bonds and notes) such greenbacks never depreciated, although the $450,000,000 of limited legal tenders once depreciated to about 35 cents on the dollar as measured in gold.

Bank-note currency depreciated to the same extent that the $450,000,000 greenbacks did, and for the same reason; that is, because bank-note currency was not legal tender money. This is further convincing evidence that the soundness of currency chiefly depends on its being made legal tender by law.

Much of this information is from "U. S. Treasury Department Circular No. 52," giving "Information respecting U. S. bonds, paper currency, coin, production of precious metals, etc.," issued July 1, 1910. Readers are advised to get and read that public document. It can be obtained free on application to "The Secretary of the Treasury, Washington, D. C.," or anyway, through a congressman or senator. Note pages 24, 27, 28 and 29 for the official facts above stated.

If it is true that making Government currency lawful money by a law making it full legal tender for all debts, public and private, will keep it always at par with gold, and that making it only a limited legal tender or non-legal tender may cause depreciation because of the discrimination, should not every dollar of currency issued under authority of any act of Congress be made, in the interest of the people and the Government's honor a full legal tender for all debts, public and private? If not, why? There is no legitimate reason.

What possible excuse is there for inflicting upon the people vast issues of bank note and gold certificate currency that under the law is not lawful money but mere optional currency, utterly worthless for paying ordinary debts if the creditor cares to refuse to accept it? The whole wretched system has been fastened upon the country by the banks in their insane greed to discredit and keep down the volume and use of Government money and increase the demand for bank credit loans and bank currency from which banks derive a steady special profit. They have for 50 years used this legal tender "joker" and had it inserted in the laws of the land because the people did not understand its baneful character and subtle evil effect. *And they have carried it to such length that only about 5 per cent of all the currency in the hands of the people is legal tender lawful money, 95 per cent being mere optional currency.*

It is time the people took matters into their own hands

and drove the banks and Wall Street out of the temple of legislation and the executive departments of their Government.

HENCEFORTH EVERY DOLLAR OF CURRENCY MUST BE ISSUED BY THE GOVERNMENT AND BE A FULL LEGAL TENDER IN ANYBODY'S HANDS FOR THE PAYMENT OF A DOLLAR'S WORTH OF DEBT ANYWHERE AT ANY TIME. There should be no letup or compromise until every dollar outstanding under the authority of any law of the United States is of this high character and quality.

National City Bank Letters.

Following is a continuation of writer's correspondence with the National City Bank of New York from the chapter "Confession of Wall Street." These letters are inserted here because they have special reference to the questions of legal-tender and currency depreciation:

"MILWAUKEE, WIS., Nov. 26, 1911.
The National City Bank,
    Wall Street, New York City.
Gentlemen: I thank you for your reply of 24th inst. to my recent letter, and for the printed matter issued by you in support of the Aldrich plan. I shall read the public addresses in advocacy of that plan made by your president with pleasure and profit.

It seems to be important that all currency be maintained at par. We all remember the evils due to the depreciated treasury notes, or 'greenbacks,' during the civil war. Were not they legal-tender to an extent at least equal to the proposed currency to be issued by the National Reserve Association? They were issued by the Government, and this currency, unless also backed by the credit of the Government, will only be secured by this private association. Do you not think this may lead to a depreciated currency?

The Aldrich plan seems in all important essentials to be practically the same as the central bank plan originated some years ago either by your bank or the New York Chamber of Commerce. Am I right in this comparison?

Again thanking you, I am,
                    Very truly yours,
                    (Signed)   ALFRED O. CROZIER."

"The National City Bank of New York.
New York, November 29, 1911.
Mr. Alfred O. Crozier,
Plankinton House,
Milwaukee, Wisconsin.

Dear Sir: Replying to your favor of November 26th, we beg to say that you are undoubtedly right in your theory that the 'greenbacks' issued during the civil war were legal-tender to practically the same extent as the currency it is proposed to permit the National Reserve Association to issue. We would, however, call to your attention the fact that the credit of the Government back of the 'greenbacks' was not sufficient to guard against depreciation in their value. It is hardly to be supposed, therefore, that placing the credit of the Government back of the notes to be issued by the Reserve Association would entirely guard against the difficulty you fear. The authorities fully recognized the danger of the greenbacks in our monetary system, and in the act of March 14, 1900, a greatly increased gold reserve was provided, and there was also inserted in that act the provision that when United States notes are presented at the Treasury Department for redemption, they must first be exchanged for gold before being re-issued. Thus you will see that an attempt was made to place the gold stock in the reserve fund back of the greenbacks.

If you will read paragraph 68 of the suggested plan for monetary legislation forwarded to you, you will see that it is therein provided that all note issues of the National Reserve Association must be covered to the extent of at least one-third by gold or other lawful money, and the remaining portion by bankable commercial paper as herein defined or obligations of the United States, but no notes shall be issued whenever the lawful money so held shall fall below one-third of the notes outstanding. You will thus see that your statement that such notes would be secured only by this private association is hardly correct. The notes will be secured by this reserve of lawful money to the extent of one-third, and to the extent of the balance will be secured by commercial paper or Government obligation. It would appear that the legal tender quality of the notes backed by these ample provisions for reserve security back of them would guard against any depreciation.

We shall endeavor to procure and send to you a copy of the plan originated some years ago by the New York

Chamber of Commerce. From this you will be able to make your own comparison with the plan now proposed by Senator Aldrich. There is undoubted similarity between the two plans, but we believe it is too much to say that they are practically the same, as Senator Aldrich has worked out, we believe, a much superior method of control of the proposed National Reserve Association than had been thought of at the time the New York Chamber of Commerce suggestion was made.

We trust this satisfactorily answers your inquiry, and are,
Very truly yours,
W. H. Tappan" (Asst. Cashier).

"Milwaukee, Wis., Dec. 13, 1911.
The National City Bank,
    Wall Street, New York City.

Gentlemen: Returning here after an absence of some time, I find your valued favor of November 29, which I have read with interest and carefully considered.

The integrity and soundness of all currency is so important to all of us; and the necessity of making no mistake in any system adopted so imperative, I am tempted to again trespass on your valuable time.

You say that the 'Aldrich plan' currency will be legal-tender to no greater extent than was the depreciated 'greenback' of civil war times, and that 'greenbacks' depreciated in spite of the credit of the Government being back of them. And you hold, if I understand correctly, that the proposed currency of a private corporation, secured only by a gold reserve of one-third and commercial paper of various private parties for two-thirds the par value of such currency, and without any obligation on the Government to maintain such currency at par, will be safe and sound and likely always to be accepted by the people at par, as would a currency issued or backed by the Federal Government and secured by an adequate gold reserve. Is this your view?

As I now recall, there was one issue of 'greenbacks' amounting to $50,000,000 put out during the civil war that were by their terms and on their face a 'full legal tender' for all purposes. Am I right in suggesting that these never depreciated like the other greenbacks that were only a 'limited legal-tender' usable for all purposes, except duties on imports and interest on the public debt? Were not those 'full legal tender' greenbacks, with nothing behind them but the faith and credit of the Government, the same as a government bond, always worth their face in gold coin even when the 'limited legal-tender' greenbacks were worth about 35 cents on the dollar?

If this is historically true, was it not the credit of the Government that kept the 'full legal-tenders' at par, and the *exception* that caused the 'limited legal-tenders' to depreciate? And is there not danger of depreciation of 'limited legal-tender' currency issued by a private corporation without the faith and credit of the Government being pledged to maintain it, even if secured by the relatively small gold reserve and commercial paper?

Under the gold standard law you cite (1900) was not the faith and credit of the Government forever pledged to maintain at par with gold every dollar of the public currency?

Will not the Aldrich plan change that gold standard act provision by authorizing an enormous paper currency, upwards of a billion dollars of it, with no pledge or obligation by the Government to maintain it at par with gold or at any figure at all? Are we not taking a dangerous leap into monetary darkness by this plan?

Hoping I may be set right if I am wrong in these matters and again thanking you, I am,

Very truly yours,
(Signed) ALFRED O. CROZIER."

"THE NATIONAL CITY BANK OF NEW YORK.
Capital $25,000,000.
Surplus and Undivided Profits $25,000,000.
NEW YORK, December 15, 1911.

MR. ALFRED O. CROZIER,
    Plankinton House,
        Milwaukee, Wisconsin.

Dear Sir: Acknowledging your favor of December 13th with reference to the Aldrich plan, we note that you class the bank note and the greenback together. We believe that you will secure a broader view of the subject from an address recently delivered in Racine by Mr. Joseph T. Talbert. While this address does not cover all the questions raised with reference to the greenback, still it so clearly differentiates the position and function of the greenback and the bank note that we believe it will be useful in clearing up

UNITED STATES MONEY vs

The National City Bank
of New York.

CAPITAL $25 000 000
SURPLUS & UNDIVIDED PROFITS $25 000 000
CABLE ADDRESS "CITIBANK"

New York,
December 15, 1911.

Mr. Alfred O. Crozier,
    Plankinton House,
        Milwaukee, Wisconsin.

Dear Sir:

    Acknowledging your favor of December 13th with reference to the Aldrich plan, we note that you class the bank note and the greenback together. We believe that you will secure a broader view of the subject from an address recently delivered in Racine by Mr. Joseph T. Talbert. While this address does not cover all the questions raised with reference to the greenback, still it so clearly differentiates the position and function of the greenback and the bank note that we believe it will be useful in clearing up doubts which you seem to have with reference to this subject.

    We take pleasure in forwarding, under separate cover, a copy of this address, which we hope will reach you promptly.

Yours very truly,

Assistant Cashier.

S-R

doubts which you seem to have with reference to this subject.

We take pleasure in forwarding, under separate cover, a copy of this address, which we hope will reach you promptly.

Yours very truly,
(Signed) THOS. A. REYNOLDS,
Assistant Cashier."

Evidently the bank could not find or give any explanation that would aid the Aldrich plan, of the historic fact it could not controvert, that the first $50,000,000 of legal tender greenbacks never depreciated while the $450,000,000 of limited legal tender greenbacks had depreciated. So the bank in its reply makes no answer to writer's letter on that vital matter, the most important question in the impending struggle, but refers him to the speech of Banker Talbert (vice-president of National City Bank and director of Continental and Commercial National Bank of Chicago) which on examination was found to say nothing whatever on that subject.

Thus we find the biggest and greatest bank in the United States, that commands the greatest expert financial minds in the country, and has upon its directing board representatives of all of the powerful Wall Street interests that dominate the entire national banking system, the mammoth insurance companies, the railroads and the trusts of the United States, actually unable or unwilling to attempt to explain why legal tender money did not depreciate while limited legal tender currency badly depreciated.

This is not criticism. It is evidence of good sense, the sudden retreat of the bank when it found the water getting too deep and it could not swim.

The Aldrich bill does not invest the proposed corporate currency with half the legal tender power enjoyed even by the $450,000,000 of limited legal tender greenbacks that depreciated. It is not to be made "lawful money" at all. It will not be a tender for the payment of ordinary debts between individuals.

The commission's Aldrich bill reads:

"Sec. 53—The circulating notes of the National Reserve Association shall be received at par in payment of all taxes, excises, and other dues to the United States, and for all salaries and other debts and demands owing by the United States to individuals, firms, corporations or associations, except obligations of the Government which are by their terms specifically payable in gold, and for all debts due from or by one bank or trust company to another, and for all obligations due to any bank or trust company."

This is all there is on this subject in the bill. The corporate currency would not be a tender between individuals, or between any individual and any corporation other than banks and trust companies. It will be optional currency, not "lawful money." Corporate currency should not be legal tender "lawful money," because that would be forcing the people by law to accept the corporation currency for the exclusive profit and benefit of the corporation. That would be a wrongful use of law. The foundation is to be laid by the Aldrich bill to work off on the people another billion dollars of currency not lawful money, and it is said not to be guaranteed by the Government, but be merely an obligation of a private corporation, the obligation or debts of which will aggregate ultimately more than ten times its entire cash capital.

No wonder the National City Bank hastily dropped the subject. In its letter of November 29, 1911, the bank itself cited the fact that greenbacks even with the whole credit of the Federal Government behind them, and only $450,000,000 outstanding, depreciated more than 50 per cent. How then can it be expected that the National Reserve Association, with only $100,000,000 of cash capital and perhaps a billion dollars of liabilities, can, without any Government guarantee or assistance, keep its billion dollar issue of currency from depreciation, and at par? Especially so, when it is not even made "lawful money," or as much a legal tender as the Government greenbacks that depreciated in spite of the support of the Government, solely because they were not made full legal-tender? It is a wildcat scheme and it will be a wildcat corporate paper currency like that emitted by the banks and worked off on the people in vast quantities before the Civil War by confidence game methods. It is a reckless, dangerous experiment.

The only possible reply is the proposed gold reserve of 33⅓ per cent "required," but with no provision or penalty to enforce it. But if such a gold reserve will make safe and sound a vast issue of corporate paper currency that is not full legal-tender and is only the obligation of a private corporation and not of the Government, then why would not the same size gold reserve make safe and sound the same size issue of Government currency that is a full legal-tender for all debts public and private, and is backed by the entire faith, credit, taxing and bonding power of the Government of the greatest nation on earth?

There! That's the conundrum. That is the one big question in all this controversy. The bank could feel it coming, so it "flew the coop" and escaped.

But the people can and will answer the question that the bank dodged, for the reasoning is simple and plain and the evidence is official, convincing and conclusive.

While they did not dare openly to propose it at first, either before the Aldrich bill becomes law or by an amendment in after years the Government will be made liable for all currency issued by this corporation, will be made an accommodation indorser on the corporation's notes for a billion dollars, even if it would not be obligated from the beginning under the statute heretofore cited. Absence of any provision in the pending bill expressly stating that in no way shall the Government be liable, is significant. And the remarkable and conflicting letters from various members of the Monetary Commission and the big banks printed in preceding chapters give the whole thing a sinister appearance.

CHAPTER XX.

REORGANIZING THE MONEY SUPPLY.

New System, Government Money Secured by Gold, Instead of Unlimited Optional Corporate Currency.

On June 30, 1911, there was in circulation $930,367,929 of gold certificates and $698,532,060 of bank-note currency, total $1,628,899,989. This is over half of the $3,214,002,595 that comprised the entire stock of all kinds of money of the United States on that date, in circulation, in the banks and in the Treasury. Yet not one dollar of those vast issues of gold certificates and bank-note currency is legal-tender "lawful money." It is all mere optional currency that anybody can legally refuse when it is tendered in payment of an ordinary debt. There are cases where this has worked great wrong and hardship. One reported instance may be cited to illustrate. Some western men had discovered and developed a valuable mine to a point where there was ore enough in sight to show to a certainty that the property was sound and of great value. They needed money to build a large plant and operate the property. They went to Wall Street. After careful investigation the New York "bankers" agreed to furnish the money. Instead of joining in the deal they put their money in as a "loan" secured by mortgage on the mine. It was made a short-term mortgage. It came due before the plant could be finished and operated to make the mine yield enough to pay the debt. Payment was demanded and the mortgage for about $150,000 foreclosed. The western men finally raised the money elsewhere and on the last day of redemption tendered it to the sheriff in settlement. The eastern lawyer representing the Wall Street people found that considerable of the $150,000 was gold certificates and some bank-note currency. These not being "lawful money" he refused the tender and demanded payment in "lawful money." There was then no time to go from the distant county to a bank in a large city to get the necessary gold or greenbacks, the "lawful money." The western men thus were robbed of their property and the rich Wall Street sharpers got it, as was their aim from the beginning, for a mere fraction of its value. The legal-tender "joker" in the law enabled them to do it legally.

Few people know that bank currency is not legal-tender, and not one in ten thousand understand that gold certificates, with 100 per cent in gold deposited in the Treasury are mere "warehouse receipts" instead of "lawful money" and are useless whenever the other party cares to refuse them. The bankers who got this joker grafted into the laws know, but the masses of the people are kept ignorant of these matters so vital to their interests and welfare. It is a shameless fraud upon the people to which the Government has been made a guilty party.

Very little gold or greenbacks are in the hands of the people. This lawful money is largely kept by the banks in their "lawful money legal reserves." It has been estimated that *of all the money in actual circulation among the people only about 5 per cent is lawful money, the other 95 per cent being mere optional paper currency.* And now the Aldrich plan would authorize a vast unlimited volume of corporate currency, not guaranteed at all by the Government, to be worked off on the people by the banks in the shape of payrolls and otherwise, not one dollar of which will be legal-tender lawful money, all being only optional corporate currency.

It is time for the people to call a halt on all this unfair and injurious juggling of their money supply and its debt-paying qualities, done by the banks for their profit and advantage; done to discredit and handicap Government currency, the people's own money, in the interest of corporate bank currency.

If present public officials are faithless and will not give relief and protection to the people against the soulless rapacity and greed of the special interests the people should make it their first business to choose new and honest public servants. There is no matter more vital to the happiness and pocket of every man, whether he carries a dinner-pail or rides in his automobile.

Now that the banks have raised the question and forced the issue upon the country, the people should demand and see that it is settled right. *Except the coined metal money, every dollar of outstanding currency, Government and bank-*

WHITE MAN'S (U.S.) BURDEN.

NEW "OLD MAN OF THE SEA."

FOR 50 YEARS THE NATIONAL BANKING SYS-
TEM BOTH LEGALLY AND ILLEGALLY HAS
PLUNDERED THE GOVERNMENT AND THE
PEOPLE. UNJUST GRAFT TOTALS COUNT-
LESS MILLIONS. THE OFFICIAL RECORD
IS GIVEN IN THIS BOOK.

*note, should be gradually replaced with just one kind of
Government currency, issued in convenient denominations.
Every dollar shall be lawful money, full legal-tender for all
debts public and private, redeemable in gold, secured by an
adequate reserve of gold, and guaranteed, the same as bonds,
by the whole faith and credit of the Government of the
United States.* This is the only practicable course if Congress, the Government, is to be fair and honest with the
people.

The $1,163,901,183.56 of gold in possession of the Federal
Treasury June 30, 1911, is sufficient, if this suggested monetary revision is adopted, to constitute a 50 per cent reserve
of gold to secure an issue of $2,327,802,366 of legal-tender
Government paper currency. This is more than enough
to replace the $930,367,929 of gold certificates, $698,532,060
of bank-note currency and $346,681,016 of United States
notes, or greenbacks, which together amount only to $1,975,-
581,005.

The promoters of the Aldrich plan can not question the
adequacy of a 50 per cent gold reserve or the soundness
of such a Government currency, for that is all they propose to "secure" a vast paper currency to be emitted by
a private corporation without any Government guarantee.
In fact the data supplied by the monetary commission attempted to show that by the experience of Europe a gold
reserve of 33⅓ per cent is ample security for an issue of
currency, and the bill of the commission now pending in
Congress permits the Reserve Association to run its gold
reserve down to 33⅓ per cent. And this 33⅓ per cent
reserve can be all greenbacks, without one dollar of actual
gold. If that is safe for a corporation surely it is for the
Government, with all its unlimited taxing power, splendid
credit, vast resources, and power to issue bonds to buy
gold without restriction or limit under the Gold Standard
Act of March 14, 1900. So without buying another dollar
of gold, using only what the Government now possesses,
$1,163,901,183, not in circulation but in the hands of the
Treasury, a total legal-tender Government currency amounting to $3,491,703,529 would be possible without the gold re-
serve falling below 33⅓ per cent. This is more paper currency probably than the country will require during the next
forty years. And when it needs more the Government can
get all the gold it wants as the world's gold production
goes on increasing each year, simply by issuing its redeem-

able, gold secured, Government guaranteed, full legal-tender
lawful money circulating notes, or currency, to pay for
same.   And each dollar of gold so bought safely can be
made the basis for two or three dollars of additional Government currency.

It is well always to keep in mind that one of the chief
objects in forming this great bank trust, this vast money
combine, is to corner and so regulate the supply of money
and credit that incorporated wealth will get all and the
people none of the benefit due to the providential increase
in the world's gold production.   If increase of gold increases
the prices of property and labor it will be offset by a general increase of interest rates when loanable funds all are
under one central control with no serious competition for big
loans.   And if later a falling gold production decreases the
prices of all property and labor, interest rates arbitrarily
can be kept high and thus automatically increase the value
of all bond wealth measured in property or labor.

This splendid volume of $930,367,929 of gold certificate
currency, and the equal amount of gold in the Treasury securing the same, all cost the Government practically nothing,
only the nominal cost of coinage.   Miners and other owners
of gold bullion for sale simply deposited their gold at the
Government's assay offices or the three mints and the gold
was paid for with U. S. gold certificates.   This automatically
increased the Government's stock of gold, expanded the
volume of the public currency and put the gold currency
into general circulation.   A gold certificate is the Government's promise to pay back on demand an equal amount of
gold.   But the miner does not want his gold back.   He
wanted to market his gold production.   And he has more
to sell each year.   He never will ask for a return of the
gold.   All he wanted was his pay in something he could
use as money at par for deposit in the bank or to pay his
workmen for mining more gold.   He puts the gold certificates into circulation.   They are payable to bearer.   They
are used as money.   Anybody can present them for redemption and get their face in gold coin.   But usually no
one wants the gold.   The paper certificates are more convenient.   Holders only want to know that they could get
gold if they desired, or that the currency is sound and
worth par.   Usually it is only when actual gold is required
to settle some international balance that gold certificates are
presented for redemption.   A very small proportion are pre-

sented and the actual gold demanded. The quantity of
money has increased faster than population. The per capita
circulation was:

1862	$10.23
1865	20.58
1878	15.32
1888	22.88
1898	25.19
1900	26.93
1908	34.72
1910	34.33

Of the United States gold production of $96,269,100 in
1911, $33,756,546 was used in the arts and $62,512,546 for
monetary purposes. As original deposits of gold made with
the Treasury in 1911, for which gold certificates were given
in payment amounted to $175,383,090, it will be seen that
much gold came from abroad, nearly two-thirds. The
$485,604,000 excess of exports over imports explains this.
Although the Act of March 3, 1863, authorized this receipt
of gold and issuance of gold certificates, on July 1, 1889,
there was only $154,048,552 of gold certificates outstanding,
or less than last year's net increase.

With this big international trade balance in our favor,
hundreds of millions annually, all settled with gold, there
should be no doubt of the Government having ample gold
to protect all the Government currency needed to replace
all forms of paper currency.

It is an unanswerable example, this creation of $930,367,-
929 of Government paper currency, gold certificates secured by a 100 per cent gold reserve, obtained practically
without expense to the Government, all of it except $154,-
048,552 since 1889. If the gold reserve basis instead of
being 100 per cent had been 50 per cent, the gold paper
currency instead of being $930,367,929 would be $1,860,-
735,858. If the gold reserve basis had been 33⅓ per cent,
gold paper currency now would be $2,791,103,787. *So there
can be no question as to the soundness of the proposed gold
secured Government currency or the sufficiency of the supply
of gold to protect the same.*

The only remaining question is the danger of overinflation. This would not affect the soundness of the currency because that is insured by the Government guaran-

tee and the gold reserve. The banks and the monetary commission concede this. But the banks are afraid that if the Government controls the issuance and volume of money the people sometime may induce it to issue so much that the people will do more business on a cash basis and less with credit bought from banks. And Wall Street and its foreign clients are afraid that increase of Government currency will tend to decrease the demand for gold and the value of bonds payable in gold, or in other words, increase the prices of securities (except gold bonds), property and labor as measured in gold. So Wall Street, the Rothschilds and the banks are unwilling to trust the people and Government of the United States to run their own affairs in a sane and rational manner and propose by the Aldrich plan that the Government abdicate and turn the whole thing over to the banks to be run for the benefit and profit of the banks, Wall street and the Rothschilds instead of the people of the United States. They want their private corporation appointed receiver or guardian of the republic. *But the people know that there is far greater danger from excessive contraction of the currency if the banks control than there is from excessive expansion if the Government of the republic continues to exercise its constitutional functions in the matter.* So THE PEOPLE MUST "STAY IN THE SADDLE" AND KEEP CONTROL THROUGH THEIR GOVERNMENT OF THE POWER TO REGULATE THE VOLUME OF THE PUBLIC CURRENCY, THEIR MONEY SUPPLY. IT WOULD BE SUICIDE TO DO OTHERWISE. We should remember that inflation of bank credit has the same effect as inflation of the currency, only it is a tenfold greater danger. It would be more sensible for the Government to grant to a private corporation for its profit a monopoly of issuing and fixing the price and quantity of all postage stamps than to grant private control of the public currency.

Wall Street and the banks carefully laid a trap for the people and now have walked into it themselves. To obtain a corporation currency under private control they have openly committed themselves so that they cannot oppose a Government currency of the kind herein proposed without making themselves ridiculous. This is what we have long waited for, and the people should not delay in pressing their advantage and opportunity to get an adequate and sound public currency under Government control.

It is only necessary to pass a simple act making all gold

certificates a full legal-tender to make them as valuable to
the people for paying debts as they were, by special act of
1907 made to the banks for legal reserve purposes. And
as gold certificates come back to the Government in payment of duties and taxes they can be cancelled and new
national currency issued in their place on a 50 per cent gold
reserve basis. As this currency gradually expands at the
2 for 1 ratio bank-note currency can be gradually called in
and cancelled and the Government bonds be paid off out
of any available surplus. The transition will be easy and
natural and do no harm or injury to the legitimate interests
of the banks or anyone else.

The law can fix the gold reserve basis as 50 per cent,
with an emergency provision by which the volume of currency can be suddenly expanded to a 33⅓ per cent gold
reserve basis, this emergency issue to be loaned to the
banks only at such rates as will insure its prompt return
to the Government when the emergency is past. This would
keep an extra emergency currency always available and
ready amounting to more than a billion dollars. The first
$200,000,000, enough to move the annual crop, could be fur-
nished during crop marketing at moderate rates, the balance at emergency rates. This plan would guard against
the danger of panics far better than the Aldrich plan; it
would not be giving private interests power by excessive
contraction to cause panics, and it would do much to prevent panics altogether by helping to remove the causes of
panics.

Providence truly has shaped events to make it possible for
the people to now free themselves from the present expensive
and dangerous bank and Wall Street domination of their
money supply. Every condition is right and the time is
ripe. A definite plan is suggested in the next chapter. The
change can be made by one simple act of Congress and with
practically no expense to the Government. This is because
the Government right now has ample gold to make the
change. It will make it possible for the Government ultimately to save nearly $10,000,000 now going as profits to
the banks and about $20,000,000 interest on the public debt
every year. And it will obtain from the banks a handsome
annual revenue by charging the banks a fair and reasonable
price for the use of Government currency for their cash
reserves and to put into circulation among the people.

There can be no opposition to this alternative plan by

any man who has faith in the soberness and soundness of the government of the republic unless that man is a banker or financier seeking unjustly and improperly to use the powers and laws of government for his private profit and special advantage. On the other hand, if the Aldrich bill becomes law, the Government will be firmly obligated to pay out $1,485,024,050 just for interest on the $963,349,-390 of 2 per cent Government bonds which the measure refunds for fifty years at 3 per cent.

CHAPTER XXI.

UNITED STATES MONETARY COUNCIL.

A New Currency and Banking Plan.

Instead of the Aldrich plan for *a private central bank* named *"National Reserve Association,"* it is suggested that Congress create *a responsible public institution* to be called *"United States Monetary Council,"* with original, exclusive and supreme authority for the Government over all monetary and banking matters. It shall not be a mere commission or board, but a new, distinct and separate coördinate or subsidiary branch of the Government with the same control over its delegated functions that the legislative, executive and judicial departments possess over their respective functions.

To that end, subject to such modification of details as may appear wise, it is proposed:

1. The "United States Monetary Council" shall be created by Act of Congress, and afterwards made permanent by amendment to the Constitution. It shall be a new, distinct, coördinate or subsidiary branch of the Government with original, exclusive and supreme authority over all matters within the functions expressly delegated by the creating legislative act. Congress shall have the same control over such council as it has over the Executive and Judicial departments, and no more. The council shall have original, exclusive and supreme control for the Government of all monetary and banking matters, and such other things as at any time may be expressly delegated to it by Act of Congress.

2. The council shall consist of seventy-five members called "governors," a majority being a quorum. The Chief Justice of the Supreme Court, Vice-President, Speaker of the House, Secretary of the Treasury and Secretary of Commerce and Labor shall be ex-officio members (each having power to appoint an alternate to act in his stead at any meeting), the other seventy to be appointed by the

A DELIBERATIVE PUBLIC INSTITUTION, INSTEAD OF A PRIVATE CORPORATION.

75 members, one representing each of the 48 states and 27 the Federal Government. It shall regulate the banking system, fix the general discount rate and issue and determine the volume of the public currency, under strict regulations and legal safeguards. It shall establish and maintain the "square deal," between the banks and the public.

President, one on the mandatory nomination of the governor or vote of the people of each state without confirmation, the other twenty-two by and with the advice and consent of the Senate. The term shall be four years, the appointed members to be so arranged that one-half of those nominated by states and one-half of those confirmed by the Senate will go out of office each two years, the President in the same manner appointing their successors and filling any vacancies. Impeachment for cause by the council shall lie against any governor or elected officer of the council. By majority vote the people of any state may "recall" its representative and substitute another "governor."

As the National City Bank has 24 directors, National Bank of Commerce 40, Continental and Commercial National 44, total 108, and the proposed National Reserve Association would have 46, it would appear that 75 is a reasonable membership for the United States Monetary Council, representing the whole country.

This plan will insure against any politics or partisanship in the operations of the council because both parties always will have influential members on the inside ready instantly to block by publicity any attempt improperly to use the powers of the council. It is a complete guard against Wall Street influences. This plan also insures to every state representation and fair treatment and will gain for the council and its acts general public confidence, and thus establish a sound, stable, permanent and elastic system of banking and currency adapted to the changing needs of the country. This deliberative and responsible public body will forever protect the country and its business against the panic-inciting and dangerous evils of excessive currency and credit inflation and contraction. It would make panics impossible.

3. The council from its membership shall elect four persons by open ballot to serve for one, two, three and four years respectively, the one having the shortest time to serve to be president and the three others vice-presidents. A new vice-president to so serve four years shall be similarly elected each year.

The council shall appoint the Comptroller of the Currency, and such other officers, agents and employees as it may deem best and all standing and special committees and shall have power to dismiss any appointee. It shall fix the salaries of all elected officers and appointees, same to be paid out of funds controlled by the council; but the salaries or compensation of governors shall be specified in the Act of Congress creating the council and paid out of funds controlled by the council. It is suggested that the position be largely honorary, without salary, each governor receiving say $25 per day while necessarily absent from his home and his actual railroad fare. This would divorce the positions from the scramble for political spoils and command from each state a man of the highest character and standing who would serve as a patriotic duty and for the dignity and high honor conferred.

4. The executive committee shall consist of fifteen members. The president and three vice-presidents of the council and the Comptroller of the Currency shall be ex-officio members, the other ten to be appointed by the council from among its members or otherwise. These ten should be trained and experienced financial experts of the highest standing and character, paid whatever their valuable services may be worth.

The routine affairs of the council and its branches all shall be under the management of the executive committee, subject to the supervision of the council and its committees and under its rules, regulations and by-laws, which council is authorized to adopt, alter or repeal, same to be not inconsistent with law or the act creating the council. This guarantees careful, efficient and intelligent business management of the highest order.

5. The regular annual session of the council shall be in February, at Washington, D. C., which shall be the headquarters of the council; other sessions can be held quarterly, or only on call. Branches established in various parts of the country for business convenience shall be organized by the executive committee on plans approved by council.

6. Every governor, officer, appointee, agent or employee of the council or person acting under its authority shall be selected because of special fitness, without regard to their political views, be deemed public officials and shall take the usual oath of office required by law. And before the annual meeting each year every such elected officer, appointee, agent and employee shall file with the council his written declaration under oath stating that during his service he has not wilfully or knowingly violated his oath of office and to the best of his knowledge and belief always has in everything been faithful to his duties and public trust. Any false

declaration shall be made perjury, punishable under the criminal statutes.

Any attempt improperly to use the powers or functions of the council by any person charged with the exercise of any of such powers or functions, and any attempt by any person to induce such improper use of such powers or functions, shall under the penal statutes be made a crime severely punishable by fine, or imprisonment, or both.

7. The council shall have full, exclusive and supreme control of the issuance and disposition of all coin and public currency, but every dollar shall be full legal-tender for all debts public and private, redeemable at par on demand, in gold when required, secured by a gold reserve of at least 33⅓ per cent.

Council may put such currency into circulation through national and state banks and trust companies on such terms, security and conditions as it may from time to time prescribe, same to be impartial and uniform throughout the United States and so far as practicable in accordance with general regulations formally adopted and publicly announced by the council. It may create a general discount market and rediscount for such banks and trust companies first-class commercial paper under proper safeguards, fixing from time to time its general uniform rate of discount, using for such purposes its currency and the deposits made with the council by the banks and trust companies and the Government, which shall be council's only depositors. The Government shall deposit all public moneys with the council and make all its disbursements through the council. The council will not be a bank and shall not do general banking business in competition with banks.

Every national bank and every participating state bank or trust company shall deposit with council all of its legal cash reserves not kept in its own vaults, and in any event at least two-thirds of its required legal reserve, the legal cash reserve of all such banks to be by law reduced to a minimum of 12 per cent of their total deposit liabilities. Banks may sell drafts against this central deposit, instead of New York drafts. The interest to be allowed to the Government and the banks on deposits, if any, and charged for currency and rediscounting are factors likely to change with changing conditions from time to time and safely can be left to the wise judgment and discretion of council and its experienced executive committee to be always adjusted

on a fair business basis with reason and justice in the light
of all circumstances then existing and by rule of the square
deal.

The council will be entirely self-supporting and also will
furnish to the public treasury a very large and steady revenue easily obtained without any unfair burden to business
or the banks, paid in return for the invaluable service and
protection rendered by the council and for the valuable immunities and privileges conferred by law upon banks under
which they have a monopoly of the right to receive deposits
and to loan at interest their mere credit to an amount averaging ten times their net cash assets. As the Government
and its laws make this possible the banks should pay to the
Government whatever such privileges reasonably are worth
to the banks. Any private business would be ruined by
such unbusinesslike practices as the turning over of hundreds of millions of Government money to the banks
absolutely free or for a nominal 1 per cent. The council
will put the matter on a business basis.

This council plan and its branches puts each city on equal
footing, breaks the financial monopoly of New York, *takes
bank cash reserves out of Wall Street,* "mobilizes" them in
"one central reservoir," there to be always ready for instant
use to extinguish a "financial conflagration" occurring in
any part of the country, and for constant daily use in all
parts of the United States where required by the ever fluctuating demands of business. Genuine and safe elasticity of
the currency, made to automatically respond to the rise and
fall of the volume of trade and commerce and the marketing
of crops, without danger of arbitrary manipulation for
selfish purposes, would thus be firmly and permanently established. With all its powers Wall Street then could not
cause general panic or endanger the banks anywhere in the
country with fatal "runs" by frightened depositors. Every
bank is left free and independent, and yet the resources of
24,392 banks and of the Federal Government are combined through the council for the protection of each bank,
depositors, business borrowers and the public generally. A
panic then would be harmless.

8. Council shall maintain the gold standard in accordance
with the Act of March 14, 1900, and a gold reserve of not
less than 33⅓ per cent of all Government paper currency
of every kind in actual circulation outside of the public
treasury and council, gradually retiring all bank-note cur-

rency, greenbacks and gold and silver certificates, substituting the uniform, full legal-tender, redeemable, gold-secured, national currency proposed by this plan. It shall have power to acquire at par from the banks 2 per cent U. S. bonds used as a basis of circulation as the bank-note currency is retired, paying for same with such new public national currency. This, in time, would extinguish the entire interest-bearing public debt ($963,340,390) with noninterest-bearing currency without materially increasing the volume of public currency. In this way the Government would save the $1,485,024,050 of future bond interest imposed by the fifty-year refunding scheme of the Aldrich plan and $963,349,390, the amount of outstanding 2 per cent bonds to be exchanged for currency, total $2,448,373,440; also the millions of currency burned or destroyed by other accident—the benefit from which under the Aldrich plan would go to the banks. And the Government also would get pay for use of its surplus revenues.

It shall be lawful for any holder of national currency to present same and demand the actual gold for any legitimate business objects, but organized raids upon the public gold reserves made for the purpose of embarrassing the Government or forcing the issuing of Government bonds shall be made a felony punishable by a fine equal to the amount of the currency presented for redemption for such purpose and by imprisonment not more than ten years. It is even more important thus to protect the Government against criminal "raids" than it is to protect banks, as some states by law do, against artificial "runs."

9. Council shall have exclusive control of the regulation of banks and may make, alter or rescind any rules and regulations for such purpose (not inconsistent with law) that it may deem necessary. And to aid in making such regulation more effective in the interest of depositors and the public, Congress shall so amend the National Bank Act that suitable criminal penalties will be imposed upon bank officials and directors who knowingly violate the law, including punishment of any bank official for accepting or demanding any commission on loans made or securities bought by his bank, or practicing discrimination between customers in the matter of interest paid on deposits or charged for loans or other service rendered by the bank; or for directly or indirectly charging a greater rate of interest than 6 per cent per annum on any kind of loan or discount; or for mak-

ing or calling any loan with the object of extortion or forcing the sale of pledged securities or property or the manipulation of the quotation prices of any security "listed" on any stock exchange.

This would stop the scandal of the use of the banks and people's deposits for unfair stock market manipulations, and of 10, 50, 100 and 1,000 per cent interest on call loans paid to entice the money of the whole country away from legitimate business and into Wall Street gambling. National banks so prohibited would in their own interest force the passage of state laws to stop state banks and trust companies charging over 6 per cent on either time or call loans, or practicing discriminations between customers, or the other evils thus made unlawful. This is designed to establish a general condition of obedience to law, common honesty and the "square deal" in the world of banking.

10. This plan, or some modification thereof, is the only possible way to create a bigger and stronger financial power than that now possessed by Wall Street and no time should be lost, because Wall Street each day is getting stronger. It would break the strangle hold the "special interests" now have on the entire banking capital of the country and through the banks upon all business, and divorce the entire banking system, state and national, from Wall Street by at one stroke making the banks independent of Wall Street and dependent for safety and currency upon a deliberate, dignified, independent, impartial, law-controlled public institution, operating in the open instead of in secret, granting as a legal right instead of a bartered favor the service and privileges of the council to each bank direct without discrimination or favoritism. This is the only way to give all the people the benefit due to increase of general wealth, regulate rates of interest, the price of money and credit, by preserving and protecting free competition for loans between separated and independent banks; instead of destroying competition and establishing complete bank and money monopoly by Act of Congress as proposed by the "Aldrich plan." This is the only way to curb or destroy the excessive, growing and dangerous financial, industrial and political despotism of high finance, emancipate the banks and all business from the multiplying and intolerable evils of the present and reëstablish industrial liberty and financial freedom in the republic. A banking and monetary reform consummated on these lines would be a great and lasting na-

tional blessing second only to the Constitution of the United States.

11. This council plan is in line with the rising spirit of the hour that seeks at all hazard to preserve popular government by maintaining or increasing direct control by the people over their own affairs and welfare. The Aldrich plan is the direct contrary. It deprives the people and even their government of any effective voice, control, regulation or restraint over the private corporation that would monopolize their entire money supply and possess powers that can be used to make or break the business welfare of every individual and corporation and the prosperity of the nation. At the very moment when the whole power of Government is being exerted to regulate and restrain lawful combines and destroy lawless trusts the Aldrich bill boldly proposes that Congress actually legalize a great money combine, a trust of the trusts. Shall the public currency forever be controlled by a council with the source of power in the people, or by a private corporation with the people and Government eliminated and the source of power exclusively in the beneficiary banks? Is it to be Aldrich's *National Reserve Association* or the People's *United States Monetary Council?* Shall it be an unrestrained private central bank or a law-controlled public institution?

The "Aldrich" bill actually is pending now. Congress soon will decide. The people without delay should make their will known. They should require every candidate for president and congress to publicly pledge himself. Take no man high or low for granted. Both parties should take a position for or against. This must be made the chief issue of the 1912 campaign. It is the only safe course, for the people.

SHALL IT BE UNITED STATES MONEY
OR
PRIVATE CORPORATION CURRENCY?

CHAPTER XXII.

THE OCTOPUS.

Coming Incorporated Money Monster.

(See Frontispiece.)

The "American Experience Table of Mortality" is about fifty years old. It was based on conditions that prevailed a half century ago. It was devised by a big insurance company that arbitrarily "loaded" same for its greater safety and profit with figures about one-third higher than actual experience. The figures have not been changed. Improved sanitation and knowledge have reduced the average death rate. The actual combined experience table of mortality of the large life insurance companies is about one-third lower than the "American Table." But the American Table has been permanently grafted into the statutes of most states and long has been used as the basis for settling estates, computing the value of dower, life estates of widows, children and men, and the amount of damages in personal injury cases. If the true expectancy of life at the stated age is in fact a third longer than that in the statute great injustice is done.

Writer has verified the above facts with the opinion of an actuary of one of the largest old-line life insurance companies.

Insurance has become a great public necessity. Rates should be equitable and administration honest, impartial and strictly for the good of policy-holders and the public. The highest and most compelling motives have induced millions of people to become regular annual contributors to these funds for the protection of future widows and orphans. Once they start they must go on steadily or pay higher rates and perhaps through ill health be unable to get new insurance at all.

The old-line companies now have over sixteen billion dollars of insurance in force. Their annual income has increased from $187,424,959 in 1890, $392,358,741 in 1900, to $703,920,542 in 1910—a sum larger than the $701,372,374

344

that comprised the entire receipts of the Federal Government in 1911.

The Equitable, Mutual Life, New York Life, Prudential and Metropolitan, five big companies controlled by Wall Street, have $9,000,000,000 of insurance (60 per cent of the total), 6,220,036 policies in force, a combined yearly income of $329,176,873 and $2,236,632,312 of assets. The assets of these five companies exceed in value the aggregate capital stock of the 7,331 national banks and the entire national debt combined. Every dollar of this immense fund has been paid in as premiums by the people.

The total disbursements for all purposes made in 1910 out of the $703,920,542 of income was only $488,781,352, leaving $215,139,190, or nearly one-third, to compound and cumulate. And every year this unused fund is getting larger. If it continues to increase at the past ratio it will take less than ten years to draw into this idle insurance fund an amount equal to all money in circulation.

Premiums are based on that spurious American Table. This collection of a third more than currently needed tends to pile up in Wall Street a vast and increasing portion of the savings and wealth of the people, except that part used for losses and dividends. These dangerously swollen funds are largely under the control of the big interests that dominate the railroads, trusts, large banks and trust companies, and with the aid of these deposit funds manipulate the stock market and its nearly thirty billions of listed securities for private gain to the great loss of the public that owns these vast insurance and bank deposits.

The law now prohibits insurance companies investing these trust funds in stocks. But it is said that millions of dollars instead of being invested in proper bonds and real estate loans are merely deposited in favored banks, thus increasing the loaning power of such banks at least 400 per cent more than the cash so deposited, these loans often being made to the trusts and big stock-market operators at nominal interest rates and used against the public in the frequent "bull" and "bear" campaigns.

January 1, 1911, the above five companies had on deposit in banks and trust companies $35,243,070 in cash, which increased the loaning power of such banks more than a quarter of a billion dollars.

More than any other agency, life insurance and its excessive premiums computed by a false table have helped to

make Wall Street the universal money mecca toward which
every one of the three billion nimble dollars in the United
States seems possessed to make its annual pilgrimage of
devotion and tribute.

Fire insurance companies have over a half billion of accumulated assets and $295,644,715 annual income. Cas-
ualty and surety companies help swell the grand total of
yearly insurance income to more than one billion dollars.
This exceeds the national debt. It is greater than the
combined capital stock of the 7,331 national banks. If
one year's insurance receipts was converted into one-dollar
bills four of them could be given to every man, woman and
child in the United States and there would be enough left
so that if sewed together end to end they would be long
enough to go around the world once at the equator and
again by way of the North and South Poles.

Other potent agencies conspire to ever increase the golden
flood that constantly sweeps into Wall Street from every
part of the country.

The Bell telephone system now ruled from New York
has a capitalization of $580,000,000 and $53,600,000 cash
or liquid assets. It has 5,882,719 stations handling 22,284,-
010 messages daily, with 120,311 employees. It controls
the Western Union telegraph with 24,926 offices and $144,-
264,443 capitalization. The Postal telegraph also has large
business and revenues. The four big express companies
controlled by Wall Street collect more than 100 million
dollars every year, paying 14 per cent to 54 per cent annual dividends. They keep in their treasuries more than
$70,000,000.

The United States Steel Corporation has $508,302,500
common stock, $369,281,100 7 per cent preferred and $596,-
351,867 of 5 per cent bonds, total $1,464,935,467. Its net
profits made in ten years exceed a billion dollars. It gathers
and draws into Wall Street every year an enormous volume
of money. It keeps on deposit in banks at least $75,000,000
cash. The tobacco trust is said to have $20,000,000 cash
on hand and other trusts a greater or less amount. The
Standard Oil interests no doubt command and draw to
Wall Street more money than any other trust because
they are in one way or another interested in and taking
profits from so many different kinds of enterprises. If as
reported, their actual net profits approximate $100,000,000
every twelve months (as much as the average annual net

profits of the steel trust), then each ten years this will add $1,000,000,000 to their liquid capital and wealth. In fact the compounding of interest and excessive profits from multiplying investments and huge speculations made doubly successful and certain because of the command of unlimited capital and bank credit may add a billion to their resources in five to eight years, and another billion each succeeding like period, the time constantly shortening as profits and capital increase at compound ratio. If these interests continue their policy of buying up control of banks in various parts of the country and thus acquire complete control of the proposed National Reserve Association with its limitless powers, the time surely will come when these interests and their allies will be able to clear a billion a year and possibly several times that ultimately, every dollar of which will be paid by the business men and producers of the United States. And the evidence is abundant and conclusive that the Aldrich plan was originated and is being promoted by the Standard Oil interests and their local and foreign affiliations.

The capitalization of industrial combines grew, 1898 to 1908, from $3,784,000,000 to $31,672,000,000. This astonishing development has its headquarters in Wall Street, to which a large portion of the cash revenues are sent.

Trust growth has injected new problems into American life. These must be met and solved. It will require patience, wisdom and courage to eliminate the bad and preserve the good, to exterminate the rats without burning the barn. There is little objection to the combinations being big. Big instrumentalities are required to accomplish big things in a big country with big resources and big-minded ambitious men. And these instruments must be in corporate form. No individual could supply all the capital. In a copartnership each partner is liable without limit for joint debts. In an ordinary corporation a stockholder is liable only for the amount he has invested. The almost universal incorporation of industry is due to the desire for permanency and to limit individual liability.

A corporation's life, unlike the human, is not liable any day to end. Practically speaking a corporation is immortal, yet it has no soul. The general incorporation of all business tends to eliminate much of the personal or human element, substituting an inanimate, driving, everlasting, heartless machine with matter-of-fact cogs and wheels and

levers, cold, metallic, selfish, sordid, and in its operations
often criminal.

There is but one way to put a soul into a corporation.
If the law will impose adequate fine and imprisonment upon
each consenting officer and director whenever their corporation does an illegal or improper act the whole attitude of the
corporations toward the public and their entire course of
business will be changed and improved and more than half
of all corporate evils and abuses instantly will disappear.

It is wholly impracticable for government to fix the
prices of numberless trust products. It would quickly lead
to Government regulation of wages, general Government
ownership and operation—state socialism. Nor can trusts
be left free to extort excessive prices from the people with
the power of monopoly. There is a middle course, simple,
easy, practicable and just to both the corporations and
public. Congress has power to regulate or suppress corporations engaged in interstate commerce that become, or
attempt to become monopolies or even partial monopolies.
It should by law take from such corporations every special
advantage and profit obtained through use of the power
of monopoly. All excessive profits due to monopoly should
be confiscated by law and returned to the people through
the public treasury. Trusts by law must be divorced from
each other, from railroads, banks, Wall Street and politics.
If this is done thoroughly and honestly trusts can be made
a blessing to the country. If this is not done trusts must
be exterminated.

But the biggest trust problem and the greatest trust evil
is the growing and dangerous monopoly of all money and
bank credit by a few Wall Street men; and the Aldrich bill
would increase this evil and danger a thousand fold.

Death always has been the chief means for redistributing
wealth and preventing dangerous accumulations in the
hands of individuals and families. The highest public policy demands the dissolution and scattering of excessive
fortunes. The English plan of the oldest son inheriting all
is made unlawful here. It was thus hoped to prevent
swollen fortunes. But by will and trustee methods this
policy is being defeated. And unless great care is exercised
the perpetual corporation will be used as the means for
perpetuating these giant fortunes, a victory over death and
the laws of nature, and they will go on growing in size
and power until they rule the Government or destroy it

altogether. Incorporated wealth is the greatest danger of this age.

The railroads annually gather vast sums, much of which goes through Wall Street, because that is the location of the principal financial office of each system. They now have 239,991 miles of track, 1,699,420 employees with eight million dependents, aggregate capital stock $8,380,819,190 and bonds $9,600,634,906 (total $17,981,454,096), and collect as gross earnings each year the enormous sum of $2,804,580,939. If all this was sent to New York and in cash the railroads annually would gather up and ship to Wall Street every dollar of money in the United States outside of the Treasury, including all the actual money in the 24,392 banks of the country.

Many railroads have vast accumulations of cash assets deposited in favored banks controlled by big financial interests that dominate the roads. Some lines have $30,000,000 to $60,000,000 of cash or liquid assets. Each million so deposited in New York banks where the legal cash reserve is 25 per cent, enables the bank to increase its credit loans $4,000,000. If the million is deposited in a country bank, where the reserve is 15 per cent, or in a state bank or trust company, and three-fifths of it then is redeposited by the outside bank in a Wall Street bank (all of which can be done in one day), that one million forms the legal cash basis for about ten million dollars of extra credit loans by the co-operating banks.

The Stock Exchange is the chief instrument used by high finance for despoiling wholesale the people of the entire country. It hides the character of the transactions and the identity of the parties. It bids up the interest on call loans and thus sucks out of the banks of the country and into Wall Street untold millions seeking usury. It causes the public each year a direct loss of more than a billion dollars by methods that might fill the prisons with high financiers but for the fact that New York for a liberal share of the ill-gotten gains shields the guilty and licenses or tolerates these crimes against her sister states and the nation.

Serious as are the above described conditions the practices of the allied banks may constitute a bigger evil and their combined power a greater danger. This because of their country-wide organization, perfect machinery, political influence and activity, control of a large portion of the ready cash and monopoly of the vastly larger volumes of bank credit. All business, individual and corporate, more or less is dependent always or at certain periods upon banks. It can not prosper without bank assistance, because gradually business has worked away from the cash basis and now 95 per cent of the entire volume is carried on with bank credit. All American business is in the hollow of the bank hand, and can be aided or squeezed according to the will of the big interests that in recent years have acquired control over the banking system.

Unless before too late business men help to check the growth of this dangerous incorporated bank power their business eventually will be swallowed up in the great money maelstrom or become food at some future feast of the all-devouring interests. And thousands who now proudly consider themselves independent bankers soon will be reduced in authority to mere clerks, hired servants, executing the orders and doing under compulsion the will of the absent Wall Street masters of finance to the lasting injury of local business, their communities, neighbors and friends.

Will the banks prefer Wall Street for master to a law-regulated public institution? It must be one or the other. The United States Monetary Council would establish justice and the square deal as the rules of action in banking, finance and business. Each bank then would keep its reserve balance with the council against which it can make and sell drafts for general business use instead of New York drafts. This will break New York's monopoly and put every other city on an equality with the metropolis. And there is nothing more important to the rest of the country than to stop the present rapid concentration in New York of power over every kind of enterprise and activity. As Rome was the Roman Empire, so New York will be the United States unless the balance of the country asserts its right to equal opportunity and speedily enforces the same with legal safeguards. A United States Monetary Council is the best instrument now available for that purpose.

New York banks have little reason for keeping a deposit in any outside bank. But the present law respecting cash reserves induces country banks to keep large balances in New York banks. Instead of keeping its cash reserve of 15 per cent of deposit liabilities all in its own vault the country bank is allowed to keep three-fifths thereof on deposit in some central reserve bank. New York pays a

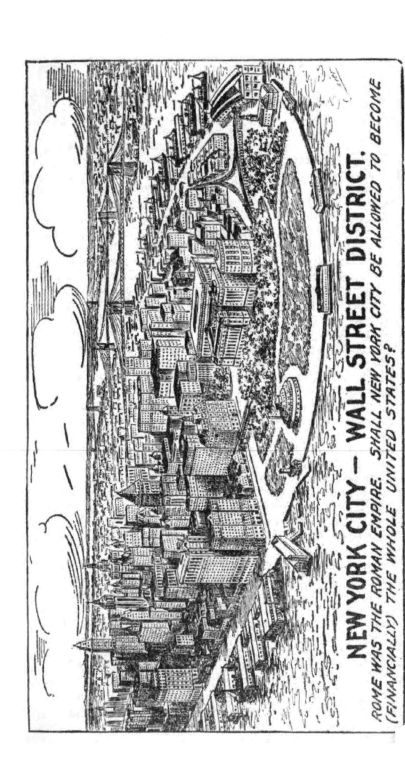

NEW YORK CITY — WALL STREET DISTRICT.

ROME WAS THE ROMAN EMPIRE. SHALL NEW YORK CITY BE ALLOWED TO BECOME (FINANCIALLY) THE WHOLE UNITED STATES?

per cent interest for such deposits. This tends to concentrate in New York a dangerous proportion of the country's cash capital. The Aldrich plan leaves this reserve scheme unchanged and most of the country's cash in Wall Street.

National banks alone on September 1, 1911, had $744,-614,305 on deposit with reserve agent banks (half of the total cash held by all banks), $399,508,977 with national banks not reserve agents and $162,271,793 with state banks and bankers, total $1,306,395,075. The actual cash in all the 7,331 national banks on that date was $941,362,369. Their credit loans were $5,663,411,073 and total resources $9,956,476,830.

The 24,392 reporting banks of all kinds on June 7, 1911, combined had $1,554,147,169 cash, $2,788,772,572 deposited by banks in other banks, $13,040,389,844 loans and $23,-631,083,382 of resources. These inter-deposits between banks often is a bond binding them together for mutual advantage and profit. In this way one bank may obtain a strong control over another. With all reserves in the United States Council, each bank will be independent. It no longer will depend for safety or profit on other banks or Wall Street.

The cash or liquid assets deposited in the banks by the railroads, express, telegraph, telephone, industrial and insurance companies that are controlled by a few men are believed to equal the $1,554,147,169 that comprises the total cash held by all the 24,392 banks. If so, then those men have power by withdrawing such deposits to force every bank to call in and cancel practically all of its loans, to force business men suddenly to pay up over fifteen billion dollars of debts to banks. That action if taken would plunge into bankruptcy most of the 24,392 banks and the borrowers of such banks and inaugurate the greatest panic in history. Probably it will not be done, at least to that extent, but the power to do it is in the hands of a few Wall Street men and every banker knows it and is afraid to antagonize the high financiers. That is the "black hand" threat that Wall Street ever holds over the financial institutions of the United States. That is the deadly power that would be abolished by the creation of the United States Monetary Council to regulate and protect the banks and the business of the country with an independent and ample supply of elastic public currency.

The bank tax on all business computed at 5 per cent

on $23,000,000,000 of bank resources exceeds a billion dollars per year, or more than the national debt. The transportation tax annually levied on business and commodities by railroads for service is nearly three billion dollars. The insurance companies collect another billion. The trusts probably as much as the railroads. These four agencies, therefore, collect from the people each year a total sum larger than the value of all crops. A large portion of this vast business is expense that is added to the cost of food, clothing and other things and thus directly increases enormously the cost of living. This is in addition to the profit and expense added by the many middlemen between producer and consumer; and does not include rent, gas, fuel and numberless other items that enter into the cost of living.

A large portion of these vast and ceaseless streams of money flows through many artificial channels extending all over the country that now converge in Wall Street, financially draining the country and carrying to that one center an ever increasing proportion of the people's income and the nation's wealth.

It was to simplify this process and make the desired results more certain that Wall Street invented the pending Aldrich plan for a vast private central bank or association that should legally and firmly and permanently bind the 24,392 banks all in one vast combine for mutual profit and advantage as against the people.

Is There a Money Trust?

A trust is an artificial condition in any line of business that restrains trade and tends to eliminate competition and establish monopoly. Complete stoppage or control of trade is not necessary. Elimination of all competition or absolute monopoly is not essential. If the artificial conditions are such as to suppress competition entirely or in part and create complete or partial monopoly it is a trust. The conditions not only must naturally operate to produce these results but they must be artificial. If the conditions are artificial, created, and naturally tend to produce such results the law will assume that those creating such conditions intended thus to form a trust. Incorporation is not an essential in forming a trust.

The growing, selfish and insolent Money Power, incorporated and unincorporated, violates every law regulating and restraining its conduct, treats the people and their government with contempt, and then invokes the protection of the laws and the courts to shield the stolen "vested rights" and privileges against violence that their own lawless course tends to incite.

Wall Street is a trust. It is a trust-manufacturing trust. Every condition there is artificial and calculated to eliminate competition and install monopoly. And it actively seeks to establish this trust condition among railroads, industries and banks. The chief object is increased profits.

There are many money trusts. In every city the banks are forming a local trust, usually by clearing-house rules or oral agreements. The object is to keep as low as possible the interest paid for deposits and as high as possible the interest charged borrowers. If bank power continues to grow in time they will pay no interest on deposits. In form and effect it is an injurious conspiracy against depositors and borrowers, the customers of banks. The agreements are identical and for the same object in the banking business as the acts in the industrial world that are made criminal by the anti-trust law. And there is less reason or excuse for these bank trusts that control the supply of money and credit than for industrial trusts and they are far more burdensome and dangerous. The prices of exchange and other bank charges often are regulated locally by trust agreement. The policy of charging regular customers exchange on out-of-town checks deposited is spreading rapidly by clearing-house agreements. A certain city that has about 500,000 population recently adopted the scheme. Next day a leading hotel was charged by its bank 15 cents "exchange" on a $50.00 check drawn by writer on a Cincinnati bank. If the same rate was charged on the whole 160 billion dollars of checks that yearly go through clearing-houses the tax on business and the extra net profits of the banks would be increased $480,000,000, or enough to pay an extra annual dividend of 24 per cent on the entire capital stock of the 24,392 banks. Banks are now making excessive profits but as their wealth and power increases they will extort more and more from business if business will permit it. All such trust agreements among banks either should be prohibited or made general and uniform by law with severe punishment for discriminations. There should either be real and unrestricted competition for loans and business among banks or a uniform scale of charges should be fixed and enforced by law. There should be no money trust at all among banks or a trust strictly regulated by law. That is the only safety, the one protection for business. Were it not for these local money trusts the general bank discount rate would be 4 per cent or 5 per cent instead of 6 per cent, with a reasonable allowance as interest on deposit accounts, and ordinary depositors of cash would get 4 per cent or 5 per cent for the money that enables the bank to loan four to ten times as much "credit" at 6 per cent. And if bank favoritism and discrimination was stopped and trusts and stock gamblers were not allowed to borrow at 2 per cent while others must pay 6 per cent, and all were treated impartially the banks could establish a uniform 4 per cent discount rate and make just as much profit. And a 4 per cent rate or even 5 per cent would wonderfully stimulate legitimate business and promote national prosperity, and greatly reduce the cost of necessities and living. Then there is a general money trust. It is not incorporated—not yet. But it is real. An artificial condition exists in the world of big finance that tends to eliminate genuine competition for loans, deposits, issues of bonds and deals requiring financing. Insiders co-operate instead of compete and they have more profits to divide and outsiders pay more and get less because this money trust condition through fear and favor has merged control of money and bank credit largely in the hands of a few men. These men by direct or indirect means dominate practically all of the important financial institutions of the United States. The will of these men is a most complete, definite, powerful and dangerous money trust. Its intangible and invisible form increases its irresponsibility, rapacity, craft and daring. A hidden power is the most dangerous and the most difficult to locate, regulate or restrain.

While a powerful and supreme money trust exists and dominates in the larger sense all American finance and business and everybody knows of this fact, it will be difficult if not impossible to reach and properly control it by direct regulating statutes. But its power for evil can be greatly diminished by indirect agencies. Laws with suitable penalties stopping all bank discriminations, usurious interest rates, margin gambling, regulating the stock exchanges, divorcing the trusts, banks, railroads and insurance companies from each other and regulating the use of their cash funds, taking the bank reserves out of Wall Street and mobilizing them in one central reservoir under Government regulation, and creation of the United States Monetary Council as a greater financial power than Wall Street, made independent and impartial by law, able and ever ready to aid and protect the 24,392 banks of the country and the business customers of such banks with an ample supply of sound elastic currency and credit will stop most of the glaring evils and abuses and bring Wall Street and its lawless element ultimately under the effective control of the Federal Government. And there is no other way to get adequate relief from present intolerable conditions. The pending Aldrich plan is a long step in the opposite direction. Instead of curtailing it would multiply the already over-swollen power of those few Wall Street men. Their money trust then would be complete, incorporated, a legal body entitled to claim the protection of the laws and the courts. Acts now evil if not criminal would be made lawful and the National Reserve Association as a vast private money trust would become the ruling power in finance and business. Shall the present outlaw money trust that now must hide in the shadows and operate in the darkness, the bandit of the financial highway, be called and crowned by Act of Congress as the supreme sovereign of finance and business, a lawful money trust, the incorporated master of 24,392 banks and of all industries, commerce and politics?

The National Reserve Association will have power of life and death over the business of every man, the affairs of every corporation, the welfare of every community and the prosperity of the nation. It will be judge, jury and executioner. By inflating and contracting its corporate currency and raising and lowering its discount rate it can raise and lower at will the prices of all securities, property and human labor. By co-operating with the private central banks abroad it will help establish a universal money trust that will eliminate all competition between banks and bankers for bonds and loans and this world-wide money monopoly will double the mortgage on all mankind by increasing interest rates everywhere.

To it Congress is asked to hand over as a free gift a billion dollars of public currency, money, the property and medium of exchange of 94,000,000 people, to be forever retained and loaned out to the people for its profit. It may have power to run the nation into debt or liability for billions of dollars as guarantor on the emissions of its printing press, on corporate currency issued without limit or effective restraint. By act of Congress the public revenues of the republic for a half century are to be mortgaged to this money trust, forty billions collected by taxation to be turned over for deposit and use by this private corporation without one cent of compensation.

By resolution adopted by vote of the five men who comprise the majority of its executive committee, it can, in secret and without notice, contract and cancel a million, a hundred million, or five hundred million of its corporate currency and at one breath thus annihilate billions of bank credit built as a tenfold inverted pyramid on such currency, forcing every bank to call in its loans and every business borrower to pay his bank obligations at whatever sacrifice. It will have power to abolish prosperity and inflict panic, plunging the entire nation into the horrors of a financial catastrophe that would paralyze industry and commerce, close the factories and turn millions of workmen out to tramp the streets without means to provide food and shelter for their helpless wives and children.

To five men, perhaps mere dummies, irresponsible, paid employees of an unregulated, uncontrolled and unrestrained private corporation, Congress is asked to absolutely and unreservedly commit for fifty years the vital destinies of the republic and the interests and welfare of its 94,000,000 inhabitants. The National Reserve Association, a great private central bank owned by the banks controlled by Wall Street, is to be invested with supreme governmental powers and incorporated as a great dominating money trust by law, independent of government and above all public authority.

That is the omnipotent and deadly octopus Congress is urged to legally set loose and install as the master of American banks, business, finance, industry, commerce and politics. Its poisonous and itching tentacles will gradually reach out and bind themselves about every home, farm, industry, bank, the public treasury, courts, Congress and the White House, gathering to itself supreme political power, sucking the wealth and substance of the people into Wall Street and dumping it into the Stock Exchange or the eager laps of the handful of men who will seek by moral if not by legal treason to rob the people of their God-given liberty, destroy the republic as a living reality and in its place erect an empire disguised as a democracy with incorporated wealth crowned as the ruling sovereign and all the people its subjects.

That is the coming incorporated MONEY MONSTER

APPENDIX.

A CENTRAL BANK TRUST.

President of the United States Gets Analysis of "Aldrich Plan" Made by Author—Position of President Taft—Letters and Inside Facts Made Public.

On November 16, 1911, the author of this volume met President William H. Taft in the White House at Washington to discuss certain proposed changes in the monetary and banking laws and particularly the so-called "Aldrich Plan" for a private central bank urged by the National Monetary Commission.

A written statement or analysis of that "Plan" then was given to the President, its receipt being formally acknowledged by his secretary in the following letter:

THE WHITE HOUSE
WASHINGTON

November 17, 1911

My dear Sir:

      I have brought to the President's attention your letter of the 10th instant, which you left with me yesterday,

Sincerely yours,

Secretary to the President

Mr. Alfred O. Crozier,
    Grand Rapids, Michigan.

In the interest of a more general understanding among
the people of the important questions involved in the suggested revolutionary changes in our currency and banking
systems, and in view of recent events, it seems advisable
and proper here to make such statement public. It is as
follows:

"GRAND RAPIDS, MICH., Nov. 10, 1911.
HON. WILLIAM H. TAFT,
    President of the United States,
    Washington, D. C.

Dear Sir: Your secretary, Mr. Hilles, at Milwaukee
suggested that I see you in Washington to personally discuss with you the proposed changes in the monetary and
banking systems and that I write out and send to you my
views on the subject. Therefore, without assuming any
want of knowledge about these matters on your part, as a
citizen and republican I respectfully venture these few
observations.

You of course know that the gold standard is firmly and
permanently established and is not an issue in the present
monetary campaign. This simplifies the situation.

Shall control of the public currency be public or private? That is the real question and about the only one
in serious dispute. On this vital issue in the immediate
future the greatest monetary struggle in the nation's history is likely to take place. It may largely overshadow all
other political problems; and the successful party of the
future I believe will be the one that takes the people's side
in this contest.

Former Correspondence.

You may recall my letter of August 20, 1909, to you at
Beverly just before former Senator Aldrich called upon
you there.

I then told you that I had information that the National
Monetary Commission would report in favor of a central
bank to issue, inflate and contract the public currency, the
institution to be a private corporation owned by the banks,
which meant ultimate control by Wall Street.

About ten days later, in a public address at Boston, a
few days after your conference with President Aldrich

of the commission, you said that the trend of the minds of a majority of the monetary commission was in favor of a central bank of issue, but that if such institution is created it must not be controlled by Wall Street or by politics. This public warning was timely, to the point and named the greatest dangers to be avoided.

It is my view that any private corporation controlling the currency supply of the entire country inevitably would in time be controlled by Wall Street and that it will use the imperial powers of the institution over all banks and through the banks over the business of every man and corporation to dominate in its own interest the politics of the states and nation. That if such an institution be needed and is created it should be a public institution under absolute public control instead of a private corporation. I am opposed to Congress taking from the Government a billion dollars of public currency used by the people as their chief money supply and handing it over as a free gift to an irresponsible private syndicate to be forever retained and loaned out for the exclusive profit of such syndicate.

The Aldrich Plan.

The revised "Aldrich Plan" put forward by the National Monetary Commission asks Congress to create a great central bank to be named National Reserve Association. It is to be a private corporation. The $300,000,000 stock is all to be owned by the banks in proportion to the size of their capital stock. For example, the National City Bank of New York, having $25,000,000 capital, will own a thousand times as much National Reserve Association stock as a country bank with $25,000 capital. Three large Wall Street banks together will own nearly as much central bank stock as half of all the national banks of the United States, taking the smaller banks. If all the stock is subscribed and only half payment is required the 4 per cent stock will net the banks 8 per cent. The big banks of course will own the central bank and Wall Street will control the big banks.

Already the larger banks are organizing side-partner security companies—a sort of financial "Dr. Jekyll and Mr. Hyde"—to acquire banks throughout the country to control the central bank. The National City Company is the Siamese twin of the largest Wall Street bank. It is reported to have already acquired more than a hundred large banks in Washington, Chicago and elsewhere. But it was too hasty or too public about it. Publicity of this illegal scheme endangers the Aldrich Plan in Congress. So we are told that at least for a time the National City Company is to put all of these bank stocks out of its hands. Presumably the certificates will go into friendly hands or remain under its control. Then, ostrich-like, it will be completely hidden from the people because its head is buried in the sand.

The elaborate and complicated system of branch boards and local associations does not fully disguise or change the potent fact that the National Reserve Association will be a private corporation owned and absolutely controlled by the special interests.

The banking fraternity is to select forty-two of the forty-six directors of the National Reserve Association. The other four are public officials representing the interests of 90,000,000 people whose entire public currency supply is to be handed over by Congress to be forever kept and manipulated by this private corporation. As four is not a majority of forty-six, the share of control allotted to the public would be a huge joke if not so dangerous. The ratio of forty-two to four in favor of the banks doubtless correctly represents the division of benefits between the special interests and the people. The general plan in most features is all right. But the scheme of private instead of public control reveals the climax of the greed and audacity of high finance.

It is conceded that the scheme originated in Wall Street and I think you will take judicial notice that "high finance" never supports a financial measure unless its interests and power will be advanced by its adoption.

Private Monopoly of the Public Currency.

The chief aim of the "interests" is to obtain through a corporation owned by them a private monopoly of the public currency. In my letter of August 20, 1909, I fully explained how at the New York meeting of the National Civic Federation, December 17, 1907, the distinguished Wall Street bankers present publicly refused to accept my amendment to their currency reform resolution, viz.:

"Provided that control of the volume of the public currency shall not be taken away from the Federal Government and put into private hands."

In that letter also I recalled the fact that in his emergency currency bill Senator Aldrich attempted to eliminate from the present law the prohibition against contracting the national bank currency more than $9,000,000 per month, and that he consented to strike out of his bill this dangerous provision allowing unlimited and sudden contraction of the entire public currency only when attention was called to the matter by the public reading of my petition in the Senate the next day after his speech for his bill. Thus every currency move emanating from Wall Street seems to be an effort to induce Congress to give private interests unlimited power suddenly to contract the currency supply—to make money scarce without warning.

The private syndicate, under the Aldrich plan, without any substantial consideration to the Government is to get nearly a billion dollars of currency used as money for about the cost of printing. This money never will be returned to the Government. Millions will be destroyed or burned by accident. The benefit goes to the syndicate, not, as now, to the people. This syndicate of bankers for its own profit is to loan this vast public currency to their own banks. If the banks are to use it as a reserve basis it will enable them to loan to the people for interest profits more than ten billion dollars of bank credit in the shape of ordinary bank loans.

For thus empowering the syndicate and its banks with relatively little extra investment to collect from the people continuously interest on about ten billion dollars of extra loans the Aldrich plan demands that the syndicate pay the Government 1½ per cent per annum on all currency issued in excess of $900,000,000, and 5 per cent on all in excess of $1,200,000,000, but nothing on the first $900,000,000! Even this apparent generosity (?) vanishes in the light of the fact that it is not expected this currency ever will exceed $900,000,000.

Many believe that this currency will not pass at par unless backed by the faith and credit of the Government and that this should be pledged. If the Government is to be responsible for the currency and a private syndicate is to issue and own it and get the profits from its use, would not the Government in effect be in position similar to a man loaning his promissory note for a billion dollars to another party who gets the note cashed and forever keeps and uses the entire proceeds?

Dangerous Currency Contraction.

Banks, as you know, loan credit, not money. This is the right to draw checks to the total of the note discounted. Borrower gets a bank-book showing his "credit." This makes him a "depositor," although he has put in no actual money. By thus increasing its loans of "credit" a bank correspondingly can increase its deposits without getting an extra dollar, almost indefinitely. About the only legal limitation is that it must have in cash in its vault an amount equal to a certain per cent of its deposit liabilities varying from 25 per cent down to 7½ per cent according to the location of the bank. The official reports show that the banks as a whole loan eight to twelve times as much "credit" as they have in cash.

I have not at hand more recent reports but the report of the U. S. Comptroller of the Currency for 1907 shows that the collective individual deposits (not including deposits by banks) of all the 19,746 reporting national and state banks and trust companies amounted to $13,099,600,000, while their aggregate cash reserves amounted to $1,113,742,316, or 8.5 per cent of their aggregate deposit liabilities due to individuals.

When the banks are fully loaned up, if by withdrawals or otherwise their cash reserves are decreased half, under the law they must decrease their total loans one-half. They must force their customers suddenly to pay up loans aggregating eight to twelve times the shrinkage of cash reserves. If a half billion thus is withdrawn from bank reserves business borrowers must pay up at once over five billion dollars of loans due to the banks (an amount more than twice the total of all the money in circulation in the United States), no matter what sacrifices of securities, properties and commodities it entails. The banks cannot do other than force such payments even if it closes industries, plunges labor into idleness, causes general distress, panic and financial ruin.

A private corporation with power suddenly to contract the outstanding public currency without limit, of course thereby could almost to any extent deplete the reserves of the banks and force them immediately to call in their loans in such volumes that general panic and financial disaster would be inevitable. Likewise by inflating the currency it could increase bank reserves and enormously and even dangerously expand the loaning power and profits of the banks.

In order that this vital and all controlling power over the banks and all business, the power to inflate and contract the public currency, might not be feared by the people as formidable, not to say dangerous, it has been given an enticing name, "elasticity." No doubt elasticity of the currency and of the loaning power of the banks is desirable. But it may make a great difference to the people and their interests who does the stretching, and for what purpose it is done.

Is it wise or patriotic for Congress unnecessarily to grant an obviously dangerous power to uncontrolled powerful private interests, leaving the people for protection only the mere hope that such interests will not use the power against the general welfare and for their own private profit?

Artificial Panics.

It is the belief of many that some panics or quasi-panics have been more or less deliberately caused for improper purposes and that most panics are due chiefly to artificial and removable causes.

Every panic in history seems to have started in Wall Street. To stop panics should we not go there and remedy the evils that tend to create panics, such as margin gambling, usurious interest rates and illegal bank practices, instead of merely legislating to safeguard the banks against the results of panics? You may know of the fact that 75 per cent of all transactions on the stock exchange are fictitious, illegal, gambling and "wash sales," and that 80 per cent of the money and credit to conduct such deals is supplied by the banks that hold the deposit savings of the people.

Congress will have to act to protect the country against these harmful things because the great state of New York for about four million dollars annually in stock transfer fees has sold to the gamblers the privilege of wrongfully despoiling on its soil the people of that state and of the United States.

Long before the panic of 1907 in writing and orally I expressed the belief that a panic might be caused to pinch the country into crying for monetary reform and accelerate in Congress the prearranged program of Wall Street. The panic and the "object lesson" came just before the Congress convened in which was first introduced the legislative measures prepared and publicly advocated by Wall Street bankers and the New York Chamber of Commerce months before the panic, including in substance the identical privately owned central bank scheme now known as the revised Aldrich plan—the National Reserve Association.

At said National Civic Federation meeting in December, 1907, when a majority present were Wall Street business men or their friends, I publicly expressed my belief that the panic of 1907 was artificial, no one present disputed the charge.

The facts about serious Wall Street moves seldom become public. But it was reported that at the recent Congressional investigation of the Steel Trust one of the most prominent financial men of Wall Street, Oakleigh Thorne, president of the Trust Company of America, on oath astonished the country by declaring in substance or effect that the panic of 1907 was artificial, was deliberately caused, and named the high Wall Street interests he is said to have sworn started the run on the banks that precipitated the financial crisis. And now the Government in its suit against the steel trust gravely charges some of these same people with illegal acts or criminal conspiracy and with using the financial institutions and capital of the country for unlawful purposes.

And these are the same interests that largely will control the National Reserve Association and its autocratic and dangerous powers, thereby creating a financial monopoly— a trust of the trusts—under express authority of Congress at the very time when the Government and the courts are trying to destroy monopoly by breaking up the trusts. A monopoly of banking and currency will give them ultimately a complete monopoly over about everything worth controlling in the United States, including Government itself.

At a recent meeting of the New York Bankers' Association, in a public address one of the most prominent Wall Street bankers virtually threatened the country with another panic unless Congress yielded to the demand of Wall Street and adopted the Aldrich central bank scheme.

After the Aldrich-Vreeland emergency currency bill had passed the Senate in 1908 I was present at a public hearing before the House Banking and Currency Committee. More than a dozen bankers, members of the Currency Commission of the National Bankers' Association, were present and spoke against the measure, as did many representatives of the larger commercial organizations of the country. Replying to direct questions by members of the committee every banker solemnly declared that if the bill passed it would cause another panic, and several said the panic would arrive in less than three months. The bill passed but no panic has occurred and more than three years has elapsed. Either those distinguished bankers were poor prophets or the change made in the bill striking out the Senate amendments that prohibited persons being both directors of a bank and of a corporation borrowing from that bank and lowering the Government tax on the emergency currency so as to make it profitable for the banks to handle it warded off the predicted panic and saved the country.

To cause a panic or even to threaten the country with one to frighten or force the people and Congress into passing laws that otherwise would be defeated is a species of duress utterly indefensible and dangerous. It is worse than the rule of the mob. For the public prediction of panic tends to cause panic, and the financial and fatal consequences of panic often are pathetic.

It is not my desire to stir up class feeling or arraign bankers as a whole. Most bankers are honest, patriotic and useful citizens. But the above incident was a public proceeding and the printed records show the facts as stated.

This would seem to be a good time and opportunity to resist the unjust and selfish legislative demands of the "interests" and thus for all time settle the question as to which is supreme and the most powerful, Wall Street or the Government and people of the United States.

Control Currency to Manipulate Prices.

The Aldrich plan grants to such private corporation direct control over interest rates by the unregulated, unrestricted and unlimited power to increase and decrease the discount rate. If it should increase the discount rate to the banks of course the banks would do the same or more to their customers. Otherwise those in control of the central bank by increasing the discount rate could instantly deprive every bank and trust company in the United States of a substantial portion of their entire profits.

Would not every banking institution in the country in sheer self-defense find itself obliged to obey the financial and political orders of those who may have seized control

of the National Reserve Association? Would not this create
a vast and dangerous political machine that inevitably would
result either in its controlling the Federal Government or
itself being abolished for political action like the old United
States Bank of Andrew Jackson's time in the midst of
universal panic and financial chaos?

The central bank simply by inflating and contracting the
public currency or by raising or lowering the discount rates
could automatically and immediately raise and lower the
prices of all securities, property and labor.

Prices of the twenty-five billion dollars of listed securities
at times fluctuate at least 20 to 50 per cent. This is partly
due to natural causes but more often it is due to unfair
manipulation by secret pools that cause interest rates to be
run up on the Stock Exchange to ruinous figures and bank
loans to be called in large volumes to aid inside operators in
their speculations against the public. And yet a drop of but
10 per cent in the average price quotations indicates a direct
and immediate loss to the holders of securities of a sum
equal to all the money in circulation in the United States.

Bidding up the rate on call loans is the effective magnet
used to entice away from local business the money of the
people deposited in banks that it may be used in "high
finance" flotations and to promote gambling speculation in
Wall Street.

Bank Discriminations.

A related evil, that should be made impossible by law
while Congress is reforming the banking system, is the
practice of many large banks of discriminating in the matter
of loans and interest rates in favor of trusts, insiders and
stock speculators.

Why should trusts and Wall Street operators usually be
able to borrow from the banks practically in unlimited quantities at 2 per cent while responsible business and commercial customers often cannot borrow enough properly to
conduct legitimate business and always must pay two to
three hundred per cent more as interest than is paid by
stock gamblers?

As the banking system is a quasi-public institution clothed
with a public interest by law, enjoying special privileges and
immunities, it should exercise its duties to the public impartially, without discrimination, and not in any way be an

instrument used to oppress individuals, corporations or communities or to promote unlawful monopolies and unnatural and improper concentration of wealth in the few to the disadvantage of the many.

International Money Monopoly.

You of course realize that whoever controls the monetary circulation to a large extent will control the credit, interest rates, prices and the business activities of the world.

A central bank issuing the public currency if a private corporation naturally will co-operate with the great privately owned Government banks abroad and comprise in effect an international monetary trust with a world-wide monopoly of money. The result if not the design will be permanently to eliminate all competition for large loans. This will make it easy to double the mortgage on mankind without a dollar of extra benefit simply by increasing the rate of interest on the nearly thirty billions of the bonds of governments and the vast quantities of state, municipal and corporation bonds as they mature and from time to time are refunded.

The revised Aldrich plan proposes immediately to increase the rate of interest and so refund the national debt of the United States, amounting to nearly a billion dollars, that it will not be paid off for half a century. It would unnecessarily mortgage the next generation before it is born. Surely this is not the desire of the people and I do not believe their Congress will do it.

In a broad sense there is always a struggle on by the great individual and corporate owners of the vast fixed income or bond wealth of the world to decrease the relative value of property and labor as measured in money by increasing the rate of interest on bonds. Thus they hope to recover what they lost when Providence unexpectedly swelled the output of gold until gold and gold bonds now will purchase much less labor or property. By bringing the large competitors for such bonds into co-operation either interest rates can be increased or the bonds be bought below par because there will be no other available market for the bonds.

The Aldrich plan will help create an international financial world power above and beyond the reach of all law that through the power of the purse will be able to rule governments and kingdoms, cause peace and war, extort from the peoples of the world an ever increasing interest toll and tend to develop a civilization where the dollar with its metallic heart will be of more importance than man with his immortal soul.

And the more war there is the greater the demand for money for armies and battleships and the higher the interest rates can be raised by the coming great international monetary combine.

An Alternative Plan.

At the New York meeting of the Academy of Political Science in December, 1910, President Aldrich and other members of the Monetary Commission being present, I suggested tentatively an alternative plan.

We had listened to the clever and astute arguments for the "Aldrich plan" by the distinguished Wall Street bankers present. One of them is a partner in a great international banking house said to represent in America the Rothschilds of Europe. He declared gravely that if dividends on the central bank stock are limited by law to 4 per cent there would be no danger of control of the institution falling into the hands of the special interests because there would not be enough temptation to make them want control. Replying, I cited the purchase of a few thousands of Equitable Life Insurance stock for $2,500,000 made by a well known Wall Street banker when the law limits dividends on the stock to 7 per cent annually and said that it was power the banker sought and that it is power the "interests" seek through a central bank under their control. I then told them that I did not believe they ever could persuade Congress to take away from the Government and grant to a private corporation an exclusive monopoly of the entire public currency.

The great issue now raised is whether control of the public currency shall be public or private. It always has been public and the Constitution so intended. The burden of proof is on those urging the radical change.

Suppose we grant the need of currency and banking reforms, consolidation of bank reserves, elasticity, a central bank or agency to issue the currency and even rediscount for the banks; in fact to do all of the things proposed by the Aldrich plan.

And as recent concentration of banking capital and power in the hands of the same few who dominate the trusts, railroads and other large activities seem to have made it now impossible to finance or conduct any important undertaking without their consent perhaps it is necessary to create a central institution with financial power greater than Wall Street to emancipate the banks and the business of the country from this tightening and dangerous grip.

But no convincing reason has been advanced why the National Reserve Association should be a private corporation instead of a public institution under public control.

Why should Congress make the dangerous experiment when the historical public control will be better and more safe? Ample safeguards easily can be provided that will keep all partisanship and politics out of the institution.

There are several ways to provide public control. One way, the plan I suggested at said Academy meeting, is to have the President appoint a board say of one hundred non-salaried governors, one on the nomination of the governor of each state. This body to select an executive committee of well paid, highly trained financial experts, sworn as public servants and divorced from all other business, to run the institution. This plan, or some modification of it, would insure representation and fair treatment to every state, guard against partisanship, and inspire the confidence of the people, which is necessary to insure the usefulness and permanency of any such institution.

It will be far safer for banks to be able to obtain adequate assistance direct from a public institution as a defined legal right, instead of begging a favor from a private corporation and perhaps on the side being forced to submit to some unprofitable secret agreement with the interests in control of the corporation by way of flotations or the purchase of securities.

The banks constantly will be in grave peril if the Aldrich plan is adopted. They will be the storm-center of such bitter partisan strife, crimination and suspicion that depositors may take alarm, withdraw and hoard money, inflicting upon the banks and the country in even more aggravated form the very evils and dangers sought to be avoided by monetary reform.

Public investigations of banks and bank practices will be frequent, demanded and conducted for partisan purposes. If my definite information is correct, and I believe it is, that the official reports on file with the United States Comptroller of the Currency show, on sworn admissions, that nearly 40 per cent of all national banks knowingly violate the law, you can see the harm to the banks and the handle that would be made politically if these reports were made public and exploited in a partisan congressional investigation of the banking system.

The exigencies of political strife might emblazon the fact that right now there are more than sixty convicts who formerly were bankers, in just' one of the many prisons, and wholly unwarranted inferences might be drawn, casting unjustifiable suspicion upon all bankers when as we know the great majority are law-abiding, upright, and useful citizens. This may excite public fear, induce runs on banks, do permanent harm to the influence of bankers generally and endanger the solvency of their institutions.

The Aldrich plan if adopted I believe will stir up class distinction and hatred more than any legislation ever proposed in the country's history. What folly to take these risks when it is not necessary.

If the banks reach for more profit and power they may have many of the special privileges and immunities they now enjoy taken away. At best the interest and power of any country bank in the central bank will be insignificant and useless.

Bankers should remember that in Andrew Jackson's time when banks became the issue in politics they suffered frightfully along with the entire country in the resulting panic. As the nation and its activities now are more extensive the calamity may be far greater.

An attempt is being made to persuade or drive all bankers into a suicidal support of the Aldrich scheme. But I know that there are very many patriotic bankers who realize the danger and will vigorously oppose the plan. Some will not because afraid of reprisals by Wall Street.

I do not believe Congress will farm out the public currency to be forever exploited for the profit of a private syndicate. If Congress insists that control of the National Reserve Association be public instead of private and those promoting it oppose and block all monetary reform because their personal interests are not served the responsibility for any resulting future panics will be upon them.

You will understand that we do not oppose the legitimate

business of Wall Street but insist that its lawless and unjust acts must cease.

The practice of the "interests" in hailing as a statesman the man who furthers their designs and crying "demagogue" when anyone objects to their unfair use of the powers and laws of Government against the general welfare has lost its effect because the people are more thoughtful, observant and alert in their own interest.

You of course realize that no monetary or banking reform is possible as a permanent solution of current defects unless it accords with the discriminating judgment of a majority of the voters of the United States.

Your commanding position, power to recommend to Congress and to veto its acts, makes it possible for you to protect the country by defeating this attempt to obtain private control of the public currency. For this reason my appeal is addressed to you with full confidence. And in this I know I voice the earnest views of very many citizens.

Mr. President, still I am an optimist. Most people are good. But in the Steel Trust suit the Government seems to think some are not so good. It is no want of faith in humanity when we object to Congress taking an obviously dangerous power from the Government and the entire people and unreservedly putting it into the irresponsible hands of the selfish few.

Very respectfully yours,
(Signed)   ALFRED O. CROZIER.

President Taft's Position.

Writer is a republican. But Lincoln, not Aldrich, is his ideal. He has admired the judicial temperament and genial personality of President Taft, and approved many of his important official acts during his long public career. He had hoped the President would take such a stand for the people and against the special interests that his reëlection would be advisable, imperative.

Believing that the crucial test of the President's courage and independence would come when the Monetary Commission reported to Congress the predetermined plan for the creation of a huge money trust to privately control the public currency and rule the banks and through them the business of the entire country, author in all fairness and in writing frequently made the President aware of the true situation so that there would be no chance of his

COMING CENTRAL MONEY TRUST

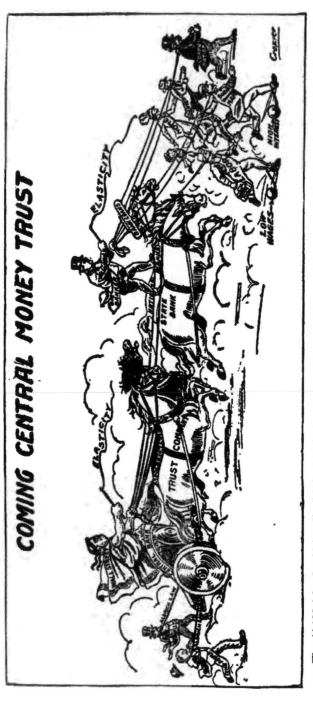

The "Aldrich plan" legally binds 24,392 banks for 50 years into one incorporated machine controlled by the banks owned by Wall Street. It will completely monopolize and manipulate all currency and bank credit. By contracting corporate currency and depleting bank reserves, Wall Street can force the banks suddenly to require business men to pay up billions of dollars of bank loans. This means panic, and general ruin.

being taken by surprise or misled. The foregoing, one of many during the past three years, illustrates.

Writer's letter of August 20, 1909, to the President was received and read just before Senator Aldrich arrived at Beverly to confer about the Monetary Commission's work and, if reports then current were correct, to urge a special session of Congress to hastily put through the central bank scheme in November, 1909. If that course was contemplated it was abandoned as unwise. About three weeks after his conference with Aldrich at Beverly the first public intimation was given that the Monetary Commission was even considering a central bank plan. This was made by President Taft in his Boston speech on September 14, 1909, the first of his 13,000-mile western trip. In that speech he said:

"It is apparent from the statements of Mr. Vreeland and Mr. Aldrich that the trend of minds of the Monetary Commission is toward some sort of arrangement for a central bank of issue which shall control the reserve and exercise a power to meet and control the casual stringency which from time to time will come in the circulating medium of the country and the world.

Mr. Aldrich states that there are two indispensable requirements in any plan to be adopted involving a central bank of issue. The one is that the control of the money system shall be kept free from Wall Street influences and the other that it shall not be manipulated for political purposes. These are two principles to which we can all subscribe."

This public declaration was what writer hoped to call out from Mr. Aldrich or the President by the letter of August 20, 1909, so the country might know what was coming. Nearly a year earlier writer had caused one of the leading press correspondents of New York to personally interview Frank A. Vanderlip, then vice-president and now president of that great Standard Oil institution, the National City Bank. Mr. Vanderlip then was reported as saying (in 1908) that the Monetary Commission would report in favor of a central bank to issue and control the currency. Because that bank had led in the fight for a central bank and to create the Monetary Commission, and on account of Senator Aldrich being the father-in-law of John D. Rockefeller, Jr., this early information was considered reliable, as now it proves to have been. That letter was as follows:

THE WHITE HOUSE.
WASHINGTON

Beverly, Massachusetts,
August 23, 1909.

My dear Sir:

Your letter of August 20th in regard to financial legislation has been received and will be brought
to the attention of the President.

Very truly yours,

Secretary to the President.

Mr. Alfred O. Crozier,
Wilmington, Delaware.

"WILMINGTON, DEL., August 20, 1909.
Hon. William H. Taft,
Beverly, Mass.

Dear Sir: I most earnestly hope that no special session
of Congress will be called prior to December to attempt
currency legislation. There would not be sufficient time
for the people and press to study and discuss so important
and difficult a subject.

There may be those who urge a special session as a means
of passing measures that could not be put through if the
country was given time to learn the true character and
effect of such a law. But I am sure you would not knowingly countenance such a course. You have in a short

time won the confidence of the masses and they trust your judgment and vigilance to guard their welfare and prevent hasty and ill-considered laws. It would seem that your responsibility in this regard is particularly heavy because the average man does not realize how his business and general welfare may be jeopardized by unwise banking and currency laws.

I had hoped it might be convenient to discuss this subject with you personally before it came to an issue but the published report of the talk of an extra session impels me to write you.

Now Mr. President, I think there is ample evidence to establish beyond reasonable doubt that there is on foot a determined movement, well concealed from the people, to take from the people's government and put into private hands all control over the volume of the public currency. This of course would mean direct or indirect control by Wall Street of the people's entire money supply. Those exercising this power to inflate and contract at will the volume of the circulating medium could thereby easily and to a large extent increase and decrease the prices of securities, property and labor. Are we ready to take a step so full of possible peril to the public welfare? Should it even be considered at a special session that can at most last only a few weeks? The power to contract suddenly and arbitrarily the volume of currency available for business necessarily carries with it power to increase interest rates, to wreck credit, derange business, endanger the solvency of banks and the security of depositors and even to cause panics. It is not sufficient to believe that such a power would not be used to that extent by human beings. Is it wise or patriotic to put such enormous power into private hands when it is not necessary?

If it is attempted I believe it will be the beginning of one of the greatest financial struggles in recent history; one vastly more intense and important than the silver controversy; one that will engender class hatred as never before; and I do not want to see the republican party committed to the wrong side.

It seems to me it is relatively less important what our money is made of so long as it is redeemable in gold and backed by the credit of the Federal Government, than it is to have its volume free from private control and manipulation and ever responsive to the varying demands of business. To get currency elasticity it should not be necessary to give individuals the power to contract when it should expand. Better no elasticity unless we can have one that will operate automatically in response to the rise and fall of natural demand.

I firmly believe if a fight for private control over the public currency is started it will lead to an irresistible demand for a Government issue of national currency exclusively, all redeemable in gold, the volume to be regulated from day to day by the Federal Government. I am not saying that this would be wise but I think it would be inevitable and preferable if the alternative is private Wall Street control, direct or indirect, over all the money of the people.

The distinguished governor of one of our largest states said to me that he could not believe any one would seriously propose such a plan. Yet the committee on resolutions at the National Civic Federation meeting, a majority of whom were Wall Street men, flatly refused in public to accept my amendment (to their currency resolution) which said merely, 'Provided, that the power to regulate the volume of the public currency shall not be taken from the Federal Government and put into private hands."

The Aldrich currency bill when reported contained a provision allowing sudden contraction not only of the $500,-000,000 of emergency currency, but also the $700,000,000 of bank note circulation, total $1,200,000,000, or nearly half of all currency in circulation in the United States.

When my petition of protest was read in open senate in the midst of the discussion of that bill, exposing this dangerous provision, Senator Aldrich instantly went privately to the Senator who introduced my petition and told him the Finance Committee would strike out the provision allowing the sudden contracting of the entire bank-note currency. But why was it put in at all? Those who drafted that bill and those in whose interest many believe it was framed are not novices.

There are those who believe that the Aldrich-Vreeland law was largely but a foil for the real measure desired and which will be revealed only when the Monetary Commission created by that law reports. And that the recent significant reorganization of certain congressional committees was part of a predetermined plan to force through Congress the mysterious measure the character of which is to be carefully concealed from the public until the last moment. If this be true the demand of the interested promoters for hasty action at a special session is explained. If information which came to me nearly a year ago proves correct the Monetary Commission will report in favor of a great central bank. This to be given absolute control of the financial business of the Government with exclusive power to issue currency ad libitum and to contract the volume at its pleasure. This institution to be called a *Government* bank, but owned *privately*. It will be thinly sugar-coated by a provision allowing the President to appoint some of the directors.

The chief fight then will be as to whether the institution shall be owned and controlled privately or by the Government. The republican party cannot afford to take the wrong side if this issue is to be forced upon the country. It will court disaster if it does so.

The people were led to expect that the Monetary Commission would be open and impartial in its investigation and hearings, giving ample opportunity to all who might desire to be heard. The hearings have mostly been held in Europe and not in the country chiefly concerned. They have been as secret as a council planning a military campaign. Those attended who were privately invited and their names have been carefully concealed from the public. The people and press of the United States have been completely ignored. And now rumor says that you are to be asked to convene Congress in extraordinary session to receive and hastily act on this mysterious report, presumably that its plan may be enacted into law before the people have time to understand its provisions and their effect or to organize and express their opposition.

I sincerely hope our fears are not justified, but in any event I am sure we can rely on the executive authority to protect the people against hasty and unwise financial legislation.

Very respectfully yours,

ALFRED O. CROZIER."

Writer has refused to credit the published reports that the President's mind was being shaped by Mr. Aldrich, and the more serious intimation that the apparently insurmountable opposition to President Taft's nomination in 1908 was overcome by a deal that resulted in the passage of the

Aldrich emergency currency bill, then supposed to be killed, the creation of the Monetary Commission with Aldrich at the head and democrats and republicans of his selection with him, the sudden change of front in Mr. Taft's favor of the most powerful banks and Wall Street financiers with the alleged understanding that if nominated and elected he could be depended upon at the last moment not to veto but to support the private central bank plan that from the start it has been known the commission was created to promote. Surely the President was not a party to any such unpatriotic deal even if it was made.

If Mr. MacVeigh, a democrat, was appointed Secretary of the Treasury at the instance of the promoters of the Aldrich plan so that a prominent democrat would be in position to help fool Andrew Jackson democrats into believing that the contemplated central bank is not a central bank, of course the President was not aware of the scheme.

Knowledge that the special interests never support anyone whom they even doubt, generally know what they are doing, take nothing for granted, exact in advance a most definite and binding arrangement, the fact that the sudden change of such interests at the last moment cinched Mr. Taft's nomination and election, the character of some of his chosen official advisers in the Cabinet and in Congress, were all incidents calculated more or less to shake one's confidence and cause grave doubts and fears. Hoping against hope, giving the "benefit of the doubt," we could only await the raising of the curtain on the final act in the great drama representing the struggle of the people against the "interests" to discover whether the President, the sworn defender of the republic, the chief actor would cast his great influence and official power on the side of the people or their enemies.

The complete confidence of Wall Street during the whole of the time since June, 1908, that its half-century-long dream of a great central money trust under its control soon would be realized, the formation of side-partner security companies by the big Wall Street banks to buy up control of enough other banks throughout the country to control the proposed National Reserve Association and many other acts in preparation for the feast of profits and power the monopoly of money and control of all credits would confer increased the feeling of uncertainty as to the real position of the chief executive of the nation.

President Taft at last has officially announced his position in his message to Congress on December 21, 1911, as follows:

"Monetary Reform.

A matter of first importance that will come before Congress for action at this session is monetary reform. The Congress has itself arranged an early introduction of this great question through the report of its Monetary Commission. This commission was appointed to recommend a solution of the banking and currency problems so long confronting the nation and to furnish the facts and data necessary to enable the Congress to take action. The commission was appointed when an impressive and urgent popular demand for legislative relief suddenly arose out of the distressing situation of the people caused by the deplorable panic of 1907. The Congress decided that while it could not give immediately the relief required it would provide a commission to furnish the means for prompt action at a later date.

In order to do its work with thoroughness and precision this commission has taken some time to make its report. The country is undoubtedly hoping for as prompt action on the report as the convenience of the Congress can permit. The recognition of the gross imperfections and marked inadequacy of our banking and currency system even in our most quiet financial periods is of long standing; and later there has matured a recognition of the fact that our system is responsible for the extraordinary devastation, waste, and business paralysis of our recurring periods of panic. Though the members of the Monetary Commission have for a considerable time been working in the open and while large numbers of the people have been openly working with them and while the press has largely noted and discussed this work as it has proceeded, so that the report of the commission promises to represent a national movement, the details of the report are still being considered. I cannot therefore do much more at this time than commend the immense importance of monetary reform, urge prompt consideration and action when the commission's report is received and express my satisfaction that the plan to be proposed promises to embrace main features that, having met the approval of a great preponderance of the practical and professional opinion of the country are likely to meet equal approval in Congress.

It is exceedingly fortunate that the wise and undisputed policy of maintaining unchanged the main features of our banking system rendered it at once impossible to introduce a central bank; for a central bank would certainly have been resisted and a plan into which it could have been introduced would probably have been defeated. But as a central bank could not be a part of the only plan discussed or considered that troublesome question is eliminated. And ingenious and novel as the proposed National Reserve Association appears it simply is a logical outgrowth of what is best in our present system and is in fact the fulfillment of that system.

Exactly how the management of that association should be organized is a question still open. It seems to be desirable that the banks which would own the association should in the main manage it. It will be an agency of the banks to act for them and they can be trusted better than anybody else chiefly to conduct it. It is mainly bankers' work. But there must be some form of Government supervision and ultimate control and I favor a reasonable representation of the Government in the management. I entertain no fear of the introduction of politics or of any undesirable influences from a properly measured Government representation.

I trust that all banks of the country possessing the requisite standards will be placed upon a footing of perfect equality of opportunity. Both the national system and the state system should be fairly recognized, leaving them eventually to coalesce if that shall prove to be their tendency. But such evolution can not develop impartially if the banks of one system are given or permitted any advantages of opportunity over those of the other system.

And I trust also that the new legislation will carefully and completely protect and assure the individuality and the independence of each bank to the end that any tendency there may ever be toward a consolidation of the money or banking power of the nation shall be defeated.

It will always be possible of course to correct any features of the new law which may in practice prove to be unwise; so that while this law is sure to be enacted under conditions of unusual knowledge and authority it also will include it is well to remember the possibility of future amendment.

With the present prospects of this long-awaited reform encouraging us it would be singularly unfortunate if this monetary question should by any chance become a party issue. And I sincerely hope it will not. The exceeding amount of consideration it has received from the people of the nation has been wholly non-partisan, and the Congress set its non-partisan seal upon it when the Monetary Commission was appointed. In commending the question to the favorable consideration of Congress I speak for and in the spirit of the great number of my fellow citizens who without any thought of party or partisanship feel with remarkable earnestness that this reform is necessary to the interests of all the people."

To avoid any possibility of doing the President injustice the following letter was sent:

"MILWAUKEE, WIS., Dec. 22, 1911.
Honorable William H. Taft,
    President of the United States,
        Washington, D. C.
Dear Sir: Referring to your financial message to Congress of yesterday, kindly advise whether it was your intention thereby to approve specifically or in a general way the Aldrich plan for a National Reserve Association owned by the banks?

Please also advise as to whether you will insist on a clear majority of the directors of such an institution being appointed by the Federal Government so that the Government will have supreme and absolute control of this private corporation?

My permanent post-office address is care of The Romaine, Middleton Avenue, Clifton, Cincinnati, Ohio.

Thanking you, I remain,
            Very respectfully yours,
                ALFRED O. CROZIER."

The reply to the above can not be published because it was marked "personal." The language of the President's message, however, leaves no hope that he will oppose the Aldrich plan or insist on Government ownership or any public control that will be effective. The following quotations from letters published elsewhere in this volume in full are more than significant, they are eloquent:

A letter dated December 27, 1911, from the American Bankers' Association says:

"Referring to your inquiry about President Taft's attitude, we have no further advices than extracts from the President's message to Congress, in which it appears that he endorses the 'Aldrich plan'."

The National Bank of Commerce in New York writes on January 3, 1912:

"The writer has not before him the annual message of President Taft, but his recollection is that the Aldrich bill was favorably mentioned therein."

New-York Life Insurance Company.
New York, N.Y.

Darwin P. Kingsley,
President

December 26, 1911.

Mr. Alfred O. Crozier,
    Plankinton House,
        Milwaukee, Wis.,

Dear Sir:—

Answering yours of the 22nd, I beg to state that in a recent address I believe President Taft substantially approved of the Aldrich Plan. I do not know that his approval went to every detail, but I believe it covered the general program of a Central Reserve Association.

I believe it is clear that public opinion is advancing along these lines very rapidly.

Very truly yours,

D. Kingsley
President.

The above is conclusive proof that Wall Street and the banks believe the President is definitely with them in the coming contest. They generally know, they do not guess, on matters so vital to their business interests.

The recent published statement by Senator Burton, said to be a close adviser of the President, his signature to the Monetary Commission's report, and the warm advocacy of the Aldrich plan in his annual report of December 4, 1911, by the Secretary of the Treasury MacVeigh, all indicate that the present administration is committed to the plan of taking away from the Government and granting to a private corporation owned by the banks all control of the public currency·of the United States. The President argues against "consolidation of the money or banking power of the nation" and then favors the Aldrich plan that would bind all banks into one great money trust by act of Congress. The pending bill permits the Reserve Association to adopt "regulations" and binds each bank specifically to obey such "regulations," present and future. This gives the central bank as much power over all banks as it would have if it owned the entire capital stock of every bank.

One has to twice read the President's statement that the National Reserve Association is in no sense a central bank to be certain that it was not intended as one of those famous presidential jokes. Anyway, Wall Street and the banks all had a good laugh over that statement, joke or no joke.

The bill reported by the commission, printed herein in full, shows that although for prudential reasons (to fool Andrew Jackson Democrats), Aldrich named it "Reserve Association" instead of "Central Bank," the corporation is to have all of the ordinary functions, powers and privileges of European central banks and of the central bank abolished by President Jackson.

President Taft, quoting Aldrich and Vreeland in his Boston speech, called it a central bank of issue. There has been no change in the functions of the institution since the New York Chamber of Commerce originated the plan in 1906, elsewhere herein fully described. The only real change was in the form of management. In 1906 it was to be a Government Central Bank with the Federal Government in supreme control. Now it is a private central bank with the banks in supreme control. Aldrich, to obscure this, has devised a complicated system of branch boards and for electing directors. He calls it a republican or democratic form of government but the people have no hand in it. The banks are the source of all power. If all public officials were elected by vote of the corporations instead of the people it would be the kind of "democracy" Aldrich devised and the

President praises for the National Reserve Association. The Government of 94,000,000 people chooses 4 and the bank fraternity 42 of the 46 directors of the central bank. The benefits are divided in about the same proportion.

It is to be a private corporation with shares of stock, receive deposits, issue notes, have a reserve, loan its credit, discount paper, buy and sell bills of exchange, charge interest, accumulate a surplus, pay dividends. The President surely must have taken Mr. Aldrich's word, for the statement that the National Reserve Association would not be a central bank is untrue and ridiculous. If all banks join it will have over 24,000 "depositors." This central bank will do for such customers (the banks) all the things an ordinary bank does for its customers. It is a central instead of an ordinary bank because the banks and Government are to be its only customers.

The President seemed to realize that there would be a big fight over the question as to whether control of the institution shall be public or private. The people are certain to resist giving control of their entire money supply into private hands.

But President Taft says, "It seems to be desirable that the banks which would own the association should in the main manage it. It will be an agency of the banks to act for them, and they can be trusted better than anybody else chiefly to conduct it."

On page 11 of the published address made by President Aldrich before the Economic Club of New York, issued by the Monetary Commission, he said: "The management of the Bank of England is in the hands of 24 directors selected largely from merchants—no bankers, in their sense of the word, being eligible for the position—and these, including the governor and deputy governor, elected by the directors from their own number, have control of the business of the bank."

Here is the greatest central bank in the world the policy of which largely influences the interest rate, supply of credit and business conditions not only in the British Empire but throughout the world, and yet not one banker ever is allowed on its board of directors or to occupy any position except as a mere hired employe. There is a reason, a fundamental one, that Congress should heed, for that English policy is the result of a century of careful experience.

The truth is the bankers always are on one side and business men on the opposite in the game of finance. The bankers loan, business men borrow. Bankers charge interest, business men pay it. The banker naturally seeks to increase his profit by increasing interest and other charges and this increases the burden on business.

But the people, consumers, pay it all, for interest and bank charges are expense included in the cost and increase by at least that much the prices of commodities.

Big bankers in a sense are parasites on business. They make all their money that way. Many are good men, honest, fair and reasonable. Elsewhere herein it is shown that very many are unfair, sordid, dishonest. As a class during all history their avarice and rapacity has increased with their riches and power. They often take advantage and abuse popular confidence and increase their profits and the public burden when trusted with power and opportunity. This is history. It is the reason banks are barred out of the management of the Bank of England. It is why the good Lord scourged and drove them from the temple. It is why 600 years B. C. Mohammed rebuked and broke with his uncles, the bankers of Mecca, for charging 100 per cent interest, taking the side of the poor and founding a religion that now has 176,000,000 followers. It is the reason why bankers should not be given by Congress monopolistic control of the public currency with exclusive power to fix the rate of discount, interest, without restraint, that all the people of the country must pay, the power to eliminate all competition for loans—a money trust.

The policy of the Bank of England means that over there business men and merchants have more influence than bankers in matters of government and legislation and therefore they have put a bridle on banks and bankers to make them serve instead of dictate to all business. Because the Bank of England issues the currency and regulates the money supply and interest rates it is managed exclusively by patriotic business men for the common good. They know that if the bankers were in control money might artificially be made scarce for the very purpose of increasing interest rates that more profits might be extorted from business men by the bankers.

To put bankers, or the dummies of bankers, in control of the National Reserve Association is to make it certain that year by year the supply of money and credit will be so manipulated that it will impose upon legitimate business all over the country an ever increasing interest burden and expense for bank accommodations. It is all right to hire the best of expert bankers to do the technical work but they should be, as in England, mere employes under the absolute control of a board composed of broad-minded and patriotic business men, Republicans and Democrats, from all parts of the country, sworn as public servants. That is the only safe plan. But Aldrich and the President would turn the whole thing, public currency, public revenues, Government funds of all kinds, all the money in the United States, over to the absolute control of a selfish private banking syndicate so that no one could get a dollar for any purpose without the consent of the syndicate and on its terms.

The President's argument that Congress need not hesitate about adopting the scheme because if it does not work well it can be amended is like urging a sick patient to swallow the unknown contents of a bottle marked "Poison" because if he don't like it and he finds it is likely to kill him the patient can just simply throw the poison up again.

Did Aldrich get the President to insert that clever suggestion, concealing from the chief executive the amending clause of the commission's bill, as follows?:

"Sec. 58. Congress reserves the right to alter or amend the provisions of this act to take effect at the end of any decennial period from and after the organization of the National Reserve Association." Note the absence of the word "repeal" in the above section. It is nowhere in the bill.

"Decennial" means "tenth anniversary." Congress is asked to bind its own hands and shackle the whole country for ten years, so that during that time the sovereignty of Government is powerless to make any change. It puts the central bank, the money trust, above, independent of and superior to law, government, the people, for ten years, and successive periods of ten years. Before ten years the promoters expect this money monster will have attained such political power that thereafter any amendments will be for the benefit of the banks and Wall Street instead of the people. This provision is typical of the whole bill, and reveals the grasping power of the special interests now bringing pressure on the whole country through the banks and otherwise to force it through Congress. And it strikingly reveals the unpatriotic course of the paid, sworn and trusted public servants of the Monetary Commission who seem to be trying to betray the people and the country into the power of the banks and Wall Street.

This is the most insolent amending clause ever inserted in a bill introduced into Congress. And the Government's paid and sworn Monetary Commission urges its adoption.

The first to start the cry of non-partisanship in the alleged hope of keeping the opponents of the Aldrich plan divided while the minority as a compact balance of power can be used to terrify both parties and extort unwilling support for the Aldrich plan in Congress among both Democrats and Republicans was Paul M. Warburg, partner in the great Wall Street banking house of Kuhn, Loeb & Co., said to represent or do business for Standard Oil and the Rothschilds of Europe. He, as the reputed author of the Aldrich plan, did this at a meeting in Wall Street of bankers and others held to advance the plan, as elsewhere herein fully shown. Mr. Aldrich took up this Wall Street cry and used it throughout the country and now the chief executive of the republic echoes it from the White House of the nation in his official message to Congress.

The President's message, however, is even more remarkable for its omissions. When it was written the President had available the official report of the United States Comptroller of the Currency made on December 4, 1911. The Comptroller (as shown elsewhere herein in full) made the most astounding and terrible charges against banks and bankers ever contained in a public document. He showed that over half of all national banks knowingly and constantly break the laws of the United States. He charged bankers wholesale with dishonesty, grafting and crime. He made his showing from the sworn admissions of the banks themselves on file in his office. He urged Congress to amend the laws, increase the criminal penalties, that he might be better able to enforce the law against the banks for the protection of depositors, borrowers and the public.

Did the President support this request of the Comptroller, did he instruct his Attorney-General to proceed to enforce the law against bankers officially shown to be law-violators? No. But he did in that message criticize federal judges for shielding a few grafting clerks of federal courts and urged Congress to enact a law giving power of removal to the President as well as to the judges.

Instead of instructing the Department of Justice to prosecute the thousands of rich and powerful criminal bankers he puts the entire machinery of Government to work to discover and punish a mere handful of misguided workingmen and then urges Congress to turn over to these very lawless bankers for their personal profit the supreme governmental function of issuing all ·public currency and the other imperial powers included in the Aldrich plan. Workingmen who break law should be punished but lawless bankers and millionaires should be treated the same way, because they have violated the same identical criminal statute, the law of the United States.

It is difficult to reconcile the former assertions of the President in his messages and public speeches that he proposed to enforce the law, every law, against all violators, rich or poor, individual or corporation, labor union or trust, without discrimination, fear or favor, with his apparent indifference to the constant violation of several different provisions of the federal law by thousands of bankers officially accused by the Comptroller of the United States.

Nor is it due to any oversight or lack of information on the part of the President. Writer personally put into the President's own hands at the White House on November 16, 1911 (two weeks before the Comptroller's report was made public on December 4, 1911), the written statement hereinbefore printed in full which contained the charge (based on evidence privately obtained by writer), that the records in the Comptroller's office showed that at least 40 per cent of all national banks were constant and intentional law-breakers.

We earnestly wish there was some possible way to explain or excuse this strange course of the President. Whether so intended or not the conduct of the present administration of Government and the law tends to constitute and classify the prosperous and powerful bankers and Wall Street financiers as a favored class, exempt and above the law, daily treating the laws and the authority of Government with utter contempt, ignoring their sworn obligations to their depositors, stockholders and the public, breaking criminal statutes with impunity and, because of the indifference of the Department of Justice or the policy of the Executive, enjoying full immunity from penalties of forfeiture, fines and imprisonment.

He has often and well said that in a republic it is dangerous to execute the laws in any but a just, equal and impartial manner. It cannot be that questions of mere political expediency would induce the learned jurist, the distinguished public servant, the sworn and trusted President to compound with or grant active or passive immunity to lawless bankers as a class because they are bankers, rich and politically influential, and even to urge Congress now to vastly increase their profits and power by law. As shown in another chapter there are 40,000 national bank officers and directors this very moment who are guilty under the laws of the United States of the crime of conspiracy, each being liable to a fine not exceeding $10,000, or imprisonment not more than two years, or both, and there is ample evidence in the Comptroller's office and elsewhere to prove the charge in each case.

Yet the Attorney-General does not act, the President is silent. Why? Politically speaking, events soon will show that if the President took his stand knowingly it was suicide; if he was deceived it was assassination. So long as the special interests get away with the plunder they waste no tears over the coffin containing the blasted political hopes of careless or faithless public servants whom they have induced to betray the public welfare into their itching hands.

GOVERNOR HARMON

William J. Bryan says that Judson Harmon, Governor of Ohio, is one of the candidates for the democratic nomination for the presidency being secretly supported by Wall Street.

This may explain why Governor Harmon ignored or did not answer a recent courteous letter by author asking him whether he was in favor of the Aldrich private central bank bill now pending in Congress. Following is the letter:

MILWAUKEE, WIS., Dec. 18. 1911.

Gov. Judson Harmon, Columbus, O.

Dear Sir:—The need of wise and practical banking and currency reform now is so important, kindly advise as to whether you favor the suggested National Reserve Association plan advocated by the National Monetary Commission. Thanking you, I am,   Very respectfully yours,

ALFRED O. CROZIER.

WALL STREET!

Alfred Owen Crozier's Great Financial Novel, "The Magnet," Is Warmly Resented by Wall Street.

The book exposes in detail the precise secret methods by which, with the aid of the Stock Exchange and the "ticker," "high finance" manipulates quotation prices on 20 to 30 billions of "listed" securities, and fleeces the public out of a billion dollars each year. Author did not expect or desire Wall Street's approval.

In "The Magnet" scrapbook was found the following letter which is here reproduced, without consultation with former publisher. Author considers it evidence that "The Magnet" hit the right mark.

TICKER
A MAGAZINE OF THE MARKETS
THE INVESTORS' MENTOR

❧ Each number of the TICKER is filled with examples, suggestions, and illustrations showing the carefully drawn plans, the shrewd methods, the accurate systems used by successful operators and investors in all markets.

THE TICKER PUBLISHING CO.
45 EXCHANGE PLACE
NEW YORK

❧ As an advertising medium for brokers, bond dealers, and firms merchandising high class goods, the TICKER tops them all
❧ It reaches out for the new people who are daily coming into the markets.
❧ Every copy is read by
A MAN WITH MONEY

New York Jan. 22, 1909.

The Funk & Wagnalls Co.,
New York City.

Gentlemen:-

We beg to return you under separate cover the copy of The Magnet, which you sent us.

We do not think favorably of this work and not caring to criticise it otherwise in our columns, we are sending it back.

Thanking you for your courtesy, we remain,

Yours very truly,

THE TICKER PUBLISHING CO.

RDW/ELW.

"THE MAGNET."

Alfred Owen Crozier's financial novel, "The Magnet," has been read by Roosevelt, Taft, La Follette, Bryan, Hughes and by many Congressmen, Governors, Supreme Judges, business men and labor leaders.   It was extensively and favorably reviewed by the daily press and magazines (see press notices on following pages).   La Follette spent an hour reading extracts from "The Magnet" to the United States Senate as part of his famous eighteen hour speech in 1908.   That book was Author's "first gun" in his campaign for honest finance and a progressive and patriotic money policy.   It was preliminary to his new volume, "U. S. Money vs. Corporation Currency."

"BOOK OF THE HOUR."

"The Magnet" is full of fun, thrilling situations, adventures and tender romance.   The Women particularly enjoy it.   The characters are pat, entertaining and almost recognizable.   Every patriotic man should read it because of the startling and true revelations and exposure in detail of the precise methods being used by Wall Street High Finance in its rapid and dangerous conquest of the American Republic.

"The Magnet" was first issued as **a high class $1.50 novel by Funk & Wagnalls Company.**   The manuscript, written in 1906, was delivered to publisher months before the October, 1907, panic, and yet the book contains a full description in detail of that panic and the way it was caused.   Its chapter, "The Artificial Panic," was surprisingly prophetic.

The Magnet Company is publisher of Mr. Crozier's new work, "U. S. Money vs. Corporation Currency."   To enable readers of the new book to also obtain "The Magnet" at very low cost, The Magnet Company has acquired the plates and all rights in "The Magnet."

These two books no doubt will be the **"Uncle Tom's Cabin"** of the present progressive crusade for the preservation of popular government and liberation of American Business, Politics and banks from the present intolerable bondage to the panic-scourging mastery of Wall Street High Finance.

"U. S. Money vs. Corporation Currency" is a powerful book of merciless facts from the official records. "The Magnet" is a fascinating romance woven about the private central bank scheme that since actually has materialized and now is before Congress. It is "Flesh and Blood in Action." It sets forth with startling and convincing realism the alliance between Crooked Big Business and Crooked "Boss" Politics, and lays bare the shady methods employed. These books were prepared at great cost by author to post the public and help prepare the people so they could successfully fight to preserve their rights and liberties. Patriotic readers are earnestly asked to help extend their circulation and usefulness. Form "Clubs of Three" so as to get the books at the relatively nominal price, as per "Special Offer to Readers," set forth on inside of front cover of this volume. The campaign of 1912 is now on, so kindly act promptly. Help start the "endless chain." Your own interests are deeply involved in a wise solution of this the greatest issue since the Civil War.

Send orders by mail with P. O. Money Order to

THE MAGNET COMPANY,

Provident Bank Building,

Cincinnati, Ohio.

PRICES—(SINGLE COPY, POSTPAID).

"The Magnet," 500 pages, 7 beautiful illustrations, Cloth, $1.00; Paper, 50 cents.

"U. S. Money vs. Corporation Currency," 400 pages, 34 striking and timely illustrations and 30 original letters from big banks and financiers, etc. Cloth, 60 cents; Paper, 30 cents.

SEE SPECIAL CUT PRICE (inside front cover) where 3 copies at one time are ordered accompanied by remittance.

Baltimore American.—An up to the minute novel, teeming with the electric thrill of the last sensation in high finance and corporate boodling, "The Magnet" will justify its title in holding the attention of the reader from start to finish. It is argument in flesh and blood. It is logic in action. It is conviction upon the anvil.

Philadelphia North American.—One of the most powerful romances which has appeared lately, and which goes to the very root of many of the current national problems.

Philadelphia Record.—"The Magnet" is a powerful story. Mr. Crozier writes with humor, originality and directness, as well as with force and lucidity.

Boston Globe.—Rills of humor, as sparkling as real rills under the kiss of summer sunshine, trickle through and make fascinating the pages of "The Magnet."

Detroit Free Press.—The financial side of this story is treated with an abandon that makes Mr. Lawson's "Frenzied Finance" seem mild as milk.

Wilmington (Del.) Journal.—"The Magnet" is more than a fascinating romance. It may make its author, Alfred O. Crozier of this city, a national character.

Cleveland Press.—Alfred O. Crozier is author of "The Magnet," a novel in which J. Pierpont Morgan and other familiar figures of Wall Street figure in thin disguise.

Cincinnati Post.—In obtaining material for his book Mr. Crozier spent months studying the hidden currents and sunken reefs of Wall Street.

Wilmington (Del.) Star.—Mr. Crozier thoroughly understands the subject of high finance, which is the underlying subject of "The Magnet." Our sympathies are with him in his war with the vampires of the nation, as they were with Lawson, and as they are with Roosevelt, all three of whom by varying methods, some wise and some doubtless unwise, have been valiantly fighting the battle of personal and corporate honesty and of financial, industrial and commercial cleanliness.

Chicago Examiner.—Mr. Crozier's new book, "The Magnet," though written in story form, bristles with philosophic discussions. Fortunately Mr. Crozier is not without the saving grace of humor, and some of his severest criticisms are modified by this human touch.

Chicago Post.—A grave novel of public affairs. The book is beautifully illustrated by Wallace Morgan, the originator of the celebrated Fluffy Ruffles Pictures.

Washington Times.—For twenty years Mr. Crozier has been a prominent lawyer. He is also a manufacturer with wide business experience and a student of financial and political affairs. For five years he was treasurer of the National Conference of Charities and Corrections of the United States. He started the modern movement for a Delaware Ship Canal and the Atlantic Coast inland waterway from Cape Cod to Carolina. He was an influential delegate at the recent National Rivers and Harbors Congress at Washington and at the Waterways Convention, Philadelphia.

Detroit News.—"The Magnet" was written by a former resident of Grand Rapids, Michigan. The story centers in Wall Street and some of the characters are almost recognizable by their names.

Minneapolis Journal.—Alfred O. Crozier, lawyer, manufacturer and man of wide experience has given another evidence of his versatility by writing a novel. It is called "The Magnet" and gives voice to views which caused something of a sensation at a recent meeting of the National Civic Federation.

Detroit Times.—"The Magnet," by Alfred O. Crozier, is a powerful and fascinating romance, interspersed with philosophic humor.

St. Louis Republic.—"The Magnet," by Alfred O. Crozier, should find many readers. It is a romance of the battles of modern financial giants, great financial matters being dovetailed into a pretty love story. The book is written in a new and original style, and is designed to appeal to the serious minds of all thoughtful Americans.

Cleveland Leader.—"The Magnet," by Alfred O. Crozier, is certainly one of the most appropriate books for the times. At a time when the country has been suffering from a lack of currency it is interesting to read an account of how one man was able to get all the gold under lock and key and actually get his hands on so nearly all of the rest of the currency that the country was nearly frenzied. Of course it all became a grand problem for the President, Cabinet and Congress, to struggle with. The metaphysical struggle with Sterling Morton, the man who actually cornered the money, is better read than described. There is an interesting love story running through the book.

Augusta (Me.) Herald.—One of the most conspicuous publications of the hour is the new novel by Mr. Crozier which is in reality an arraignment of the evil forces at work in Wall Street.

Chicago Tribune.—Mr. Alfred O. Crozier, an attorney of Wilmington, Delaware, has written a novel called "The Magnet" which attacks Wall Street and its methods. Mr. Crozier is the member of the Civic Federation who so badly baited August Belmont at the meeting in New York a month or so ago.

Kansas City Star.—"The Magnet" is by Alfred O. Crozier, a distinguished lawyer of Wilmington, Delaware, who has decided views on Wall Street's "panic making machine" and the other manifestations of modern finance.

Grand Rapids (Mich.) Herald.—Mr. Crozier has studied his subject from several view points. It should be read to be appreciated, for an outline of the plot does not give the fullness of the tale.

Seattle (Wash.) Post-Intelligencer.—Mr. Crozier has written a polemical novel whose ideas may be gleamed as follows: "Congress should go slow on currency legislation. The recent artificial panic was to scare the country into forcing Congress to act quickly and blindly. Selfishness instead of patriotism seems to be the inspiration of every proposition emanating from banking sources. They want elasticity, a rubber currency. This means simply the power to expand and contract the volume of money. But in every plan the banks demand the exclusive right to exercise this dangerous power. They are unwilling to let the people's government have any say." Mr. Crozier is much in earnest and very zealous.

New York Sun.—There is a passage in "The Magnet" describing Wall Street at page 55, which makes us think that Mr. W. J. Bryan must have read the book before making his speech at Carnegie Hall last Tuesday evening.

Montreal (Canada) Witness.—"The Magnet" can not fail to arouse at least a determination to discover how much of truth is contained in its vigorous and fearless denunciations.

St. Louis Christian Advocate.—"The Magnet" is a book of 497 pages, and in matter is a strongly written romance, really thrilling in many of its scenes and incidents.   It is intended to expose the crooked ways that mark the methods of Wall Street and corporations generally, and in a powerful climax shows what may come to pass under existing conditions.   We recommend the book as worthy.

Brooklyn Eagle.—Mr. Crozier is a lawyer of Wilmington, Delaware, and a student of finance.   He certainly knows Wall Street in all its ramifications, and is not afraid to speak out against it, as he proved about a month ago, when he attacked high rates of interest and margin gambling at a meeting of the National Civic Federation.

Dallas (Texas) News.—The serious minded will feel repaid to plod through "The Magnet" for the unquestionable value of its revelations. It strips naked that hideous panic making agency, the destroyer of confidence and credit, the wrecker of fortunes and happiness, the enemy of society, humanity and the republic—Wall Street.

Cleveland Town Topics.—No other work of fiction will be published within the twelve months which will prove so absorbing, so powerful, so revealing—which will touch so boldly upon so vital a subject as "The Magnet."   It is a book which deals with financial problems and with no weak or uncertain touch.   There has been no hesitancy in the mind of the man who wrote it, no hedging of facts, no cringing to the powers that be.   Those who enjoy fiction of the highest class and of the most absorbing interest should read this book.   Having once opened it they will become bound by its spell.

New York World.—Our novelist (Mr. Crozier) sets out to popularize the arguments against the Wall Street Gamble, and he does this with eloquence and force.·

Louisville (Ky.) Western Record.—"The Magnet" was an agreeable surprise.   The story is one of great interest, one's attention is closely held.   Yet the indictment against many of the methods of modern finance is strong and clearly put, so that the average man who knows little of these things can understand.   How Mr. Crozier managed to make such an absorbing story out of his dry and unpleasant facts remains a mystery.

Madison (Wis.) Journal.—The evils of Wall Street gambling, elastic currency schemes, political conspiracies, etc., are laid bare in a new Novel by Alfred O. Crozier.   Many of the reforms urged by President Roosevelt in his last message to Congress, were previously incorporated in this book.

Charleston (S. C.) News and Courier.—In his book, Mr. Crozier has written in powerful and fascinating way about a question of intense practical moment, weaving into his romance a great deal of delightful philosophic .1umor, and telling the story in a new and most original way of he conditions which so nearly affect not only the business life of the country, but its social and domestic happiness as well.

Omaha World Herald.—The author of "The Magnet" states that he has written the book with the hope that it may induce public thought and discussion, and thus do some good by helping to defeat the designs of lawless and incorporated wealth.

Portland Oregonian.—"The Magnet" is a cleverly constructed audacious Novel.

Albany (N. Y.) Argus.—Mr. Crozier has been creating sensations in financial circles and columns of interviews in the newspapers, with his radical views on Wall Street and the worship of the Golden Calf.

The Banker, Chicago.—The recent Boston address (before the City Club) on banking topics by Alfred O. Crozier, has attracted attention anew to his powerful novel, "The Magnet." Crozier is a born enemy of the trusts and his fighting blood was up, a la Sterling, when he wrote this wonderful story of Sterling the promoter, Helen Morton and John Hays. As a description of a venture in high finance it is worthy of a place in any library. It teaches a useful lesson for those who risk all for money. The plot and counterplot are clever, with a grand climax and a moral victory to conclude. Buy it and read it.

Des Moines (Ia.) Register and Leader.—"The Magnet" is a delight to the jaded reader who has wearied of the conventional and purposeless drivel which seems to have usurped the romantic market. Mr. Crozier, first of all, writes with a defined object in view. His theme is drawn from important public questions of today.

Glasgow (Scotland) News.—Read in the light of the recent money crisis in the United States, "The Magnet" is well calculated to cause grave searchings of heart among those who realize how much of the world's future is bound up with the developments—political and financial—of that country. It is decidedly dry reading, but it is deeply instructive.

Indianapolis News.—The author of "The Magnet" possesses a great mass of useful and timely information.

Milwaukee Sentinel.—"The Magnet," by Alfred O. Crozier, is a powerful novel, dealing with current affairs, containing a fascinating romance and illustrated by Wallace Morgan.

Dayton (Ohio) Watchword.—Whether the resignation of General Dupont as head of the Speaker's Bureau of the Republican National Committee was voluntary or was forced by President Roosevelt will probably remain a secret. In this connection, however, it is significant that a few days previous to the General's resignation President Roosevelt received a communication from Alfred O. Crozier, the Wilmington lawyer, whose book, "The Magnet," has caused such a sensation in political and financial circles. He called attention to the serious handicap that General Dupont's presence upon the executive committee was likely to exert upon Mr. Taft's election.

Detroit Advocate.—The author has original views on various subjects. It will set one thinking to read Mr. Crozier's book.

New York Christian Herald.—"The Magnet" is a timely romance of the battles of modern business giants and the fatuity of living merely to accumulate material riches.

London (England) Globe.—"The Magnet," by A. O. Crozier, comes from America, and proves to be yet another novel lustily lashing the trans-Atlantic overweening craze for making money by any means, honest or dishonest, and showing how it demoralizes the national character. American financiers and other worshippers of the almighty dollar have no lack of mirrors in which to see their unlovely selves. The story ends with a novel act of restitution.

Detroit Times.—"The Magnet" is certain to attract attention and make its impress on the coming National Campaign.

Colorado Springs Gazette.—Unlike Lawson, Crozier is not a speculator, and his insight into Wall Street affairs has not been gained in a rough-and-tumble mix-up in the battles of the street. His has rather been the attitude of the student and the investigator. For years he has studied the game as it is played, until the study has become his hobby, his passion. He fairly oozes statistics. To illustrate the accuracy of his knowledge of the trend of banking and currency affairs, one of the chapters in his novel, "The Magnet," although written more than a year ago, describes with remarkable fidelity the recent money panic, giving in detail, months in advance of their actual occurrence, many of the facts which are now a part of current financial history.

Portland Bulletin.—The characters in the story are splendidly portrayed, and reveal some excellent word drawings on the part of the author. The private schemes in Congress regarding elastic currency are laid bare. The methods and powers of Wall Street are exposed. The author of "The Magnet" tells how panics are created, and their effect. He also tells of methods regarding the regulation of railroads and trusts and other kindred subjects. This book is well worth perusal, not merely for its romance but for its timeliness, in so far as present political and industrial conditions are concerned.

Syracuse Herald.—Mr. Crozier has written a novel of modern business, in which men talk in billions, and the merger has been carried to the ultimate. The author says the book is not a reservoir of panaceas, but he hopes it may induce public thought.

San Francisco News-Letter.—At close range, Mr. Lawson may present a prettier picture to the eye—his graces of person, his immaculate taste in dress, with its touch of the esthetic in the always conspicuous boutonniere, being well known, but when it comes right down to physical bulk, Crozier makes an impressive eyeful. He is a fair specimen of what we have come to expect a fighter should look like. When standing on the ground, he stretches in straight, solid fashion nearly six feet into the air. The scale would probably register his weight at 225 pounds. His head, surmounted with a stiff growth of that peculiar copper wire hair which we are wont to associate with unusual physical strength, tops off a face that is as grim and relentless as a Pilgrim Father's. Two lean, muscular jaws jutting away, like the sides of a gunboat, from a somewhat long and inquisitive nose, terminate in a firm and knotty chin. In platform speech these jaws snap shut at impressive intervals, and it is then that the man's strength and fixity of purpose is revealed at its best. A close friend says his eyes are gray. Perhaps they are, but if so, they are the coldest, steeliest pair of gray eyes ever set into a man's head. If you or me were to be pulled suddenly from a dark room into the light, our eyes would blink and blur until they became accustomed to the changed condition. Perhaps Crozier's eyes would act likewise, but they do not convey that impression. They strike one as eyes that would gaze at you steadily and unblinkingly under almost any conditions.

Boston Globe.—"The Magnet" is the magic and attractive title of an up to the minute novel by Alfred O. Crozier, published by Funk & Wagnalls Company. In a style which holds the interest of the reader from beginning to end the author deals in a logical, convincing and entertaining way with high finance and boodling.

New York Christian Observer.—In this novel ("The Magnet") of nearly 500 pages the machinery of Wall Street is uncovered to the public eye, revealing its diabolical methods and the tragedies that result.

Fourth Estate, New York.—"The Magnet" is a book of 500 pages, so magnetic, so fascinating that the reader, having once begun it, will not be ready to lay it aside, until he has finished it.   The story is one of so called high finance, related in a captivating style.   An overwhelming desire to secure the power which wealth is supposed to give possesses a man of apparently strong character, who is described as playing a desperate game to obtain the control of national finance.

Love, hatred, fear, intrigue and other passions skillfully interwoven play their parts.   Fortunately love gains the ascendency over the greed for gold, and a moral victory is won.   Traits of American life and manners are graphically pictured in this romance of the battle of giants that figure in modern finance.

New York Commercial.—Mr. Crozier lives in Wilmington, Delaware, is a well known lawyer and is also a successful manufacturer. He is intensely in earnest, and this very earnestness gives him a poise and ease of demeanor that never desert him, even under trying circumstances.   During the recent meeting of the National Civic Federation in New York, at which were present Andrew Carnegie, August Belmont, Seth Lowe, Samuel Gompers and scores of other notable figures in American public life, the discussion had ambled along in a dignified and orderly, if somewhat desultory manner until near the close of the meeting, when Crozier slowly arose from his seat, and in his characteristic way fired a question at Belmont.   The question was simple in itself, but it was not just the kind of question that members of that august body were accustomed to have put so bluntly, and it created a stir.   A battery of well bred stares was focused in Crozier's direction, but it did not quail him.   He serenely waited his answer—and he got it.   The incident is characteristic of the man.   He impresses you as one who will get what he goes after.

Although not indorsing all the conclusions reached by Mr. Crozier President Roosevelt, with whom Mr. Crozier has conversed on the subject uppermost in his mind, is following a similar line of reasoning, as is evidenced in the President's recent remarkable special message to Congress.

New York American.—Alfred O. Crozier, the big Wilmington (Del.) lawyer, who furnished the three "explosions," which made the recent convention of the National Civic Federation the liveliest in its history, did not speak his whole mind on the sins of Wall Street and capital in the Federation session.

On Monday he chastised Wall Street as a panic making machine, and made some of the big financiers present squirm.   Tuesday he "stood up" August Belmont on the charge of capitalizing franchises, and wrung from him his first public defense of the Interborough Metropolitan Merger.   He then tried to inject a "saving clause" into the elastic currency resolution proposed by Isaac N. Seligman.

Since he startled the staid Civic Federation there has been no little curiosity as to just who Crozier is.   He comes from New York stock and was born in Grand Rapids, Michigan.   He graduated from the University of Michigan in 1886 and has been a lawyer for twenty years.

San Francisco Call.—In the opening chapter of "The Magnet," which antedates the story about 30 years, the upbuilding of the plot is well outlined.

New York Tribune.—Alfred O. Crozier, the Delaware delegate to the National Civic Federation, who was appointed to draw up resolutions of thanks to retiring President August Belmont, together with Isaac N. Seligman, after he had tilted with both of them at Monday's and Tuesday's meetings, is anxious to bring about an organized effort to do away with margin sales and call loans at exorbitant rates of interest. Mr. Crozier said last evening that only by these means did he think that panicky conditions could be securely guarded against.

New York World.—A bomb was dropped into the placid councils of the National Civic Federation yesterday and the echo of its explosion had not ceased to reverberate at the annual dinner, held last night at Hotel Astor.

The man who had the temerity to raise this storm was Alfred O. Crozier, of Wilmington, Delaware, a lawyer and the author of "The Magnet," a book attacking Wall Street. Face to face he told the financiers they caused the money panic.

New York Herald.—August Belmont, chairman of the Boards of Directors controlling the surface lines and traction facilities above and beneath the earth in New York City, made the longest impromptu speech of his life yesterday in defending traction companies and mergers.

He took the position that, since the obligation to operate cars was laid so heavily upon the corporation, the employee also should be made to feel, when he accepted a position with the transportation company, that he was in the service of the public and should not be permitted to leave his post without notice.

"Mr. Belmont," asked Mr. Crozier, "if an employee entering the employment of a public service corporation at a modest wage thereby, incurs an obligation as a servant of the public, should not the corporation which receives the franchise from the public free—a franchise which is not property, but a mere license—should it not also have an obligation to the public and be prevented from capitalizing that franchise for $100,000,000 and then charging the public higher rates so as to pay dividends on such capitalization?"

Mr. Belmont was astonished by the long hypothetical inquiry and a wave of red swept over his face. Some of the labor element in the room applauded Mr. Crozier.

Many more press notices from other leading papers and magazines, and strong endorsements of "The Magnet" by men prominent in public life, could be given, but space will not permit.

To many, Mr. Crozier seems to be an extreme radical, but the fact is he is a cautious and careful conservative. His radicalism is only the radicalism of naked truth, which he states bluntly and always without qualification or apology. He believes the time to temporize with dangerous national evils has passed, and that the only way to prevent the swing of the pendulum to a dangerous extreme is to quickly establish justice and a square deal in finance, business and politics and between capital and labor. That is all he seeks. He would not harm any legitimate business, big or little, not even that of Wall Street. But he thinks the only way to safeguard legitimate business is to destroy the evils.

Mr. Crozier and family went to Cincinnati, Ohio, because of the unsurpassed school system of that city, and that his two daughters might complete their education in the splendid university and art school of that town.

He also has established there the headquarters of his Cement Products Company that supplies special machinery and erects plants for the manufacture of brick with ordinary "wet process" cement-concrete under the "Crozier system" of which he is inventor and principal owner, the product being known as "Crozite" stone and brick.

But for years Mr. Crozier constantly has pushed the non-partisan progressive campaign for the preservation of popular rule and to retain in the people and their government control of the country's supply of money. He has freely and gladly expended very many thousands of dollars and years of time and personal effort in making the investigations and collecting the information now made public for the common good. The relatively nominal price put on his new book has been made possible by him. If Congress instead of adopting the "Aldrich Plan" will take up the "Crozier Plan" for a U. S. Monetary Council it will prove a great and lasting national blessing.

THE MAGNET COMPANY.

Regular Order Blank
(Single Copies)
THE MAGNET COMPANY
Publisher
PROVIDENT BANK BUILDING
Cincinnati, Ohio

Date_____1912

Dear Sirs:—
    Enclosed is *P. O. Order* for $_____. Send (postpaid) indicated books to the following address:
(Cross out Book and Binding not desired)

Name_____

Street_____

Town_____

State _____

"The Magnet" } Cloth $1.00 / Paper .50

"U. S. Money vs. Corp. Curr." } Cloth $ .60 / Paper .30

(Mail to Publisher with *P. O. Money Order* payable to The Magnet Co.)

······················(Cut Off Here)······················

Regular Order Blank
(Single Copies)
THE MAGNET COMPANY
Publisher
PROVIDENT BANK BUILDING
Cincinnati, Ohio

Date_____1912

Dear Sirs:—
    Enclosed is *P. O. Order* for $_____. Send (postpaid) indicated books to the following address:
(Cross out Book and Binding not desired)

Name_____

Street_____

Town_____

State _____

"The Magnet" } Cloth $1.00 / Paper .50

"U. S. Money vs. Corp. Curr." } Cloth $ .60 / Paper .30

ORDER BLANK

(Three Copies)

(As per "Special Offer" on inside front cover of this book)

THE MAGNET COMPANY

Publisher

PROVIDENT BANK BUILDING

Cincinnati, Ohio

Date_____1912

Dear Sirs:—

Enclosed find *P. O. Money Order* payable to you for $_____

This is to pay for *three copies* as per your "Special Offer" printed elsewhere herein. Send (postpaid) the books to the following addresses.

(Cross out Book and Binding not wanted, after each name)

	Book	Binding

Name _____

"U. S. Money vs. Corp. Curr." — Cloth / Paper

Street _____

"The Magnet" — Cloth / Paper

Town _____

State _____

Name _____

"U. S. Money vs. Corp. Curr." — Cloth / Paper

Street _____

"The Magnet" — Cloth / Paper

Town _____

State _____

Name _____

"U. S Money vs. Corp. Curr '" — Cloth / Paper

Street _____

"The Magnet" — Cloth / Paper

Town _____

State _____

(Fill out this blank order and mail to publisher with *P. O. Money Order* payable to The Magnet Company)

Lightning Source UK Ltd.
Milton Keynes UK
UKHW022100090522
402738UK00003B/202